hollywood flatlands

animation, critical theory and the avant-garde

———

esther leslie

VERSO

London • New York

First published by Verso 2002
© Esther Leslie 2002
All rights reserved

The moral right of the author has been asserted.

Verso
UK: 6 Meard Street, London W1F OEG
USA: 180 Varick Street, New York, NY 10014–4606

Verso is the imprint of New Left Books

ISBN 1–85984–612–2

British Library Cataloguing in Publication Data
A catalogue record for this book is available from the British Library

Library of Congress Cataloging-in-Publication Data
A catalog record for this book is available from the Library of Congress

Designed and typeset by Illuminati, Grosmont
Printed and bound by Ajanta Offset, New Delhi, India

contents

 **prelude**

This book hosts a number of encounters between animated films, figures of the avant-garde and modernist critics. The study was motivated by frustration at the phoney war between high culture and popular or low or mass culture. This combat has played out in various contributions to the (ill) discipline of cultural studies. In various discussions the attitude to popular culture on the part of avant-gardists, critical theorists and modernist artists is often parodied. A generally accepted line declares over and over that high culture and popular culture have been – for so long – enemies. To declare an intimacy between modernism and mass culture is too far-fetched for the professionals of popular culture (just as it is for the pro-ponents of a sealed-off lofty culture by the privileged for the privileged). From such a perspective, it is impossible to imagine the personal and critical rendezvous between Eisenstein and Disney, or to acknowledge that Siegfried Kracauer, Theodor Adorno and Walter Benjamin sat amongst cartoon audiences and developed their thoughts on representation, utopia and revolution in relation to Disney or Fleischer output, or to entertain the idea that the flattening of surfaces and the denial of perspective troubled simultaneously New York art critics and *New Yorker* cartoonists, not to mention myopic Mister Magoo.

Modernist theorists and artists were fascinated by cartoons. And those who took cartoons most seriously were political revolutionaries. As such they were anxious to develop new vocabularies for cultural and social forms within a totality that also contained possibility. They were modernists, not 'high modernists' and all that implies, but proponents of a demotic modernism that was open to base impulses and ever curious about the shadow side, the mass market of industrialized culture. For the modernists, cartoons – which rebuff so ferociously painterly realism and filmic naturalism – are set inside a universe of transformation, overturning and provisionality.

Modernist curiosity about animation combined with animadversion; that is to say, modernists watched as an anarchic and utopian form exploded into the culture scene, its little strips bouleversing logic and order and propriety, only later to be betrayed by the most successful makers' insistence on developing a coy bourgeois 'realism'. Cartoons – especially in their dominant Disney version – reformed, nestled up to the culture industry and changed their shapes correspondingly. The ideal reality that took on contours in Disney's fairy-tales showed nothing other than the momentary arrest of all possibilities for revolutionary social transformation. The idealized world moulded in Disney's fairy-tale reels made graphic the suppression of revolutionary hopes for social transformation in the 1930s and 1940s. Cartoon lines outlined political stances. Cartoon shapes and fantasies modelled social situations and the frustrations and joys that accompanied them. That there was a political edge to the cartoon line was expressed most dramatically in the now love affair, now skirmish, between Disney and the Nazis. The uses and abuses of the 'European' fairy-tale were at issue in the 1930s, as Nazi cabinet members, fascist filmmakers, communist critics, Europeans and Americans tussled over the bequest. These tussles, and others, reset the meanings of mass culture.

Postmodern orthodoxy claims that 'intellectual' interest in popular culture comes into being in the post-war period (after years of modernist elitism), with the inauguration of postmodernism's own discourses. But, in fact, it seems that the *productive* relationship between (modernist) intellectuals and popular culture is by then already a thing of the past, terminated in that very period, discredited by the historical advent of ugly mass movements and spurious mass parties substituting themselves in the name of the mass. The beneficiary of this pacifying of the mass became, eventually, the mass as consumer category. The early-twentieth-century relationship between intellectuals and popular culture was *productive* in the sense that both intellectuals and mass culture producers recognized, in some way, that all was to play for, that transformation was a virtue, a motive and a motif, that dissolution of form, including the form of the mass itself, was on the agenda, indeed that there was a chance to return to the drawing board of social formation. Animated popular culture was seen to redraw relations, and to propose something extraordinary – its own abolition, the abolition of the division between 'high' forms and 'mass' forms and, necessarily, the abolition of the social divisions that sustain cultural divisions. The postmodern post-war version of the intellectual encounter with mass cultural forms tends, in contrast, to an affirmation of what is, whereby the mass (and its cultural forms) is made positive as mass *in itself* and is not expected to be self-conscious, critical and *for itself*.[1]

This book presents some key arguments about mass culture and technical and formal innovation. These do not appear as a succession of elitists arguing about the virtues and vices of slumming it with the masses, but as their attempts to discern fully the possibilities of technological and popular culture, from wherever it came. The book filters technological culture – represented by its special delegate animation – through the theoretical writings of artists and critical theorists, and zooms in on those places where the writers address cartoons head on – or at least scoot past them, in ruminations on drawing, colour or caricature, the meanings of fairy-tales and talking animals or humans as machines. This book does not claim to provide a complete history of animation or even of Disney output, let alone all the other studios and individuals.[2] It does not even always move through time chronologically. Rather, it spirals and twists through special scenes that have been out of focus too long: a reminder that convincing analysis requires both wide-angle and zoom shots. It is a polemic against the limp sociological positivism that would like to erect impermeable bulkheads between mass culture and critique.

It is presupposed here that artefacts – such as the cartoon, the suprematist canvas, the fairy-tale – can be understood only in the context of the whole scope of culture. Just as it is recognized that the pursuit of realism in painting smashed into the invention of photography, so too coloration in painting comes to make sense in relation to the possibilities of Technicolor. Drawing signifies only in relation to all forms of drawing, and only thereby can a politics of the line be discerned. Early animation's energies of negation captivated the Dadaists, who then carried out their own experiments. Time, duration and the representation of movement were issues for both futurists and cartoon-industry in-betweeners. Flatness and depth-illusion concerned vorticists and inventors of the multiplane camera. Eisenstein understood this when he shunted his points of reference from Piranesi to Tenniel to Disney, or discovered Engels's dialectical evolutionary science affirmed in the wiggly line of a *New Yorker* cartoon. All this and more is expanded in what follows.

preclusion: experi-mental

phantasmagoric

An animated cartoon drawn by hand was shown in Paris in the summer of 1908, before an audience of buyers from London. Titled *Fantasmagorie*, it was made by Emile Cohl and lasted for less than two minutes.[1] After the corporate trademark of Gaumont had flashed by, a white line surfaced on a black background. The artist's hand appeared and, like a music hall lightning sketcher, speedily drew a clown, suspended from a bar. Drawn into life, the clown releases the bar, which descends and forms a box. The box contains a gentleman wearing a top hat and carrying an umbrella. The man's accoutrements reshape themselves into a cinema interior. The clown begins to tease the gentleman to the point of exasperation, and the gentleman, in turn, goes on to torment a lady topped by a large plumed hat, who is seated in front of him. She is fully absorbed in the film footage of marching soldiers, and is crying and laughing at the reel of events. The gentleman slits the screen. Another film is projected and it shows abstract shapes in motion. Finally the gentleman sets the lady alight with his cigar, and her head swells into a sphere. For the next forty-seven seconds the clown is abused – first by the Michelin man, then by a soldier, then by a flower. The clown's head is ripped off his shoulders and a bottle-shaped man bounces it up and down in a diabolo cup. The bottle-man turns into a bottle, and fires its cork. Then it swallows up the clown, only to turn into a lotus flower and then into an elephant and finally a house, into which the clown is locked by a policeman, but he escapes, cracking open his miraculously regained head in the process. The torture stops. The artist's hands intervene again with a drawn paste pot to mend the clown, who, once repaired, swells up like a balloon and floats away. The cartoon ends. It has presented an illogical narrative of cruelty and torture executed by people and things at war with each other. But the violence is painless, dreamlike, as if it were more of a utopian transfiguration of actuality's discord. And, at the end, the clown, suffering no after-effects from being decapitated twice in one minute, floats off in an undefined spatial void. From the very first, animation, self-reflexive and unmasking, establishes a circuit of life and destruction. Animation, the giving of life, battles with annihilation, and always overcomes, always reasserts the principle of motion, of continuation and renewal. Cohl with his *Fantasmagorie* forges an illusion, but disabuses viewers too. Through the intervention of the artist's hand, through the knowing play with surface and depth, and through an ac-knowledgement of screen, simulation and situation, Cohl reveals the deri-vation of the over-lively objects. The illusion struggles against the illusory.

Cohl, together with Jules Lévy, had been a prominent member of a gang of artists and journalists called the Incoherents. He orbited the stars of the avant-garde scene in the 1880s. Where the decadents and symbolists accented the morbid, the Incoherents exhorted laughter and ludicrousness. They were an avant-garde assemblage beating out the path that the Dadaists and surrealists would later track. They loved the cabaret and caricature. On 1 October 1882, Jules Lévy's home hosted an exhibition called *Arts incohérents*. This was a follow-up to his earlier show of drawings by people who did not know how to draw. *Arts incohérents* showed work by profes-sional artists who used all sorts of eccentric and everyday found materials – for example, there were sculptures made out of bread and cheese. There was a monochrome painting by the poet Paul Bilhaud. Its title was *Negroes Fighting in a Cellar at Night*. After the group had disintegrated, Cohl main-tained its absurdist and irreverent attitude, but now in the infant medium of film.

The name of Cohl's cartoon – *Fantasmagorie* – invoked a type of optical amusement that was just then slipping into obsolescence, as film displaced it. Phantasmagoric machineries were popular nineteenth-century spectacles that projected a cortège of spectral bodies before spectators' believing–disbelieving eyes. Phantasmagoric representations revelled in their techno-logically enabled ability to contrive a fraudulent presence. A Belgian showman who called himself Robertson ran the first major magic lantern show in a Paris theatre in 1797. It was called the 'Fantasmagorie', and he made pictures come to life by mounting a magic lantern on wheels and pushing it closer and further from the screen, sometimes through clouds of smoke. Optical machineries and then photographic equipment were contributions to a new and growing techno-culture industry. In the seventeenth century Isaac Newton had used persistence of vision to demonstrate the composition of white light. Over a century later, following Peter Mark Roget's experiments with persistence of vision in 1824, the devices began to multiply. In 1827 the English physician John A. Paris invented the thaumatrope, a disc that spins to combine two images – a bird in a cage perhaps. In 1832 the Belgian Joseph Plateau invented the phenakistoscope: a gyrating disc of images viewed through an eye slot, before a mirror. Then, in 1834, came the zoetrope, a spinning drum with strips of images spied through slits. Scary, commercial magic lantern shows were popular from 1874 to the outbreak of the Great War. Sometimes these played with illusions of size or tricks of presence and absence. By 1880 Emile Reynaud had invented the praxinoscope, a zoetrope with a drum of mirrors inside. A few years later he developed better machinery and demonstrated before an audience of family and friends his 'théâtre optique'. Projected onto a larger-than-life screen were several hundred coloured images, a combination of background imagery and moving image strips. But it was not photographed for mass reproduction. In 1892 he showed *Pauvre Pierrot*. It was made of five hundred drawings, was thirty-six metres long and lasted fifteen minutes. It was a sound film

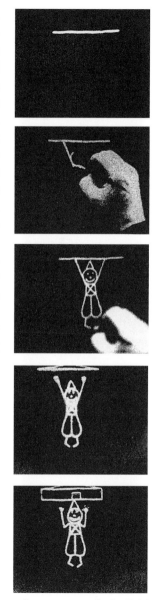

Fantasmagorie, Emile Cohl

with bells, beating sticks and a mandolin. The image strip had tiny silver tongues attached which, in contact with the electro-apparatus, triggered sound effects. Eventually Reynaud conceded that he could not compete with cinema and is said to have thrown his image strips into the River Seine despondently. These were the years of patent mania. As the nineteenth century concluded, hundreds of optical machineries were invented, registered and died virtually unused. And others found a place and ever more opportunities for display. Film had the virtue of diversity. It could be real. It could be fake. It could imprint the world outside the window or the world in the studio. It reprised topical events, such as Queen Victoria's Diamond Jubilee celebrations. It had scientific uses for it could be used to reproduce movements and shapes too slow or too tiny to be perceived by the unaided eye. It could be magical and absurd, in drawn form or using the object world that it found, staged and manipulated. The possibility of manipulation meant the possibility of film's use for analytic purposes.

Photography reproduces the fragment of a moment, and this alone provides material for analysis – the structure of an object, the relationship between an entity's parts in only one sliver of time. When the broken fragments of time are set next to each other, the analysis of movement is made possible. The frame by frame of a filmstrip emerges in the last decades of the nineteenth century out of the experimentation around still photography. In 1874 Pierre Jules César Janssen invented the photographic revolver, which he used to track the various phases in the course of Venus. The movements of the stars and planets were to be recorded in these vision machines, lending such projects a utopian scope. Indeed, in thesis 83 of *Society of the Spectacle*, Guy Debord posits a relationship between utopianism and astronomy:

> As Sorel observed, it is on the model of *astronomy* that the utopians thought they would discover and demonstrate the laws of society. The harmony envisaged by them, hostile to history, grows out of the attempt to apply to society the science least dependent on history. This harmony is introduced with the experimental innocence of Newtonianism, and the happy destiny which is constantly postulated 'plays in their social science a role analogous to the role of inertia in rational mechanics' (*Matériaux pour une théorie du prolétariat*).[2]

But investigations into cosmic and celestial bodies – and certainly their utopian import – waned as war on earth loomed.[3] These photographic tools that made patterns of movement visible found military uses, when, for example, Ottomar Anschütz received a commission from the war ministry to do a ballistic calculation of gunfire. Anschütz had a camera that could take extremely rapid exposures ($1/1000$th of a second) and with this he had photographed marching troops, gymnasts and jumping horses. In 1884 he devised ways of photographing birds in flight. A bird and bullet soaring through the air could both be mapped. From 1882, Etienne Marey, a doctor, used chronophotography as an observation instrument for physiological examination, inspired by Eadweard Muybridge's horse photographs, which in 1879 had revealed for the first time the way that a horse trots – most strikingly when transferred to a praxinoscope and set once more in motion with the viewer controlling the horse's speed. Marey had been developing machineries of time and motion study, whereby mechanical or pneumatic devices attached directly to the subject and activated a pen resting on a band of moving paper. Convinced by the uses of chronophotography, he designed and built a camera in the shape of a 'rifle', which he used to take multiple frames of birds in flight. Marey could move with the bird through the air, in a type of panning. He turned his camera on people too. But Marey did not record natural movement so much as make a graphic representation of it. He dressed his assistant Demëny in a black costume whose one arm and leg were traced in white lines. Demëny moved through space and the camera recorded in time-lapse a geometric figure, an abstraction of a human who looks strangely like rows of Reynaud's moving pauvre

pierrots. These were images whose analytic, dissecting eye would a few years later be discovered by artists, such as Marcel Duchamp, and restrung in his cubo-futurist static, defamiliarizing meditation on movement through space, as in *Nude Descending a Staircase*.

Marey's deployment of chronophotography was analytical, to be used by physiologists and other scientists, and yet visually it invoked the illusions and trickery of popular spectacles such as the phantasmagoria. Film's animation of life, or of the effect of life, seemed, indeed, to engender life. That was magical. That was what seemed magical. That was why it could so quickly and easily represent magic, trick effects, the trickery of sorcery and supernaturalism. The filmstrip was even more effective in allowing the analysis and the illusioning of movement, and Muybridge could only really prove the value of his machinery when he turned the fragment images back into moving film. After vivisection his victims come back to life.

These toys and these illusory projections and early filmic experiments were popular, and consequential. They did not go unnoticed by social diagnosticians. For example, the notion of the phantasmagoric machinery enters Marx's description of the fetish commodity.[4] In *Capital* Marx writes:

> the existence of things qua commodities, and the value relation between the products of labour which stamps them as commodities, have absolutely no connection with their physical properties and with the material relations arising therefrom. There it is a definite social relation between people, which assumes for them the phantasmagoric form of a relation between things.[5]

The commodity, through the processes of commodity fetishism, Marx states, acts according to its own laws as an actor on a shadowy stage. It attains a 'ghostly objectivity' and leads its own life. In the reports from the stock exchanges cotton 'rises', copper 'falls', corn is 'buoyant', coal 'slack' and the markets 'animated'. Things have made themselves independent. They take on human characteristics.[6] The fetish commodity is anthropomorphized. And the relationship between the worker and the means of production is altered too. Marx details how the machinery uses the worker – and the producer of things empathizes with the manufacturing machines, with its 'fetishistically driven objects', so much as to supplant its own self as their 'soul'.[7] Fetishism's processes freeze humans in the icy air of reification: humans become things; things become humans. Marx uses the example of the table. As soon as it steps forward as a commodity it is transformed into a sensuous–non-sensuous thing. It stands not only with its feet on the ground; in relation to other commodities it stands on its head, and develops, Pinocchio-like, out of its wooden brain grotesque ideas, far more wonderful than if it began to dance of its own free will. Marx's footnote to this point reminds the reader of how the tables began to dance in China, as the rest of the world stood still: *pour encourager les autres*, he adds. This cryptic reference, according to an annotated edition of *Capital*, suggests that Marx is referencing the anti-feudal liberation revolts in China, which occurred at the same time as the European bourgeoisie succumbed to a spiritualist fad for table-raising in the fallow period after the defeat of the 1848/49 revolutions. In the absence of political progress, European citizens turn mystical – it was indeed the case that the modern worldwide spiritualist movement was inaugurated in a 'haunted house' with table-rapping in Hydesville, New York, on 31 March 1848 – while at the same time in China struggle breaks out, indicated in the phrase 'dancing tables', a synonym for revolution. The coming to life of inanimate objects, through the action of commodity fetishism as well as in Marx's rhetoric – those dancing tables of revolution and the European farcical imitation in spiritualist table-turning – is an illusion. In China it is the people who turn the tables on their rulers, and in the spiritualist fad it is the projection of a class unable or unwilling rationally to understand the world in which it takes up its place. But it seems, to reified consciousness, that the things themselves propel their own movement. It seems as if sign-things acquire an occult power over producers and

consumers. The sign-things are fetishized, invested with powers that make them animate, more animated than us, who, in relation to them, become mere things, lifeless. And so it seems in animation too, whether drawn frame by frame or photographed, then brought to life in projection.

In the 1935 'Exposé' of the *Arcades Project*, Walter Benjamin cites Marx's analysis of commodity fetishism. According to Benjamin, phantasmagoric commodity fetishism reaches its apex in the spectacular technological junkyards of the nineteenth-century world exhibitions.[8] Here, claims Benjamin, it appears as if things have more personality than their frequently faceless and nameless makers. Benjamin's *Arcades Project* was to be some sort of Marxian retelling of a fairy-tale, in which the Sleeping Beauty is awoken from the nightmare-dream sleep of capitalism's commodity phantasmagoria. In 'Pariser Passagen', an early collection of notes for the *Arcades Project*, Benjamin refers to youth as a slumbering princess, suffering an experience akin to that of dreaming. Youth – that is, the future – sleeps, while the objects sizzle. Twentieth-century souls must wake up to the objects of the nineteenth, wake up to the broken promises of abundance, and face, in full consciousness, the alluring objects in the stores of attractions. Benjamin stresses how the *Arcades Project* is an attempt to write up the 'technique of awakening'. And yet, necessarily, the peculiar liveliness of objects must be tabulated, and the social utopian fantasies invested in objects noted.[9] Brecht criticized Benjamin's animation of the world of things as mysticism, as a childish attempt to undo the fetishism of commodities by taking it seriously. It is, after all, a child's impulse to awaken life in petrified things. But Benjamin is insistent: it is objectively true; things are not what they used to be.[10] In industrial modernity, things sidle onto centre stage. And once the thrill of the world exhibitions dulls, cartoons and the movies are the next screen to flaunt the super-animation of fetish things.

Benjamin identifies an early form of cartooning as a visual exemplar of this fantastic state of affairs. Grandville, the nineteenth-century caricaturist – and as such a producer of mass art, whose caprices fuse and confuse nature and fashion items, people and commodities, animals and people – is labelled by Benjamin the sorcerer-priest of commodity fetishism.[11] But, says Benjamin, Disney's scenarios too, albeit without Grandville's seeds of mortification, indicate, through their robust liveliness of inanimate objects, just how autonomous our objects seem to us.[12] Given this, it was no surprise that animators – inheritors of Grandville's transmutation skills – would immediately sell their skills to advertising. In Britain Arthur Melbourne Cooper is said to have produced an animated commercial for Bird's Custard Powder in 1897. He also pioneered propagandistic uses in his animation of matches in *Matches: An Appeal* (1899). This was a petition to the public to donate matches to soldiers fighting in the Boer War. An artist quick to make an art of objects moving was Méliès. He animated the letters of the alphabet for adverts in 1898. Méliès had been at the first performance of the Lumière Brothers' film at the Grand Café in Paris. Three months later he obtained a camera and began making films. Méliès animated the moon, stars, rockets; it was a cosmos in movement, in specially built sets, often with trapdoors and scenery shifted by pulleys. He did not effect the frame-by-frame illusions of liveliness. Méliès had spent time in London and visited 'the home of mystery', the Egyptian Hall, headquarters of theatrical magic and illusion. In his book *Der Kampf um den Film* (*The Struggle for the Film*), finished in the late 1930s, Hans Richter wrote of Méliès:

> The world in which his films took place was the set of his *Théâtre Robert Houdin*. But that set was no longer a flat surface *in front of* which conjuring tricks were performed, it was a *space*. The naivety of the decors reminds one of the Douanier Rousseau, their romanticism of Delacroix, whose powerful frames Méliès broke by having the shadows of real clouds pass over Delacroix's romantic canvases.[13]

The fantastic and the documentary were combined. And in Méliès, as in Disney later, the scenery becomes an active character. The development of this technique quickly led to the bestowal of personalities on the superlively objects. J. Stuart Blackton, an innovator in the one turn, one picture method, made the theme of objects possessed of life explicit in 1907 in *The Haunted House*. The 'old spirit world' had not been abolished in the United States – it provided amusing material for entertainment. Blackton had been animating lightning sketches such as *The Enchanted Drawing* in 1900 and, in 1906, *Humorous Phases of Funny Face*. This showed a face and a neck, drawn by hand, just as the lightning sketchers had done. It showcased their emphasis on speed, on the displacement of a line, the adding of a dot, a deletion here or there. Then, without the sketcher's hand being visible, a woman appears and then a man. Smoke obliterates the woman – and the hand appears again to rub it all out. A fat body emerges; a mess turns into two faces. They disappear again, replaced by a clown, playing with a hat and baton. A white poodle enters and jumps up. A big hoop appears. The hand rubs out parts of the image but the unerased part of the clown keeps dancing, as if it were clinging onto every bit of life, in any part. So then the hand rubs the rest out. But Blackton's ghostly story of the haunted house was different. It used real-world objects. The little house's door and windows start to wobble. Inside, objects move of their own volition. The food on the table is cut by a knife, the tea pours itself and the sugar cubes jump into the cup. A clown emerges from a jug. The room tips to one side and furniture slides, and then the room goes into a spin – by now of course it is the camera that does not just record frame by frame, but also produces the illusion by slanting and rotating. The following year a Spanish cameraman Segundo de Chomon performed a similar trick in *Hotel Elettrico*. (Eventually, these mobile objects develop fully fledged personality. Walt Disney's studio was later remarkable for its drawing of 'furniture with personality'.[14]) Cohl was employed by Gaumont to attempt to work out how Blackton made *The Haunted House*. Animators and producers and audiences were not simply seduced by the magic. They all wanted to know how the magic was done; that is to say, they were spellbound and wanted, at the same time, to break the spell through enlightenment. Of course, for some this was in order to repeat it for profit.

Cohl did not follow Blackton's animation of objects. He took another direction. Blackton had included the real world in his cartoons. Cohl stuck with the drawn universe. His cartooning shunned photographs of 'reality', remaining instead inside the graphic world and inventing a fluid plastic language of ideographs. There were, however, real-life shots of the artist's hands. Cohl's humour was black, unlike that of Reynaud, whose *Pauvre Pierrot* exuded the atmosphere of a French fairy-tale. In contrast, Cohl's influences were burlesque, grotesque, and derived from the circus and vaudeville. His characters were often circus attractions, jugglers and magicians. In *Un Drame chez les fantoches* (1908) a little white stickman goes to a door. Above the door is a window and curtain. He points at the window with his stick. A woman throws a bucket of whiteness on him. He leaps in through the window. There is an explosion. She runs out for help. He tumbles out of the window and runs away. A policeman comes with a big truncheon. He gives it and his cape to her. They jig a little. A bearded man comes and knights the policeman. On walks a man with a wardrobe. He opens it to show a pedal machine. It explodes. A tower grows with a plant pot. A woman comes, and the policeman comes again. Then a serpent is there. The woman falls down. The man falls down in grief. A vase grows around them. He ascends. Then he is in a cell, and he tries to escape by reaching the window. A ladder appears. A fight breaks out. And so it goes on – no reason but dream reason and the endless battle with the state, with other people, with objects. The 'hero' Fantoche, who fights the world and nature, was the retarded ancestor of Charlie Chaplin.

The animation market was competitive and international. The Éclair studio employed Cohl, and so he moved to their American site in 1912. He worked on the animation of a comic strip called *The Newlyweds*, and the Éclair studios coined for these 'drawings that move' the name 'animated cartoons'. These took their place in a burgeoning market of American product. America was the home of magic, of spiritedness, after all, since 1848 and the toe-cracking, table-rapping Fox sisters at Hydesville. Marx alluded to the American fascination with spirits in his *The Eighteenth Brumaire of Louis Bonaparte*:

> in countries with an old civilisation, with a developed formation of classes, with modern conditions of production and with an intellectual consciousness in which all traditional ideas have been dissolved by the work of centuries, *the republic* signifies *in general only the political form of the revolutionising of bourgeois society* and not its *conservative form of life*, as, for example, in the United States of North America, where, though classes already exist, they have not yet become fixed, but continually change and interchange their component elements in constant flux, where the modern means of production, instead of coinciding with a stagnant surplus population, rather compensate for the relative deficiency of heads and hands, and where, finally, the feverish, youthful movement of material production, which has to make a new world its own, has left neither time nor opportunity for abolishing the old spirit world.[15]

The spiritualist movement was given a boost when the Theosophical Society was founded in the state of New York by Colonel Olcott and the

Russian aristocrat Helena Blavatsky in 1875. Engels kept an eye on it in the 1870s and after, if only to mock.[16] In a letter to Friedrich Adolph Sorge in Hoboken, written in 1886, he noted the ideological function of spiritualism and other 'old world' hangovers:

> the Americans, for good historical reasons, lag far behind in all theoretical matters; true, they did not bring with them from Europe any medieval institutions, but instead a mass of medieval traditions – religion, English common (feudal) law, superstition, spiritualism – in short, every kind of balderdash that was not immediately harmful to business and now comes in very handy for the stultification of the masses.[17]

Engels's critique of spiritualism's politically anaesthetizing effects was one that would be echoed later in attacks on cinema. For Marx, in the 1850s, that the 'old spirit world' remained had to do with time, the too speedy pace of change and buoyant invention, which meant that inherited and immigrated ways of life and belief had to be circuited into life in the republic. The rapid pace of change, the feverish activity, did not relent. America, land of immigration, site for the building of new lives and fortunes, continued to host a flurry of quacksalving and cure-alls, gadgets, machineries, techniques and fantastic claims. In America, inventions were patented and styles transformed constantly. Animation was invented and reinvented. In 1913 Raoul Barré devised the peg system, for the easy registering of drawings by holding one on top of the next with standard perforations. He also concocted the slash system with Bill Nolan. Here the foreground character was cut out, obviating the need to keep redrawing repeated elements of the background. In 1914 John Randolph Bray patented the use of printed background scenes and the application of grey shades. The next year he patented the use of transparent paper to split the moving figures from the static background. In 1915 Earl Hurd introduced celluloid plates. Bray's and Hurd's inventions produced the cel system, which became the dominant mode of cartoon production by the mid 1920s. These devices evoked Taylorized assembly-line methods and were essentially labour-saving cycles. But time and labour saving was not a universal aim. Winsor McCay represented another strain. He used no labour-saving methods. His animations were detailed, beautiful, and took many months to produce. McCay's story of an animal tamer and his dinosaur, *Gertie the*

Ko-Ko Chops Suey

Dinosaur, was first shown in Chicago in 1914. A later effort, *The Sinking of the Lusitania*, made in 1918, was a cartoon that imitated the rhythm of newsreels; 25,000 drawings depicting the final hours of an ocean steamer sunk by a German submarine shimmered their elegant lines on the screen. At twenty-five minutes in length, it was the longest animation so far.

But the bulk of cartooning was finding its form as short character-based sketches, emerging from studios. In 1915 began the *Out of the Inkwell* series by the Fleischers, who invented the rotoscope, a method of converting live-action sequences into drawings frame by frame. It allowed an animator to copy live-action film frame by frame onto a piece of translucent glass set into a drawing board for tracing onto animation paper. One of the Fleischer figures was a clown called Ko-Ko, who always opened the show by exiting from an inkwell. Ko-Ko knew that he was made of ink – and in the early days his story was often one of the struggle for corporeal existence. The show started typically with the animator's hand drawing Ko-Ko from a few inkblots. Then Max Fleischer is seen at work in the studio. Action cuts between the studio and the cartoon world, until the story takes off, playing with the different planes and realities, further confusing things by creating illusions of depth through exaggerated perspective drawing. Otto Messner cut between live action and drawing too in 1916 in *Trials of a Movie Cartoonist*. As he draws, the figures rebel and refuse to do what he tries to make them do. They contradict him, insisting he has no right to make slaves of them, even if he is their creator. The *Out of the Inkwell* series innovated in episode after episode – developing new techniques to thrill and bamboozle and amuse the audience. Consciousness of the medium was part of the entertainment. Social satire mixed with reflections on the relationship between animator, studio and figures. For example, *Ko-Ko in 1999* (1924) opens on the animator dipping his brush into an inkwell. He draws a block with a hole. Suddenly the animation springs into life. A head pops through. A hand lobs body parts at the head. Like inkblots they land and form a hand, a bell-bottomed trouser leg. He sticks his tongue out and snubs his nose. Ink splats him in the face. He fashions it into the rest of his body. The focus is back on the animator, who is playing with paper to make another figure. And then three more. A question mark springs from Ko-Ko's head for he is puzzled. 'Hey! What's the idea of the freaks?' he asks of the weirdly dressed figures. 'They are not freaks', says the animator. 'That is what people will look like in 1999.' Ko-Ko hates them. Old Father Time and he have a fight, and they whizz through the ages to a futurist world of skyscrapers and automation. A series of nightmarish encounters ends with an automatic marriage machine. 'Crickity-crack-clink-g-tr-r-r-buzz-wife? Do you this sap...' it whirrs, and then the instant babies arrive and the first matrimonial spat occurs. To end it all, bits of paper are tossed in the air and they turn into real live women cleaners, cleaning up a vast desk with an inkwell in the animator's studio.

In 1919 Pat Sullivan's Felix the Cat – or, better, a prototype called Master Tom – appeared in a short called *Feline Follies*.[18] It was four minutes and ten seconds long. Before *Felix* the studio had been making a series of Charlie Chaplin cartoons in 1916 and ones based on a cartoon strip about a 'sambo' figure, called Sammy Johnsin. *Feline Follies* opens on Master Tom as he hears a female cat meowing in the distance. He is intrigued, and his long black upright tail curls into a question mark. Later it becomes a toothbrush. It is a detachable prop, and inventively transformable, as are other things in this cartoon world: musical notes from the cat's wooing

Feline Follies

serenade become parts of a scooter, the tail its baseboard. But this is no children's fairy-tale. The world is cruel, and when the cat, framed by the mice, seeks solace in Miss Kitty White, only to find she has a brood of wailing kittens, he goes to the gasworks, puts a gas pump in his mouth and lies down to die. Felix, like Chaplin, is a victim. But he could not die just then. This was just the beginning for one of the first cartoon characters to be successfully and massively merchandized. The cat's success leeched on Chaplin's. Felix the Cat copied many of Chaplin's moves, the funny walk, the subtle movement or gesture. In the 1923 *Felix in Hollywood* the cat detaches his tail and uses it as a cane. He develops a moustache, and shrugs as he turns into Chaplin. This larking around comes to a halt when a 'real' cartoon Chaplin intervenes, accusing the cat of 'stealing my stuff'. In 1925 Felix hallucinates inside a refrigerator in a parodic short called *Felix the Cat in the Cold Rush*. But, unlike Charlie, Felix the Cat always finds solutions to problems beyond Chaplin's capabilities, for Chaplin is trapped in the physical world, as actor, despite all the tricks that post-production might be able to conjure up. Chaplin may have recognized his essentially cinematic character, but he also might have known that he could not fully dissolve himself into the celluloid world. He is supposed to have once remarked that he envied the perfect timing of animated cartoon gags because they never had to take time to breathe.[19] Their deadness made them seem so much more alive.

avant-cartoon

Just as cartooning was taking off in New York, Walter Benjamin wrote a tiny fragment called 'Negative Expressionism'. In this, he digresses on the figure of the eccentric. The Eccentric was a name adopted by avant-garde Russian circus performers. These were a type of clown who performed ludicrous novelty numbers. They appeared in the early years of Soviet theatre, arguing that the new tempo of life demanded a new type of acting, a new type of writing – gag-based – a new direction, in all a new type of show. They invented a system of acting, reliant on an intentional violation of logic, of sequence and ambiguity. Inspired by formalism's assault on habit and its disrespect for inherited consciousness, they set their clownish faces against emotion, innerness and psychology. Psychology is turned head-over-heels. The dramatist is a coupler of gags, a stager of stunts and tricks. The Eccentrics negated expressionism, with its talk of soul and psyche. Benjamin jots down some notes on these new figures:

> Eccentrics – clown and natural peoples – overcoming of inner impulses and the body centre. New unity of clothes, tattoos and body. Promiscuity of clothing of man and woman, of arms and legs. Dislocation of shame. Expression of true feeling: desperation, dis-location. Consequential search for deep possibilities for expression: the man, who has the chair he is sitting on pulled away from under him, and stays sitting. – Genderlessness, complete disintegration of vanity. Masculine genius at prostitution.[20]

Benjamin concludes by affiliating this anarchic, popular modernist form with Dada art, asserting the Eccentrics' connection with Francis Picabia. The eccentrics Kozintsev, Trauberg, Yutkevich and Kryzhitsky launched a manifesto in 1922. It declared:

> WE ARE ECCENTRISM IN ACTION
> 1] Presentation – rhythmic wracking of the nerves
> 2] The high-point – the trick
> 3] The author – an inventor-discoverer
> 4] The actor – mechanised movement, not buskins but roller-skates, not a mask

but a nose on fire. Acting – not movement but a wriggle, not mimicry but a grimace, not speech but shouts

We prefer Charlie's arse to Eleanora Duse's hands

5] The play – an accumulation of tricks. The speed of 1000 horse power. Chase, persecution, flight. Form – a divertissement

6] Humped backs, distended stomachs, wigs of stiff red hair – the beginning of a new style of stage costume. The foundation – continuous transformation

7] Horns, shots, typewriters, whistles, sirens – Eccentric music. The tap-dance – start of a new rhythm.[21]

European culture is to be abandoned in favour of American technology. The new techno-culture is one of pulp-fiction book jackets, Keystone Cops, circus posters, rollercoaster rides and the amusement park. The electric siren of contemporaneity bursts with a mighty roar into the perfumed boudoir of artistic aestheticism! The manifesto puts forward some proposals, amongst which are calls for the production of cartoons, caricatures and *revue*.[22] The Eccentrics loved Chaplin, and he appears throughout the manifesto: 'Protest is inevitable, just like Charlie Chaplin's moustache'; 'Risk, bravery, violence, chase, revolution, gold, blood, laxative pills, Charles Chaplin, wrecks on land, sea and in the air, surprise cigars, operetta prima donnas, adventures of all sorts, skating-rinks, American books, horses, struggle, *chansonettes*, a *salto* on a bicycle and thousands and thousands of events that make our Today beautiful.'[23] Eisenstein, also in 1923, remarked on Chaplin's 'attractional' mechanics of movement, with its particularly lyrical effect.[24]

Benjamin returned to the figure of the Eccentric in 1935, deeming it a relation of Chaplin and Mickey Mouse. Circus, Dada, Chaplin, cartoons and Disney form an absurd file that bounds and shimmies through modernism. The Eccentrics were adamant that American modernity was a greater source of ideas and attitude than European high art. And the theorists of formalism concurred. Shklovsky praised Chaplin in 1923.

Chaplin's movements and all his films are not conceived in words or sketches but in the flashing of black and white shadows. He has broken finally and completely with theatre and for that reason he does of course have the right to the title of the first film actor.

It is interesting to note that Chaplin never says anything on film and no explanatory titles appear on the screen between the individual reels of his films.

Russian film actors have told me that, in order to link the disparate elements of cinema movements with emotion, they speak suitable phrases under their breath. You can observe this if you look at their lips. Chaplin does not speak on film: he moves. He works with cinematic raw material and does not translate himself from theatrical to film language. I cannot at the moment define the essence of the comic nature of Chaplin's movement but perhaps it lies in the fact that it is mechanical. You can divide Chaplin's acting into a series of passages, each passage usually ending with a full stop, a pose.

Resorting perhaps to metaphor, we might say that Chaplin's movement is dotted. Chaplin himself is obviously well acquainted with all the 'steps' in his art. We can divide his acting into a series of 'constant movements' repeated with varying motivations from film to film. I shall enumerate a few: Chaplin walks (laughter provokes the actual moment he moves from the spot), Chaplin on a staircase, Chaplin falls off a chair (head over heels and then he stays like that), Chaplin smiles (for three beats), Chaplin is shaken by the collar, and so on.[25]

Chaplin's films were the best that cinema had produced till then. They were pure cinema, and 'in all probability classical cinema will derive from them', Shklovsky presumed.[26] Turning to the future of cinema, Shklovsky suspected that Chaplin's stunts were looking too well worn and his art was changing. He noted the various paths that cinema might take. Horror films with the requisite chase, murders and temporal transpositions; the American film with even more stunts, train crashes, animals, all turning into a sort of cinematic vaudeville. The high-society psychological film, reminiscent of theatrical form, he hoped would die out. But the future of cinema, he concluded, might belong to animation.

There is one more line that the development of cinema might follow and that is the animated trick film. I have seen several and I am convinced that it has as yet quite unrealised potential. The interesting thing about it is the awareness of the toy-like quality of the animated image moving on the screen. The feeling of illusion was a very important feature of the old theatre and they knew how to use it, suppressing it one moment and resurrecting it the next. Cinema is, of course, very conventional just as photography itself is conventional but we have trained ourselves to perceive the world through photography and we scarcely notice the conventionality of cinema. Hence one of the opportunities for artistic construction is disappearing: the play with illusion. Perhaps the animated film can be combined with the photographed film? But what will be will be.[27]

All sorts of anti-academic and experimenting artists found that cartoons touched on many things that they too wished to explore: abstraction, forceful outlines, geometric forms and flatness, questioning of space and time and logic – that is to say, a consciousness of space that is not geographical but graphic, and time as non-linear but convoluted. In short, cartoons were not tempted to imitate theatre, to produce an illusion in three dimensions. Some artists threw out their oil paint and abstract canvases in order to devise films. In Germany around 1921 the painter Walter Ruttmann turned to abstract 'absolute' animations, melding film with avant-garde art. Dadaists George Grosz and Otto Dix and company had already moved into an art of caricature; turning painterly expressionism into cartoon on canvas or paper. Take George Grosz's image of Oscar Panizza's funeral (1917–19): a skeleton emerging from a coffin into a chaos of architecture and half-animal, half-human creatures. And Otto Dix's painting *The Matchseller* included dialogue in a comic strip bubble, just as had William Randolph Hearst's early pre-1918 cartoon strips. This exchange is a discussion between graphic designers, in peculiarly nihilistic and yet quixotic times, about how to represent the modern world and how, through that representation, to destroy its apparent coherence. Both seek pictorial and verbal languages that spurn bourgeois humanism. Their visual language hoped to shock and surprise and make the viewer ask: What will they try to pull on us next? How repulsive can they make my environment seem? This ugliness and flatness and motility that they portray – does it lay bare how all this civilization is merely a façade? And a façade ready to be overhauled? When Rodchenko decided in 1919 that the line stands firm against pictorial expressivity, that it has revealed a new conception of the world – truly to construct and not to represent – he could have been describing cartoons' flexible and cavalier attitude to representation.

René Clair included a whimsical cartoon in *Paris qui dort* (1923), and some animated matchsticks in *Entr'acte* (1924). And the other sections of the film, devised by Francis Picabia, portrayed gags, loosely sequential according to a Cohl-like illogic. The film was to be shown in the intermission of Picabia's ballet called *Relâche*. The programme declared: '*Entr'acte* does not believe in very much, in the pleasure of life perhaps; it believes in the pleasure of inventing, it respects nothing except the desire to *burst out laughing*.'[28] Léger animated a Charlie Chaplin cutout in *Ballet Mécanique* (1923–24) in a sequence called 'Charlot cubiste'.[29] Other portions of the film featured extreme close-ups of domestic items. The simple act of close-up in itself acted as an animation of objects, an endowment with life and personality. As Léger wrote in *A New Realism – The Object* (1926): 'Enormous enlargement of an object or a fragment gives it a personality it never had before and in this way it can become a vehicle of entirely new and plastic power.' Emile Cohl's derangement of narrative endeared him to the anarcho-surrealist sensibility of Jean Vigo. Vigo's *Zéro de Conduite* of 1932 has a scene in which a villainous school inspector enters a classroom of naughty schoolboys. He looks at a drawing lying on the teacher's desk. It was drawn while the teacher was doing a handstand. The stickman drawing comes to life. Vigo's homage to Emile Cohl dances.

Other intellectuals noticed the inventions and transformations that were occurring in the cartoon world. In the *Observer* of 8 May 1927 W.O. Brigstocke reflected on Felix's curves – developed steadily since Bill Nolan, the originator of rubber-hose animation, had drawn Felix from 1922 to 1924, the volume of work being too much for Messmer to cope with alone. Huntly Carter reported on Brigstocke's idea in his study of 'the new spirit in the cinema':

> Fantasy, which has for so long been accepted as an expression of the whimsical state of mind, is, of course, within the legitimate sphere of the Cinema. On the screen it is seen at the gayest and best in a small line that assumes thousands of fantastic shapes that comprise the Cartoon. In the Cartoon, which is one of the most popular and in some respects the best medium of cinema expression, the human atom and its belongings undergo whimsical changes that cause a continuous stream of images to form in the mind, and that throw an abundance of rich crumbs to the imagination. But the Cartoon never departs from the actual. It consists of an elastic line in evolution. Shapes grow out of it with which we are familiar even though they are distorted and battered by a sort of recurrent earthquake.
>
> In other words, the Cartoon of the Mickey Mouse, the Krazy Kat, the Felix the Cat, the Inkwell, the Adventures of Sammy and Sausage, or the Oswald Sound Cartoon kind, is simply the caricaturist playing with line that has the elasticity of gas. It shrinks and expands, collapses and recovers, behaves like a spring winding and unwinding, and at the same time assumes the shapes and characteristics of human beings, animals, insects, of animate things, and inanimate ones made animate. These extraordinary puppets of all sorts, that fall to pieces in heaps and reunite, and outdo even an India-rubber ball in diversity of shapes; that speed through space with a velocity that has no parallel outside the

Cinema, have a distinct sociological value. They exhibit man in society caught in a network of events undergoing or trying to escape the consequences. They are in fact a comment, a very witty instructive and biting comment on the absurdities of Man and other living things seen in the light of materialism. At the same time they are human, tragic and comic. According to Mr W.O. Brigstocke, of the Education Department of the Liverpool University, the Cartoon has a valuable educational side owing to its elasticity. He has suggested that the moving line of a Felix Cartoon can serve to teach architecture. 'Felix could illustrate in a film such difficult conceptions as that of thrust in architecture. Suppose the teacher turned two other Felixes into pillars at his side and then constructed a Felix arch. It would be easy and amusing for him to show stresses and how they could be met. You could see the arch sagging at the knees or wherever it would sag. Gothic cathedrals which demonstrated in the light of all men where they were weak and where they were strong, by bending, writhing and even falling down, promise infinite amusement. In the same way what could not be done with maps? Let Felix be taken up to a great height and let him behold all the kingdoms of the world with their pomp and vanities, not to speak of their trade and transport; then drop him a given number of feet, or let him use up one of his nine lives and drop him all the way; in this manner it would be easy literally to see what scale means, both in space and time values. When one thinks of Felix and mathematics – cones sliced in lovely sections, curves developing in a panoply of perpendiculars, and tangents to illustrate the secrets of growth and motion and form – why, in these lines we could have all the joys of Felix, Professor Einstein and the Zoo simultaneously.'[30]

Carter's defence of *Felix* cartoons was based on a perception of their scientific potentials. They traced the flexible line of evolution. They made visible the convoluted complexities of modern bureaucratic society. And they explained physics by visualizing, twisting and assailing its principles. Physics and Darwin parlayed in the cartoon cosmos. This seemed to extend the type of satirical-pedagogic investigation into geometry that English headmaster Edwin Abbott Abbott devised in the 1880s in *Flatland*, an adventure story that begins in a two dimensional world, populated by a socialized hierarchy of regular geometrical figures:

Imagine a vast sheet of paper on which straight Lines, Triangles, Squares, Pentagons, Hexagons, and other figures, instead of remaining fixed in their places, move freely about, on or in the surface, but without the power of rising above or sinking below it, very much like shadows – only hard and with luminous edges – and you will then have a pretty correct notion of my country and countrymen.[31]

A. Square from Flatland, a land of two dimensions, undertakes a journey with A. Sphere, a being from three-dimensional Spaceland and they visit Pointland, a land of no dimensions, where A Point exists, certain that he is everything for he comprises the whole of his universe. They tour Lineland, a land of one dimension, where the longest line is the King. They enter three dimensions for a short time, enjoying the new perspective afforded. But such experience only turns his fellow shapes, the low-rank circle-women, the triangles and the many-sided masters, against him. A satire on Victorian hierarchy melds with mathematical instruction and an Einsteinian dimension beyond the earth's three dimensions is struggled for imaginatively.

Dedication
To
The Inhabitants of SPACE IN GENERAL
And H.C. IN PARTICULAR
This Work is Dedicated
By a Humble Native of Flatland
In the Hope that
Even as he was Initiated into the Mysteries
Of THREE Dimensions
Having been previously conversant
With ONLY TWO
So the Citizens of that Celestial Region
May aspire yet higher and higher
To the Secrets of FOUR FIVE OR EVEN SIX Dimensions
Thereby contributing
To the Enlargment of THE IMAGINATION
And the possible Development
Of that most rare and excellent Gift of MODESTY
Among the Superior Races
Of SOLID HUMANITY

In 1927, the vogue for *Felix the Cat* films in France spurred art historian Marcel Brion to remark on Felix's expressiveness. Brion indicated a similarity between the films' permutable world and the visions of the surrealist movement. He called Felix a 'sur-chat', unlike everyday cats.[32] Felix converts objects all the time: question marks turn into skyhooks, his tail a Chaplin-style walking stick or a ship mast or a car crank, horizon lines become tightropes, and the titles become objects in the story. Felix can turn into a holdall bag, if the situation demands it. Resourcefulness is the most important thing. In *Felix Dopes it Out* (1924), a lion's roars appear as rings of sound. These then get used as lasso-like restrainers. Everything in the drawn world is of the same stuff. This is shown most graphically in the opening title, when Felix the cat sucks ink from the animator's nib, in order to form his tail, the tail that is so flexible and useful. Felix's ideographic playfulness recalled magical experiments with words, the phonetic and graphical transformational games present in the literature of the futurist, Dadaist and surrealist avant-garde of the second two decades of the twentieth century. Such typographical play – as in Apollinaire's calligrammes, a visible lyricism where there exists a graphic figurative correspondence between the poem in print and the sense of imagery of that poem – brings words to life and produces something syncretic, an object between a poem and a picture. Apollinaire was aware of the transformation that such an approach wreaks on narrative. He wrote: 'Psychologically it is of no importance that this visible image be composed of fragments of broken language, for the bond between these fragments is no longer the logic of grammar but an ideographic logic, culminating in an order of spatial disposition totally opposed to discursive juxtaposition ... it is the opposite of narration.' The ideograph, word-image, holds up the narrative flow, much as does the gag, basis of the short cartoons.[33] This fitted well with distributors' demands – for the number of gags was correlated to the number of laughs – which was, after all, the measure of a film's success.

Walt Disney's first Laugh-O-Gram cartoon in 1922, 'a modernized version of that old fairy-tale' *The Four Musicians of Bremen*, used transformation and typographic effects too. Perhaps Disney's embrace of the modern age through the old, inherited form of the fairy-tale mimicked L. Frank Baum, author of *The Wizard of Oz* and countless other 'modernized' or 'electrified fairy-tales'. Musical notes float on the air. The word 'ouch' emanates from a tree, as does the word 'idea' from a fish's head, and, in a nod to Felix, the cat removes its tail and uses it as a bat to parry attacking artillery fire, before riding off on a cannonball as if it were a motorbike. Walt Disney began to make cartoon films at the beginning of the 1920s. Walt Disney could not draw very well, but he had an aptitude for characterization, for developing cartoon 'personalities' and also for structuring *fabula*. He based his stories on fairy-tales as they were out of copyright, but even so they did not make much money. The *Out of the Inkwell* series from the Fleischers had made animated drawings act in the real world, but Disney turned it around in the mid 1920s for *Alice in Cartoonland* and put a real girl in the animated world. Always have a hook, always do the new thing, was the motivation of the time. *Alice's Fishy Story* (1924) opens with a little girl involuntarily at piano practice. She escapes by getting her dog to tinkle on the keys, and so deludes her mother into thinking it is she who plays. Animals are children's willing helpers in the cartoonworld, just as they are in fairy-tales. In a dream sequence, which fades into cartoon, she visits the North Pole. A cat is there with a skate on his tail and two on his back legs. As he slides the same backdrop goes by again and again. The big story, reported in *The Arctic Breeze* newspaper, is that the fish have gone on strike, and so the Eskimos are starving. 'Idea!!' radiates from the cat's head, as he uses his tail to drill into the snow. But the fish fight back, as a swordfish cuts a circle around him. Live Alice turns up to save the day when the rescued cat is sent to the wrecked Hesperus, to dredge up chewing tobacco from 1854. He chucks in plugs and when the fish come up to spit it out, he bonks them on the head with his detached tail. The real world materializes at the end – all film and no more drawings – and Alice and friends are chased off the private land they have occupied. The end is always the return to reality – the reality of the law, property, school, home.

In 1927 Disney produced *Oswald the Lucky Rabbit*. Machinic and tinkering, he was a Buster Keaton-type figure, in a world of automation. Critics preferred animated Oswald in an animated world to Alice. They relished the accelerated pace, tauter construction and the dynamic use of space. Construction was modelled on live-action conventions: cutting patterns, iris masks, point-of-view shots, diagonal angles, multiple camera set-ups, shadows, games with fake perspective, all the effects known from Fairbanks, Lloyd, Chaplin and Laurel and Hardy films. But, importantly, in Oswald's and Alice's world, it was always a question of movement, of animation, all the more apparent if images of the inanimate world were represented: hand props, buildings, lampposts and anything that was supposed to be still or fixed in shape had to be tweaked, squashed and stretched. Again the cartoon world was violent and cynical. *Great Guns* (1927), for example, was about a war draft. It showed piles of mouse corpses and heads blasted off – only to be redrawn in place again. There was sexual innuendo too, with guns once they have been blasted falling limp. It was adult and stupid.

Its grim humour was a riposte to the 'educational' short *Silent Gun of the Future*, a feature on the Goldwyn–Bray studio animated newsreel. A title announces 'a tremendous report and a great recoil follow the firing of the big guns now in use'. Then a picture follows of a big cannon on the battlefield. This is the electro-magnetic gun, the silent powderless weapon of the future. An animation demonstrates the electro-magnetic principle of passing current through coils of wire to set up a magnetic field. This is then shown in operation along a gun barrel. The coils charge one at a time, propelling the shell until it is fired. The shells are shown exploding nowhere, in a no-man's-land. The war of the future is unmanned and will be powered by self-loading, self-firing lively machines. This captured in an image the strange logic of animation. Animation was a world of life without humans. Objects came to life on their own accord. Animals spoke or re-created the social community that humans thought was reserved for them alone. Without humans, but full of life, it could only remind audiences of their superfluity, of their death perhaps. Death through absence – as in the self-loading gun, which shows the skill of killing without victims or perpetrators. And yet, at the same time, there might be compensations in death. The realm of the dead is the realm of the overlively – just as ghosts are too lively and have too much energy and a desperate desire to communicate and just as the spirit that objects possess makes them mischievous and meddling, not quiet and subservient.

it's mickey mouse

After the studio which was distributing the Disney cartoons appropriated the Oswald character, Walt Disney created Mortimer Mouse, and then changed the mouse's name to Mickey. Animated by Ub Iwerks in less than two weeks, Mickey Mouse's first role was motivated by Charles Lindbergh's transatlantic flight. *Plane Crazy* (1928) mustered all the lunacy of techno-logical modernity. This was graphically represented by the plane as it circled and swooped, and also in the cartoon's look, in the multiple changes of angles of vision, and the speed of movement of things and the fast pace of actions. The audience twists and turns with the plane or with the line of vision that follows the plane. The whole image surface is animated. It is not one single activity that we follow, but a dispersed scene – it cannot all be taken in at one viewing. And the whole world is alive. A church spire crumples itself up to avoid the passing plane. Bodies elongate and detach parts at will. Substance mutates. Reality, objects, are always working to solve problems, efficiently. So, Mickey is able to yank a fan-tail from a turkey to place on his new airplane. Human relations are brutal too. Minnie has to be terrified into kissing Mickey. Then came *The Gallopin' Gaucho* (1928), with Mickey Mouse in a Douglas Fairbanks pastiche, but distribu-tors showed little interest. The first film to get a release, *Steamboat Willie* (1928), would have to present a special selling point. *Steamboat Willie*, which premiered in November 1928 in the New York cinema Colony Theatre, was an exercise in strange literalism: a goat eats a musical score and then its tail is cranked to produce music, which appears on the screen as notes floating through the air. And when the cow is fed hay it immediately assumes the size and shape of the bale it is fed. A ratty Mickey Mouse was made of a rubber-hose-type torso, which did not snap back into place when stretched, but dangled for as long as was necessary for the gag. The special selling point of the first successful cartoon film with Mickey Mouse – the thing that hooked the crowds – was its sound.

The Disney team was not the first to use sound. Through the 1920s the Fleischer brothers experimented with soundtracks for *Song Car-Tunes*. Paul Terry, producer of more than two hundred silent *Aesop's Fables* for Amadée Van Beuren, made a synchronized sound film called *Dinnertime* in the summer of 1928. When Disney's third film was underway, *The Jazz Singer* was being talked about in Hollywood and elsewhere. But it was obvious to many that animation had a particular affinity to sound and music. Music and film both move through time, but in cartooning, with its frame-by-frame fully controllable structure, the links between sound and image could be drawn so tightly that a symbiosis, a perfect rhythmic synchronization,

Mickey Mouse in Disney's *Steamboat Willie*

could occur. Music was often visualised in the silent animations, in count-less scenes of misbehaviour in the dance halls, or more inventively, as in *Alice the Firefighter* (1926) when a rag piano player uses musical notes to climb up to a hotel window. *Steamboat Willie* presented the tensions between brutish Peg-Leg Pete, Minnie Mouse and Mickey Mouse. Many of the gags involved sound – the cow whose mouth is prised open, so her teeth may be played as a xylophone, for example. A 'bar sheet' was used for *Steamboat Willie*. This was a chart for each musical action or phrase – every toot and whistle and melody – linking it to a description of the screen action it was to accompany. The camera operator's exposure sheet was prepared before the animators set to work. Everything was precisely charted to allow syn-chronization. This system, in its more evolved form, came to be known as 'Mickey Mousing'. This sonic universe accepts no differences among sounds, no hierarchies of tone. All noises take their place on the sound-track and get their turn. A violin phrase is no better than a cracking walnut or a squelching kitten body. The art lies in the arrangement of materials, from wherever they stem. Simultaneously, in Vienna, twelve-tone analysed the issue of democracy in sound. Kurt Schwitters knew of the democracy of materials too and put its principles into practice in his Merz collages. His was an art of the ragpicker and it knew no hierarchies of stuff, for, as Hans Richter relates in his autobiography, Schwitters had a habit of foraging in rubbish bins for scraps to use in his collages. One memorable ripe cheese paper rescued from a bin stunk out an entire first class hotel in Switzerland.[34] Léger imported the ragpicking technique to America, telling Richter one day that he painted American landscapes: 'Americans throw everything away into the landscape, and I paint it.'[35] But Disney and the Fleischers and Sullivan and the others were already doing this, re-imaging the landscape, bringing the abject back to life, giving it all voice, from the tin cans to the tom cats to the rednecks.

Disney was sure that sound could be used even more effectively in his cartoons and so he set about devising his Silly Symphonies series. The gags were milder. The point was the synchronicity of sound and image. The cartoons were more slowly paced than the slapstick knockabouts. Here the music really did seem to be antecedent. *The Skeleton Dance* (1929) was the first Silly Symphony. Ub Iwerks drew it and Carl W. Stalling composed the music. It opened with two huge disc-eyes, and crashing music. The view draws back to reveal an owl. There is the sound of caterwauling in the graveyard and it sounds like a curious music. All the movements are synchronized with sound and music. Stretchy and squashy skeletons dance in formation. One skeleton borrows the bones of an-other's legs to play him as a ribcage xylophone. A cat's tail is played as a cello. Everything is in movement all the time. *The Skeleton Dance* was perhaps the most successful of all the Silly Symphonies. Jean Prévost, in a 1938 article from *Vendredi* entitled 'Walt Disney, the man who never had a childhood', noted that it had been made without worrying about audience reactions. Yet public and critics alike were charmed. Dorothy Richardson had praised Felix in the modernist film journal *Close Up* in August 1928,

The Skeleton Dance

and *transition*, the house journal of the modernist avant-garde, went so far as to print a still from *Steamboat Willie*. In a special programme on 10 November 1929, the rather dandyish London Film Society, under the direction of Ivor Montagu, and before an audience that included Eisenstein, John Grierson and Aldous Huxley, showed Jean Epstein's *The Fall of the House of Usher*, Grierson's *Drifters* and Eisenstein's *Battleship Potemkin* together with Disney's *The Barn Dance*.[36] Eric Walter White, in a study of silhouette animations by Lotte Reiniger, put out by Leonard and Virginia Woolf's Hogarth Press in 1931, defended animation as 'pure cinema':

> At the present moment the cartoon film is by no means confined to the United States. Countless imitations of Mickey Mouse have sprung up in France and Germany; and Russia (as might be expected) has turned out a series of modernised *Aesop's Fables*, in which the human roles are played by machines and the moral emphasises the necessity for collectivist as opposed to individual action. It is not improbable that in the near future musicians will be found writing scores for short trick film operas; a pair of collaborators like Bert Brecht and Kurt Weill, who produced *Der Flug der Lindberghs* for radio performance in 1929, are certainly capable of inspiring such a musical trick film, in which they could remedy all the unfortunate errors made by Pabst in the screen adaptation of their *Threepenny Opera*. However that may be, the trick film in its original form

remains one of the purest manifestations of cinema, and there is no doubt that a century hence (if the films have not perished by then) the best work of Walt Disney and Lotte Reiniger will be looked upon as primitives in the same way as the present generation looks on the paintings of Simone Martini and Sassetta or the music of Byrd and Monteverdi.

White explained Disney's speciality:

> The important discovery made by Walt Disney in his cartoon films concerns the unexpected relations that exist between visual and aural phenomena. For instance, when a stream of bubbles appears on the screen, Mickey will almost certainly prick them with a pin, and as they explode they will play a tune in which the frequency of the wave-vibration of each note will be inversely proportional to the size of the bubbles. Other purely visual discoveries are the spectacular entry made by the plaice in the opening submarine scene of *Frolicking Fish*, where the plaice, having swung in from the side, reaches the centre of the screen, turns round and reveals the fact that it is as thin as a lath, and the solo dance of the frog in the Silly Symphony, *Spring*. This particular frog is dancing by the bank of a stream, and at first his shadow dances with him in obedience to the physical laws of light. But suddenly the frog and his reflection part company: as the frog dances to the right, his shadow dances to the left, and *vice versa*. This piece of optical nonsense is as purely cinematic as the Oceana Roll in the *Gold Rush*; and many other instances (often more vulgar) can be found in Walt Disney's work.[37]

This was not just children's stuff, and certainly not sugar-sweet. Whether they were for adults or children was indeterminate. They were simply for anarchists of any age. Cartoons, for all their slapstick playing, seemed to appeal to intellect and imagination. Critics noticed that those made prior to 1928 were primarily concerned with ideas. Robert Feild, who spent time at the Disney studios in the late 1930s and wrote the first 'serious' study, *The Art of Walt Disney* (1942), understood the cerebral nature of animation. Film, he notes, has the ability to overcome the limitations of time and space to which we are normally subjected. The imagination of the audience can be appealed to in such a way that it is freed from the restrictions of the physical world.[38] 'What is Mickey anyway but an abstract idea in the process of becoming?'[39] Philosophy and animation unearth each other.

Lack of speech, but presence of noise, facilitated the cartoons' success on the international market. By 1930 Disney's mouse was an international phenomenon. Mickey Mouse conquered Germany in 1930. In January of that year the first Mickey Mouse film seen was *The Barn Dance*. In February five more were shown including *The Skeleton Dance*. Disney was conquering Europe. The actions portrayed in these early Disney films were irrational and physics-defying, sometimes violent and raucous, but only one ran into problems with the censors: *Barnyard Battle*, a farmyard knockabout based on the World War of 1914–18, where the Hun are German cats, defeated ignominiously by the French Mickey-style mice. National pride was at stake: the film's German censors justified their decision to ban the film by arguing that it besmirched German honour. With a world market to sell on, Walt Disney Enterprises had been established in 1929. It was a licensing agency. Felix the Cat was the first animated character to become a success-ful toy, and Little Nemo, Krazy Kat, Mutt and Jeff, The Katzenjammer Kids and others had all appeared. There were plenty of Disney character effigies and images, from various unlicensed sources – some more, some less similar to their on-screen counterparts. Such markets were open for expansion, and studios saw opportunities for tie-in products, from Holly-wood fan magazines and fashion lines to games and toys. In 1929 the rights to use Mickey on school writing tablets were sold to a company in New York. In February 1930, Walt Disney agreed a contract with the George Borgfeldt Company for the international licensing, production and distribution of Mickey Mouse merchandise. Borgfeldt made Mickey Mouse toys that tumbled and squeaked. He made Mickey Mouse sparklers and spinning tops – and often from the cheapest materials of celluloid and tin.[40] Mickey Mouse's popularity in the years of depression convinced Disney that more revenue needed to be generated through character merchandising, and Herman Kamen was employed to consolidate and expand sales – in-house – through merchandise tie-ins, cinema decorations, badges, posters, masks, balloons. It might have been the merchandising, and a toy market to exploit, that compelled Mickey Mouse to become cuter, more toy-like, but also a vehicle for good behaviour – at the Saturday afternoon Mickey Mouse Clubs, children learnt how to cross the street, wash behind their ears and respect their elders. Children were formed into conformist adults.

In any case Mickey Mouse changed. He became a person, rather than a rat, by the time that *Plow Boy* appeared in 1929. He adopted white gloves in 1930. In 1931, in *The Mouse Hunt*, Mickey Mouse turned into the un-sophisticated boy, and he went around with his dog. He was supposed to be an average boy of no particular age, fun loving, clean living in a small town. Freddy Moore introduced a new plastic style of drawing to the Disney studios as the 1930s drew to a close, and so Mickey Mouse became cuter, softer, rounder, of flesh and blood. Moore gave the face more character and definition, and his pliable body had a constant volume. His pear-shaped body could be better 'squashed and stretched', though never too traumatically; this allowed for a world of cause and effect matched by psychological validity.[41] Now his eyes had irises and pupils, which meant that they looked more realistic, more human and could effect a greater range of expression, perhaps it might be imagined that Mickey Mouse was also in possession of a soul. By now animators had worked out ways of endowing a character with apparent weight, ending staccato, jerky and unanchored movements. Weight and weightlessness had begun to preoccupy Disney's animators, though it had not been at issue for Cohl, in his world of hot-air balloons and vaporization. Where once gravity-defying tricks were the essence of cartooning, a realist injunction was now invading the look. But could all that embodiment and all that personality keep the wolf from the door? The Disney Studio was in financial crisis in 1934. The headline of the *New York Telegraph* reported in late 1933 that Disney's three little pigs were scoffing all the profits. In March 1934 the *New York Herald Tribune* declared: 'Mickey Mouse as actor a dud at making money'. Still, by then, Disney had other ideas – feature films, human beings – in mind, and animation already had a history, if, at points, an unrespectable one.

zeros, dots and dashes: drawing and the european avant-garde

we could be zeros

In January 1923 a journal published 'Thank you, Francis!' by the international Dadaist Francis Picabia. Railing against an 'imbecilic age' in which, since the war, 'morality' is the new contagion, and artists strive to be taken seriously, he insisted:

> What I like is to invent, to imagine, to make myself a new man every moment, then forget him, forget everything. We should be equipped with a special eraser, gradually effacing our works and the memory of them. Our brain should be nothing but a blackboard, or white, or, better, a mirror in which we would see ourselves for a moment, only to turn our backs on it two minutes later.[1]

Picabia flaunted speed, impermanence and the virtues of erasure. The brain might be a blackboard or white board, visioned like the drawing pads of the lightning sketchers, where images appear, mutate, disappear. He wanted to erase his self, reinventing for each moment a new man, memoryless. The eraser rubs out him and it rubs out his works too. The self with brain as screen and built-in effacer – this image reworks Hegel's description of brainwork: thinking is always the negation of what we have immediately before us.[2] This endless deletion, considered from Hegel's dialectical point of view, leads not to nothingness but to movement; just as it does in cartoons' formal mechanism of obliteration of the previous cel (sometimes achieved through a rubber-in-hand cancellation of lines). Cartooning is made up of frames and what happens 'in between', between each frame. Its principle is obliteration. Dada too proposed an annulment, a critical, dialectical one, the negation of the negation, the invalidation of invalid values. In 'Cannibal Dada Manifesto' Picabia proclaimed to the first French Dada audience in 1920 that Dada 'smells of nothing, it is nothing, nothing, nothing', like your hopes, your heaven, your idols, your politicians, your heroes, your artists, your religions. Picabia attacked value, artistic and monetary. He could not resist rubbing the bourgeois nose in commodity logic and its need for an art alibi: 'In three months my friends and I will be selling you our paintings for plenty of francs.'[3] Hugo Ball described Dada as a 'clownery out of the void'. It was an absurd art of trash for a world whose official values proved to be corrupt. Huelsenbeck's crazed Dada poem *End of the World*, a protest against hellish militarism, proposes a cartoonish scenario of anthropomorphics and lunacy:

> This is what things have come to in this world
> The crows sit on the telegraph poles and play chess
> The cockatoo under the skirts of the Spanish dancer
> Sings as sadly as a head waiter's bugler and the cannon lament all day.

Dada's voiding of value was not simple, as indicated by participants' stance towards their own 'movement' – Hans Richter's lecture at the Dada Soirée in Zurich in April 1919 was titled 'Against Without For Dada'.[4] And Dada may have meant refusal, meaninglessness, nix, but it – that is to say, the word itself, in Tzara's Romanian – also meant yes, yes.

Dada's visual practice ransacked trashy mass materials, the wrappings and promotional materials of mass reproduced culture. So, Hannah Höch snipped images of ballerinas and fashion mannequins from illustrated magazines such as *Die Dame*, and set them with and against scraps of her sewing pattern designs from her day job at the handicraft division of Ullstein Press, words cut from newspapers, reproductions of highly rated works of art and advertisements for commodities. Grosz–Heartfield made collages in 1919, such as 'Sonniges Land' (Sunny Land) and 'Dada-merika' with scattered references to the new art movement and snips of national-political press ideology segued into images of Wilhelmine Germany, advertising and the machine world. George Grosz continued the practice of recombining or respinning mass materials with a postcard in 1921. He altered a standard format tourist shot called 'Steilkuste am Nordufer der

Insel Hiddensee' (Shelving coast on the Northern bank of Hiddensee Island), by adding in pencil a tree, a flag, a moon, a Zeppelin and two boats. This was described by Dadaists as 'corrective practice'. Grosz and Heartfield vandalized a reproduction of a work by Picasso, renaming it 'La Vie Heureuse, Korrigiertes Meisterbild' (The Happy Life, Corrected Master-piece). Marcel Duchamp corrected a reproduction of Leonardo da Vinci's *Mona Lisa* (1919), adding a moustache and a punning title. High art booty and mass imagery alike were used; important only was the collage materials' reproduced status, which foreordains a lack of intrinsic value, a negation of existing values, coupled with easy accessibility and an unavoidable modernity. This anti-art had to be modern. Elsewhere art became modern differently, but a technological motive was often close at hand.

A few years after, in the later 1920s, Moholy-Nagy indicated how he had seen one of Malevich's white boards, a white on white square, as the perfect screen on which to project reflected moving images. Broadcasting the arrival of the new kino-culture of 'colour and light', Moholy-Nagy flagged up a crisis of art brought on by technological change:

> Symptoms of the commencing decline of traditional painting – I am not refer-ring to the terrible economic plight of the artists at the present time – are already apparent in a number of directions. The development of the suprematist Malevich may serve as an example. His last picture: a white square on a square white canvas is clearly symbolic of the film screen, symbolic of the transition from painting in terms of pigment to painting in terms of light. *The white surface can serve as a reflector for the direct projection of light, and what is more, of light in motion.*[5]

Malevich's experimenting had used painting to delete painting. Suprematism had begun with the *Black Square*, painted perhaps in 1913, or maybe later, during the Great War, and repeated at least twice over the next fifteen years. Suprematism upheld the supremacy of geometric form over figurative representation. The black square was first shown in the 'Last Futurist Exhibition', '0.10', in St Petersburg in 1915. It marked a full stop to a naturalism-hungry painterly process that the avant-gardists decreed had begun long ago with the savage's attempt to produce a self-image. An end had been put to all this by a future-oriented practice, which hoped to interrupt time itself, the continual flow of ever-same representations. Malevich wrote 'From Cubism to Suprematism in Art to New Realism in

Painting, to Absolute Creation', a pamphlet to accompany the exhibition, in which he declared: 'I have transformed myself *in the zero of form* and dragged myself out of the rubbish-filled pool of Academic art.'[6] Zero was the cipher. Zero could wipe out history and memory. The counter could be reset to zero. A letter to the painter and composer Matyushin, written in May 1915, mentions a project: 'In view of the fact that we are preparing to reduce everything to nothing, we have decided to call the journal *Zero*. Later on we too will go beyond zero.'[7]

By 1923 it was not clear that Malevich had yet moved beyond zero, for his manifesto 'The Suprematist Mirror' declared that everything – God, the Soul, the Spirit, Life, Art, Labour, Movement, Space, Time, and so on – is infinite and so equal to nothing.[8] Zero is still everything and nothing at once. White square on white square was another move in the game of eradicating the inessential, in order to discover painting as an end in itself. One version from 1918 showed a white square, filling up all of the canvas, backing another white square, almost invisible, fixed at a slight angle. Art must hit the zero point to reconstitute the world. In this world or out of this world was the argument. Malevich turned away from the detritus of everyday life in order to return to the world – that is, the world of pure forms, unalloyed, ahistorical geometry. Others were immersed in the rhythms of the world. Whether they looked at the world – and translated it into photography, montage, direct imprints – or whether they looked through it to the world of pure forms and essences, they were all looking for solutions to a problem called 'modern art'.

Moholy-Nagy's enthusiasm for the white on white square converted Malevich's negation into a plus, rescinding the quest for artistic autonomy by positing the painter's canvas as a surface for something else, a screen. The zero of form is made to greet the age of multiplication. In 1919 Hans Richter produced some Dada portraits for Hans Arp's magazine *Zeltweg*, selecting not the drawing but its direct imprint in blue on carbon paper, and so indicating the reversal of rank that subtends left modernism: 'I made the original drawing but the essence was really the copy, the copy was the original.'[9] This version of the copy, the reproduced, was just one of the experiments in replication that Richter staged in 1919. Together with Viking Eggeling he began to make scroll pictures, long strips of paper, broken into frames. One drawing was repeated with variations again and again. These were not the first scroll pictures of course, for the practice existed in the Chinese calligraphic tradition. In modern times, members of the Bloomsbury Group had come upon the idea, too. In 1914 Duncan Grant had worked on a series of *Abstract Kinetic Paintings with Collages*, on a scroll, several yards long and unrolled through a light-box in time to music by Bach. He conceived of this experiment as the preliminary stage of a film. His antagonist Wyndham Lewis, who flaunted his futuristic credentials, did not seize the technology of the future, but his *Tyro* portraits, from 1920 and 1921, with their garish colours and angular distortions, possessed that flatness and emptiness characteristic of the cartoonish. As Lewis wrote in the *Daily Express* of 11 April 1921: 'The Tyro is raw and underdeveloped: his vitality is immense, but purposeless, and hence sometimes malignant. His keynote, however, is vacuity; he is an animated, but artificial puppet, a "novice" to real life.' For Richter and Eggeling, their repetition of the same element with major or minor variations formed a chain and a relationship not only in space but also in time. Eventually this mock film negative strip demands to be translated to film: 'The scroll looked at us and seemed to ask for real motion. That was just as much of a shock to us as it was a sensation. Because in order to realize movement we needed film.'[10]

Avant-garde film surfaced out of the extension of problems posed in the fine arts: how to represent rhythmic processes not just in space and on a flat surface but also in time. And, once film-literate, they hoped to create a pure language of cinema, a cinematic specificity, labelled by Louis Delluc, in 1920, after Daguerre, *photogénie*.[11] While some saw the move of art into film as anti-art, others saw it as art's fulfilment, an absolute art, evading psychologistic experience, in favour of pure willed forms, non-referential, loaded with metaphysical significance.[12]

Hans Richter's abstract films were conceived as a light-play of positive and negative. He, like Malevich, reduced form to its simplest element, which, he claimed, happened to be the rectangle or square, a shape that corresponds to the standard canvas as well as to the screen. He was keen to argue that this shape really was the simplest form and was not chosen because of some assumed metaphysical importance, as was the case for

Doesburg or Mondrian. His films *Rhythm 21*, *Rhythm 23*, *Rhythm 25* project on to the square of the screen more squares and rectangles. The projection screen is the object under analysis. His shapes break it up, squash it, negate it. *Rhythm 21* opens with a shot of the dark film screen, and then it is pressed together from the sides until it is completely white. The process reverses, until the surface is completely black. Black wipes out white, white black, in a play of polarities, a facsimile of musical counterpoint. Squares and rectangles shrink and grow and shift, as if moving through a three-dimensional space, yet foregrounding the mechanism of that particular illusion. *Rhythm 23* has more squares, jostling each other on the square screen, some quite small, some elongated, so that they begin to look like Malevich's coloured suprematist paintings with small bars and rods and rectangles criss-crossing the picture plane. It is no surprise that, in 1927, Malevich and Richter discussed the idea of making a suprematist film.[13] This discussion took place while Malevich was visiting the Bauhaus, where he met Moholy-Nagy. Gropius's Bauhaus could well stimulate reflection on film, for film experimentation was part of the teaching syllabus. Through the 1920s Moholy-Nagy broadcast light-plays there, baring the apparatus during the performance. And from 1921 Schwerdtfeger and Hirschfeld-Mack developed and demonstrated 'reflecting moving pictures'. These investigated the variable behavioural possibilities of geometrical form.[14] A screen caught the light of multicoloured lamps, shaped by movable stencils, and hitched to a score. Viewers on the other side of the screen saw apparent shifts of movement and colour or the illusion of different spatial concepts. Hirschfeld-Mack, recollecting a film he saw in 1912, noted a disgust with its tasteless scenario and literary content, but also the unmissable statement of the 'primary means of filmic representation': 'the alternating abrupt and long drawn-out movements of light-masses in a darkened room, light varying from the most brilliant white to the deepest black'.[15] The 'reflecting moving pictures' experimented with the effects of direct coloured beams combined with music to 'evolve into a new artistic genre'. It just needed to be recorded, in order to diffuse out of Weimar into the world.

Cinema was impermanence, lodged in the permanence of its reproducibility. It offered a chance to break with tradition – or to found a new one that exploited film's motility, change, movement, and its ability to be everywhere and anywhere at once. That is how it was understood. The manifesto of futurist film insisted in 1916: 'we prefer to express ourselves through the cinema, through great tables of words-in-freedom and mobile illuminated signs.'[16] In 1916 the futurists pledged the self-rule of kinetic art:

> The cinema is an autonomous art. The cinema must therefore never copy the stage. The cinema, being essentially visual, must above all fulfil the evolution of painting, detach itself from reality, from photography, from the graceful and solemn. It must become antigraceful, deforming, impressionistic, synthetic, dynamic, free-wording.[17]

Its imperative was unavoidable, and not just for the futurists. In 1918, in 'L'Esprit nouveau et les poètes', Apollinaire had suggested that all art will become photographic in time:

> It would have been strange if in an epoch when the popular art *par excellence*, the cinema, is a book of pictures, the poets had not tried to compose pictures for meditative and refined minds which are not content with the crude imaginings of the makers of films. These last will become more perceptive, and one can predict the day when, the photograph and the cinema having become the only form of publication in use, the poet will have a freedom heretofore unknown.[18]

For the futurists film had to be storyless. It must be a filmed dreaming of objects, animated, humanized, baffled and dancing objects, removed from their normal surrounds and put into abnormal states to expose their amazing construction and non-human life. The futurists delighted in the idea of filmed dramas of disproportion, scenes such as a man drinking dry a lake with a tiny straw in an instant. That was a gag, essentially. They promoted unreal reconstructions of

Hans Richter, *Rhythm 21*

the human body, and suggested flirts, fights and marriages of funny faces, such as the big nose that silences a thousand congressional fingers by ringing an ear, or the two policemen's moustaches that arrest a tooth. They wanted linear, plastic, chromatic equivalences of men, women, thought, events, music, feelings, weights, smells and noises. And rhythm was the watchword – linear, plastic, chromatic rhythms so that with white lines on black can be shown the inner physical rhythm of a man who discovers his wife's adultery, and chases the lover – 'rhythm of soul and rhythm of legs'. Dramas of humanized or animated letters, geometric dramas, typographical dramas could all be imagined. Using all these ideas and others, they hoped, in 1916, to 'decompose and recompose the universe' according to their 'marvellous whims'.[19]

Eventually Malevich perceived a problem. Cinema had not heeded futurism's advice. The trouble was that this copying machine was copying other forms. In 'And Images Triumph on the Screens' (1925) Malevich censures film's refusal to escape the grip of tradition and its adherence to the 'monkey's habit' of considering 'man's ugly mug' and 'all its everyday rubbish' to be the aim of art.[20] The following year Malevich wrote in 'The Artist and the Cinema' about two sets of artists. There were the objectivists (concretists), easel painters, reproducers of everyday life, who did not clarify in their own mind the essence of art, and there were the non-objectivists (abstractionists) who clarified the essence of art and rejected the portrait and reflection of everyday life.[21] Cinema, he had expected, would overturn the whole of imitative culture, once the abstractionists with their 'new flash of consciousness' participate.[22] Artist-painters in the West, he notes, are now entering cinema using abstraction, soldering the joint between painterly and kinetic art, and 'so beginning with our future source of new forms'.[23]

Malevich's zero-sum game played with the matter of form and the negation of traditional artistic values. Hans Richter, in contrast, in his 1928 film *Inflation*, recalculated the zero as a matter of monetary value, an issue of exchange – that is to say, a political issue, bound up with the history of the Weimar Republic. One moment of that history was the spinning of zeros out of control, as if they had a life of their own. Zeros had a new currency. In 1923, zero, the super-sign, had taken on a life of its own in

Germany, in the Great Inflation. Proliferating zeros take on obliterating significance. The inflation began in the war, because the German government launched a borrowing programme, hopeful of swift military victory and favourable repayment conditions. Victory did not come, and defeat came slowly. The government printed more and more notes. Prices doubled in the war years. This quick-fix solution of mass reproducing notes continued after the war. In 1922 a great inflation kicked in. The inflation reached its peak by the late summer of 1923. One dollar cost 31,700 marks on 1 May. On 1 July it cost 160,400 and on 1 August it was 1,103,000. From then every few hours prices doubled. Workers rushed out to spend all their money before it bought only half as much again. Million mark notes were used more usefully as wallpaper. Value was in freefall.

This episode of German history coincided – not coincidentally – with Walter Benjamin's turn to Marxism. The book that Benjamin wrote as this turn was taking place was *One-Way Street*. One of its key sections was begun during the inflation, and was titled 'A Tour of German Inflation'. The tract was a cry against the way in which money had taken over, and had become the only theme – a situation that was far worse probably than anything that the money-critic Georg Simmel, who died just before the war's end, might have imagined possible. In his 1903 essay 'Metropolis and Mental Life' Simmel had posited a link between the money economy and domination by clock time. Money and clock time alike are numerical measures – these common denominators produce a social organization cemented by a deadened impersonal standard. So Simmel insists that the modern mind is a calculating one. Benjamin extends this in 1920s' Germany, where money inflates and time is rationalized:

> All close relationships are lit up by an almost intolerable, piercing clarity in which they are scarcely able to survive. For on the one hand, money stands ruinously at the centre of every vital interest, but on the other, this is the very barrier before which almost all relationships halt; so, more and more, in the natural as in the moral sphere, unreflecting trust, calm, and health are disappearing.[24]

In this society, and never more obviously than during economic crisis, people are joined together by paper chains of zeros. Shame marks the bearing of those who have money, and they hand out tokens to beggars in order both to mask their guilt and to conceal the sight of inequality: 'It is impossible to remain in a large German city, where hunger forces the most wretched to live on the bank notes [*Scheinen*] with which passers-by seek to cover an exposure that wounds them.'[25] *Schein*, the word for banknote, is also the word for appearance (as opposed to essence, in a Hegelian sense) and carries intimations of falsehood. Hyperinflation exacerbates the centrality of money, and, as numbers of zeros multiply, life itself seems to become more and more insignificant, less and less essential. 'Tax Advice' notes the following connection between money and lived life:

> Beyond doubt: a secret connection exists between the measure of goods and the measure of life, which is to say, between money and time. The more trivial the content of a lifetime, the more fragmented, multifarious, and disparate are its moments, while the grand period characterizes a superior existence. Very aptly, Lichtenberg suggests that time whiled away should be seen as made smaller, rather than shorter, and he also observes: 'a few dozen million minutes make up a life of forty-five years, and something more.' When a currency is in use a few million units of which are insignificant, life will have to be counted in seconds rather than years, if it is to appear a respectable sum. And it will be frittered away like a bundle of banknotes.[26]

Monetary inflation possesses a moral dimension, and also operates as a political wake-up call to elements of the middle-class intelligentsia, including Benjamin, who, in this time as almost always in his adult years, had money problems. Runaway inflation and its crisis of establishing value accentuates – for all, and particularly for the slightly better off – a principle inherent in capitalism: the discrepancy between use value and exchange value. And it throws into relief the question of time. Marx's discussion of the difference between production time and labour time inaugurated modernist reflection on modern time, whereby time is understood as a variable. Specific types of production (for example, wine-making and agriculture) require longer production time for natural processes to function; therefore the production time is longer than labour time.[27] Likewise, natural conditions such as fertility of the land and weather affect production time and the quantity and quality of commodities.[28] These processes are relevant in a capitalist economy, as in a feudal one, and yet it seems to commentators as if labour time or the time of capital is the

only time. 'The bourgeoisie is attached to labour time,
which is liberated for the first time from the cyclical',
notes Guy Debord in thesis 140 of *Society of the Spectacle*.[29] The unity of social production and nature is
mystified in capitalism by the domination of exchange
value over use value. Nature's contribution to the
production of use value is screened out, and labour
time becomes the measure of value under capitalism,
and so nature – apparently a free gift for capital –
becomes a mere object of labour. Nature's time and
capital's time exist in contradiction. Capital's time is
one of numerical calculation. Revolutionary time is the
effort to break with calculated, quantifiable capitalist
time – not in order to return to natural time (production time) or to labour time as measure, but to
produce something else: a time that is full, fulfilled,
malleable, subjective. Malevich's zero had been one
effort towards that refusal, in resetting the counter. As
he wrote in March 1918: 'install the new rhythm of
time' and 'we form our own time, with our time and
forms'.[30] Malevich's aesthetic insistence on resetting
the counter had become a social insistence in the new
Soviet Union of the post-revolution, where the question was pertinent: could capital's domination over time
– through wage-labour – be escaped.

In 1928 Hans Richter made *Inflation*, an introduction to a UFA feature film, *The Lady with Mask*. The
opening title describes the film as 'a counterpoint of
declining people and growing zeros'. It is a montage
of inflation scenes cut across by dollar signs and multi-
tudes of zeros whose multiplication signals the shrinking value of the Deutschmark. Commodities flash up,
a house, a car, a sewing machine, an ornate clock,
shoes, alcohol, a book, a cigarette, burning up as smoke
and ash.... More and more money buys less and less,

Hans Richter,
Inflation

as prices depreciated by the hour and the $1.00 exchanged for billions of marks. Exchange is a dizzying substitution. From the black and white strip, people stare out, their heads arranged into zero shapes, revealing the nothings that they have become. The people act beneath the superimposed zeros of the super-inflated banknotes. Dollars are the new hieroglyphs, their equivalence value unfixed. Through money social life is organized only around the binding and divisive power of currency. Human community is replaced by mathematical exchanges. Everything is represented through a third term, a figure, a cipher, that is an abstraction, a substitute as well as being a token of materiality, of what is real in a world subject to a money economy. Inflation is inflating, spreading, growing – the zeros are like a virulent life form – but is, at the same time, its opposite, depreciation. Life is reduced to zero, not as a negation of a negation as in Malevich's zero-formation, but as annulment of human value. Exchange value takes on a life of its own, a life of multiplying zeros, and a measure of time. These zeros link into history again, as signs of the devaluation of human life in the mass mobilizations that had been and were to come, ciphers of thousands of men deployed in war, and the millions who would die. In a reflection on these years, Richter mentions how on 30 January 1933 the Nazis burned down the Reichstag, and how, on the same day ten years later, 100,000 men surrendered in Stalingrad. Clippings from American newspapers relating this battle were collaged into Richter's scroll painting *Victory in the East 1943–1944*.[31] But there were many more lives to be spent before the victory over fascism could be declared.

If, in Weimar, the economy could not be saved, and capitalism could not be significantly reformed, then at least cinema might be a candidate for reconstruction. Richter's film experiments were to save cinema from itself. He was certain that the avant-garde had rediscovered cinema year zero. In *The Struggle for the Film* he noted that, 'Twenty years after the possibilities of the camera had been discovered, they were rediscovered by the avant-garde.'[32] And he cited as examples of this René Clair's slow-motion funeral in *Entr'acte*, Disney's shooting organs, and his own flying hats. His flying hats appeared in *Vormittagsspuk* (*Ghosts before Breakfast*), and their trick animation was a utopian revolt against the inevitability of subject–

Hans Richter,
Ghosts Before Breakfast

object relations. Objects – hats, neckties, coffee cups – rebel against
routinous everyday life. *Vormittagsspuk* had original music by Paul Hindemith.
Hindemith was a great fan of *Felix the Cat* and wrote a score called *Felix
at the Circus*. For Richter, the trick film was the confutation of Hollywood's
narratives and naturalism. Richter thought film was only worth the effort
inasmuch as filmmakers studied all of its possibilities. In his protest against
bad films, *Filmgegner von Heute – Filmfreunde von Morgen* (*Film Enemies of Today
– Film Friends of Tomorrow*), written in 1929 as a manifesto for the Stuttgart
Film und Foto exhibition, he begins with the basics of cinematic form,
outlining the 24-frames-a-second principle, then moves immediately into
the tricks of slo-mo, speed-up, superimposition, lens distortion, animation.
It is the camera as box of tricks that makes film an artform, and Richter
reinforces this by listing camera operators, not directors, in his filmography.
The camera as box of tricks can lead the assault on naturalism: 'It is the
case, then, that the same is true of film as has long been proven with every
other art form. To be bound to nature is a restriction.'[33]

What was immediately before the eyes had to be deleted. The camera
must reinvent the world. This could be taken in many directions. Hermann

Warm, the set designer on Robert Wiene's studio-bound *Cabinet of Dr Caligari*, had said that 'films must be drawing brought to life', and so he painted in the shadows and shapes in a crazed rejection of imitative objectivity. The studio film re-images the world fantastically in its sets. The absolute filmists were more literal in their understanding of what it meant to bring a drawing to life: Viking Eggeling with his geometrical compositions in rhythmic movement, Hans Richter with his flashing squares, Walter Ruttmann's primal polarities.

Eggeling, Ruttmann and Richter were painters and it seems that, at least at first, they hoped that animation could be, above all, painting's salvation rather than film's. The first film that Ruttmann saw was a cowboy film, shown at a fairground. Later he wrote articles about film as art, but they always came back to him with a rejection note from the editor and the comment that it has been proven that film is not an artform. Sometime between 1913 and 1917 he wrote *Kunst und Kino*, where he defended film as art, though he was still interested then in the use of plot and actors. The laws of film art were those of painting and dance.[34] In 1919 or 1920 Ruttmann wrote an essay entitled 'Malerei mit Zeit' ('Painting with Time'). Speed and tempo are the age's defining characteristics, and so a new art form was necessary, an art placed 'midway between painting and music'. Film's optical forms – light and dark, movement and rest – are arranged by 'time-rhythm'.[35] Moving painting is invented. This time the movie-painting is abstract, referencing nothing but the values of shade and speed. Ruttmann's animations, made between 1921 and 1926, used abstraction as a negation of reality. The animations showed twenty-odd Mondrians a second – and as many copies of the 'original' artwork, the celluloid strip, as could be made. This was conceived as a liberation, from naturalism, from nature. He called each strip a *Lichtspiel*, play of light, but this was also the German word for movie. In early April 1921 Ruttmann showed his short filmstrip of colour *Lichtspiel Opus I* for the first time before a small group. The film critic Bernhard Diebold wrote a newspaper article on 'the new art':

> Until now film was crafted photography, ersatz-novels, ersatz-theatre, and as a photographic vehicle, it remained but naked naturalism. Even certain retouchings could not alter that. But now the artist paints his film. He no longer obeys the

naturalism of actors, of landscapes, horses, donkeys, palm trees, and real rough cast walls, but rather the stylistic will of a creator of motion, who, like the musician, lends expression to his soul through ornaments that move in time.[36]

It is 'eye music', as Diebold called it, audible light, visible music, a synaesthetic implosion of the senses. It was the confirmation of his answer to his question posed in the *Frankfurter Zeitung* in September 1920: how is film going to overcome naturalism? It must strive for painting in motion. Sky blue, sunset red, lush green geometric dancing in rhythmic succession, budding and disintegrating. Spiny forms protrude from the edge of the square and shapes and colours flutter, jitter over the screen. Diebold saw a red sun throbbing in its orbit, emitting a pulsing coloured ray, and cube forms smashing toward the centre while waves ebb and flow. The action evoked for him by this amorphous spectacle was the Creation.[37] Ruttmann made more: *Opus II* (1921), *III* (1924) and *IV* (1925). Critics' commentaries on the strips raced to reveal the variety of shapes and colours and tried to imagine ways of anecdotalizing their activities. After seeing *Lichtspiel Opus II* Diebold had remarked that the new 'eye music' would not be easily assimilated by 'the public', but it would be more readily accepted by them if 'clever business people' would choose the painted film as a vehicle for advertisements, for the public would appreciate the 'compromise' between art and business.[38] Soon the advertiser moved in – Julius Pinschewer, the pioneer of German advertising films[39] – and Ruttmann made the first part-abstract colour adverts for Excelsior tyres and Kantorowicz liqueur. Precisely the enchantment that commodity retail sought was ruled impermissible by the state, which in 1922 was waging an enlightenment campaign against hypnosis. The Munich film censor slapped an X-rating on *Lichtspiel Opus II*, a clash of spiked wedges and curved blobs like knives and body organs, for fear it might induce hypnotic states. One critic noted the strong erotic associations and the films' excitement of lust, and thought that was cause enough for the censors' rancour.[40] *Opus III* was less organic and more geometric. Composed to a sharp mechanical rhythm, it concentrated on rectilinear forms and diagonals, coinciding more directly with the geometry of the screen. *Opus IV* was geometric too, but its use of patterns aimed at optical effects, rather than screen dissection. The viewer was being worked on.

Lotte Reiniger,
The Adventures of
Prince Achmed

But there was always the danger that the absolute film was not a research tool in contemporary perception but a new decorativeness. Diebold, back in 1921, had worried about an Arts and Crafts taint to Ruttmann's work. And the expressionist Alfred Kerr saw in *Lichtspiel Opus 1* the kind of prettifying surrealism that would indeed full-bloom in Disney's *Fantasia* methodology. Kerr described how 'a violet worm thing grows into a bent cob of corn; rolls itself into an Edam cheese; a moon; an even smaller Edam; a small orange. Fish-like, an unknown magical beast, all kinds of colourful forms slide soft as ribbons in elegant curves over the flickering surface... A strip of sun, lemony, sweeps like a broom from left to right, pales, fades away.'[41] Perhaps Ruttmann was aware of a seductive charm in his animations and so abandoned the production of beauty for an observation – and investigation – of the actual in reality-montage. The new decorativeness and cutesifying of the imagery was something that Oskar Fischinger would take to the United States and later sell to Walt Disney for use in *Fantasia*.

At the public premiere of *Lichtspiel Opus I* Diebold introduced Ruttmann to Oskar Fischinger, who had been working on a wax-slicing machine. Fischinger's device cut slivers off swirled coloured waxes while a camera

Lotte Reiniger,
*The Adventures of
Prince Achmed*

shutter, synchronized with the movement of the blade, filmed the changing features traced by the multicoloured whorls and striations of wax. In projection, the wax came to life. Ruttmann bought a licence to use Fischinger's device for commercial purposes. He used the wax-cutting machine for some trick effects when doing the backgrounds for Lotte Reiniger's silhouette film *The Adventures of Prince Achmed*. Reiniger was keen on utilizing technologies to produce effects. In his book on Reiniger, Eric Walter White described the trick table that made much of her work possible:

> Roughly speaking, a trick table measures about four feet by three feet; it is made of glass and lit from below by a lamp or lamps, whose light is diffused by a shade of frosted glass. The camera is set above the table in a framework which enables it to be adjusted horizontally and vertically. Its shutter is controlled by a bulb similar to those used by studio photographers. Each shot is taken singly, and as quickly or slowly as the producer wishes. It should be noted that although the producer exposes his material and works with it on a horizontal plane, the finished film is of course projected vertically, and great care must be taken to ensure that the figures in it appear to be obeying the laws of gravity.[42]

Reiniger faked depth in two-dimensionality, turning flatness into a figment of 3D form, while variegated tones suggested an illusion of distance. She was concerned to create a world of conventional physical laws. Gravity and perspective ruled. Changing scale simulated close-ups. However, naturalism could only go so far. This was all, after all, presented in a curious side-on world that could only seem magical to a viewer. But working with Reiniger on fairy-tales was not what Ruttmann wanted to do. When the collaborators assembled to watch the marked print of *The Adventures of Prince Achmed* for the first time, Ruttmann exclaimed 'What has this to do with 1923?'[43] (The inventor of the wax-slicing machine might have had occasion to pose the same question, for he found himself in debt, having – at the height of the inflation – been defrauded by a business partner with whom he ran a small animation firm in Munich. Financially devastated, he walked to Berlin.) What did the filigree shadows, trapped in a flat world of genies and demons, backlit and caught only with sidelong glances, have to do with the collapse of the economy, or with the logic of modernism? They had something to do with modernism's logic, if only in terms of the oscillation between a stark flatness and the exploration of depth through its fakery. The varying tones of grey suggest retrogressions and make the viewer accept the shadow for the substance. Like Picasso's paintings of plaster busts in 1924, as Eric Walter White argued, the third dimension is abandoned and the scene is translated into two dimensions.[44] In the first years of the century, numerous artists imaged a two-dimensional universe. Exemplars in every cultural form attempt to depict flatness and loss of volume, and there is much talk of platitudes, façades, layout, display, surface, dabbing, plaques, plate, panels, effacing, flattening and film. The surface overlays the content, form is torn into deformation, and, frequently, colour glares out instead of delighting in delicate modulations of hue.

The absolute filmists refused to accept the flat surface, setting up investigations into the illusioning of depth. Ruttmann's shapes grew and shrunk in ways that made it look as if they were bursting forwards or zipping backwards towards a horizon that did not exist. Duchamp's *Anémic cinéma*, begun in 1924, showed a series of glass discs painted with geometrical segments and lines, and these were spun to create an illusion of spatial extension. Flat forms were used to probe the illusion of depth. The effects were the results of probing certain problems in the physiology of vision. It was scientific research into perception. Duchamp was interested in stereoscopic photography, a kind of ideal construction, synthesized by the viewer. The stereofilm did not succeed, but some of the rotoreliefs and revolving spheres used for it were recycled in *Anémic cinéma*. This was art and science, with a new basis for both. The zero had wiped the slate, in order to begin anew. The canvas was white. The film negative was a minus, a negation of canvas. Then, as Malevich insisted, they had to go beyond zero. So they made a point in space, the dot, one dimension. The dot became a line, and, in cartoons, it began to walk. It walked into two dimensions. Eisenstein went down this route too. In 'How I Learned to Draw' Eisenstein quotes Wang Pi, a Chinese writer from the third century BC: 'What is a line? A line speaks of movement.'[45] Line is dynamic movement, process, a path. When Eisenstein stops drawing, he turns to film, and there he composes the 'lines of actors' movement "in time"'.[46] For Paul Klee, too, movement inheres in the line, for it is a dot that has been taking a walk. In his teachings at the Bauhaus, between 1922 and 1925, Klee lectured on the basic forms of the triangle and the square and conceived their emergence as the result of the line's erotic activity.[47] The basic geometric forms were more pliable and analytical; 'and anyway ...', noted Klee, 'I do not wish to represent the man as he is, but only as he might be'.[48] In 1924, in 'On Modern Art', Klee wrote of the artist's disinterest in natural form, for the process of formation is more valuable than final forms:

> He is, perhaps unintentionally, a philosopher, and if he does not, with the optimists, hold this world to be the best of all possible worlds, nor to be so bad that it is unfit to serve as a model, yet he says: 'in its present shape it is not the only possible world.'[49]

In Klee's work any schoolish division between modernist geometrics and expressionist mood-work is exposed as scam. Such geometrics are the cosmos reimagined as utopic.

lines walking

Another rectanglist, Piet Mondrian, took a different route. Like Malevich, he spread colour patches, but also elevated the line, pointing, in 1919 in an imaginary dialogue on his New Plasticism, to its moral standing: 'The

straight line tells the truth'.[50] But Mondrian had no time for the changeable. For him the relationship of two straight lines perpendicular to each
other expressed the immutable. The same year Rodchenko also ascribed
a firmness to the line. The line stands firm against pictorial expressivity.
It has revealed a new conception of the world. The line constructs, not
represents. The line is the fundamental element of constructivism, of rebuilding art, or seeing, from scratch. Rodchenko exhibited paintings of
black on black, non-objective paintings of swirl and shadow, in 1919, in
an exhibition where Malevich's suprematist white-on-whites also hung. He
painted a series of lines in 1919. And, in 1921, he wrote a manifesto called
'Line', where the history of art was shown to follow a line from imitation
to abstraction, and abstraction turned out to be itself, in its most stripped-
down form, a line. The brush thrown out, the new tools are the press, the
roller, the drawing-pen, the compasses.[51]

> The significance of the LINE finally became quite clear – on the one hand its
> function as boundary and edge, and on the other hand – as a factor of the
> principle structure of any organism in life, the skeleton, so to speak, (or basis,
> frame, system). Line is the first and the last, both in painting and in every
> conceivable form of construction. Line is the route of passage, movement,
> collision, boundary, connection, intersection. Thus line conquered everything
> and destroyed the last citadels of painting – colour, tone, facture and plane. Line
> erected a red cross over painting.... Having put line at the forefront, as an
> element without which it is impossible to construct and create, we thereby
> reject all aesthetics of colour, facturality and style, because everything which
> hampers construction is style (for example Malevich's square).[52]

The line went back to the drawing board, then, and a re-evaluation of the
elements of drawing took place, after the years of avant-garde experiment
with colour and plane. It was time for a starting point, to go beyond zero.
Lines allowed the return to basic elements – but the word too, as
Rodchenko well knew, had political resonance, as in the 'party line'. And,
in addition to that, walking the line, wire-walking, evoked the avant-garde
humourism and funambulism of the artist as acrobat, a dehumanized
human, a mechanized vitality.

The last Dada soirée in the Saal zur Kaufleuten in Zurich in April 1919
included a speech by Eggeling, co-signatory of Dada manifestos, on elementary Gestaltung in abstract art. Dada was ending, and Eggeling, Janco,

Arp, Giacometti, Baumann and Hans Richter were about to convene the Radical Artists' Group, a formation of abstract artists, responding to the November Revolution in Germany and determined to turn destruction into construction. Their manifesto, drafted by Eggeling,[53] appeared in a Zurich newspaper.

> An artists' manifesto. From a group of artists who call themselves 'radical artists', we have received the following manifesto with a request to publish it. 'Deep and uniform views must prevail if great decisions are to be taken for the longer term. Intellectually and materially we make the following demands.... We artists, as representatives of an essential part of the entire culture, want to place ourselves "in the thick of things", and take our share of responsibility for the coming ideal development of the State. That is our right. We announce that this law of artistic movement in our time is already to hand in a comprehensive formulation. The intellectuality of an abstract art means an enormous expansion in the human sense of freedom. The aim of our faith is fraternal art: a new mission of human beings in the community. Art in the state must reflect the spirit of the entire body of the people. Art compels unambiguity, should form the foundation of the new human being, should belong to every individual and to no class; we want to gather the conscious power of each individual's productive energy in the fulfilment of his mission into a uniform achievement. We fight against the enervating failure to be systematic. Our supreme viewpoint: Aspiring to a comprehensive basis for the intellectual horizon. That is our duty. Such work will guarantee the people the highest value in life and undreamed of possibilities. The initiative for this belongs to us. We shall lend expression to the powerful trends, give tangible direction to the scattered efforts.'

Eggeling worked on the surface, his scroll paintings and movies shunning depth in favour of filmic thinness. Eggeling's starting point, Richter noted later, was

> the most elementary pictorial element, the line, and he was working on what he called its 'orchestration', (a concept first used by Gauguin in speaking of colour). This was the interplay of relationships between lines which he had arranged (as I had done with positive and negative surfaces), in contrapuntal pairs of opposites, within an all-embracing system based on the mutual attraction and repulsion of painted forms.[54]

Eggeling presupposed a unity of opposites with forms placed in context only by their opposites and brought to life by the establishment of an inner relationship between these two opposites. Reconstruction of culture was to begin with the line. Eggeling set the line in motion. His films are like warped Emile Cohl cartoons that have gone beyond figuration, lines twisting and turning, forming spirals, musicless because the movement of the shapes is in itself a visual symphony and needs no accompaniment. These spirals hold the centre of the screen, and the film frame seems like the space of a concert hall. A master shape and its variations are traced onto paper or tin foil, or painted on thin sheets of rubber, and animated under the camera by slicing away minute strips and shooting in stop-motion a single frame after each slicing. As in music, modelling from nature was to be excluded. Eggeling devised what he called a *Generalbass der Malerei*, a 'thorough bass of painting'. Since polarity reconciled Analogy with Antithesis, polarity was conceived as its unifying principle. The likeness and unlikeness of component parts of any artwork need to be displayed for the whole work to figure a unity. If the work is incomplete, its identity is destroyed. The shapes shift position, light intensity, proportions, at varying speeds, all transpiring in strict regulated sequence. Dominants alternate. With the elaboration of one motif, in rhythmic counter-movement, another dwindles.

When Eggeling began working on the preparatory drawings for such a conception, he likely did not know that another man was in Switzerland working on these questions, through a study of Hegel. The two would end up in 1916 in the same street, one in the Cabaret Voltaire, the other across the road in his exile home at 12 Spiegelgasse. By then Lenin – who, coincidentally, some fifteen years before went by the name of Richter to throw the tsarist police off his trail – was working on his pamphlet on imperialism. He determined in the course of that study that the process of revolution could only be thought in conjunction with his studies of dialectics.[55] Lenin too, via Hegel, had grasped the powers of negation, pressing beyond the common-sensical tenet that negation is of no import, that it is 'merely negative': 'The negative is to an equal extent positive – negation is something definite, has a definite content, the inner contradic-tions lead to the replacement of the old content by a new higher one.'[56]

Lenin's studies also placed the accent on motion, on development and movement, destruction of the old and the emergence of the new out of that old. In 1915, in a meditation on the question of dialectics, the unity of plus and minus in science and social science (the class struggle) is entertained, and the play of opposites shown to be conditional, temporary, transitory, relative:

> Development is the 'struggle' of opposites. The two basic (or two possible? or two historically observable?) conceptions of development (evolution) are: development as decrease and increase, as repetition, *and* development as a unity of opposites (the division of a unity into mutually exclusive opposites and their reciprocal relation).[57]

And, following Hegel's representation of knowledge as a series of circles, he portrayed dialectical knowledge dynamically as 'living', many-sided, with the number of sides progressively increasing, with an infinite number of shades of every approach and approximation to reality, with a philosophical system growing into a whole out of each shade.[58] Lenin rejected the concept of knowledge as a straight line, preferring the series of circles, a curve, a spiral, parts of which can, at any moment, be transformed into an independent, complete straight line. But down that excisionist route he saw obscurantist dangers inherent in rectilinearity and one-sidedness, woodenness and petrification, and the forms of subjectivism and subjective blindness that arise from seizing on a part of the whole, from cutting up the flow of movement and development.

In 1922 the constructivists forged international links. Their energies fed off revolutionary developments in the Soviet Union, and the promise of revolution elsewhere. 'Art today is international … We stand at the outset of a great creative period.'[59] Object builders of the world unite! In Germany members of the Novembergruppe and other avant-garde groups attended a Congress of International Progressive Artists in Düsseldorf. Van Doesburg, Lissitsky and Richter, Eggeling and Janco immediately formed a faction, in opposition to the expressionist-dominated majority of subjectivists and individualists. The constructivists and the Dadaists came together for the first time, and the constructivists had to put behind them attacks on Dada, such as the one voiced by Lissitsky: 'The days of destroying, laying siege and undermining lie behind us.… Now is the time to build on ground that has been cleared.'[60] Construction, rebuilding, was the idea. Such passion manifested itself in a new internationalism of signs.

Moholy-Nagy pushed the Bauhaus to adopt clear, nonhistorical, non-traditional printing fonts made of circles and straight lines.[61] Herbert Bayer even designed elegantly rational one million mark, two million mark and billion mark notes – without 'cupids frolicking about numbers … ornamenting the façade of hell'[62] – for the Thuringian money coffers in 1923's inflation period.[63] They have no pictorial elements, just a blockish, characteristically Bauhaus script and a dominating row of zeros, and the standard legal refrains. Put into circulation on 1 September 1923, they were not as serviceable as hoped, for immediately after their appearance higher denominations were already necessary. This was circulation at top speed. But a rational language (even in an irrational system) was the aim.

In the same rational-modernist spirit Viking Eggeling and Hans Richter wrote a funding-seeking pamphlet entitled *Universal Language*. They sent the pamphlet to Einstein, who commended their work. Eggeling, who, aiming for general validity, never dated his productions, thought that he was creating a universal language. Richter agreed, for the interrelationship of elementary forms and laws of perception tapped something universal. Eggeling's alphabet or lexicon of graphic forms was to provide the basis of a new visual language. This attempt rested on abstraction from nature, governed by a conceptual system based on polarities and analogies. The result was geometrical forms. It recalled a watchword of Richter's gleaned from Schopenhauer: 'for him, the cosmos, looked at from a blessed star, should appear like a solved geometrical problem'.[64] The universalization of language had been prompted before, at the time of the French Revolution, when discussion of the reconstruction of the French language elicited proposals for a 'rectangular' reform of the language, erasing all foreign elements, purifying provincial dialects. Eventually it was suggested that the words of the language be analysed in a system of sound coordinates, assembled into mathematically exact sound groups corresponding to the semantic level, so as to produce a clarified French. Another revolution demanded another attempt.

Eggeling's research into shapes, forms, and relationships between points in space and lines insisted on the Adamic, Edenic. Hans Arp first saw Eggeling's compositions as a hieratic writing. And, after all, the Cabaret Voltaire founder Hugo Ball had relayed the uselessness of conventional spoken and written language, proposing abstract painters as advocates of a supra-natural sign language: 'Is the language of signs the actual paradise language?'[65]

benjamin on the line

The sign swung into view in the 1920s. There was Malevich's fascination with the 'look' of words, the relation of white page and black script, or blank sheet and obscure oblongs, the latter, in a suprematist brochure from 1921, seemingly erasures of misprints, but effectively cancelling out grammatical and syntactical coherence.[66] This layout style – what Vladimir Markov, in 1923, evoking the synaesthetic effect, called 'sound-painting' – could also be seen in the constructivists' page design experiments, such as the emancipation of words on the pages of Kruchenykh's and Ilia Zdanevich's booklets. El Lissitzky, typographer, artist, poster maker, photographer, architect, worked on signs and designs, sometimes the geometric architectural paintings of *Proun*, sometimes politics as signage in his *Beat the Whites with the Red Wedge* (1919), sometimes dynamic design in book and journal covers and layout, furniture, architectural interiors and exhibitions. The sign was in cinema too, for Kuleshov had insisted that 'A shot must be treated like a sign, like a letter.'[67] All this obsession with signage was mainstay of a formalism that Trotsky chastised as a new religiosity in the early 1920s, noting how the formalists believe 'In the beginning was the Word. But we believe that in the beginning was the deed. The word followed as its phonetic shadow.'[68] Trotsky was sticking with Faustian Marxism.

Someone else was taking signs seriously. The jacket of Walter Benjamin's book *Einbahnstraße* (*One-Way Street*), of 1928, showed a montage of street furniture, with superimposed instances of his title photographed from street signs by Sascha Stone. And many of the subheadings of the paragraphs inside were taken from the language of street paraphernalia and billboards. Benjamin was translating his preoccupation with mystical language, hieroglyphs and cabbala into a reading of secret writings, the signatures of things in the urban world. He analysed city space and city writing, noting that printing is pitilessly dragged out onto the street by advertisements, forced to leave its supine position in books. The newspaper lives in manipulable multiplanes, predominantly the vertical plane, and the film and billboard live in the perpendicular. In short, he notes, in the city writing turns graphic, a picture writing developing towards an international moving script.[69] All this was an extension of earlier thoughts on drawing. In 1917 his short article 'Malerei und Grafik' ('Painting and Graphics') had pondered the spatial alignment of different types of imagery.[70] These thoughts were the results of Benjamin's intention 'to follow the difference between painting and graphics to its very root'.[71] A picture is vertical before the observer. A mosaic is horizontal at the observer's feet. Benjamin argues that drawings are too often viewed as paintings – that is to say, in the upright plane. Painting presents a longitudinal image of the world, representational and containing the world's objects. Drawing shows the world's cross section, and so is symbolic – that is, it contains signs. Drawing is like writing, and should be flat before us. Though, he concedes, it might be writing's return to origin – signs on stones – if it stands upright. Such considerations about the proper plane of drawing were fundamental to the animator's art, where horizontal drawings rise onto vertical screens.

In 1918 Benjamin wrote a short piece entitled 'Uber die Malerei oder Zeichen und Mal'.[72] Its title exploited the ambiguity of signs, for it meant 'On Painting or Sign and Mark', but *zeichen* was the root word of drawing, and *Mal*, mark, was the root of the word for painting. Gershom Scholem's memoir *The Story of a Friendship* reveals how in 1918 Benjamin voiced a preoccupation with ideas of perception 'as a reading in the configurations of the surface – which is the way prehistoric man perceived the world around him, particularly the sky'.[73] Later, in 1933, in 'On the Mimetic Capacity' Benjamin asserts that reading is older than spoken language, for entrails, stars and dances were semiotic systems. After them came the runes and hieroglyphs, limbs of mediation of a new reading.[74] Benjamin's early fragment on drawing begins with an analysis of the sign. The sign is characterized by the role that the line plays in it. Benjamin distinguishes the different lines – the line of geometry, the line of the letter, the graphic line and the magic line of the absolute sign. The last two are of interest to Benjamin. The graphic line is defined by its contrast with the surface, which it forces to become an *Untergrund*, an underground. It can only exist on this underground, which is why, were it to cover the entire surface, it would cease to be a drawing. The graphic line lends its underground an identity, unlike the geometric line. This identity is not that of the white paper surface, but something else, another layer. That is to say, the white paper could (theoretically) be removed and the white underground – as clouds or white surf – remain. Then Benjamin characterizes the 'absolute sign', a sign that tends to appear on inanimate things, and he uses examples: Cain's sign, the sign on the Israelites' doors in the tenth plague in Egypt, Ali Baba and the forty thieves. All this is seen to contrast with the absolute mark. The sign is imprinted. The mark emerges. The mark, often tied to guilt or innocence, usually appears on the animate – Christ's wounds, blushes, birthmarks, leprosy – and is always absolute. What holds for the mark, *Mal*, also holds for the medium of painting, *Malerei*. The painting has no *Untergrund* and no graphic line. Paintings may contain recognizable configurations, but these are not graphic – that is to say, the painting points to something other than itself, something higher, the name, the word. This analysis of image, medium, surface showed up one practice that synthesized the two – the watercolour, the only instance in which colour and line coincide, where the pencil outlines are visible, the paint is transparent, and the *Untergrund* remains, though coloured.[75]

For Benjamin, Klee was the only gratifying modern painter. This was precisely because he confounds distinctions. It was unclear whether he was a painter or a drawer. Benjamin reveals in a letter to Scholem in March 1921 that he can 'depend' only on the painting of Klee, Macke and Kandinsky.[76] Elsewhere Chagall is mentioned, but Klee is singled out as the only one who has some sort of connection to cubism, itself a form of art that is positioned somewhere between painting and drawing, an artform in which the 'linear structure' dominates the image.[77] The presence of the line connected the image to the sign, and to writing – as Adorno was later to emphasize when, in 'Engagement' (1962), he labelled Klee's art *écriture par excellence*.[78] Painting as *écriture* is best articulated in poem-pictures such as *Einst dem Grau der Nacht enttaucht...* (1918) in which each letter of the poem occupies a coloured square of the divided grid, divided through the middle by a strip of silver paper. The image is the letters, the letters are the words and the whole is a picture. Klee did not paint in the traditional manner. He used techniques similar to those used by the absolute filmists. For example, *self-portrait monsieur Perlenschwein* (1925) deployed a spray technique, sprinkling watercolour in pinks and greys over a stencil. The pig face had two eyes, one square, one rhomboid. Klee was making reference to physicist-philosopher Ernst Mach's 1905 treatise *Die Analyse der Empfindungen und das Verhältnis des Physischen zum Psychischen* (*The Analysis of the Sensations and the Relations of the Physical to the Psychic*). Mach showed that the square and the rhombus are geometrically similar, but are not perceived as such. The rhombus appears dynamic and larger. Klee cheated in this game of perception, by making the square eye larger. Optical illusion outwits illusioning the real.

In April 1921 Benjamin went to an exhibition of Klee's works in Berlin, and at the end of May he went to Munich and bought one of Klee's watercolours, *Angelus Novus*, created in 1920. This image was later, in 1940, described by Benjamin as a frozen representation of impotence in the face of a ceaseless flow of catastrophic progress. In 1922, when the century's worst horrors had yet to be committed, Benjamin named a journal project after his new picture. He concludes the journal announcement with an explanation of the image and the title. It is a presentation of ephemerality. Benjamin refers to Talmudic legend and the angels, created anew in every moment in countless hordes, in order then to cease to be once they have sung their hymn to God, dissolving back into nothingness. It is quite an image of animation.

Klee's scratches are a type of writing, a hieroglyphics ready for decipherment. Their surfaces become testimonies of what will have been. His lines plug into the unconscious, pre-conscious reception of the world and its traces, evading the elaborate machinery of illusive representation. Perhaps his images were scribbled on the 'Wunderblock', the 'mystic writing pad' that children and Freud adored. In his essay 'A Note upon the "Mystic Writing-Pad"', written around 1924, and published in 1925, Freud outlined the systems of consciousness. It is a peculiarly self-conscious essay, right down to the title, which might be read as a pun (Freud puts his own notes upon the mystic writing pad) and as such adds another layer to the intricate model of the unconscious, overwriting what had been there previously.[79]

In this essay he conceives a psychic apparatus, which 'has an unlimited receptive capacity for new perceptions and nevertheless lays down permanent – even though not unalterable – memory traces of them.'[80] He then refers to his earlier work in *The Interpretation of Dreams*, from the turn of the century, where he said that there is a system of perceptual consciousness, which receives perceptions but retains no trace of them, so that it can react like a clean sheet to every new perception; while the permanent traces of the excitations that have been received are preserved in 'mnemic systems' lying behind the perceptual system. In *Beyond the Pleasure Principle* Freud refined this model and added that consciousness resides in the perceptual system rather than the permanent traces. In 'A Note upon the "Mystic Writing-Pad"' Freud describes an apparatus that has come onto the market. As he sees it, its mode of working is analogous to the way that consciousness works. The toy perfectly replicates the operation of the psychic system. It is called the 'mystic writing-pad'. It plays with the visible and the invisible, with revelation and concealment. Freud goes to some length to describe this device, a writing tablet from which notes can be erased by an easy movement of the hand – and yet which retains permanent traces of the etchings that have been made upon it. He tells us of its structure and materials – wax, translucent paper, celluloid. A pointed stylus scratches the surface, making impressions on the waxed paper. This writing stands out darker than the surrounding grey. Freud even troubles to tell us that the current version of the device works slightly differently, but is in principle the same. The device's celluloid sheath protects the paper that receives the impressions. When the top sheet is lifted and cleared still a permanent trace remains on the underlying wax slab, and is legible in certain lights. The mode of operation of this device mirrors the workings of consciousness, which also divides the two functions of receipt and preservation between two types of consciousness. Freud is constantly concerned with the appropriateness of his analogy. He worries about the fact that no use is made of the permanent traces of impression on the wax block, but then insists that that does not matter. It does not matter for the use of the writing pad, which truly would be mystical were it able to 'reproduce' the writing from within, as can memory. Freud then pushes the analogy even further – revealing that it agrees with a notion that

hitherto he kept to himself. This relates to the way in which consciousness, like the writing pad, constantly stretches out to the world and receives impressions, only then to recoil, to withdraw once the excitations
are sampled. Indeed the pad and consciousness are both active, opening
up to the world and then shutting down. Freud chose as metaphor a toy.
It was a device that belonged more to the genus of the nineteenth-century
hand-operated toy than to the modern world of electrical film, but the
mechanism – the repeated opening up and closing down – was the same
as in the camera shutter mechanism. This particular idea of opening up
and shutting down is picked up again in the 1925 essay 'Negation' where,
altering his terminology slightly, Freud asserts that the ego periodically
forays through the perceptual system to sample external stimuli, only to
withdraw.[81] The unconscious never admits negation, but the unconscious
is revealed by negation constantly. Repression works in so devious a way.
Freud also asserts the way in which perception of real objects can be an
internal process – not a checking that an object exists in reality, but rather
re-finding the object in memory in order to assure oneself that it is truly
real.[82] The machinery of memory vouchsafes the actuality of the event.
Freud's model of consciousness as a whole, as evidenced in 'A Note upon
the "Mystic Writing-Pad"' and 'Negation', is a dialectical model. Its elements, as in Hegel's dialectic of *Aufhebung*, are receipt, preservation, negation and overcoming.

Freud's analogy had not come from out of the blue. Various theorists
of the modern tied optical devices and new toys together with processes
of consciousness. Marx had evoked at different times the *camera obscura*
and the *phantasmagoria* apparatus in the nineteenth century to model consciousness, and this practice of seeing consciousness and the unconscious
through optical devices does not abate in the following century. Indeed,
the analogy between optics, optical devices and memory takes us into the
heart of modernist aesthetics in the 1920s, when the technology of recording comes to the fore: registering traces in film, in photography, on record
and in other technologies of imprinting, of receipt and preservation.

Benjamin constantly evokes optical devices or effects to model memory
and the reception of modern experience in general; for example, the section titles of his book *One-Way Street* include 'Imperial Panorama', 'En-

largements', 'Technical Aid' and 'To the Planetarium'. This is not surprising, for *One-Way Street* is all about Benjamin's own change of focus, and the adoption of a new urban, political, modernist perspective that undertakes the recovery of the extraordinary poetry of banality – the poetic psychopathology of everyday life. Benjamin titles one subsection 'Stereoscope', and so sets us in mind of a later piece in 'Berlin Childhood around 1900', also called 'Imperial Panorama', which includes the description of a favourite optical entertainment device with its three-dimensional town views. All these optical devices are toys or experiences from his childhood, but they also become tropes through which to reimagine his infant years and to confront memory and history. In 1932 Benjamin alludes to a proto-cinematic device – a thumb cinema – in a little fragment that was to be part of a lecture on Proust.[83] Freud used a child's toy to envisage the unconscious. Benjamin, along with Freud and many others, had recently asserted the great seriousness enacted in child's play. The thumb cinema figures in a rumination on death. Benjamin had planned to kill himself in a hotel in the South of France in 1932, but instead he decided to speak about memory and how the past can be viewed. The lecture touches on dying in connection with the cliché of an image strip zipping past a dying person's mind's eye. Memory is seen as an image, or more specifically as a photograph. History too, Benjamin notes in the *Arcades Project*, decays into images, not stories.[84] The tendency to visualize, to snapshot, to freeze or bring a tableau – Brechtian style – to a standstill infuses Benjamin's history writing. He disrupts temporal flow. He suggests that the key images in our lives develop later, after the event, as does a photograph. Remembering is the glimpsing of a set of flickering images that are bound up with their moment of recognition. Time is shunted backwards and forwards in Benjamin's memory work. The old traces – such as the inventory of the room imprinted on his child-mind that Benjamin mentions in his memoirs – need to be accessed.[85] And their imprints need to be developed in the light of subsequent development.

It was recording's – imprinting's – play with time that fascinated Benjamin. Temporal and spatial interrogation come to the fore in Benjamin's studies of film, where there too could be found an unconscious, an 'optical unconscious'. This 'optical unconscious' is first mentioned in

1927 where Benjamin argues that in film there 'arises a new region of consciousness', through which people get to grips with the ugly hopeless world, comprehensively (*faßlich*), meaningfully (*sinnvoll*) and passionately (*passionierend*).[86] Rather than an ocular toy providing the occasion to envisage the psyche, as in Freud, the optical device produces a psyche and restructures it, as well as providing a way of knowing a previously unseen, unrevealed world of actions and connections. The receipt of the world then preserved in film and photography provides access to a different nature than the one already known. 'A Small History of Photography' details the 'different nature' available to the machine-enhanced perception of the 'optical unconscious'. Benjamin writes:

> A different nature speaks to the camera than speaks to the eye; most different in that in the place of a space penetrated by a person with consciousness is formed a space penetrated by the unconscious. It is already quite common that someone, for example, can give a rough account of how a person walks. But he would not be able to describe their position at the fracture of a moment of stepping out. Photographic aids: time-lapse, enlargements, unlock this for him. He discovers the optical-unconscious first of all through it, just as the drive-unconscious is discovered through psychoanalysis. Structural compositions, cell formations, with which technology and medicine deal – all this is more fundamentally allied to the camera than the atmospheric landscape or the emotion-seeped portrait.[87]

Whether we have a better view or a deeper view or simply see differently is not resolved – but photography and frame-by-frame procession appear to provide an occasion for scientific analysis (just as they had for the chronophoto experimenters of the 1870s and 1880s). Textures of forms and patternings of cells open up to the camera eye. Something invisible to the naked eye is brought to light. It is worth a foray into the history of science to probe this point further. It has been argued that the debate over the usefulness of microscopic vision was indicative of scientific self-confidence about explaining the world.[88] Sceptics like Locke and Berkeley mocked the popularity of play with microscopes. It was only the introduction of cell theory – a unified explanation of organic process, both plant and animal – that gave meaning to microscopic research. It was Robert Hooke, the author of *Micrographia: Or Some Physiological Descriptions of Minute Bodies Made by Magnifying Glasses with Observations and Inquiries Thereupon*

(1665), who began this and coined the word 'cellulae' as he observed through a microscope what seemed to be small chambers or tiny monks' cells in thin slivers of cork. These appeared to be dead cells; it was not until Matthias Schlieden looked more intently through the microscope in the nineteenth century that their living nature was understood. On this footing Theodor Schwann could claim that all organisms are made of one cell or more, and that the cell is the basic structural unit for all living organisms. Concentrated analytic perception finds its social analogue. Marx locates the momentousness of the commodity – the 'cell' of bourgeois society. In so doing he demonstrates that close attention to minutiae is not myopic but diagnostic. Lenin writes of this discovery:

> In his *Capital*, Marx first analyses the simplest, most ordinary and fundamental, most common and *everyday* relation of bourgeois (commodity) society, a relation encountered billions of times, viz. the exchange of commodities. In this very simple phenomenon (in this 'cell' of bourgeois society) analysis reveals *all* the contradictions (or the germs of *all* the contradictions) of modern society. The subsequent exposition shows us the development (*both* growth *and* movement) of these contradictions and of this society in the sum of its individual parts, from its beginning to its end.[89]

Lenin accentuates Marx's interest in the commodity as the cell of bourgeois society. It is meaningful only in its mobility, in its circulation, its movement through exchange, a billionfold. This cell is present too in film, sometimes dropping one 'l', the cel is the simplest and most fundamental element of animation. It, too, gains full meaning in its interrelationships with others.

The worlds exposed by photographic means may have existed previously, but then again perhaps only in dreams, suggests Benjamin. It seems that there has been found a 'scientific' way of appropriating new worlds. It is optically unconscious and brought out through filmic devices, just as Freud found in the toy a way of seeing, or knowing, the psyche better and differently. But it is not just the external world that is discovered through film. Photography allows the observer to come to grips with interiority. This most external of artforms – the thin celluloid strip of surface imprints whirring through the projection apparatus – relates to the interior. Benjamin uses the word 'interior' in preference to the word 'innerness' –

the realm of the emotion-seeped portrait – for he likes its intimation of the language of motor cars. What is this interiority? It is a psychic unconscious. It is the world of dreams, the shadow world, the underside that does not surface in instrumental rationalism.

These optical devices – from mystic writing pad to film – allow a renewed and fantastic understanding of the contents of consciousness. In some fashion this knowledge, in a Hegelian manner, is always based on the negation of what simply is. In Freud's model, negation, or withdrawing from sampling the world's effects, is necessary for function. In Benjamin's understanding of film, negation of what is occurs through the trickery of in-betweens and manipulations, of stretching space and time, or setting off non-apparent relationship through montage, and all that dreamwork that might appear psychotic. All these procedures could be described as a Freudian dreamwork, but are in fact the better seeing on the part of the receptive 'optical unconscious', which, on closer inspection, gives up the real for analysis. Film and photography, the camera arts, are arts of tracing, etching with light and silver. Just as the unconscious retains traces – as can be imaged in the mystic writing pad – so too does the camera. It was obvious that its first uses would be analytical, and would indulge in a scrutiny of its materials: its wax, colours, shapes, lines, traces and their in-betweens and absences, movement and disappearances.

city symphonies

Walter Ruttmann, after he had abandoned his animation of abstract shapes, put forward a zero thesis too. *WEEKEND* (1930), an eleven-minute film without images – 'a blind film' as Ruttmann called it – was strictly a radio broadcast recorded onto the optical soundtrack of film prior to the invention of audio tape.[90] Ruttmann was influenced by the Russian constructivist Dziga Vertov with his idea of 'Radio-Ear', and his concept of radiophonic montage. Richter notes that developments on the acoustic level had to be made independently of images, as that would give sound a greater freedom to explore possibility.[91] Ruttmann insisted that acoustic montage demanded greater levels of precision than visual montage. Acoustic montage had a different tempo. Ruttmann claimed that it was faster than visual montage, and 'depended on $1/5$th of a second'.[92] Montage is always a question of time itself.

WEEKEND was a documentary montage of street sounds, an acoustics of 'jazzy' end-of-day work noises, the journey home and away, words, sirens, cash registers and birdsong. Six scenes were recorded over three days – the scenes were either documentary recordings in factories, underground stations, railway stations and so on, or were derived from work with amateurs. The production of the piece is consistent with its subject matter – Ruttmann travelled the city just as did the subjects he represented. He gathered documentary material by riding across Berlin with a mobile recording machine. The piece moves from the end of the working day – what Germans call *Feierabend* – to Monday morning. The first scene is called 'Jazz of Work', and the sounds come from typewriters, telephone bells, cash machines, hammers, saws, bosses giving dictation, all syncopated, strongly contrapuntal, and designed to express the oppressive, overbearing nature of machinic work. This scene gives way to 'Feierabend'. The clock strikes and work is over. Other clocks strike and factory sirens blare out, bringing – through montage form – the conception of time into line with the tempo of labour. Now everything closes – desk lids, shutters, cupboards; key bundles tinkle. 'Freizeit', free time, begins. There is a journey into the countryside – into the open air – or 'Freie' – the free – as the Germans call it. This journey is not one that escapes the mechanization of the everyday so apparent in work and city life. It is mechanized too – undertaken by car, train, bus, and also managed according to external dictation, as railway guards shout 'climb aboard' and 'hurry along'. 'Pastoral' is the next scene, with bells as the dominant motif – church bells, cow bells, while in the distance cars pass by, a marching band approaches, children sing. Then work begins again after this short interlude – the church bells are interrupted by factory sirens, calling the workforce to labour. Alarms and telephones ring out and the motifs of the first two scenes 'Jazz of Work' and 'Feierabend' play again.

Ruttmann's imageless film raised the time of work and free time, 'necessity' and 'freedom', as social issues. (Though it is not true to say that it is imageless for the filmmaker. Each sound has a *Tonbild*, a shape that it impresses on the filmstrip – a siren has a line thin as a strand of hair, a hammer beating imprints broader strokes, and heavy bars denote the rumbling approach of a locomotive. Sound turns graphic, but only for the montagist here.) Its orchestration of sounds was part of a conscious, constructivist montage practice. The intensive labour of the piece is not gathering materials but montaging them together rhythmically – attempting to discover the true rhythm of modernity. Sometimes the connections are of a logical nature – a telephone call is put to the operator: 'Dönhoff 204'. This segues into a child counting, '4 times 4 is…', which cedes to a department store lift announcement, 'fourth floor ornaments'. Or again, another 'logical' set of associations: a woman implores 'please permit me', an outraged man shrieks 'who gives you permission …', and then a dictation takes place – 'and we permit ourselves to…' In these rapid but motivated shifts through scenes linked by words all levels of the social totality are connected.

In the montaging together of the city scraps and constructed scenes an interrogation of modern time takes place, which is also a commentary on the available social structuring of time. *WEEKEND* is an attempt to generate a rhythmic pattern of modernity. Tempo increases as work approaches, but the rhythms of free time are not utterly distinct from the rhythms of work – both are subjected to mechanization and external determination. Of course, this is not just about time – for Ruttmann was keen to express also spatial arrangement through this medium, using closeness and distance of sounds in order to generate three-dimensionality. Film itself is spatial – this one 250 metres long – but it runs through time, or transforms into time. In any case, the film is stuffed with sounds, more than a hundred of them – spatialized sounds, sounds that clash and interrelate. It relays a time made full again, exposing banal reality as potentially rhythmic, and it was understood to be the most modern thing. The time it re-presents is mechanized, and not organic, but this proves to be the resource of new rhythms and new experiences. Its modernity, of course, resided in its technological form, which was apt, given the subject matter. A technological machine records the noises of other technological machines and represents a reality suffused with technology. But it uses the capacities of the technological recording machine in order to intervene in reality, in order to reconstruct reality and engage it in a dialogue that intimates freedom and potential. The battleground is time. The questions include, to what extent do machines – work machines, transportation machines – set a tempo for humans, and how does this differ from or mirror the time of free time and the ritual, of the church, of the country walk?

There is work time and there is free time. Other German intellectuals – notably Siegfried Kracauer – came to realize, at this same moment, that one comes to be conceived increasingly in the image of the other. In Kracauer's studies of Weimar culture, for example, Taylorization and Fordism transfer to the cultural sphere too. Kracauer's urban employees had formed as a direct consequence of technical and administrative rationalization. Kracauer focused on the rootlessness of the white-collar employees. Their own preferred culture turned into aesthetic play the reality of their big-city lives: the drill and routine of the working day. Kracauer supposed a mirroring of rationalization of the production process in the ordering of spare time. Glittering revues were signs of the unstoppable demythologization of society by capitalist rationality in the cultural realm. The Tiller Girls and other leg-kicking dancing troupes – more strictly geometric than the sexy French chorus-line cancan dancers – turned mass production and standardization into pleasure in the production of a mass ornament that was an aesthetic reflex of the conveyor belt. Melancholic love songs on piano are the same in structure as typists tapping out dictations. And, for Ruttmann, even if the dash to the countryside for a little pleasure can escape the determinations of mechanical work time (though still reliant on its technologies of transportation and its world of money and commodities), that free time is defined by its opposite, which exists always as a limit. The title of Ruttmann's 'blind film' may be important in this respect. Its title, the English word 'weekend', was perhaps to be heard as 'weak end', prefiguring the final word on the soundtrack – *Null*, zero. This zero signals the weekend's end and the beginning of the working week. The weekend is the interval between work. It is between time. The soundtrack's concluding zero negates the freedom of the weekend, which is not really a freedom but a controlled space of recuperation, over once business insists it must end. It was in the same style, with the same commitment to direct imprinting of the real world, as Ruttmann's documentary films from that era. But it was no mimetic construction. Its orchestration of sounds was part of a conscious, constructivist montage practice.

By 1926 Ruttmann had almost abandoned his experiments with abstract animations. He chose to transmit montaged, and so reworked, imprints of the industrial world. But even then, his most famous documentary film, *Berlin, Symphony of a City* (1927), opened with an abstract sequence of wavy lines in motion, gradually becoming straight and then merging with the railway lines on which the train to Berlin speeds into the city. These abstract figures are reflected in the rest of the film, in the spinning signs in shop windows and the shadows cast by street furniture. It was not so much that Ruttmann forsook abstraction for the direct imprint of the real world, but that this metropolitan space could be its own formal critique. Reality is a composition of rhythms and lines and shapes in motion. Human-made, urban, industrial actuality contains the abstract forms, the parallel lines, the right angles of geometricism. Willy Haas described Ruttmann's film, in a Berlin film journal in 1927, as a fusion of camera tricks, image antitheses and swift reportage. Ruttmann's essay in the film programme mentioned 'counter-point', implying that this was the musical, rhythmic principle of the film, though Haas thought the film more like a blurry Wagnerian *Gesamtkunstwerk* than a strict composition by Bach. Kracauer found the film too intellectual, too crassly 'composed' out of a series of oppositions.[93] In 1929, the Bauhaus design quarterly, the *Zeitschrift für Gestaltung*, classifying the film as one of a number of avant-garde films that used a 'rhythmized optic of movement', spoke of Ruttmann's 'shaping' or design (*Gestaltung*) of reality in motion. But the Bauhaus members were disappointed. Ruttmann was too static. He did not move his camera enough. He did not shape reality enough, but left it dead. It is only when the street itself begins to move that the film wakes up, woken by reality's own dynamism. And from then on the tempo is too speedy, unmodulated, unrhythmic. Bauhaus compared the film to Ruttmann's abstract animations. The 'rhythmic dynamic of the abstract filmstrips' and the 'hacked-up flicker' of the Berlin film are not different because of a change in Ruttmann's *Gestaltungsmethode*, but because of a change in the object being photographed. The camera is passive in both, registering what occurs before the lens. But the discrepancy lies in the fact that whereas the photographed world is mobile, the world of the single drawing is static. Ruttmann's animation brought the drawing to life, and so was adequate to the task; extensive depiction rather than intensive shaping, arbitrariness rather than control, exploration of the elements at hand rather than the chance registration of too much detail in the world. Bauhaus looked at Viking Eggeling's short film bequest, praising his precise, controlled, constructionist commitment, but accusing him of having a painter's eye, flattening out the spatial possibilities of film, its optics of depth, to the two-dimensional surface of the canvas. In the end, they said, Eggeling's *Diagonal-Symphony* (1919–24) (his second film – the first was called *Horizontal-Vertikales Orchester*) looked like a series of tryouts for a drawing.[94]

city traces and movement

The Russians had a word for engagement in the world with the intent to change it – *byt* – a word that meant more than just everyday life; rather the engagements of material life, everyday life as something to be constructed, manipulated, transformed, something conflictual and changeable. The idea of *byt* was used by revolutionaries, such as Trotsky in his 1923 collection *Problems of Everyday Life*. The Russian Revolution had brought the concept of the everyday into sharp focus, for the slate was as black as a suprematist canvas and everything had to be rebuilt – language, industry, social relations, familial relations, education. And the word *byt* was used by avant-gardists, too, as a critique of culture and its contents: as Boris Arvatov wrote in *Art and Production* (1927), new Soviet productivism means 'the melting of artistic forms into the everyday'.[95] Rodchenko, for example, with his sloping camera angles and multi-perspectivism, wanted only that the everyday be seen again, the familiar defamiliarized, in order that it might be consciously known. As he said in 1928: 'I am expanding our conception of the ordinary everyday object.'[96] Rodchenko and comrades in the Productivist wing of the Soviet avant-garde questioned – by redesigning – everyday objects and also ways of seeing objects.

For the avant-garde, filaments connected the Soviet cities and Berlin. This materialized in debate, lectures, exchange, exhibitions and translations. Where Russia had had its successful revolution, Germany, with Berlin as its vanguard city, looked set to follow. Until 1924: then it was the Soviet Union alone, its internationalist perspective replaced by the Stalinist philosophy of 'Socialism in One Country'.[97] But still the Berlin revolutionaries came to see, just in case a new structure of the everyday had been established. That was why Walter Benjamin went to Moscow at the end of 1926, just when the Left Opposition was entering its dwindling but still exuberant stage. Had the everyday been reinvented? Had seemingly eternal structures and patterns been trashed? The visit to Moscow was a test of life under Communist Party rule. Benjamin noted observations about life in the capital in a diary.[98] It was the basis for a city portrait titled 'Moskau' (1927).[99] In his diary Benjamin notes that the left is losing out, and yet there is still a palpable energy infusing Soviet society.[100] Everything is still uncongealed a decade after the revolution, from all sorts of laws to the placing of bus stops. New ceremonies for christening and marriage are presented in the clubs and at research institutes. Those who live there are unconditionally ready for mobilization, decampment, transformation – the days are full with meetings and committees, the venues makeshift. Russia and the Russian avant-gardists participated enthusiastically in the reinvention of daily life and the remodelling of cityscapes. Various utopias were devised, to match and better the one that had supposedly been instated. Dreamers and planners imagined and implemented spatial reorganization and altered social relations. *Byt*, everyday life, is moulded, provisionalized – all this can be seen in Moscow in 1927. Benjamin writes:

> Each thought, each day, each life lies here as on a laboratory table. And as if it were a metal from which an unknown substance is by every means to be extracted, it must endure experimentation to the point of exhaustion. No organism, no organization, can escape this process. Employees in their factories, offices in buildings, pieces of furniture in the apartments are rearranged, transferred and shoved about.[101]

Movement is a principle of life. *Byt* is a political matter. Everyday life is being reinvented, and yet some of the old structures hang over or are indeed being reinstated. Benjamin in 1927 was catching all aftershocks of a revolutionary experiment as it petered out or was even sent into reverse. What goes into the published city-portrait is a more encoded response to the challenge to capitalist relations posed by the Soviet Union. Moscow is Berlin's critique. That much is clear from the opening lines of the Moscow city portrait:

> More quickly than Moscow itself, one gets to know Berlin through Moscow. For someone returning home from Russia the city seems freshly washed. There is no dirt, but no snow, either. The streets seem in reality as desolately clean and swept as in the drawings of Grosz. And how true to life his types are has become more obvious. What is true of the image of the city and its people applies to the intellectual situation: a new perspective of this is the most un-doubted gain from a stay in Russia.[102]

Later he says that the person who returns home from Moscow

> will discover above all that Berlin is a deserted city. People and groups moving in its streets have a solitude about them. Berlin's luxury seems unspeakable and it begins on the asphalt, for the breadth of the pavements is princely. They make of the poorest wretch a *grand seigneur* promenading on the terrace of his man-sion. Princely solitude, princely desolation hang over the streets of Berlin.[103]

All this Benjamin compares to Moscow and its choc-a-bloc streets, with goods bursting everywhere from houses, hanging on fences, on pavements, in little sleighs, sheltered from the snow by colourful woollen blankets. Berlin, in contrast, is a 'freshly swept, empty racecourse on which a field of six-day cyclists hastens comfortlessly on'.[104] Benjamin's city analysis hopes to draw from language something akin to imagist visual portraits, conveying readings of space through intensely described forms, little scenes, in which significant roles are played by light and colour and – montage-like – the crashing together of disparate things. In 'Moscow', Benjamin writes:

> [I]n the evening they switch on brighter lights than are permitted in any other great city. And the cones of light they project are so dazzling that anyone caught in them stands helplessly rooted to the spot. In the blinding light before the Kremlin gates the guards stand in their brazen ochre furs. Above them shines the red signal that regulates the traffic passing through the gate. All the colours of Moscow converge prismatically here, at the centre of Russian power.[105]

Here, as often in Benjamin, colour is emphasized. In Moscow, says Ben-jamin, 'The eye is infinitely busier than the ear. The colours do their utmost against the white.'[106] Experience is coloured – in Moscow maybe most of all, for it unfurls against a backdrop of white snow, or under the blinding glare of the light of power that invades all spaces and allows no private life. Red is everywhere. The red light that regulates traffic is the light of the East, communism. It picks up the colour of glowing coloured rags, Chinese paper fans, paper kites, glazed paper birds, and solid coloured wooden toys – all the stuff for sale on the boulevards.

Benjamin is brought back to life again in Moscow. Street life reinvigorates the senses. He is like Marx's new post-revolutionary human, the sensations reborn. In Moscow Benjamin relearns smell and sight and colour and taste and acoustics. And, more than that, he has to try to learn a language, while the slippery ice forces him to learn to walk again.[107] It is like being reborn, daily life and life in general reinvented. Experience is augmented, and the roster of what counts as experience is expanded too. As the avant-gardists with their found materials of daily life redeployed them to make material experience significant – rejecting the blandishments of the sublime – so too Benjamin demands and denotes an openness to the happenstance of experience. Rejecting Kantian schemas, Benjamin searches instead for meaning crumpled in the contingencies and constellations of experience. Moscow is a bounteous playground for that. Such a Kantian fundamental as time is remoulded there, too, for its unit of measurement is *seichas*, which means 'at once': you hear it a hundred times a day, until the promise is eventually carried out.[108] 'This makes each hour superabundant, each day exhausting, each life a moment.' What is only there for fantasy, in fantasy, is as much a part of the cityscape. If time is shattered by too much fullness, too much activity, then space too may be disrupted – modernistically – for in Moscow, the icy North, screens at a photographer's stand on the boulevard beneath bare trees show palms, marble staircases and southern seas.[109]

Vertov's *The Man with the Movie Camera* was a formalistic experiment in representing this city space and the everyday life of flux. Its form was documentary and yet it turned the cityscape into a graphic field of shapes and lines in whirl or cutting across the screen surface and blurs as the lens jumped in and out of focus. Film tends to drawing, again. In 1929 Siegfried Kracauer wrote of Vertov's cinematic practice in *The Man with the Movie Camera*:

He glides through the town at dawn, eavesdropping on people's sleep and the fragmentary existence that is silently moving. The town wakes up, stretches itself. Teeth are brushed, shutters go up. Trams and buses announce the day. It is movement, one huge powerful movement, melting together all the hitherto fragmented elements and forcing them into the rhythm of the whole.[110]

Vertov's film was a rejoinder to Walter Ruttmann's city film of Berlin. It was a part of a wider German–Soviet dialogue about the representation of contemporary urban life, carried out in lectures, film shows and art exhibitions.[111] According to Kracauer, Ruttmann's film could only set image next to image, without a strong sense of the connections. For Kracauer, Vertov, as totalist, as Marxist, had invented better ways of representing and interpreting than Ruttmann.[112] The Soviet avant-garde knew of German formal experimentation. And, from the first years of the revolution, co-inciding with the beginning of the Weimar Republic and intermittent soviet republics in Germany, the German avant-garde had kept an eye on Russian ambitions to restructure and revolutionize daily life. The German avant-garde began to deploy with enthusiasm in their art and art criticism the concept of *Alltag* or *Alltagsleben*, which developed alongside knowledge of the Russian idea of *byt*. But an earlier inspiration was found, too, in the exploration of daily life as symptomatic in Freud's *Psychopathology of Everyday Life* from 1901. Benjamin writes: 'This book isolated and made analysable things which had heretofore floated along unnoticed in the broad stream of perception'.[113] This is *Alltagsleben* as analysable symptom. For the modernist confections that took this symptomatic reading of the incidental into account, the city becomes not just a place where everyday life is spent, but the prime site chosen to play out critical, analytical representations of everyday experience. The animated exchanges between Vertov, Ruttmann and all the rest, and the claims and counter-claims, took place between members of an artistic community who knew that the modern city could only be represented by harnessing and interrogating its latest technologies, photography, film, montage and the reanimation of reality.

Analysis – reflection, recomposition – of everyday life in the city was carried out ardently in the photographs and paintings of the New Objectivists. It was also explored in Döblin's *Berlin Alexanderplatz*, a rejoinder to those other city studies, *Petersburg* (1916–22) by Bely, Joyce's *Ulysses* (1922) and the America tales of Dos Passos. It appeared in the animated film sketch by Moholy-Nagy titled *Dynamic of the City* (1921). This combined graphic collage, architectural-style drawings of buildings, letters of the alphabet, mathematical symbols. It attempted to convey in abstracted form the speed of a traffic junction passed by traffic streams, underpassed by tube trains and overlooked by communication technologies such as radio towers. Flicker and movement, kinematic principle and city constituent, were key. The city fascination was most concentrated – because daily, that is, everyday and immediate – in the feuilleton work of journalist Siegfried Kracauer, in the city portraits of freelancer Walter Benjamin, in Egon Erwin Kisch's reportage – the classic Weimar genre – and the skits of Franz Hessel, the Berliner who had, notes Benjamin in *Berlin Chronicle*, been his city guide, teaching him how to see his home city, as well as how to wander Paris.[114] Benjamin begins his city portraits around the same time as he unfastens himself from his German home, in the late 1920s. His city gaze stays with him as he scrutinizes the arcades and the archives and, ten years later, looks back on Baudelaire as a city lyricist who poeticizes the destructive processes of industrialization and technologization, violent forces that overtax and shock city dwellers' bodies and psyches as they go about their everyday lives in a sign landscape of increasing complexity. This opulent complexity translates into the search for new methods of representation in his own work in *One-Way Street* and countless city sketches.

In Weimar Germany, Berlin more specifically, and in the Soviet Union, it was in the middle to late 1920s that the focus on city representation and everyday urban experience through film, photography and journalism was most intense. In Germany, it reached a climax at that moment when the city space, city streets, had become a zone of political class struggle. Far from being a product of Weimar's much-vaunted flâneuristic urbanism, the city descriptions of the feuilletonists and Döblin and Ruttmann and co. were salvos in a war over the occupancy of space and the formulation of everyday life. This city genre was not a harmonious part of Weimar, but hacked out of it. For it was clear to those who tramped the streets, who had an eye to how life was changing, or not changing but rolling back-wards, that 'Weimar' was dead before the 1920s were out. And the Weimar chroniclers were already packing their suitcases. It was after Hitler's victory that Walter Benjamin wrote in a letter in February 1933 of an air that suffocates, but in November of the previous year he had already revealed that he was too frightened to walk the streets.[115] A consummate recorder of detail, Siegfried Kracauer described this panic superimposing itself on Weimar streets in the late 1920s and 1930s. Editor of the Berlin feuilleton office for the *Frankfurter Zeitung*, he wrote pieces day after day about life in the metropolis or the life of the metropolis. He edits the uneasy scenes into filmic mini-sequences, panning, irising out, focusing in on a civil war as it transpires. Kracauer's city scenes were a systematic attempt to read and write everyday spaces politically and socially. His piece 'On Labour Exchanges: Construction of a Space', of 17 June 1930, stated that he had visited labour exchanges in order to measure what place the unemployed actually adopt in the system of our society. The arrangement of space speaks more truth than statistics or government reports because, he writes, 'the space of the labour exchange is posed by reality itself'. He continues:

> Every typical space is brought into being by typical social relations that express themselves in it without the interfering intervention of consciousness. Everything denied by consciousness, everything that is otherwise intentionally overlooked, participates in its construction. Spatial images are the dreams of society. Wherever the hieroglyphs of a spatial image are deciphered, there the foundations of social reality may be identified.[116]

Tensions and contradictions shape spaces. The cityscape, the image of the city, can be read for political significance. In Kracauer's city skits, spaces are 'posed by reality itself' and 'spatial images are the dreams of society'. And on the streets the contradictions of everyday life, its tensions and breaking points, could be recorded. 'Scream on the Street', of 19 July 1930, catalogues a dread.[117] Kracauer relates a particular incident near the Kaiser Wilhelm Remembrance Church. He watches as a National Socialist troop, convinced it is being mocked by the clientele in a café, home of course of the famed Weimar culture, climbs over the balustrade and begins to fight the customers, until the police show up. But this act of violence is only a sudden synthesis made of a more pervasive crisis on the streets. The screaming is constant. People pretend not to hear the screams. A drunk screams but pretends he has not when Kracauer startles. A woman screaming transforms herself into a lover on the chill moonlit asphalt. A scream of blue murder is muffled behind a door slammed shut. Even the streets are screaming. The whole city is hustling with electric tension while the façade of lights from the illuminated monuments bedazzle with phosphorescence, and the neon signs flicker advertisements which blind for an instant, halos of illumination exuding glistening fuzziness, dousing thought, setting up a gauze between cognition and perception. Against this, the efficacy of sensory perception has to be reasserted. Signals of crisis loom like the masts of a sunken ship above the mirror-flat surface, writes Kracauer in July 1931 in 'Under the Surface'.[118] These are the Golden Twenties turned into the Tarnished Thirties. The experience is of sensuous overload, surface dazzle, always for him without meaning. Where in the proletarian quarters the street demonstrations forge together in solidarity masses with a purpose, in the West End only a disintegrating, disunited crowd flows, directionless, irrational. And 'The Subway', published on 11 March 1932, reflects on the crowds of people, all little parts, uncoordinated splinters of a whole that does not exist. This was a more sinister gloss than that relayed in 'Analysis of a City Map', written in 1928. There Kracauer, witnessing graphically, records the patterns formed by the flowing crowds. Where bourgeois society hopes to regulate and mark out straight lines, the crowds themselves jostle and agitate in open spaces, making patterns that continuously decompose. The swarming crowds love their constant disintegration: it holds them on the edge of life; otherwise there is just the abyss.[119] But, in retrospect, more sinisterly, Kracauer's 'The Mass Ornament' of 1927 seems to foretell that these same throngs might eventually find a more drastic recombination in their mass ornamentation, at the price of relinquishing all autonomy.[120]

Berlin was a hard city to map. Changed too quick, always changing, it existed, thought Kracauer, in unhistorical space and empty historical time. In 'Street Without Memory', of 16 December 1932, he notes a sortie into the battle zone of the everyday that the façades on the old West End apartments are stripped of ornament. This seems to concretize a frightening loss of memory – 'the bridge to yesterday' is cut away. He tells of his searches for two favourite cafés on the Ku'damm. All he finds of one is a hollowed-out interior. And the other, now a confectioner's, so represses the earlier memory of the café that it is as if it had never been there. Only the present exists.[121] 'Repetition', written the same year, continues the theme of existence formed anew each day, but always similar, like the newspaper, in the hand of the reader. Has not the everyday, the avant-gardist, manipulable space of reconstruction and decision, turned into a Sisyphean task, an arduous daily reinvention, just to stay alive? The concept of the everyday has lost its utopian edge. In the last days of the Weimar Republic the everyday is a battleground, and the revolutionaries are on the losing side. It was little different in Moscow. Benjamin, for one, found a new figure of utopia. It was not a new regime, but came in the form of a four-fingered warder of the collective dream and it was mouse-shaped.

mickey mouse, utopia and walter benjamin

wish mouse and marx

In 1931 Mickey Mouse was denounced in a Nazi journal published in Pomerania titled *The Dictatorship*. Under the headline 'The Mickey Mouse Scandal', the writer thundered:

> Blonde, freethinking urban German youth tied to the apron strings of finance Jews. Youth, where is your pride? Youth, where is your self-consciousness? Mickey Mouse is the shabbiest, most miserable ideal ever invented. Mickey Mouse is a stultification device sent over with the Young-Plan capital. Healthy instinct informs every decent girl and upright boy that the vile and dirty vermin, which import bacteria into the animal kingdom, cannot be made into an ideal animal type. Have we nothing better to do than decorate our garments with dirty animals because American commerce Jews want profit? Down with the Jewish bamboozlement of the people, kick out the vermin, down with Mickey Mouse, and erect swastikas![1]

For this Nazi, Mickey Mouse represented Aryan youth's antithesis. Its Americanness was synonymous with its Jewishness, and its Jewishness was proof of its trashiness and degeneracy. The Nazi anticipated the associations that the Nazi propaganda film *Der ewige Jude* would excite, with its footage of the common ghetto dwellers, rats and Jews. But, in 1931, this was just another laughable opinion. The report was quoted mockingly in the film journal *Film-Kurier* on 28 July 1931, where the counter-critics argued that Mickey Mouse should be taken up as a symbol of reason, against 'swastika and persecution'. Instead of the swastika emblems, patrons of Disney films were advised to buy the little Mickey Mouse pins from the cinemas and wear them to make an anti-Nazi statement. Mickey Mouse was the swastika's converse. The Nazi bluster and the studio cash-in were responding to a Mickey Mouse mania that was sweeping Germany. After the first Mickey Mouse film programme, in Berlin in February 1930, the press was wildly enthusiastic. The film company Südfilm produced a newspaper advertisement just after the showing, which proclaimed: 'An mein Volk, Heil sei dem Tag, an dem ich euch erschienen. Es war ein Sieg auf der ganzen Linie!' ('To my people, hail the day that I appeared before you. It was an out-and-out victory!') Curiously the language used pre-empted, maybe mocked, the self-aggrandizing rhetoric of a later Volksführer. The advertisement quoted all the favourable press reviews, with their praise for the 'Akkuratesse' of the action, 'the unmatched optical rhythm', the fact that 'great art triumphs in the narrowest frames', the 'glittering slapstick'. It cited the verdict of the film journal *Licht–Bild–Bühne* that the cartoons are 'a fairy-tale of the current moment, the jazz epoch'. The *Vossische Zeitung* raved about the cartoons' dalliance with complete madness in the course of re-securing the natural order of things.

In the same year that the Pomeranian Nazi maligned the verminous Mickey Mouse, Walter Benjamin wrote a fragment titled 'Zu Micky-Maus' (1931). These few jottings provide a defence of Mickey Mouse's unmasking of social negativity. Benjamin perceives in the cartoons a rejection of the 'civilized' bourgeois subject.[2] Early Mickey Mouse cartoons feature a pesky, ratty creature creating mischief, indulging in vaudeville and low-life; and, as the *Film-Kurier* put it in February 1930, he was a beast living in jazz rhythm – every step a dance move, every movement syncopated.[3] He was a spirited and insubordinate animal in a world of lively things. Mickey Mouse was not respectable. Whether Jewish or Negro, he was America's immigrant heart. In countless images and maquettes Mickey Mouse appeared as a bandy limbed, pointy creature. Sometimes he even had rodent teeth. Promotional photographs, such as Olga Tschechova's photo for the fans, caught in their frame a beautiful actress and a ratty fabric Mickey, all legs and snout, amorously clinging to the star. Benjamin responded gleefully to Mickey Mouse's nonconformist insolence. As Benjamin observes in his essay 'Karl Kraus', also from 1931, the prototype for emulation for any self-respecting modernist is not the *Übermensch* but the *Unmensch*, the un-person, the barbarian.[4] The satirist is the guise that the cannibal adopts in contemporary society – he devours his adversary, in the mimicking of styles and in the savagery of his wit. He eats up his fellow men, in order to show just how much the world will indeed almost tolerate. He takes the measure of the humanity of fellow men, and steps just beyond it. This is the world of Swift's modest proposal concerning poor children, and of Léon Bloy, who stretched credulity only a little in suggesting that landlords might be allowed to sell the flesh of their insolvent lodgers. Such brutal imagination was imported the same year into Walter Benjamin's short sketch 'The Destructive Character':

> The destructive character is young and cheerful. For destroying rejuvenates in clearing away the traces of our own age; it cheers because everything cleared away means to the destroyer a complete reduction, indeed eradication, of his own condition.... The destructive character has the consciousness of historical man, whose deepest emotion is an insuperable mistrust of the course of things and a readiness at all times to recognize that everything can go wrong.[5]

The destructive character sees nothing permanent, and, in always forcing a way through, reduces what exists to rubble. Benjamin was casting around for other destroyers. The lines that comprise 'Zu Micky-Maus' are notes from a conversation between Benjamin, the composer Kurt Weill and Gustav Glück, a bank official and friend. The three men discussed how the cartoons were to be understood through Marxist categories. Benjamin notes: 'Property relations in the Mickey Mouse film; here, for the first time, one's own arm, indeed one's own body can be stolen.'[6]

Like fairy-tales and unlike the likes of Maeterlinck or Mary Wigman, Mickey Mouse presents important, vital experiences without misty symbolism, and without melodramatic pretension.[7] The cartoons humour no illusions. This is satire, testing the limits of the possible or probable. Benjamin recycles a line from his Karl Kraus commentary: 'In these films humanity prepares to survive civilization.' In 'Zu Micky-Maus' the line describes a mankind that has run out of tears but not out of laughter. In 'Karl Kraus', it announces a programme of 'materialist humanism', against the classical ideal of humanity. For Kraus, this materialist humanism manifests itself in the child, notes Benjamin, and its face is turned to destruction of what exists, which is at the basis of all labour, as Adolf Loos says, and which is necessary to conquer the 'empty phrases' of bourgeois ideology. Kraus is the avenging angel, who must further debase the already debased. He must negate the negation. In the notes on Mickey Mouse, again, classical *Humanität* and idealist humanism are unmasked as cover stories for the powerful. 'Mickey Mouse shows that the creature remains, even when it has expunged everything humanoid. It breaks through the hierarchy of creatures designed from the human perspective.' This observation links with another point made that same year in a review essay on 'Literary History and Literary Studies', where Benjamin attacks the 'false universalism' of the traditional humanities, in whose 'privileged thinking' the rise of Western man was assumed and his interweaving of exploitation and mission in the oppression of other peoples and races dissembled.[8] Here, in thoughts on Disney, the oppression extends to animals.

For Walter Benjamin and friends, the cartoons depict a realist – though not naturalist – expression of the circumstances of modern daily life; the cartoons make clear that even our bodies do not belong to us – we have alienated them in exchange for money, or have given parts of them up in war. The cartoons expose the fact that what parades as civilization is actually barbarism. And the animal-human beasts and spirited things insinuate that humanism is nothing more than an ideology. Human species-arrogance is questionable. Benjamin reveals a pedagogical aim. All Mickey Mouse films, in essence, teach audiences about the workings of fear; they do this, as does the Grimm fairy-tale, by making them leave home.[9] He continues: 'So it is not "mechanisation", not the "formal", not a "misunderstanding" which is the basis for the massive success of these films, but that the public recognises their own lives in them.'[10] The cartoons are object lessons in the actuality of alienation. Disney's cartoon world is a world of impoverished experience, sadism and violence. That is to say, it is our world. Their recognition of dehumanization is a visual analogue, maybe, to Marx's 1844 words, rediscovered the following year – but foreseen already in Georg Lukács's *History and Class Consciousness* – on alienation and the exploited worker. There Marx writes of the workers' loss of control over their labour's production, evoking a key theme of cartoons – the animal–human fusion, and in the context of that other cartoonish feature, fetishism:

It belongs to another, it is a loss of his self. The result is that man (the worker) feels that he is acting freely only in his animal functions – eating, drinking and procreating, or at most in his dwelling and adornment – while in his human functions he is nothing more than an animal.[11]

For Benjamin, Disney's cartoon world outlines this world of impoverished and brutal experience – as Adorno and Horkheimer, too, would later underscore in analyses of Donald Duck and the culture industry. But, importantly, its projection is educative and enlightening. Benjamin's reflections on Mickey Mouse were not off the cuff. They nuzzled at the core of Benjamin's analysis of experience in the 1930s.[12] One line of 'Zu Micky-Maus' noted: 'These films disavow, more radically than was ever the case before, all experience. It is not worth having experiences in a world like this.'[13] Benjamin would repeat this sentiment in other writings; it is not sheer pessimism, but, rather, an attention to contemporary exigencies for representation. Adorno and Horkheimer later insist, in *Dialectic of Enlightenment* (1944), that Sade's radicalism exists in the fact that he exposes the brutal truth of unequal exchange, cold unfeeling and thingness at the heart of capitalism, unlike the bourgeois ideologues who seek to conceal this fact. For Benjamin, Mickey Mouse performs a similar function. The mouse portrays, unmasks and makes available for criticism.

Experience – *Erfahrung* – is on the wane. Benjamin continued this theme in 'Erfahrung und Armut' ('Experience and Poverty'), written in 1933. There he comes to the conclusion that circumstances on the battlefields of the Great War made the continued existence of experience as *Erfahrung* infeasible.[14] War's technological traumas instate experience as *Erlebnis*, as adventure, as shock. Experience is impoverished, not just for individuals but for humanity. Because of this – because of his realism – Benjamin counsels that the poverty of experience be recognized so to make a new beginning, through a 'new positive concept of barbarism'.[15] Artists should not ignore or mourn experience's impoverishment, but retransmit it, precisely by imitating the technology that gives rise to alienation. 'Experience and Poverty' applauds cultural producers who do this, who incorporate formally, in various ways, capitalism's alienating 'barbarism'. These are all 'constructors' who cleared the decks, in order to begin again. They wanted a drawing board – a more practical version of Malevich's 'zero of form', perhaps. The constructors, post-humanists to a man, all reflect frankly the cessation of bourgeois humanism: Brecht with his social-political drama-turgy of alienation, Adolf Loos with his glassy unornamented buildings, and Paul Scheerbart with his utopian fantasies which envisage how tele-scopes and aeroplanes and space rockets transform people and how they may live new mass and public lives inside those glass houses.[16] Also present in the roll call is Disney with his deranged world of spirited technologies and animals. Art is the *last* repository of value. The cubists drew on mathematics to reform the world stereoscopically. Paul Klee drew on the work of engineers, his figures, says Benjamin, 'conceived on a car's drawing board', and, just 'as a good car in its bodywork obeys above all the neces-sities of the motor', they obey 'their interior in the expression on their faces. The interior more than inwardness: that is what makes them bar-baric.'[17] Klee's figures are like cars: they are mechanical and possess in-teriors rather than innerness, or souls. They are like the new mass audiences. An unpublished version of 'Experience and Poverty' titled 'Erfahrungs-armut' ('Poverty of Experience') details the new experience-free mentality of the audience.

> It is a type of dreadful and very cheerful cannibal attitude, related to the bar-barism of children. One can tell them fairy-tales again, in which the world is as fresh and as new as for children. Best of all filmic fairy-tales. Who could better corroborate experiences like Mickey Mouse has in his films? A Mickey Mouse film might be incomprehensible to the individual, but not to a public. And a Mickey Mouse film can direct a whole public rhythmically.[18]

The laughter that the films set off can sound inhuman, but, Benjamin notes, perhaps the individual must have an element of inhumanness so that the mass audience, the collective, that was so often inhuman, might become human. Redemption then – utopia is glimpsed again. 'Experience and Poverty' builds its conclusion from reflections on Mickey Mouse's redemptive function. The exploited crave some dreamy form of compen-sation in the teeth of new barbaric experience. Emerging from savageness, Disney's mouse is also its antidote.

> The existence of Mickey Mouse is just such a dream of today's people. His existence is full of miracles, which not only outdo technical wonders, but make fun of them too. For the strangest thing about them is that they all emerge from

> Mickey Mouse's body, from his partisans and persecutors, from ordinary furniture as much as from trees, clouds or sea, without machinery, improvised. Nature and technology, primitiveness and comfort have become completely merged. And in front of the eyes of people who have become tired of the endless complications of everyday life and to whom the purpose of existence seems to be reduced to only the most distant vanishing point in an infinite perspective of means, a redemptive existence appears.[19]

Mickey Mouse films mock the technology that rules over people, but they also understand the utopian impulse that this technology plugs. This is not the sleek techno-fetishism of New Objectivity. Technology as such is banished. The films turn technical invention back into a feat of nature. In so doing they oblige audiences to confront how technology rules over them as a second nature. In his city sketch of Moscow, written after his return in 1927, Benjamin described existence in the Soviet capital in terms similar to existence in the Disney world. A disorienting, crowded ride in a bus demonstrates how the world-historical experiment in the new Russia rests on the 'complete interpenetration of technological and primitive modes of life'.[20] Such interpenetration reinvents along new lines and maybe better lines. Russia, too, is a place that generates a 'curious tempo' and sets for its peasant population a 'rhythm'. Benjamin is convinced of the rightness of Charles Fourier's utopia – essentially an improved nature of lemonade seas, extra moons and anti-lions. This utopia, he says, Marx recognized, and Russia has begun to implement[21] – but only begun. Mickey Mouse films can exceed the privations in Russia. Its new negotiation of second nature changes tempo and physics even more dramatically to the benefit of cartoon citizens.

> At every turn this existence pleases itself in the simplest and, simultaneously, most comfortable way, in which a car does not weigh more than a straw hat, and in which the fruit on the tree ripens as quickly as the gondola of an air balloon.[22]

Disney's cartoon world is a utopia, a world where the alienating technological apparatus is banished by a reformulated nature, a nature permeated by technology, sign of the historicity of nature. This new nature can pull off astonishing feats, and reveals the utopia to be gained if technologies are mastered and partnered. But now we are poor. Technology is a monstrous dominator. Culture, and humanity, in their ideological forms that rule over us, are sham. The new barbarism endures. What culture is needed in barbarism? Benjamin proposes siding with culture producers prepared, if need be, to survive culture with a laugh that might at times sound barbaric:[23] not culture or barbarism, but the barbarism of culture, and, in its wake, the recognition of technology. The 'human' is a lie. Existence is technoid; that is to say, an understanding of technical life is the starting point for social theory. This is Benjamin's conclusion. He found it confirmed in a magazine article by Eberhard Schulz, which he clipped out and kept. It was titled 'The Great Laboratory, Ways of Film', and in it Schulz asserted that film was the attempt to integrate publics into the great technical laboratory in which we all seem to be accommodated today.[24] Produced and consumed collectively, it was training for life in the present.

Benjamin was not alone in such thinking. Jean Charlot, in his book *Art from the Mayans to Disney*, of 1939, also characterized animation art as a legitimate product of a modern epoch of disillusion. It was concise because it had to be: today time was of the essence. It contrasted flatness and depth, and in so doing solved problems posed by cubism and impressionism. Charlot observed the paradox that,

> without the benefit of critical appraisal, and whipped into form by the pressure of the balance sheets and the profit motive, the animated cartoon is nevertheless the unexpected flowering of the cubist seed. In the cartoon the impersonality of a work of art has been captured, the cult of the 'original' has been smashed. The drawings are manipulated by so many hands from the birth of the plot to the inking of the line that they are propulsed into being more by the communal machinery that grinds them out than by any single human being.[25]

Benjamin's perception of technical existence – technical art, technologies of labour – draws him on to a study of the inassimilable countercurrents of bourgeois ideology as it develops in tandem with an advancing technology and a wilting prospect of human autonomy. In the ongoing note-taking for the *Arcades Project*, Benjamin ponders the significance of the Marquis de Sade, whom he identifies as a theorist of machinery. But Sade does not theorize domination by the machine so much as the reinvention of man as machine. Sade's is a crude materialism. Sade suggests a deep intimacy between sadism and fetishism and a desire for the inorganic, the machinic, such that man becomes what he desires. Benjamin writes:

> The discovery of the mechanical aspect of the organism is a persistent tendency in sadists. It is possible to say that the sadist attempts to subordinate the human organism to the image of machinery.[26]

In sadism, according to Benjamin, the machine substitutes for the human organism. Benjamin assumes this because he wants to place this tendency historically in the epoch of machinery, the bourgeois industrial epoch. The utopian socialist Charles Fourier, another materialist philosopher, follows Sade. Sade's cruelly mathematical copulation equations are twinned with Fourier's utopian socialist imaginations of a perfectly meshed system of complementary passions, which is, in essence, a 'machine made of people'.[27] These two animators of the inanimate were both entirely of their epoch, and that is one, Benjamin tells us, that was delighted by automata. Such automation, and *Unmenschlichkeit*, inhumanness, reminds Benjamin of La Mettrie, whose *L'Homme machine* (*Man a Machine*) conjures up the revolutionary weapon, the guillotine, which rudimentarily tests materialism's truths.[28] Descartes and disciples constructed a dualistic world-view that severed matter from thought, like body from head. Matter mechanically obeyed the laws of force and motion decreed by God; thought, a substance independent of matter, gave human beings a supernatural power, and animals are machines. La Mettrie's *Man a Machine*, written in 1748, commends Descartes for being 'the first to prove completely that animals are pure machines'. Claiming that thought is like electricity, he goes on to insist that all living organisms are machines whose 'soul is but a principle of motion or a material and sensible part of the brain'. Animals and humans are, in essence, the same. And both are machines. The entire universe is matter (just as all cartoons that are made up of cels consist of lines on celluloid) and it is all equally energized. This was an ill-mannered materialism, but it was echoed and transformed in Fourier's programme, which propagandizes for a rebellion, through ridicule and buffoonery, against the tyranny of the organic and tyranny over the organic, the partnered antinomies of bourgeois rule. The Fourierist utopia's secret cue is machines. But Benjamin is keen to note that Fourier's utopia does not propose the exploitation of nature by man. Rather, 'technology appears as the spark that ignites the powder of nature'.[29] Drawing on Fourier, Benjamin delineates his own politics:

> Fourier's idea of the spreading of phalansteries by explosions compares with two aspects of my 'politics': the revolution as an innervation of the technical organs of the collective (compare this to a child that learns to grasp by clutching at the moon). And the 'blasting open of the teleology of nature'.[30]

'*Innervation*' was a Freudian term for a rush of energy through the nervous system. It was as if the electricity supply had been connected directly to the human body, or rather a collective body, such as might be found in the cinema audience, laughing as one, weeping as one, directed 'rhythmically'. The Fourierist phalansteries spread across the cosmos in chain reaction, like dynamite exploding and setting off more explosions, as each spark triggers another detonation. The technical interference, escalating the 'natural' course of things, is as fantastic as the child's refusal to recognize the size of space. Such an attitude refuses natural order, in the name of something more ambitious, if not entirely serious. For Benjamin, this attitude connects Fourier and Mickey Mouse:

> In order to explain Fourier's extravaganzas Mickey Mouse must be brought on; here, just as his ideas imply, the moral mobilization of nature is completed. Here humour tests out politics. It proves how correct Marx was to see in Fourier, above all, a great humorist. Cracking open nature's teleology happens according to humour's plan.[31]

Of course, occurring between Fourier and Sade, on the one hand, and Benjamin and Mickey Mouse, on the other, was the invention of cinema, which emerged out of an analytical approach to motion – Muybridge's chronophotography and zoopraxiscope – that was itself born of a renewed tendency to conceive the body as mechanism, as in Etienne Jules Marey's *La Machine animale* (1874). This analytical approach sought the truth of movement. This assault on teleology is less concerned with truth and more concerned with possibility. Nature, cracked apart, is reconceived, for Fourier and Sade, and for Benjamin, as negation, as movement, as dynamic. Nature cracked apart is visualized in Mickey Mouse's scenarios of animate nature and unnatural deeds, as well as in the analytical approach, the divisible attack on the visible field, which is film's action. Laughter is crucial, once more. Re-presenting the animation of nature, as revolt against its muteness, and the animation of machinery, livelier than its operators, signals at one and the same time effects of fetishism and its critique from the perspective of utopia. Cracked nature evoked an image that Benjamin had used over a decade before in describing Paul Scheerbart's invented asteroid, Pallas, and the life on it. In Pallas all relationships are left out that could lead to confused innerness, interpretation and explanation. All is objectivity, and there is no sex, no gender. The new Pallasians are found in nutshells in the depths of Pallas and their birth is the smashing of these shells. The children are named by the first words they utter on seeing light. Like Scheerbart's curiously named characters, Benjamin notes, the new Russians give their children 'dehumanized' names such as *October*, *Pjatiletka*, after the Five-Year Plan, or *Aviachim*, after an airline. Pallas is a society without property or institutions. Its inhabitants have a transformed relationship to nature: natural needs are met through adaptation to environment, yet they continue to pursue technological projects that are meant to embellish not exploit the planet. Scheerbart's purpose was to disabuse people of the base and vulgar opinion that they are called on to exploit the forces of nature. He wanted to portray a world in which technology liberates humanity and the rest of creation along with it. In Scheerbart's 'utopia of the body' earth and humanity in communion form a single live body. Technology is a friend of both. This is what cartoons play through too – in their narratives of lively machineries, vocal nature and stretched physics, as well as in their technological, cinematic form of presentation.

play and transformation

In this utopia of reinvigorated social and natural relations, the thing most apparent is the reinvigoration of the object world, of that which is normally inanimate, or inarticulate. This is what Benjamin thought found voice in surrealism, as is evident, for example, in the 'primal scene' of his *Arcades Project* – the moment when he read Louis Aragon's description in *Paris Peasant* of a window display of walking sticks that comes to life in the Passage de l'Opéra. Surrealism supercharged objects, endowing them with energy, autonomy and life. Bertolt Brecht upbraided Benjamin's interest in the animation of the world of things, suspecting it of mysticism. But for Benjamin such an attitude was not only grounded historically in Marx's detection of the commodity fetish; he also thought that the wish to awaken life in petrified things was the impulse of children, and so of anthropological value. The desire for animation was a sign of children's proximity to utopia. The child's perspective is inquisitive and nonconformist, suspending disbelief. Youth's experience is infused with possibilities and hope. Through children, each epoch sustains some share in fabulous dreaming.[32] Transformation is at the heart of children's play as, rousing their mimetic capacity, they become the objects they observe and those objects in turn become other things. In adults such mimetic capacity has decayed.[33] Reflecting on the child's relationship to objects, Benjamin notes how they are drawn to places of production. In 'Old Forgotten Children's Books' (1924), he notes

> Children are fond of haunting any site where things are being visibly worked on. They are irresistibly drawn by the detritus generated by building, gardening, housework, carpentry, tailoring or whatever. In these waste products they recognize the face that the world of things turns directly and solely to them. In using these things they do not so much imitate the works of adults as bring together materials of widely differing kinds in a new volatile relationship. Children thus produce their own small world of things within the larger one. The fairy-tale is such a waste product – perhaps the most powerful to be found in the spiritual life of humanity: a waste product that emerges from the growth and decay of the saga. With the stuff of fairy-tales the child may be as sovereign and uninhibited as with rags and building blocks. Out of fairy-tale motifs the child constructs its world, or at least it forms a bond with these elements.[34]

Do these childish endeavours sound like Kurt Schwitters's Merzbau and any junk epic of modernist rubbish redemption? Because of what they offered, because they appealed to a sensibility attuned to detritus and utopian transfiguration, Benjamin collected children's books and toys, and he wrote about his collections. For example, in 'Cultural History of the Toy' (1928), a feuilleton piece written for the literary supplement of the *Frankfurter Zeitung*, he tracks the history of toys, from the time when they were produced by artisans, wood carvers and pewterers, on the side, as miniature reproductions of objects of daily life, and so contained traces of the adult world, to the industrialization of toy production in the nineteenth century when toys become, he insists, ever more distant from the adult world. But his observations are not tied to the factuality of the object under scrutiny. Benjamin imagines the object in a universe of handling. In a blow against naturalism, he makes the point that it is the imaginative act of play, culturally and class-determined of course, that makes the toy, not the toy that determines the play. The study of toys was just one of several that Benjamin wrote through the 1920s. In these short articles – on alphabet books, Russian toys, long-forgotten children's illustrated books – that appeared in newspaper supplements, literary journals and illustrated magazines, Benjamin worked out ideas about play and the enchantment of objects. It is significant that his ideas about play – essentially ideas about cognition – are worked out for the pages of newspapers and journals, transitory forms of text, passing through on their way to become detritus. These articles catch spores of what later blooms in the autobiographical memories: play as transformation, play as magical, play as mimetic and primitive. 'Toys and Play' (1928), written for a literary journal, reveals how Benjamin, like the children he studies, was intrigued by fairytales' and toys' traces of an animistic, primitive sense; the rattle, for example, he claims, is an instrument that wards off evil spirits. Accompanying these socializing and supernatural facets is always a sense of the transformative aspect of play and childish perception.

At their high point, children's books – a secret collaboration between the artist-illustrators and the young readers, behind the backs of pedagogues – bore an affinity to Baroque emblem books, pictographic combinations of allegorical objects.[35] Benjamin divulges the stimulus of his visual thinking, his thinking in images; which means his theory is so often an exchange between image and word. The Baroque emblem books had an infant equivalent, in later eighteenth-century alphabet primers that collated images of objects on one page that were related only by the fact that their names all began with the same letter. This image-word universe had a longer history in children's literature, going back to seventeenth-century picture books:

> At the beginnings of children's literature we find – in addition to primers and catechisms – illustrated lexicons and illustrated alphabet books, or whatever name we wish to give to the *Orbis Pictus* of Amos Comenius. This genre too is

XXXIX.
The Head and the Hand.   *Caput & Manus.*

the Cheeks 10.
and the Chin. 13.
The Mouth is fenced
with a Muftacho, 11.
and Lips ; 12.
a Tongue and Palate,
and Teeth 16.
in the Check-bone.
A Mans Chin is co-
vered with a Beard; 14.
and the eye,
(in which is the white
and the Apple)
with eye-lids,
and an eye-brow. 15.
The Hand being
closed, is a Fift ; 17.
being open, is a
palm,18. (hollow 19.
in the midft, is the
of the Hand ; the extre-
mity is the Thumb,20.
with four Fingers,
the fore-finger,21.
the middle-finger, 22,
the Ring-finger, 23.
and the little-finger,24
In every one are three
joynts a.b.c. (d.e.f.
and as many knuckles
with a Nail. 25.

Gena (Malæ) 10.
& Mentum. 13.
Os feptum eft
Myftace, 11.
& Labiis; 12.
Lingua cum Palato,
Dentibus 16.
in Maxillâ.
Mentum virile
tegitur Barbâ ; 14.
Oculus verò,
(in quo Albugo
& Pupilla)
palpebris
& fupercilio. 15.
Manus contracta,
Pugnus 17. eft ;
aperta,
Palma, 18.
in medio, Vola, 19.
extremitas, Pollex, 20.
cum quatuor Digitis,
Indice, 21.
Medio, 22.
Annulari, 23.
& Auriculari. 24.
In quolibet
funt articuli tres a.b.c.
& totidem Condyli d.e.f.
cum Ungue. 25.

In the Head are,
the Hair, 1.
(which is Combed
with a Comb, 2.)
two Ears, 3.
the Temples, 4.
and the Face, 5.
In the Face are,
the Forehead, 6.
both the Eyes, 7.
the Nose, 8.
(with two Noftrils)
the Mouth, 9.

In *Capite* funt
Capillus, 1.
(qui pectitur
Pectine 2.)
Aures 3. binæ,
& *Tempora,* 4.
Facies, 5.
In facie funt
Frons, 6.
Oculus 7. uterque,
Nafus 8.
(duabus *Naribus,*)
Os, 9.

Orbis Pictus, J.A. Comenius

one that the Enlightenment appropriated after its own fashion, as exemplified by Basedow's monumental *Elementarwerk*. This book is a pleasure in many re- spects, even textually. For next to long-winded, encyclopaedic learning, which, in the spirit of its age, emphasizes the 'utility' of all things – from mathematics to tightrope walking – we find moral stories that are so graphic that they verge, not unintentionally, on the comic.[36]

These illustrated picture books, picture lexicons and encyclopaedias brought image and word into the closest proximity. They stimulated and exploited a fascination with the object world and the myriad names for all its com- ponents. They seemed to make the world come alive again by naming it. Comenius and Basedow were pedagogues. *Orbis Pictus,* of 1658, and the *Elementarwerk* of 1774 were designed by reformers to educate children, to bring them to enlightenment. Comenius was a millennialist and a pan-sophist. He did not wish to present to children a safe and cosy world, but rather showed and named the horrors of torture, the nightmare of war on land and sea, which he knew well, for he had suffered in the Thirty Years' War. Comenius's theory of knowledge and education was materialist, and derived from Aristotle and Francis Bacon. The 'golden rule for teachers' was that 'everything should, as far as is possible, be placed before the senses'.[37] In his study *Great Didactic* Comenius argued that it is only 'when a thing has been grasped by the senses that language can fulfil its function of explaining it further'. In addition, 'the truth and certainty of science depend on the witness of the senses', and, furthermore, the senses are 'the most trusty servants of the memory'.[38] Sense experience is an active engagement with the world of nature; that is to say it is transformative, for it involves forming, building, tending the materials of nature. It is that involvement and adaptation that equals true knowledge. This is similar to Benjamin's emphasis on knowledge as practical. Authentic experience is conceived as close and practised knowledge of whatever is at hand. The hand handles, and so possesses practical experience of life. Benjamin's descriptions of experience use the words *taktil*, *taktisch*, *Taktische* ('tactile', 'tactics', 'the tactical'), from the Latin *tangere*, touch. To touch the world is to know the world. Pottery – one of the crafts that features in *Orbis Pictus* because the trades know the world better than the 'cobwebs of learning' – provides a model and a metaphor, because it is a type of *Handwerk*, hand work or artisan labour.

The hand marks out genuine experience, Benjamin announces in his essay 'The Storyteller' (1936). This practical knowledge needs to be guided. That was Comenius's contribution and the reason why he devised the picture books. He believed, too, that sight was the chief of the senses, and through this insight he was able to turn his belief in direct sense-experience into a matter of representation. Pictures were a second best to objects, and could not appeal to so many senses, but a picture was easier to make or obtain and could be stored forever. It might also present a clearer image, more assimilable to the mind and more attractive to the senses. To perceive a thing is to imprint its image on the brain. The mind is like a mirror suspended in a room. As the eye craves light and images, so the mind thirsts for objects to know. It reflects all around it, and all those things must be made lucid by being named and ordered and understood. Those 'little monkeys' called children love to imitate, notes Comenius – and this is the next stage of embedding knowledge of the world.[39] Infants have direct sense experience, but they cannot order those sensations. Ordering depends upon the use of language, so that objects are associated with words. Each thing must be named and expressed in all its parts, so that the senses may be trained for 'right perceiving'. Comenius, like Benjamin, was convinced of children's naive curiosity and their delight in novel experience.

In play, and in learning, children animate objects, and Benjamin re-animates the objects of the world in describing this process. In reanimating them he brings to life past energies now slumbering in objects. The reification of commodities is to be dissipated in the process. The motif of reanimation of energies and meanings now slumbering in objects recurs in the tiny vignettes sketched in Benjamin's *Berliner Kindheit um Neunzehnhundert* (*A Berlin Childhood Around 1900*) of 1938. In 'Cabinets' (*Schränke*) Benjamin associates the reanimating act of recollecting and the activities of collecting. As his childhood years passed his mother gave him the keys to more and more cabinets in the family home, and each time he was given a present he had to choose whether it was worthy of placement in the most recently accessible cabinet. He reflected that things put under lock and key stayed new for longer, and yet he also knew that it was not the newness that he wanted to preserve. He wanted rather 'to renovate the old'; in that he, as newcomer, made it his own.[40] Such regeneration was also the feat of his collections of stones, plucked flowers and pinned butterflies.[41] Collecting aims not at the stockpiling of inert objects, but rather an ingenious transmutation of objects into desired deposits. To have dislodged the drawerful of precious remnants, he notes, would have demolished a construction made of thorny chestnuts that doubled as morning stars, tin foil that was a cache of silver, building bricks that were caskets, cacti that were totem poles, and copper coins that were shields. His childhood assets grew and disguised themselves. Here mimesis and play are more important than factuality. The objects imitate other objects, just as Chaplin did in his films when he became a lampshade or a fairground horse, and just as Felix the

Cat did so much better when he curled his parts to form a motorbike or an umbrella or a climbing hook or when he imitated Chaplin.

An essay titled 'Insight into Children's Books' (1926), published in a literary journal, acknowledges the transformative impulse of children as they play to learn. The trick books that Benjamin cherished, with their shifting page orders, where words appear in costume, and where hidden flaps reveal concealed figures, and ribbons or tabs are tugged to trigger or resolve episodes, up the stakes on Comenius's show-and-tell games. These trick books demonstrate how much seeing and knowing is tied to touch. The trick books reinforce the sense in which knowledge of the world is practical, interventionist. Rebus puzzles, Benjamin informs us, were once thought to take their name from *rêver*, to dream, not *res*, thing – conjuring up all dreamwork's action of transfiguration, condensation and antithesis.[42] Such imaginative work of renewal of matter signals to Benjamin an originary impulse to revolution that exists in the child. Perhaps the Disney films promised the reawakening of decayed capacities in adults – the ability to empathize as much with objects as with people, as much with animals and trees as with machinery; they also relied on the delight in play and absurdity. Benjamin must have been aware of the audience profile for Disney films, such as that depicted on the front cover of the *Kölnische Illustrierte Zeitung* of 27 December 1930, as it promoted its presentation of the first Mickey Mouse comic strip in the German press: an auditorium of adults, mainly men, all leaning forward and laughing, while superimposed on them is an oversized Mickey Mouse.

Benjamin loved the illustrations in children's books. He wrote about the drawings in the books that formed his collection. He devised theories of how colour enticed children into dream worlds – that is, into themselves – while monochrome introduced children to the waking world of script, drawing them out, making them complete the image. Benjamin shared an interest in the fairy-tale with, amongst others, Ernst Bloch, Hugo von Hofmannsthal and the German Romantics, all of whom had figured in his reading and critical analyses. Amongst Benjamin's collected papers left behind in Paris when he fled the approaching Nazis was an essay by Jean Cassou, from *Revue de Paris*, titled 'On the Art of the Fairytale', with a handwritten dedication to Benjamin. The essay described the German fairy-tale, as characterized by the Romantic author Novalis. It was the 'canon of poetry', presenting the natural state of nature, the time that preceded our world, but, at the same time, a future, a plenitude in which the antinomies – of idea and life, world and thought, imagination and necessity – are resolved. The fairy-tale is the greatest work of 'magical realism'. Its wisdom is immanent. Cassou writes: 'The crowning purpose of magic is not therefore at all to teach us to dominate the real by magic, but that even the real, actually because of its reality, is magic.' Such a thought touched on Benjamin's own sur-realization of the ordinary, the magic of the everyday, and the everydayness of magic. But Benjamin needed a historical underpinning for this idea of enchanted, supernatural reality. He looked for the truth in the most extreme and the most throwaway representations, such as were cartoons and caricatures. For Benjamin, Disney's drawings took their place in a longer tradition of caricature, a tradition that had an inferior status within art history at that time. Indeed he pondered the question of caricature's lesser status in an essay on the Marxist collector of caricature Eduard Fuchs. Benjamin notes of Fuchs that it is not joy in the beautiful which motivates his interest in art, but an interest in truth. 'Truth lies in extremes' and caricature is, to some extent, the form from which all objective art rises.[43] The caricature, torn between drawing and thought, is a mass art. It comes into its own with reproduction, asserts Fuchs, and Benjamin agrees. Fuchs adored Honoré Daumier, and Benjamin too had devoted one of the many files that comprise the *Arcades Project* to Daumier. For it, he copied out quotations from Fuchs's 1921 book on caricature. 'Not only did caricature intensify the means of drawing immensely, … it was always the form that introduced new subject matter into art. Through Monnier, Gavarni, Daumier, the bourgeois society of this century was unlocked for art.'[44]

But it was Grandville who truly attracted Benjamin, and revealed to him the secrets of bourgeois society and the ruling classes' view of nature. One file in the *Arcades Project* was titled 'Exhibition, Advertisement, Grandville'. Here Benjamin drew the nineteenth-century cartoonist into a discussion of commodity fetishism. Grandville, a Saint-Simonian who fought on the streets of Paris in July 1830, lived in the city when lithographic art was at its peak. Drawing on established French tradition, he sometimes sketched animals in human clothes and stances, such as in 'Les Métamorphoses du Jour'. Sometimes the animal's point of view was the one from which the reader was to take a lead, as in 'Tribulations' with its black poodle a barometer of the day's events. Benjamin called Grandville the 'magic priest' of the fetish commodity.[45] He saw his work as visual analogue of Marx's fetish commodity: 'Grandville's subtleties are a good expression of what Marx calls the "theological caprices" of the commodity.'[46]

In the same file of the *Arcades Project* Benjamin expands on the relationship between Grandville's animating fantasies and Marx's theory of fetishism. It is not only the commodity that possesses a fetishistic independence, but also, as the following passage from Marx shows, the means of production that is fetishized, to the point of substituting for the human being:

> 'If we view the production process from the perspective of the labour process, we see that the worker relates to the means of production ... as mere means ... of his purposeful activity ... It is different, as soon as we look at the process of production from the perspective of the valorization process. The means of production immediately turn into means for sucking in alien labour. It is no longer the worker who employs the means of production, but the means of production that use the worker. Instead of being consumed by him as the material elements of his productive activity, they consume him as the driving force of their own life process.... Forges and work buildings which rest at night and do not suck in living labour are "pure loss" for the capitalist. That is why forges and work buildings lay "a claim to night labour" of the labourers.' This insight is to be drawn on for an analysis of Grandville. To what extent is the wage labourer the 'soul' of his fetishistically spirited objects?[47]

In the same bundle of notes Benjamin discusses the theorist Toussenel, who, in the 1840s, worked out systems of animal symbolism. A Fourierist, Toussenel also attributed meaning to shapes, the circle, the curve, the parabola. All were seen to bear human characteristics, human significance: the circle represents friendship, the ellipsis love, parabola is family sense and the hyperbola is ambition. Shapes and animals adopt human characteristics.[48] This happens in as droll a mode as it does in Grandville's 'graphic utopia'. Toussenel, notes Benjamin, classifies the animal world according to the rule of fashion – and just as the animals enter into an agreement with women, allowing their plumes and pelts to be used for beautifying purposes, so woman decorates and tends the animals' world:

An exhibition gallery from
Grandville's *Un autre monde*

'the lion likes nothing better than having its nails trimmed, provided it is
a pretty girl that wields the scissors'.[49] In the nineteenth century, it would
seem as if everything comes to life, takes on personality, anthropomor-
phizes – animals, shapes, machines – all more lively than humans. And,
reversing the gesture, human life is made repetitive, unhistorical. Grandville's caprices turn historical events into a facet of nature, and so parody
the history of humanity. Just as Adorno assaulted both myth and enlightenment in his vignette of Odysseus as 'the with-it hobbyist', antiquity's do-
it-yourselfer, proud of his bedroom construction,[50] so too does Grandville
upturn and mock human pretension in his depiction of *Un autre monde*'s
hero Krackq in pagan heaven. Charon's ferry trips across the river Styx are
spoilt by the construction of an iron bridge, just as were Paris Seine
cruises at the time.[51] Eternal verities are a joke. Modernity's self-styled
newness is a lie. Walt Disney pulls off the same trick in 'The Pastoral
Symphony' section in *Fantasia* (1940). 'Centaurettes', as Disney called them,

like Lolitas, simultaneously coy and seductive, turn nature – two doves, a strip of bark, a water lily – into the latest 1940s fashionable hats, while the college hunk centaurs woo them; and that, confusingly, in a world imagined to be from Greek mythology. Grandville's caprices – nature's brilliant accommodations to fashion, the present in the past, the past in the present – are all mobilized, maybe not as a critique of enlightenment, but as another way of asserting eternal verities as gag, a spoof, the inescapability of conformism.

In making the commodity existence of nature explicit, Grandville's nature resists by taking its fetishism so seriously that it unmasks it. It takes revenge in grotesque ways, with human beings reduced to only their fashionable accoutrements, and marine life pre-empting fans, wigs, combs and brushes.

> Grandville's dressing up of nature – of the cosmos as well as the animal and plant world – in the style of the fashions that ruled in the middle of the century, allows history, in the figure of fashion, to emerge out of the eternal circulation of nature. When Grandville presents a new fan as *éventail d'Iris*, when the Milky Way is an avenue lit at night by gas candelabras, when 'la lune peinte par elle-même' reclines not on clouds but on fashionable plush cushions – history has been as mercilessly secularized and brought into connection with nature as allegory managed to do three hundred years ago.[52]

What is also learnt, as a second version of this passage notes, is that, 'in this most arid, unimaginative century, all the dream energy of a society has fled with redoubled vehemence into the impenetrable silent foggy realm of fashion, where reason is unable to follow'.[53] Grandville reveals the dialectical drama of fashion, that fashion is the oldest trick in the book of capital, and the newest always recycles again in the shape of the oldest, of what has been, of what is most familiar. It looks new, but it reinvents the old, for it can never genuinely break with the past, and is condemned to repeat it, if in a banalized or farcical way. Marx knew it too, when he noted in 1848 that the bourgeoisie merely wished to dress the tyranny of the old feudal order in modern apparel, reducing once brave revolt to bathos. The bourgeoisie would transform the intoxicating 'grace of god' into a sobering legal title, the rule of blue blood into the rule of white paper, the royal sun into an astral table lamp.[54]

From Grandville's *Un autre monde.* Charon's boat on the Styx is filled with farcical figures from art and literature. The sign reads, 'Toll 5 centimes per soul.'

Benjamin read 'Grandville le précurseur' by Pierre MacOrlan in the journal *Arts et métiers graphiques* 44, an issue that appeared in December 1934.[55] There, alongside stills from Méliès's animations, paintings from Dalí and a frame from Disney's *La Cigale et les Fourmis* (The Grasshopper and the Ants), MacOrlan quotes Baudelaire: 'Il y a des gens superficiels que Grandville divertit, quant à moi, il m'effraye' ('There are those superficial types who are amused by Grandville. But, me, I am frightened by him.') MacOrlan is sure that Grandville's animated insects and coleopterans would make an excellent 'film cinématographique'. He notes that a tragic line marks many of these engravings of a sur-natural world.[56] Tragedy stems from the fact that they provide evidence that 'our' epoch will indisputably come to an end, even if it is difficult to specify the elements that will bring it about. MacOrlan also makes the link between Grandville and the early films of Méliès and Disney's cartoons – setting all in the tradition of surrealism, an attribution endorsed by Benjamin.[57] But Disney is not melancholic. He does not possess one seed of mortification. In this he is distant from Grandville's humour, which always carried within itself the presence of death.[58] Benjamin quotes this last remark in the *Arcades Project*.[59] Reading MacOrlan had perhaps confirmed Benjamin's idea of Mickey Mouse as a rather utopian figure, a compensatory image, consolation for the nightmare of modern life. Mickey Mouse was a 'wish symbol'.

Benjamin's 1935 'Exposé' of the *Arcades Project* pinpointed the political significance of 'wish symbols'. The Paris study is a riposte-history of the nineteenth century, a 'dialectical' narration of an old 'faerie-scene'. The alarm of class struggle is to awaken Sleeping Beauty from the nightmarish sleep imposed by capitalism's commodity phantasmagoria.[60] Class struggle is tracked as a dreamy conflict over technology's possibilities. Utopian urges nestle in the 'collective consciousness'.[61] Marx stimulates Benjamin's reference to a 'collective consciousness'. The motto for 'file N', the epistemological core of the *Arcades Project*, is clipped from Marx's 1843 letter to Alfred Ruge. Marx wrote to Ruge: 'The reform of consciousness consists solely in … the awakening of the world from its dream about itself.'[62] Marx depicts consciousness as a dream, and so dispenses a philosophic-political methodological basis for Benjamin's dream interpretation of the 'collective consciousness'. In 'Pariser Passagen' ⟨1⟩, Benjamin duplicates Marx's thesis about a bourgeoisie unable to come to consciousness and trapped by dreams or mystification about the social order.[63] The sleeping, dreaming collective is the bourgeois collective. Technology's reflection in the collective's imagination shows a utopian face. It does this by communicating with pre-technical elements and far-off ontogenetic and phylogenetic memories.[64] Benjamin draws on Marx:

> In the collective consciousness, images in which the new is intermingled with the old correspond to the form of the new means of production which to begin with is still dominated by old forms (Marx). These images are wish images, and in them the collective attempts to transcend as well as to transfigure the incompleteness of the social product and the deficiencies of the social order of production.[65]

The same 'collective consciousness' ensnares the proletariat. It shares the dreams about technology and nature, but there is a difference. As class it boasts the facility to awaken collectively, if it becomes class conscious, acting for itself. And this waking up to its own reality coincides with an actualization of technology's potential. Fetishized 'collective consciousness', congested with the quixotic dreams in which all classes participate, specifically dreams about technological and social utopia, is cracked open and grasped only by the proletariat with its distinct relationship to technology and techniques. These give it the ability to wield technological means to make the dream a reality.

The reinvention of nature and physics lay at the heart of Benjamin's concept of utopia. He had learnt from the utopian geophysics of Fourier, and was still insisting in the late 1930s that nature could be reformulated. Around the middle of the nineteenth century the bourgeoisie stopped being interested in the future of the productive forces that it had unleashed. Now, he says, the pendants to the great utopias of Tommaso Campanella and Thomas More appear. Those utopias had greeted the rise of a class seeing its interests as identical to the demands of freedom and justice. They were expansive, progressive utopias, keen to overturn modes and relations of production. The new utopias are those of Edward Bellamy and Tony Moilin, in which, claims Benjamin, the main issue is the adjustment of consumption and its charms, large warehouses and credit cards. The bourgeoisie cannot think about the real human future of their productive forces because they would have to renounce their lust for profit. The only true utopia must be the one that imagines even nature fundamentally altered by the new arrangement.

> The dream of begetting children is, of course, a poor stimulation where it is not penetrated by the dream of a new nature of things, in which these children live or for which they should fight. Even the dream of a 'better humanity' where children 'are better off' is just Spitzwegian musing, which is basically not the same as the dream of a better nature, in which they should live. (Therein lies the illimitable right of Fourier's utopia, which Marx recognized – and which Russia has begun to implement.) This is the living source of the biological power of humanity; the other is nothing but the cloudy pond, out of which the stork brings forth the children.[66]

Utopia is an improved nature – and an improved relationship to nature, such as imagined by Fourier – and approved by Marx. The new Soviet Union incubates it. In the Western world, film previews it.

mickey mouse and 'the work of art'

In the first version of Benjamin's essay 'The Work of Art in the Age of its Technical Reproducibility', written in 1935, one section is titled 'Mickey Mouse'.[67] From the mid to late 1930s Benjamin collected press clippings on Mickey Mouse and Walt Disney from French and German newspapers. There was a lengthy article by Jean Prévost in *Vendredi*, published on 17 June 1938, titled 'Walt Disney, the Man Who Never Had a Childhood'. It began with a lachrymose tale of Disney's hard childhood, and detailed the many difficulties he faced in the early days. Prévost was particularly impressed by the musical innovation that was characteristic of Disney's work: 'Walt Disney had a new idea: the idea of a great primitive or a great child. To the same rhythms, *it is the universe that is going to dance.*'

Prévost notes that the Silly Symphonies are precursors of a new artmusic form, similar to opera or ballet, but with much greater possibilities than both of those. This was a familiar theme in the mid 1930s. Adrian Stokes compares classical ballet and Walt Disney's Silly Symphonies and Mickey Mouse in his book *Tonight the Ballet*. Anthony Asquith in an essay on filming ballet in 1936 cites Disney's Silly Symphonies as an example of 'ballet constructed in film terms'. In 1934 Arnold Haskell's *Balletomania* claimed that 'Mickey Mouse seems to provide the ballet need on film; a strong personality artificially created out of a pattern. Musically, too, it would be difficult to imagine a more perfect screen ballet.'[68] Another article in Benjamin's collection, probably translated from Chicago's *Esquire*, concentrates on the 'exactitude' of the timing in Disney's cartoons, but also profiles the wages and the division of labour at the studios, focusing on the in-betweeners, and the copy-girls, each assigned a different colour to fill in and waiting for their marriage proposals. *Le Temps* carried a story on 1 January 1936. It noted that Georges Duhamel had been ruing the fact that people no longer read books, and countered that it was not the case that people were less curious than in previous years, but that they satisfied more and more their need for knowledge without having recourse to books. Instead they turned to radio and cinema, technologies that 'take not only a large place in the distraction of man in the twentieth century, but also in the apparent formation of his being'. Benjamin snipped the report from the newspaper. It coincided well with his own suspicions.[69] The new technologies of culture could satisfy the search for knowledge, but in doing so they fundamentally changed the audiences. This was no less true of the film star Mickey Mouse.

The section of 'The Work of Art in the Age of its Technical Reproducibility' titled 'Mickey Mouse' opens with the claim that the social function of film is to inaugurate a harmony between persons and machines: 'One of the most important social functions of film is to reinvent the equilibrium between humanity and the apparatus.' This equilibrium necessarily contributes some sort of subjectivity or agency to the cinematic apparatus. It is fetishized, anthropomorphized. The device of the 'optical unconscious' compounds the bequest of human faculties to the machine. The 'optical unconscious' switches a space consciously discerned by people for an unconsciously discerned space inspected by the camera eye.[70] A 'new region of consciousness' is summoned by film, contracted only in conjunction with technology. The harmony between humanity and machinery is brought about by the new modes of presentation of self as performer to cinematic apparatus – impersonal, external, de-auraticized, watched by a machine not a human audience – and it emerges also through the ways that the apparatus obliges viewers to see the world. Enlargements, emphases of miniature details, the focus on banal, everyday milieus – all this increases our knowledge of the necessities that govern our existence, but also procures for us a detailed giant and unsuspected *Spielraum*, a pun in German on the notion of 'room for manoeuvre' and 'space for play'. The enlargement of an object not only renders more precise what was already visible but unclear: it divulges wholly new structural formations in the material. This was the service rendered by microscopes from the seventeenth century onwards, when Antony van Leeuwenhoek saw animalcules in a drop of pondwater.[71] This was scientific research, and Benjamin imagined that filmic analysis could set itself equally scientific aims. The techniques of disclosure available to film are many. Slow motion not only presents familiar qualities of movement but discloses in them altogether unknown ones. It becomes obvious that a different nature speaks to the camera than speaks to the eye. The technological nature that bares itself to the camera implies an altered nature. This nature encompasses not only the creaturely and physical but also the man-made and the historical. The nature that reveals itself to the camera is unlike the unmediated nature that flaunts before the eye. Technologies of camera and film, camera movement and film editing, are the new human gestures. The contents of the psyche are externalized in technological effects. Technology pre-interprets the material on display. Adventurous travellers are offered a multitude of trips through widely strewn ruins in a world turned anti-physical. The dynamite of the split second explodes this world. Space is expanded and shrunk by montage, and time is stretched and contracted by time loops.[72] The way of seeing that the 'optical unconscious' effects is like the mode of perception in psychoses, hallucinations and dreams. Objective camera vision links to the actual subjective human perception of non-rational types, psychotics or dreamers:

> For the manifold aspects that the recording apparatus can reclaim from reality lie for the most part only outside a *normal* spectrum of sense perceptions. Many of the deformations and stereotypes, the transformations and catastrophes, open to detection by the world of optics in film, are actually found in psychosis, in hallucinations, in dreams. And so those methods of the camera are practices, thanks to which collective perception appropriates the individual ways of seeing of the psychotic or dreamer. Film stands against the old Heraclitean truth – that those who are awake share a world, while those asleep each possess a world for themselves.[73]

The dreamer, notes Benjamin elsewhere (following Novalis and Baudelaire), like the poet, endows inanimate objects with aura – that is, with the ability to return the gaze.[74] That psychotic or dreaming mind was one open to chance, horrifyingly vulnerable to randomness (even if that contingency was motivated by actuality), as the first theorists of dementia praecox noted in the one case and Freud in the other. Proust's cake-eating narrator in *À la recherche du temps perdu* taught Benjamin that the worst thing would be never to come, by chance, upon the object that releases synthetic, involuntary experience, the only kind worth having these days.[75]

Proust compared memory to a photograph, or rather to multiple photographs: perhaps each day a different photography of the same person is displayed in a shop window of the mind, he thought. But, ultimately, for Proust, photographs were inadequate matches for the shocking variety of unbidden remembering, and at best supplements, *aides-mémoire*, which threatened to substitute for the fullness of non-technical memory.

trotsky, photography and likeness

In his *Second Notebook*, written between 1933 and 1934 while exiled in France, Leon Trotsky was also keen to compare the photograph, filmic form and the working of consciousness:

> Consciousness acts like a camera: it tears from nature 'moments' and the ties and transitions among them are lost; but the object of photography, the living person is not broken up into moments. Rather, motion-picture film gives us a crude 'uninterruptedness' satisfactory for the retina of the eye and approaching the uninterruptedness of nature. True, cinematic uninterruptedness consists in fact of separate 'moments' and short breaks between them. But both the former and the latter are related to the technology of the cinema, which exploits the eye's imperfection.[76]

Photography rips a moment from the flow of events (and in this – formally – film is no different, for it too is a sequence of 'stills'). The eye's imperfection re-creates the illusion of smooth movement. Trotsky's interest would sharpen and darken against Stalin's photographic falsification techniques, when the war on memory was declared.[77] Consciousness ripping nature to shreds is partnered by historical consciousness in turn subjected to assault.

Perhaps these allusions to photography were prompted by Trotsky's contemplation of photographs of Lenin, which are also described in the *Notebooks*. The photographs, reproduced in Soviet journals and illustrated history albums, were taken at a time when Trotsky was still active in the Russian revolutionary movement. Trotsky held on to the images in exile. The jottings on dialectics, consciousness and photographic perception were interfiled in the *Second Notebook* with descriptions of the snapshots and notes for a biography of Lenin. The biography was a major project of

Trotsky's. Its relevance grew as the years went by and Stalin and the Stalinists increasingly manipulated knowledge of the past, of the story of the Revolution and its aftermath. Trotsky's contemplation of snapshots of Lenin in prison provided the first stimulus for the Lenin biography.[78] Despite his suspicion that photography was a non-dialectical form, a form that ripped things from their interconnections, Trotsky hoped that scrutiny of Lenin's celluloid imprint could reveal knowledge about him and the state of the revolutionary movement. The photographs were an *aide-mémoire*, but they can also be read as predictive. In them, that is to say, in their imaging of Lenin's pose, and in the mien of his face, the direction of history is revealed. Of some snapshots of Lenin from 1915 reproduced in a journal, Trotsky writes:

> The photograph is not stagy, like a portrait, but contingent, accidental. This is its weak side. But it is also sometimes the very source of its power. The features of the face acquire a definition that they did not have in reality. The total absence of a beard accentuates even more the sharpness of the features of the face. The face is not softened by irony, slyness, good nature. In its every feature there is intelligence and will power, self-confidence, and simultaneously tension in view of the enormity of the problems of 1915. The war. The International had collapsed. He had to start all the work over again, from the beginning. Lenin in 1921 (in the same issue) is much more relaxed, less tense, one senses from the figure that part of its vast work is already behind it.[79]

The photograph imparts knowledge of broader historical developments, though not by simply mirroring apparent reality. It cannot show the real softness of Lenin's features, or those subtle characteristics – irony, slyness, good nature – that are mobilized when the real human being acts across time. Trotsky seems to open the possibility that photographic seeing – at least this unstaged, contingent, snapshot type of photography – might access something beneath the surface, something essential.

Elsewhere in the *Second Notebook* Trotsky draws another analogy between photographs, the movies and consciousness. This time he wants to illuminate dialectical thinking, and his disruptive understanding mirrors Benjamin's hopes for the transformative abilities of film and the recombinable elements of consciousness:

Contrary to a photograph, which is the element of formal logic, the film is 'dialectical'. Cognizing thought begins with differentiation, with the instantaneous photograph, with the establishment of terms – conceptions, in which the separate moments of a process are placed but from which the process as a whole escapes. These term-conceptions, created by cognizing thought, are then transformed into its fetters. Dialectics removes these fetters, revealing the relativity of motionless concepts, their translation into each other.[80]

Clearly Trotsky suspected photography, and saw it as potentially an un-dialectical form, a form that mirrored static thinking. Static thinking postulates that '*a* equals *a*' and it splits the world into motionless elements, snapping the connections between things. Dialectics, in contrast, is seen by Trotsky as thought that fondles the curves of change, of flux, where a doublethink advances simultaneously the propositions '*a* = *a*' and '*a* = not *a*'. Dialectical thinking enables the universe to be conceived in its connections and in its tendency towards transformation. The photograph is like the Hegelian *Verstand*, understanding, whereas film is Hegelian *Vernunft*, reason. Perhaps Trotsky's more positive disposition towards film denoted an awareness of filmmaker Eisenstein's correlation of filmic montage and dialectics, whereby one shot is conceived as a thesis colliding with the next shot, its antithesis, generating, in the mind of the spectator, a synthesis. Yet, he was critical of film's invitation to be passive, its vicarious presentation of life. In *Lessons of October*, from 1924, the section on 'The October Insurrection and Soviet Legality' castigates 'a fatalistic, temporizing, social democratic, Menshevik attitude to revolution, as if the latter were an endless film.' This is history as something that happens behind closed doors, ordained by other powers than the mass, consciously. And he also knew that film, as wanted by that mass, fulfilled certain basic needs. In 'Vodka, the Church and the Cinema', of 1923, Trotsky explained that

The longing for amusement, distraction, sight-seeing, and laughter is the most legitimate desire of human nature. We are able, and, indeed, are obliged, to give the satisfaction of this desire a higher artistic quality, at the same time making amusement a weapon of collective education, freed from the guardianship of the pedagogue and the tiresome habit of moralizing.

The most important weapon in this respect, a weapon excelling any other, is, at the present day, the cinema. This amazing spectacular innovation has cut into human life with a successful rapidity never experienced in the past. In the daily life of capitalistic towns the cinema has become just such an integral part of life as the bath, the beer-house, the Church and other indispensable institutions, commendable and otherwise. The passion for the cinema is rooted in the desire for distraction, the desire to see something new and improbable, to laugh and to cry, not at your own, but at other people's misfortunes. The cinema satisfies these demands in a very direct, visual, picturesque and vital way, requiring nothing from the audience; it does not even require them to be literate. That is why the audience bears such a grateful love to the cinema, that inexhaustible fount of impressions and emotions. This provides a point, and not merely a point, but a huge square, for the application of our educational-socialistic energies.[81]

For Benjamin, in film's modernist montage-land first steps are taken for a reconfiguration of our world. The analytic aspect of film appeared to be dependent on film's indexical relationship to the materials of the world. Filmic time-loops slow down movement in the actual world. Lenses magnify previously invisible structures. And yet Benjamin overturns his commitment to imprinted reality in relating all film to Mickey Mouse antics, the world as drawn universe. It was because cartooning takes anti-physics for granted, and because it outbids the individualism of madness and dreams in its 'figures of the collective dream such as the earth-encircling Mickey Mouse', as the first version of the 'The Work of Art in the Age of its Technical Reproducibility' claims.[82] Benjamin may have recalled an image from a newspaper clipping in his possession. It was titled 'Comment naît un dessin animé', and was illustrated with an image of Mickey Mouse, the size of the globe, perched atop the world. This cosmos of detonated physics requires Mickey Mouse as occupant, for his function is curative. Benjamin continues:

If one thinks about the dangerous tensions which technicization and its consequences produce in the masses – tensions which at critical moments adopt a psychotic character – one comes to the conclusion that this same technicization has created the possibility of a psychic inoculation against mass psychoses through certain films, in which a forced development of sadistic fantasies or masochistic delusions can hinder their natural and dangerous maturation in the masses. The pre-emptive and curative outbreak of such mass psychoses is represented by collective laughter. The huge masses of grotesque happenings that are consumed in film at the moment are a drastic sign of the dangers occasioned by the repressions that endanger humanity and that civilization brings with itself. American funnies and the Disney films effect a therapeutic explosion of the unconscious.[83]

Through a grim and mimetic humour, Disney provides the safe release from daily collective experience – the threats of urban life, the mad and lively and overwhelming machines, the cars, the steel foundries, the punchups. The predecessor of Disney characters and the American slapsticks is the Eccentric. He takes up residence in film in the figure of Charlie Chaplin. If it is true that Chaplin once said that he envied the perfect timing of animated cartoon gags because they never had to take time to breathe, then the envy was reciprocated. The article by Jean Prévost in Benjamin's collection of Disneyana, called 'Walt Disney, the Man Who Never Had a Childhood', emphasized that Charlie Chaplin was Mickey Mouse's predecessor. Wyndham Lewis would have agreed with the association, placing Chaplin in his 1927 book *Time and Western Man* in the company of a virulent American culture of infantilism (where Gertrude Stein and Anita Loos were also to be found). Lewis despised Chaplin's smallness, his 'wide-eyed naïf' look, his charmed life, his child persona, his role within the spread of weak 'mass-democracy'. Artificially respired in the culture of the infant were these '*eternal* sucklings'.[84] Lewis disliked Chaplin because he represented the democratic impulses of modernity. Chaplin became its symbol, universally visible as sign. But he was a symbol, too, in his very being. When he moved on the screen, Chaplin was a semaphore, with clarity of gesture, wrote Prévost. This was a 'universal language'. This was what Mickey Mouse's animators strove after too; it was the project of modernist 'abstraction'.

In 1927, the release year of *Trolley Troubles (Oswald und die Straßenbahn)*, the first Walt Disney film to be screened in Germany, distributed by Universal Pictures, Benjamin wrote his 'Retort to Oscar A.H. Schmitz'. In this polemical reply to Schmitz's attack on art that flaunts its political tendency, Benjamin first alleged the development in film of a 'new region of consciousness'.[85] Film, he states, rips apart the prison world of factories and pubs with the 'dynamite of the split-second'. Film smashes up the surface sense of the everyday. It reorders and disorders natural vision. But it runs into problems – that is, it negates its immanent form – when it attempts to make a logical narrative peopled by fully rounded characters. Such narrative and personality-fixated dramas squeeze film back into the confines of bourgeois theatre and so ruin it. What film needs, claims Benjamin, is a tendency. The Russian films of the post-revolutionary period have a political tendency. American funnies have a tendency too – they adopt a consistent attitude towards technology. The humour of these films, relayed by gags and stunts, is directed against an unleashed and overactive technology such as assails Chaplin or the Keystone Cops; their audiences are the working class, who most need to see the technological apparatus they daily face acknowledged, mocked and reworked. The strange thing about the American funnies is that 'the laughter that these films provoke hovers over an abyss of horror'.[86] The funnies are the flipside of the deadly technical power on show in Eisenstein's *Battleship Potemkin*, where modern technology, in the shape of military technologies, the battleship and the weaponry of the army, is fought over and with. Benjamin claims that the best films, the superior films, themselves technological products, take as their theme the workings of technology, a technology that is more lively than humans, a technology that has the power to control, hurt or amplify the living. And these films show collectives in their struggle to master and reclaim machinery, and set it to productive, not destructive, uses.

Disneyworld, then, is a restitutive utopia: a world that compensates for the effects of the current means and relations of technical production, by offering therapy for damaged lives. The slapstick films and the short cartoons seemed to offer this therapy more effectively than the German studios' main features – new objectivist melodramas, for example – which mirrored the darkness of the days, the 'tragedy' of unemployment and the misery of fallen women. The cartoons and the slapstick gags were loved all the more for breaking with dull naturalism, and yet still addressing the anxieties of modern times. *Film-Kurier* had voiced as much of cartoons in 1930:

> The propulsive action develops out of pictorial ideas. In place of plot steps the stream of associations. It mediates a relaxation. It offers spectators the opportunity to give themselves over completely, without the intellect being in any position to take control.[87]

The therapy that the slapsticks and the cartoons provide is offered, however, without a demand to alter relations of production, though maybe hinting at the potential unleashed by such reorganization.

In the epilogue to 'The Work of Art', fascism's aestheticization of politics (its making politics mysterious, distant, humanity-denying and a creation of geniuses and great men) was set against against communism's need to politicize art (its making art close, manipulable, playful, educative and actively consumed). An abandoned first version of the epilogue stressed the idea of inoculation. Massive changes in the political and the aesthetic realms are connected to changes in the masses, and their conscious or unconscious shoving onto the historical stage. This change finds a direct response in the two crucial shifts of the age, articulated so well in fascism: the decline of democracy and the preparation for war. Benjamin asks how a curative function might be expected of forces in the realm of art which in the realm of politics lead to fascism? And he proposes that the answer lies in art's social status, that art functions as a making manifest of symptoms and an inoculation against identical developments in the social world.[88] The first version of 'The Work of Art' is concerned specifically with the ways in which the new masses come to terms with the technologies that rule over their lives. Cinema and film is another such technology. Benjamin draws parallels between the working lives of the city employees and the production conditions of their leisure activities. The camera operator occupies the same spot as a supervisor who overlooks workers in a factory or office. The supervisor is there to ensure that the majority of people at work in offices and factories are 'alienated from their humanity'. When the working day finishes the same masses go to the movies, so that they can vicariously take revenge on the apparatus, by watching actors assert their humanity (or what appears to the audience to be their humanity) in front of the camera, and also by making that apparatus serve the actors' own triumph. Aesthetic practice articulates the pain of human alienation from self and others. It is a remedial process. The theme of healing representations had long made sense to Benjamin. In 'A Small History of Photography' he argued that Adget's photography conveys aesthetic expression of the contusions of human alienation, in order that these be made amenable to a 'curative' analysis by the 'politically educated gaze'.[89] Here it is remodelled as filmic therapy.[90] 'Through representation by the apparatus, the person's self-alienation has found a highly productive utilization.'[91]

Mickey Mouse hovers over the first version of 'The Work of Art'. In naming the section on the 'optical unconscious' after Mickey Mouse, Benjamin implies that animation is the film form that has most legitimacy. All film is a type of drawing – a drawing or a writing in light that manipulates the reality it records. It abstracts from it. Object animation intensifies the montage effects of the film. Drawn animation makes the abstracting principle graphic. Animation is not a slavish imitation of the world. It is not imitative because it places a drawing between the lens and reality. Animation should be unresponsive to the salvage operation of psychology and the necromancy of appearances. It uses techno-progress without believing in it. Its basis is humour, always a good sign.

By 1933, 104 cartoons from the Disney Studios were in the hands of German distributors. Despite the protestations of the *Gauleiter* from Pomerania, forty-six more were to play in film programmes between 1933 and 1938. With the annexation of Austria in 1938, the Reich's film censor requisitioned another thirty-one Disney shorts. These, too, were shown in the film programmes of the Greater German Reich. Their showing was aided by the Disney studio's decision not to flaunt Disney's 'Jewish' middle name 'Elias' in Nazi Germany, and the studio also shrank the production credits right back – in case other suspicious names might offend (or maybe they diminished the roll-call in order to inflate the boss's reputation). German film distributors reciprocated. Fleischer cartoons were shown to audiences in Germany, but the 'Jewish' forenames Max and David were changed to Kurt and Karl.

Roy Disney, the businessman of the firm, devised plans to go over to film rental instead of sales, and he wrote a letter to the European distributor on 22 May 1933. Here he let it be known that the studio was working on a feature-length film that would have excellent market potential – particularly in Germany. That year, the first year of Nazi rule, a second Disney film was banned in Germany – *The Mad Doctor*. This is the tale of a mad scientist who straps Pluto to an operating table and attempts to cross him with a hen. It is as if the censors acted on a presentiment of some of the cruelty that Nazi doctors, and only most famously the Auschwitz 'angel of death' Josef Mengele, were soon to inflict through their experimentation in medical science. Other Disney products with less politically controversial themes were approved. In December 1934 a Bavaria Filmverleih advertisement appeared in *Licht–Bild–Bühne*. It advertised a short-film programme in Berlin's Marmorhaus cinema, including *The Pied Piper*, *The Night Before Christmas*, *Mickey's Mechanical Man*, *Three Little Pigs*, *Giant Land* and *Father Noah's Ark*. Something about the films forced an emphasis on their international appeal, their cosmopolitan modernity, traits that sat quite oddly in Nazi Germany. The ditty coined to promote *Mechanized Mickey Mouse* went like this:

> Willst du einmal fröhlich lachen
> sei's auf deutsch, französisch, spanisch
> Micky kann es spielend machen,
> Denn sie kommt dir heut mechanisch.

> (If you really want a laugh,
> be it in German, French or Spanish,
> it's child's play for Mickey,
> for today he is coming to you mechanically.)

But current events had bestowed a curious ring to another ditty, the one that publicized the once German story of *The Pied Piper of Hamelin*:

> Ein Musikant mit einem Spiel
> Vertreibt der Stadt die Ratten
> Den Bürgern war der Lohn zu viel,
> Seht, was sie davon hatten.

> (A musician plays a game
> to expel rats from the town.
> The cost was too high for the citizens.
> See what came of it.)

dancing hooligans

Notes for 'The Work of Art in the Age of its Technical Reproducibility' were drafted in the autumn of 1935. The first version of the essay was completed by the end of 1935. Straightaway Benjamin began to rework what he had delineated in a letter in October 1935 as 'an exemplary set of materialist axioms of art theory'. Alterations emerged out of discussions with Max Horkheimer in Paris, and, on 29 January 1936, Adorno sent a postcard to Benjamin from London, requesting a version of 'The Work of Art' immediately, for the passages from the first version, shown to him by Horkheimer, had unleashed reservations that could only be 'vindicated or liquidated' when seen in the context of the whole.[92] The second version, completed in February 1936, was a rewrite of the first version, and it included extra material and a number of additional concepts. This version was what Benjamin wanted to see published. Benjamin's letter to Adorno on 7 February reassured Adorno that his discussions with Horkheimer were amicable and productive, and that several issues raised by Adorno had formed their basis. Adorno's influence, he notes, is to be found in the footnotes, which are 'cuts through the political-philosophical substructure of the constructions given in the text.'[93] The comments on Disney's thera-peutic effect were supplemented by a footnote. Benjamin now states that a full analysis of these films must not repress their counter-meaning. A dialectical reading has to acknowledge that these same materials can work comically or horrifically. Comicality and horror are closely connected, he tells us, referring to the knowledge of children's reactions. Benjamin had long been keen to underscore the beastly nature of childish play. Benjamin resented the books that painted a happy world for children, who were seen to be innocent and delicate. In an essay titled 'Old Toy' from 1924 he criticizes kid-glove pedagogy: 'While pedagogues, pious as lambs, still cling to Rousseauesque dreams, writers such as Ringelnatz and painters like Klee have grasped the despotic and dehumanized aspect of children. Children are world-distant and immune to the cold.'[94] Another version of the footnote gives the death mask as an example of something that can work to comic or horrific effect.[95] If comicality and horror are closely linked – in dialectical relation, as he puts it in the other version of the footnote – then what determines which effect predominates? Placing his understanding of the Disney films in the context of Nazi victory in Germany, Benjamin considers the latest *Mickey Mouse* films, which 'make this question appear justified':

(Their dark fire-magic, for which colour film has provided technical precondi-tions, underlines a trait, which until now was only present in hidden ways. It shows how comfortably fascism – in this realm too – can appropriate so-called 'revolutionary' innovations.) What surfaces in the light of the latest Disney films is actually already present in some older ones: the tendency to locate bestiality and violence quite comfortably as accompaniments of existence. This calls on an older and no less terrifying tradition; it was introduced by the dancing hooligans which we find in mediaeval pogrom images, and the 'ragged band' in Grimms' fairy-tales form their imprecise, pale rearguard.[96]

Nothing is unrecuperable – and the Nazis have produced and legitimated a certain environment, a certain violence. Violence is now revealed to be less a critical metaphorical dismantlement, and more a way of life, a realistic representation of everyday brutality. The films provide training in brutal behaviour – mimesis turns bad. The violence and bestiality, basis of the humour of the cartoons, turn vicious. Humour might be transforming into the sadistic collective laughter that Adorno would come to fear. The assault on the values of bourgeois humanism and species arrogance could turn out to be misanthropy and an accommodation to punishing those defined as outsiders, freaks. This addition nudges Benjamin's thesis closer to Adorno's pessimism concerning mass culture.[97] Benjamin anticipates the criticism of Disney cartoons in *Dialectic of Enlightenment*, written by Adorno and Horkheimer a decade later, with their critique of 'Donald Duck in the cartoons', who, 'like the unfortunate in real life, gets a thrashing so that the viewer can get used to the same treatment'.[98] The films accustom audiences to a violence which civilization will mete out to them, and hopes they will mete it out in turn. The violence of the films is evidence of a bad infantilism – and it most clearly finds its form in the fascist bully whose character Adorno will later outline in his psychological survey on the *Authoritarian Personality*. Adorno hoped to cast a dark shadow over Disney and over the mimetic capability. He cautioned Benjamin against using concepts like the collective dream or collective unconscious, which he perceived to be derived from the irrationalist, and fascist-tinged, work of Carl Jung.

So the Nazis could use Disney – though a look into the workings of the *Reichsfilmkammer* in 1935 would have shown that, under pressure from the propaganda ministry, a campaign was being waged against such a predominance of American shorts in the German film market: 'We need more self-produced short films, fairy-tale films, culture films and, above all, drawn animation films.'[99] The gentlemen from the ministry were, however, under no illusions that they could compete with American product. At the end of 1936 the public's favourite christmas-time film package was a series of Disney shorts. The same was true in 1938. Copies of Disney films were shown until 1940 or 1941.

Adorno responded to the second version of 'The Work of Art', initiating a debate about the relationship of autonomous avant-garde art and technological kitsch to aura and myth. He asks, which art unmasks more effectively the barbaric circumstances that we inhabit? Both the highest, Kafka and Schoenberg, with their non-auratic, technically advanced and barbaric art without pleasure, and the lowest, Disney, Chaplin and the art of philistines, bear the stigmata of capitalism *and* elements of change. The two critics agree that the culture of least interest is the middlebrow art between Schoenberg and the American film. But Adorno distrusts the laughter of the funnies' audience, finding in it elements of the worst sadism and brutalism. And indeed he claims that all commercial films, not just those magical-filmic fantasies which try to turn the film into art, but Mickey Mouse too, have auratic aspects.[100] Mickey's magic magics away the urgency of social transformation.

The drama of footnotes undercutting the foundations of Benjamin's main theses in 'The Work of Art' presents a dialectical spectacle. It dramatizes the ambivalence in Benjamin's understanding of mass culture, or popular culture. One thesis in the 1936 essay on Leskov, 'The Storyteller', notes the importance of the fairy-tale. The first true storyteller is the teller of fairy-tales, a form that could offer good counsel. 'The fairy-tale tells us of the earliest arrangements that mankind made to shake off the nightmare which myth had placed upon its chest.' Myth is from the realm of the religious, of oppression and dominance from above. Here there was no disagreement between the two critics. Adorno asserted this, too, in his study of Wagner of 1937–38. When he was a revolutionary, Wagner had wanted to compose an opera based on a Grimm fairy-tale. This did not happen and instead *Siegfried* and *Lohengrin* exemplify the 'regression of fairy tale into myths', a sacrifice of the fairy-tale 'to what has existed from time immemorial'. This, he reveals, allows myth to be connected to bourgeois ideology: both insist that 'the power of what simply exists becomes its own legitimation'.[101] Benjamin, ever the optimist, foregrounds how the fairy-tale, in contrast to myth, relates to resistance and play. The animals that come to the aid of the child show that nature prefers to be aligned with humanity, not to fight against it as in the myth. 'The wisest thing – so the fairy-tale taught mankind in olden times, and teaches children to this day – is to meet the forces of the mythical world with cunning and with high spirits.'[102] Nature is complicit with liberated humans. In 1937 Benjamin wrote 'Eduard Fuchs, Collector and Historian', an essay on the Marxist journalist and collector of pornography and caricature. There he analyses how the bourgeois taboo on sexuality has imposed particular forms of repression upon the masses, thereby fostering the development of sadistic and masochistic complexes which can be used to deliver people up to domination.[103] Benjamin was admitting Adorno's psychic pessimism that sees authority as internalized. The writing pad of the psyche turns into a rulebook.

In the spring of 1936 the second version of 'The Work of Art' was translated into a shorter French version, commissioned by the Institute for Social Research, and titled *L'oeuvre d'art a l'époque de sa reproduction mécanisée*. While the essay was being prepared for a troublesome work of translation the wrangles began. The quarrels were largely over suggested edits. Hork-heimer, aware of the Institute's chancy position as an exile grouping in New York, was anxious to defuse the committed politics of the essay. Defusing the politics meant striking out references to Marx and Marxism, and clouding comments addressed to communists. The essay, already undercut by its footnotes, was now cut apart. During the translation of the second version, Benjamin began a third version, described by him as a 'work-in-progress' in 1938 and again in 1939. Some theses and concepts from the second version of the essay were deleted in the third version. It also provided several reformulations and some new material: notably references to Brecht's *Der Dreigroschenprozeß*, and some additional quotations from Paul Valéry, Alexandre Arnoux, Rudolph Arnheim and Georges Duhamel. Brechtian elements were elaborated, perhaps as a recalcitrant act against Adorno, who, in a letter to Benjamin, had voiced fears that 'Brecht's sun' would refuse to sink 'into exotic waters'. Though Brecht looms larger, the references to Mickey Mouse and Disney were abandoned. Instead he reflects on Paul Valéry and Rudolph Arnheim. Benjamin no longer wanted to accent a surrealist-derived notion of film as arational dreamwork, and his recognition of the 'usability of Disney's methods for fascism' curbed any affirmative reference to Mickey Mouse. In the third version of the essay, Benjamin cuts back emphasis on the fantastic nature of film's optical unconscious, presenting the camera rather as a scientific, analytical tool.

The third version of 'The Work of Art in the Age of its Technical Reproducibility' was revised, in part, as a result of Adorno's critique of the second version. Adorno voiced a number of objections, including an insistence on the brutalizing sado-masochism of the 'funnies', which, he claimed, kept the masses down rather than revealing utopia to them. Adorno hoped to cast a dark shadow over Disney. He was suspicious of film in general. Benjamin's analogy between films, dreams and madness may have been excised in response to Adorno's effort to persuade Benjamin that the dominant aesthetic in film, from the mid 1930s onwards, was not a modernistic series of explicit shocks, disruption and trick effects, but rather a realist aesthetic of invisible editing and naturalism.

Mimesis was turning bad. In writings on Baudelaire, Benjamin invokes Freud's *Beyond the Pleasure Principle*, in order to consider the body as itself, in a most Kafkaesque way, the site of mimetic trauma in modernity. The penal colony traces its punishment onto the skin. The body itself receives and retains the traces, quite crippling physical and psychic traces, of labouring in industrialism. Benjamin's monism, consciousness as a product of material, interactive transactions with the world, refutes the idealistic dualism of Locke and Berkeley and co. Technology and its modes of operation have motivated a 'crisis in perception'.[104] Furthermore, technology has submitted the human sensorium to a complex training.[105] In the last *Arcades Project* entries and writings on Baudelaire, Benjamin extends his anthropology of industrialized humanity by introducing the neurological category of shock into discussion of the experience of work. From the factory to the battlefield the experience of shock, physical and psychic, constitutes the norm.[106] Technology dictates a syncopated, dislocating rhythm. Workers must permanently react to this rhythm. Citing Marx, Benjamin describes how in the factory system workers learn to coordinate their 'own movement to the uniform and unceasing motion of an automaton'.[107] But such mimetic adaptation was more widely demanded. The city itself is a cauldron of shock effects. These shocks daily assault the dismantled individual – bombarding him or her, rapid stimulations flinging themselves at the receptive organs. The Lunapark fairground is described as the place where workers become accustomed to the drill of the factory.[108] Photography is one of the most significant instances of shock-experience, Benjamin contends in 'On Some Motifs in Baudelaire':

> Amongst the various gestures of switching, inserting, imprinting etc. the photographer's snapping has been the most consequential. One press of the finger is enough to fix an event for an unlimited time. The apparatus delivers the moment, so to say, a posthumous shock. Haptic experiences of this kind were joined by optic ones, such as are supplied by the advertising pages of a newspaper or the traffic of a big city.[109]

And to survive all this, this is where Freud comes in – he realizes that there is a psychic shell of consciousness that protects the organism against stimuli and the threat of excessive energies. Shocks that are registered on this shell are seen to be less traumatic, since it is able to act as a buffer. The buffer, posited by Freud, enables the modern unskilled worker, claims Benjamin, to function.[110] Workers adapt. They conform. They buckle down.

While Benjamin and Adorno argued, Disney's films were changing. In 1937, with *Snow White and the Seven Dwarfs*, the cartoons turned illusionistic, and the feature-length films to which the Disney studio devoted its time were striving consciously to produce an animated imitation of realist cinema – in terms of content and form and morality. In abandoning Disney, Benjamin was rejecting something that had changed anyway. The featurelengths, from *Snow White and the Seven Dwarfs* onwards, reinstitute the laws of perspective and gravity, and lead a fight against flatness, while producing traditional dramaturgical characters. They no longer appear to explode the world with the surrealistic and analytical cinematic dynamite of the optical unconscious. There is no doubt about their 'naive realism' – a derogatory tag that Adorno and Benjamin had devised together. Cartoons, whatever they were before, surrender through commercialism – and become Adorno's commodity form that offers a false appearance of integration and wholeness, and that magically conceals the labour which went into its production. They distance themselves from the art of the avant-garde, which takes fragmentation and disintegration into its law of form, making clear how constructed not only it is but also the social world – ripe for transformation. Along with deep space and gestures towards illusionistic realism come melodramatic values and sexual repression – the Hayes Production Code affects cartoon characters too. And not just Disney's. With its introduction in 1933, vampish Betty Boop, a favourite of Adorno, was re-dressed with a longer skirt and a higher neckline. *Snow White and the Seven Dwarfs* provided a clear-cut and priggish morality, a virginal and highly sanitized ideal. As it became naturalistic, moralistic and tamed, the cartoon was turned respectable, a regular part of the studio system for the middlebrows.[111] Disney turned from flatness to depth.

Even in 1937 there were those who were prepared to state quite publicly that film could have taken another trajectory. An article titled 'From Technical Art to Art Industry', of 14 March that year, snipped out of a German newspaper by Benjamin, noted that the remarkable thing about film was the victory of the *Spielfilm*, the narrative drama, which took film away from its original 'expositional and scientific function' ('schaustellerische und wissenschaftliche Anwendung') of showing the diversity of the world – its waterfalls, tribes, jugglers, dancers and so on. If the narrative drama was a pathetic outcome for filmic possibility, then the drawn version of the same was an even more ridiculous concoction.

leni and walt: deutsch–amerikanische freundschaft

leni meets walt

In 1938 Leni Riefenstahl voyaged to America, aboard the luxury liner *Europa*. She was escorted by Werner Klingenberg from the German Olympic Committee and her press agent Ernst Jäger, editor of the *Film-Kurier*. She claimed that the trip was a holiday, although the German government financed it. Riefenstahl hoped to sell her latest film, *Olympia*, to an American distributor, and she began her search for American powerbrokers while still at sea. In her luggage, which was branded with the pseudonym Lotte Richter (perhaps derived from the verb *richten*, to direct), there were three different prints of *Olympia* and numerous copies of the book *Schönheit im Olympischen Kampf* (*Beauty in the Olympic Struggle*) and other publicity material. The *Europa* docked in New York on 4 November 1938.

The film of the 1936 Olympic Games in Berlin premiered on 20 April 1938 as a treat for Hitler's forty-ninth birthday. From then until October 1938, *Olympia*, a film paid for by the Propaganda Ministry and the Film-Kredit-Bank, had enjoyed accolade after accolade, as Riefenstahl escorted it from venue to venue across Europe. Riefenstahl's international reputation had already been established by the success of her previous film, *Triumph des Willens* (*Triumph of the Will*), shown at the Universal Exposition in Paris in 1937 and awarded the *Diplome de Grand Prix*. This purported to be a documentary record of the 1934 Nazi Party rally in Nuremberg, though in fact there was a certain amount of restaging for the cameras. On 1 May 1938 propagandistic motives allowed the next film, *Olympia*, all-too-new and little seen, to be awarded the German National Film Prize for 1937–38. In late August it was shown at the Venice Film Festival and received the Coppa Mussolini. Riefenstahl's *Olympia*, as much as its subject, the 1936 Berlin Olympics, successfully promoted New Germany's public image abroad. The 1936 Olympics was designed to be a widely broadcast spectacle of peace, but in some ways the games mirrored better the Spanish Civil War, begun in the same year. (An alternative Games, 'the People's Olympics', was planned for the last two weeks of July in Barcelona, but on the morning of the opening ceremony Franco's reactionary forces plunged Spain into civil war.) Here, as there, there was a testing out of power and strength, an enforcement of the ideology of struggle, a pitching of peoples against peoples. This was not far distanced from the original sentiment of the neo-Olympics, asserted in De Coubertin's Sorbonne speech in 1892, in the epoch of high imperialism. De Coubertin's oration praised the sublimity of hygiene, sport and their telos, war, while gesturing towards peace in its conclusion.[1] In Nazi Germany in 1936 there was phoney peace-seeking internationalism in the air. The German press, for the duration of the festivities, which were attended by people from across the world, printed pages in three or four languages for international visitors. The cinema programmes included international movies and short films. In other respects, though, the event was all too Nazi German – swastika flags draped the Olympic stadium, in place of an international array of colours. But, as the 1936 Games drew to a close, Nazi-style 'normality' returned to everyday life. The cessation of the officially backed Jewish persecution, prompted by the attention-seeking and attention-garnering Games, was wound up and Hitler prepared for a public attack on the Jews at a party rally in September 1937. There he accused them of Bolshevism and support for the republicans in Spain.[2] This harangue unleashed a violence that culminated just over a year later in the horrors of *Kristallnacht*. It turned out that pacific, kind, cosmopolitan Germany had been an illusion for the cameras. There were clues to the truth. Three weeks prior to the Olympics, a Berlin cinema announced on 6 July 1936 a selection of Disney shorts, accompanied, amongst other things, by a Nazi film that did not have peace in mind. *Waffenträger der Nation* (*The Weapon Bearers of the Nation*) showed the army, the navy and the air force exercising to rousing tunes. Two years

Olympia, Leni Riefenstahl

later the opportunity arose, with Riefenstahl's new film of the events, to flaunt further an image of peace, as war drew closer. Riefenstahl's American trip was fashioned to consolidate a peaceful image of Germany abroad, and bring in multi-dollars.

On the third day of Riefenstahl's sojourn in the United States the Anti-Nazi League began a campaign against her. The campaign was further boosted by horrified responses to *Kristallnacht* on 9 November 1938. In Detroit, on 18 November, she met with modern factory-*meister* Henry Ford, an industrialist who felt some affection for Hitler, and who four months earlier had received the Grand Cross of the German Eagle, the highest honour bestowed on a foreigner in Nazi Germany. Ford was revered across Europe. In the Soviet Union, too, Taylorism and Fordism were eagerly studied for their contributions to improving labour efficiency.

But the Bolshevik admiration for Fordism was not reciprocated. Ford's sympathies lay elsewhere. As Riefenstahl put it, he 'quickly made us realize how sympathetic he was towards Germany' and, she says, Ford requested that she inform the Führer of his plans to meet him at the coming party rally in Nuremberg.[3] The admiration was mutual, for, in 1931, Hitler had informed a Detroit newspaper that he regarded Henry Ford as his inspiration, and he avidly read the anti-Semitic tracts written by Ford. He had a life-size portrait of Ford in his Munich office. The company Ford was well ensconced in the German car market. Like other automobile firms, Ford had vast business interests in Germany. The German subsidiaries of Ford and General Motors controlled 70 per cent of the German car market in 1939. For this reason Ford was not keen for war to be declared on Germany, although the company was quick to shift production to war materials in America and in Germany when the call to arms did come. As emissary from the Nazi regime, Riefenstahl was well received by Ford. Perhaps they discussed a subject close to both their hearts – the role of the artistic elite versus the malleable masses, as set out in Ford's 1922 bestseller *My Life and Work*, which had also been a big hit in Germany:

> If a man wants a field for vital creative work, let him come where he is dealing with higher laws than those of sound, or line, or colour; let him come where he may deal with the laws of personality. We want artists in industrial relationship. We want masters in industrial method – both from the standpoint of the producer and the product. We want those who can mould the political, social, industrial and moral mass into a sound and shapely whole.[4]

Riefenstahl headed for California, via the Grand Canyon. In Hollywood the Anti-Nazi League called for a boycott of Riefenstahl, running an advertisement in the *Hollywood Reporter* on 27 November. It declared: 'There is no room for Nazi agents!!'[5] There were also posters with the same sentiment on the streets. At first it seemed as if stars and studios would warmly welcome Riefenstahl, but then one by one the appointments were cancelled. Walt Disney was the only Hollywood celebrity to receive her. She visited him on 8 December 1938 and enjoyed a three-hour tour of the Disney studio.

In her memoirs Riefenstahl writes of the encounter: how they looked at sketches for the sorcerer's apprentice sequence in *Fantasia*, and how they discussed screening *Olympia* in Disney's private theatre.[6] Disney did not dare to do so, for his projectionists were unionized and might have contacted the Anti-Nazi League, an action that could have led to political shaming and boycotts. Indeed, three months later Disney felt compelled to claim that he had not known who Riefenstahl was when she visited him. Riefenstahl, for her part, after her return to Europe, talked with a reporter from the *Paris-Midi*, on 28 January 1939, and her words were reported in the *Film-Kurier*.

> Question to Mrs. Riefenstahl: 'And so the film industry did boycott you?' 'Yes, apart from one film producer. Walt Disney was the exception. He has his own studio and his position is so strong that he has nothing to fear by receiving me.' 'And so was Walt Disney the only colleague that you saw?' 'No, but he was the only one who, so to say, received me officially.'[7]

Fascists had their eye on Hollywood. Hollywood had been described by Il Duce's son, the bomber and filmist Vittorio Mussolini, as the 'centre of political agitation against the fascist idea'.[8] However, *Snow White and the Seven Dwarfs*, which had premiered on 21 December 1937 at the Carthay Circle Theater in Los Angeles, was still breaking box-office records in Rome at the end of 1938. It was to be one of the last Hollywood hits. American films were being phased out in Mussolini's Italy. The same was to occur in Germany. The *Film-Kurier*, in February, stressed that the Anti-Nazi League was a Jewish organization that was part of a 'Jewishified film industry'. On her return to Germany, Riefenstahl gave a detailed report of her American trip to Goebbels, who then noted in his diary, on 5 February 1939, an extraordinary reversal of fact. In America, according to Riefenstahl's report, things look bad – 'The Jews are ruling with terror and boycotts' ('Die Juden herrschen mit Terror und Boykott'). Goebbels voiced uncertainty about whether or not to ban American films.

The meeting between Disney and Riefenstahl was not a first. They had been brought together before – in Fascist Italy – at the Venice Film Festival, where *Olympia* had won the Coppa Mussolini. Disney's *Snow White and the Seven Dwarfs* (1937) had been a strong competitor for the prize. Indeed British and American representatives, hoping for an award for Walt Disney's cartoon, went home from the festival in protest. Disney was represented at the film festival by six films. One of the Silly Symphonies,

Music Land (1935), was the star event of the opening evening. Two short films were also shown, one of which was based on a Grimm fairy story – *The Brave Little Tailor*. After her visit to the United States, when asked why she met with Disney, Riefenstahl indicated that the Venice film competition had provided a logical connection between the two: 'And why not! … Disney and I have never met before but our pictures – *Olympia* and *Snow White and the Seven Dwarfs* – were the two outstanding successes in many outstanding countries.' And she goes on to suggest an aesthetic logic to their association: 'He has the German feeling – he goes so often to the German fables and fairy-tales for inspiration.'[9]

This claim, the attribution of 'the German feeling', demands exploration. Disney's aesthetic, especially in the first feature-length films, *Snow White and the Seven Dwarfs*, *Pinocchio* (1940), and *Fantasia* (1940), with its 'Sorcerer's Apprentice' tale from Goethe, might be called Germanic, drawing on both Romanticism and a folkish Gothic woodcut tradition. *Snow White and the Seven Dwarfs* was based on a fine Grimm fairy-tale, though Disneyfication of the ending involved omitting Snow White's coughing up of the poisoned apple lodged in her throat.

> It chanced that a King's son came into the wood, and went to the dwarfs' house, meaning to spend the night there. He saw the coffin upon the mountain-top, with little Snow-White lying within it, and he read the words that were written upon it in letters of gold. And he said to the dwarfs: 'If you will but let me have the coffin, you may ask of me what you will, and I will give it to you.' But the dwarfs answered, 'We would not sell it for all the gold in the world.' Then said the Prince, 'Let me have it as a gift, I pray you, for I cannot live without seeing little Snow-White, and I will prize your gift as the dearest of my possessions.' The good little dwarfs pitied him when they heard these words, and so gave him the coffin. The King's son then bade his servants place it upon their shoulders and carry it away, but as they went they stumbled over the stump of a tree, and the violent shaking shook the piece of poisonous apple which had lodged in Snow-White's throat out again, so that she opened her eyes, raised the lid of the coffin, and sat up, alive once more.[10]

Disney romanticized the ending, stressing the efficacy of a prince's love, and so Snow White came back to life through an awakening, reanimating kiss transferred from the Grimms' *Sleeping Beauty*. This was a theme that Riefenstahl, too, had deployed to lyrical effect in *Triumph of the Will*:

'Deutschland Erwache!', 'Germany wake up!', as the city of Nuremberg awakens to the emergence from the clouds of Hitler the charmer.

The German sourcing of Disney's feature-length films was a major topic of discussion in German film journals. Critics wanted to know who would guarantee that Disney would treat his German material well.[11] The *Film-Kurier* of 30 June 1938 published an article under the title 'Fairy-tale Film, a German Affair'.

> There is probably hardly a German person who does not have a profound and heartfelt relationship to the fairy-tale, hardly anyone for whom – on hearing even just the word – images of children do not well up and the romanticism and the secretive magic of the fairy-tale world roll out before him again.[12]

The writer goes on to claim that incontestably the fairy-tale is a German affair, and so the fairy-tale film must play a greater role in German film production:

> If Walt Disney can present to the Americans his drawn and colourful animation of 'Snow White' and can do excellent business with it (in the land of 'business' and of the technical-mercantile orientation, in which generally that which is externally successful is acknowledged!!!) – then we must only regret that until now we have not had anything like it – for there would be even more interest here.[13]

An article in *Film-Kurier* on 26 August 1938 asked whether 'our old folk-fairytales should be used to create colour animations which are directed solely towards humour, and in some countries are not to be seen by children because they could terrify young sensibilities too strongly'.[14] This was a reference to the 'horror scenes' in *Snow White and the Seven Dwarfs*. The film press was fascinated by the British censors' decision to bar admission for children. It appeared to confirm that Disney had abused the German original.[15] Disney, while not at one with the ban on child admissions to the film in Britain and the Netherlands, had, for commercial reasons, insisted that only full-price tickets be sold in the USA. The film contains one scary scene. Snow White is lost in a dark forest. She runs in panic as the gnarly and knotted roots and branches of trees stretch out to clasp her. Nature is a nightmare from which Snow White struggles to awake. When she does awaken, next morning, she finds that nature is benevolent and that the animals, like the little people she is soon to meet, want only to help her and to love her.

Disney's 'German feeling' was not enough for some. In December 1938 an article in *Film-Kurier* decided that Disney's film was lacking in comparison to the Grimm story.[16] The debate on Disney's use of that Germanic contribution to culture, the fairy-tale, went back a few years. In May 1935 *Film-Kurier* considered Disney's *Three Little Pigs*, with its elements of the Red Riding Hood story. The 'deep significance' of the German fairy-tale is translated into 'naive American slapstick mood'.[17] Disney is entertainment, not art. It does not appeal to inner emotion but to something more external, and draws out '*Erlebnis*' – adventure, sensation – rather than wisdom, wrote the critic.

The sources for the look of *Snow White and the Seven Dwarfs* were certainly European. In 1935 Walt Disney and Roy Disney had been in Europe to pick up Mickey Mouse's League of Nations Medal for making the world's children happy. (This was just one of many accolades in the period. For example, in 1936 Disney was commended to the French Legion of Honour for 'creating a new art form in which good is spread throughout the world'.) They nipped from Paris down to Rome, where Mussolini received them in his office, and while travelling through Europe Disney picked up a number of children's books with illustrations of little people, bees and small insects. He wrote a memo to his staff: 'This quaint atmosphere fascinates me and I was trying to think of how we could build some little story that would incorporate all of these cute characters.'[18]

It was from this fancy that *Snow White and the Seven Dwarfs* emerged. The Disney animator Albert Hurter, a Swiss immigrant, influenced the story's rustic Germanic setting through his try-out sketches. Hurter was responsible for producing a style for the film – its settings, architecture, props, interiors. For inspiration he turned to a wealth of illustrated books.[19] The cottage's prototype came from Ludwig Richter, who illustrated *Schneewittchen* in a Grimm edition in the middle of the nineteenth century, and Hermann Vogel, who in the 1890s illustrated Grimm in colour. Vogel's renditions of lavishly carved Bavarian woodwork and hand-hewn furniture carried over into Hurter's sketches for the settings, in which Snow White – her prototype a blonde in Richter's version and in the early modellings – was to move. (After the film's success, workers at the studio presented Disney with a backyard playhouse for his two daughters; it was a child-size copy of the cottage – this was all turning quasi-real.) Snow White was not a child of twentieth-century modernity. Pre-Raphaelite illustration and the late Romantic drawings of Ludwig Richter, Moritz Retsch and Arthur Rackham influenced her look. The characters were also drawn from European illustrated sources. The queen's raven derived from Wilhelm Busch's 1867 drawings of *Hans Huckebein, der Unglücksrabe*. The wizened bearded gnome dwarfs were purloined from the Swedish illustrator John Bauer – though Disney handed Hurter's sketches of the dwarfs to Fred Moore with the instruction to give them more 'personality'. In later sketches and in the finished film they became more rotund and infantile. (He fattened up and made Mickey Mouse cuter too.) The animators watched live-action film reels of people with achondroplasia, and then translated this into small spheres placed atop large spheres. The Swede Gustaf Tenggren was hired in 1936 for the later stages of the film's design. He was responsible for the watercolour washes. These were soft, like Biedermeier era books. Disney's syntax, based on painting, took its rooms and forest settings from nineteenth-century German fairy-tales and eighteenth-century German interiors. Biedermeier was an art of the interior. It showed the cosy domestic idyll. Its look was realist, but its sentiments sheer fantasy.[20] In turn, the style and techniques invented by the animators at the Disney studio for *Snow White and the Seven Dwarfs* influenced German animation like no other American film.

The Germanic references in Disney caused confusion in the Third Reich. Some of the gentlemen from the Propaganda Ministry saw in them only a typical American kitsch rendering of the German *Märchengutes* – the 'fairy-tale assets'. The film press reflected these views, in part, but also regretted the failings of German fairy-tale films in comparison.[21] Despite the criticisms of the American mentality, the authorities were keen to show the film in Germany. A long and complicated process of negotiation was set in motion in an attempt to get hold of *Snow White and the Seven Dwarfs* for German distribution. At the same time, Hubert Schonger, the 'only German fairy-tale film maker',[22] was working on a German 'Snow White' film. In an interview with *Film-Kurier*, on 2 December 1938, he remarked on how shocked he was by the fact that *Snow White and the Seven Dwarfs* was directed at adults. Schonger thought that the Grimm Brothers would be spinning in their graves if they knew what had been made of their 'touching fable'. The Americans, he admitted, would always be a nose length ahead of the Germans, but the problem concerned the amount of respect that should be shown to poetry. Schonger had his own ideas about how to film the fairy-tale:

> So, there should be then a thoroughly contemporary and positive use, which not only fructifies children's fantasy, but also stimulates thought. In this sense every fairy-tale can be politically upright, without one having to violate the poetry, or doing what was suggested to me for the Snow White film – lending the evil stepmother Jewish features. For one must never forget, our audience is not yet or only just of school age, and so as a result of that would simply not understand at all adult concepts.[23]

Yet, while some in Nazi Germany were disappointed with Disney's translation of the fairy-tale, it could not be denied that Disney had tapped into something dear to the Teutonic 'soul'. 'The German feeling': is this what united *Olympia* and *Snow White and the Seven Dwarfs*,[24] and allowed them to be internationally regarded as the summit of filmmaking in 1938? 'The German feeling' denoted a concoction of the romantic, the Gothic, elements of the neo-classical, everything that was not the technical experimentation of the avant-garde of the period. In this era, for Riefenstahl and for Disney, the 'German feeling' was a code word for restitution. It acted to wipe out the futuristically propelled avant-garde. The avant-garde in art explores the technically experimental and promotes, in one way or another, the politically utopian, railing against what is in the name of something universally better. In the grim 1930s, this avant-garde faded from view, suppressed and in hiding in the 'totalitarian world' and stamped out by the dumb violence of economic facts in the 'democratic world'. The avant-garde was occluded by its antithesis. The American theorist of high modernism Clement Greenberg defined this antithesis, this 'rear-guard' of the avant-garde, in his 1939 article 'Avant-Garde and Kitsch'.[25] For Greenberg, this rear-guard of kitsch comprised both American commercial culture and the totalitarian art of Nazi Germany and the Soviet Union. Kitsch, the culture of the industrialized masses, explains Greenberg, in its commercial and totalitarian guises, exploits tradition. Kitsch is that which is recognizable. Kitsch is a heightened reality that is made dramatic.[26] Kitsch bears traces of yesterday's avant-garde, diluted.[27] In the Soviet Union this kitsch was represented by Socialist Realism, an idealized naturalism. In Nazi Germany it was monumentalist art, once again illusionistic and illusory. In America its quintessence was surely Disney.

neither here nor there

Theodor Wiesengrund Adorno arrived in the United States in 1938, general release year of both *Snow White and the Seven Dwarfs* and *Olympia*. Adorno's preoccupation with domination and forms of culture in his homeland of Nazi Germany and his appalled fascination with the American commodification of culture commingle in the study that he wrote with Max Horkheimer, *Dialectic of Enlightenment* (1944). Here they perceive a duplicate dialectic of instrumental reason at work in cultural forms in Nazi Germany and in the democratic USA. Enlightenment has collapsed in on itself. Adorno and Horkheimer write:

> With the abandonment of thought, which in its reified form of mathematics, machine and organization avenges itself on the men who have forgotten it, enlightenment has relinquished its own realization.[28]

Liberal capitalism and totalitarian state capitalism alike generate a reified social order, cemented and reflected through cultural forms. In both zones culture is manufactured in accordance with principles of exchange and equivalence, identical to those that reign in the sphere of production. The economic condition of monopoly unites the production of culture across the two political systems. Monopoly turns culture into industry. They comment:

> Under monopoly all mass culture is identical.... The people at the top are no longer so interested in concealing monopoly: as its violence becomes more open, so its power grows. Movies and radio need no longer pretend to be art.... They call themselves industries...[29]

Disney has come to epitomize this tendency in culture, with the Disney trademark to this day a controlling stamp on large portions of US cultural commodity production. *Snow White and the Seven Dwarfs* marked the inauguration of this process. This first feature-length animation caused Disney to massify production, occasioning the move to a 24-hour factory of distraction production. He tripled his staff, paying for at least three million working hours, producing two million cels, though only about 250,000 were finally chosen for the feature-length film. This was the mass production of mass culture, and it was intensified once the new studio at Burbank was finished in 1940. Indeed Disney adapted Fordist methods – such as an extreme division of labour – for the field of mass (culture) production. He knew and liked the man too. Disney first met Henry Ford while on a promotional trip in Detroit, during the showing of *Snow White and the Seven Dwarfs*. Ford apparently liked Disney for being a self-made Protestant in a field dominated by Jews.[30]

Following Disney, many companies divided the labour of animation and standardized the output. Figures, dimensions, gestures, all the chief features of characters, were fixed on a model sheet for reference. Various teams would work under a director, with distinct groups devising the scripts and gags. The cel process was now the dominant mode of production, and this enabled the distribution of tasks among director, scene designer, chief animator, animator, in-betweener, department of colouring and buffing. Given this highly developed state of organization, there were few possibilities for ad-libbing or spontaneous invention. 'Typage' was a key word. Animators adopted a common dictionary of physiognomic traits – such as were relayed in a 'how to' manual by Preston Blair, one of Disney's animators – which pinpointed the look of 'cuteness', of 'screwballness', of 'heavyness' and so on.

Disney's move to the Burbank studio was completed on 6 May 1940. Here were twenty-five buildings on fifty-one acres, and the epicentre of the production process was the earthquake-proof Animation Building. Inside, the miscellaneous phases of the animation process proceeded smoothly along a filmmaking assembly line. The animation desk in pastel surroundings was designed to eliminate wastage in time and motion. It was proclaimed a workers' paradise. The buildings nestled on capacious lawns where employees could play baseball, badminton and volleyball. There was a penthouse with a lounge, soda fountain, sun deck, gymnasium

and showers for the animators and executives. The atmosphere was supposed to be relaxed. Walt insisted that everyone use first names. But that
did not mean that things were truly harmonious. Pre-trade-union Fordism,
spreading out from America to Germany and the Soviet Union, and based
on the speeding-up assembly line, armed security in the workplace and
extensive propaganda, had been, because of its dramatic overhaul of conditions of labouring and shop-floor relations, the most talked-about labour
form of the 1920s and 1930s.[31] Unionization at Ford in 1941 was the result
of militant rank-and-file activity, which Ford had been unable to break.
The same battles took place at Burbank in the same year. Some were later
to observe a parallel between the organization of the Fordist factory system
and the arrangement of the concentration camps.[32] Sometimes there really
was no difference. When the US army liberated the Ford plants in Cologne
and Berlin, foreign workers were found enclosed behind barbed wire.
They were forced labourers. Company documents praised the genius of
Hitler, and the production of military vehicles appeared to have been
approved by head office, according to a US investigator in 1945.[33]

Leni Riefenstahl was part of a monopolistic – state-controlled – culture
industry.[34] She played up the tensions between her aims and those of the
state later in her memoirs, claiming, for example, that Goebbels, a man
whose sexual advances she had spurned, harassed her by requesting that
she discharge some of her staff. She claimed that he wanted her to edit
out black athletes from the footage, and once threatened repossession of
the film, because of a small debt incurred at the Film-Kredit-Bank. But
she was not really so alienated. Indeed, in order to complain she went to
the top and her friend Hitler removed her from Propaganda Ministry
jurisdiction, placing her under the administration of Rudolf Hess and the
'Brown House'.[35] The state's favour mandated her a virtual monopoly on
filming at the Olympic Games. In consequence, all cameramen at the
Berlin Olympics wore official Nazi Olympics uniform; all foreign cameramen had censors by their side; US companies filming were forced to use
German sound equipment; and Riefenstahl was given access to all film
footage shot. These monopolistic conditions had been made possible by
actions taken early on in the Nazi reign. In March 1933 film was put into
the Reichsministerium für Volksaufklärung und Propaganda, and on 29

March 1933 the prominent film company UFA decided to dissolve all contracts with Jewish workers. Like Disney, Riefenstahl could indulge in an aesthetics of superresourcing. Both were prominent members of their national film industries. Along with Eisenstein, participant in another mighty culture industry, they were trying out the latest technical developments in soundtrack production: allowing sound and music, rather than images, to be at times the organizing force in their *Gesamtkunstwerke*. Disney and Riefenstahl treated their films as grand projects, buying in new cameras, new technologies. Both bent back the practices of the avant-garde, whose animus had been an experimentalism that twisted and turned the materials at hand and confounded convention, comprising not the development of technology but a progression in technique.

Walter Benjamin had spoken of the camera operator as dissector, as surgeon, in 'The Work of Art in the Age of its Technical Reproducibility'. For Benjamin, the segmenting, annihilative effect of the cinematic look can slice through the natural appearance of everyday life like a surgical instrument, contravening the tendency of film to mirror the surface. For Benjamin such dissection – an investigation of the world in close-up, production of links between things through montage, analysis of movement through slow-motion and so on – is part of a critical, scientific approach to the world. This is accompanied by an anti-naturalist, utopian rebuttal of physical laws and 'natural' constraint. The image becomes a multiply fragmented thing, whose parts reassemble themselves according to new laws.[36] Such critical dissection – a metaphorical dismantling – was not the goal at Burbank, nor at the Reichsfilmkammer; something more violently real was at stake.[37] Film succumbs, in this era, it might be said, to the victory of technology over technique, or more precisely, technological manipulation on technical consciousness. Technology's victory is flashed in photographic immediacy's commanding ideology of naturalism. This constrains film in the service of reflecting an apparent vision of an elevated real. The originary critical effects of recording technologies have been assuaged by ideological overdetermination. In his article 'The Work of Art in the Age of its Technical Reproducibility', Walter Benjamin aligns the rape of the masses with the rape of technology forced into the service of cult values.[38] While Hollywood is shown to be cranked up to polish the disempowering cultish and dazzling commodity glow through its charismatic stars and mythic histories, Benjamin's chilling commentary on fascist aesthetic cultism ponders the Nazi use of recording machines at vast rallies, monster meetings, mass sporting events and in war. The latest technologies are deployed by the Nazis to make representations of the masses at play, at work, at war. Manipulated emotion is the currency in Hollywood and at the Reichsfilmkammer alike:

> Mass reproduction complies well with the reproduction of the masses. In the huge rallies, the monster meetings, in mass sporting events and in war, all carried out these days in front of recording machines, the masses look themselves in the face. This process, whose import cannot be emphasized too much, is closely connected to the development of reproductive or recording technology. Mass movements appear more clearly to the apparatus than to the human eye. Hundreds of thousands of cadres are best seen from a bird's eye perspective. While this perspective is just as accessible to the human eye as it is to the apparatus, the image that the eye carries away with it is incapable of enlargement, unlike the photograph. That means, then, that mass movements, and, at their pinnacle, war, represent a form of human behaviour that is especially fitted to the apparatus.[39]

Fascist monumental art is hammered for the masses and structured out of the mass shapes that they are made to form. News items, strung together in the *Wochenschau* productions and the like, with their bird's-eye dictator's eye, are constructed to accentuate the great dimensions of the spectacular shows, the rallies and sportive-military events.[40] The camera dispatches aerial views of precisely organized patterns procured of 'human material'.[41] Benjamin's acquaintance, Siegfried Kracauer, back in 1926 in 'The Mass Ornament', had registered that the Americanist Taylorization and Fordization of entertainment operated to similar effect.[42]

Riefenstahl's film was a paean to the new possibilities of movement and body dissection offered by recording technologies. The Olympic Games itself was an opportunity to exalt technologies of mass culture and technology per se. The Olympics were held in Berlin in an 85,000-seat stadium. The fittest bodies and the latest in industrial machines were on display. Not only Riefenstahl's film but television, too, mediated the events. Some 160,000 television viewers watched the Olympic Games in Germany, enthusiastically submitting to the techno-reproduction of bodies, in 400-

seater television viewing halls – Goebbels and the first Reich director of broadcasting, Eugen Hadamovsky, believed that propaganda was most effective when received in collective audiences, which produced the added effect of peer pressure to conform. The Olympic Games paraded Nazi organizational abilities – the mass event, the pageantry, the draperies, the whole spectacle, ordered, efficient and mass. For Adorno, sport provides a model for mass culture, and is pivotal in the establishment of totalitarian rule:

> Sport itself is not play but ritual in which the subjected celebrate their subjection. They parody freedom in their readiness for service, a service which the individual forcibly extracts from his own body for a second time. In the freedom which he exercises over his body the individual confirms what he is by inflicting upon this slave the same injustice he has already endured at the violent hands of society. The passion for sport, in which the masters of mass culture sense the real mass basis of their dictatorial power, is grounded in this fact.[43]

The fixation on the body, on training, on displaying, measuring and venerating is seen by Adorno to be part of that process of the oppressive dialectic of reason; the philosophy that abandoned human affinity with nature in the name of an exploitative objectivity. The fascists do it best of all. Adorno writes:

> The 'tragic' philosophy of the Fascist is the ideological party which precedes the real blood wedding. Those who extolled the body above all else, the gymnasts and scouts, always had the closest affinity with killing, just as the lovers of nature are close to the hunter. They see the body as a moving mechanism, with joints as its components and flesh to cushion the skeleton. They use the body and its parts as though they were already separated from it. Jewish tradition contains a disinclination to measure men with a foot-rule because the corpse is measured in this way for the coffin. This is what the manipulators of the body enjoy. They measure others, without realizing it, with the gaze of a coffin maker.[44]

The tragic philosophy is deadly. And part of this disciplining is the application of technology to the body, an effect redoubled in sport's reproduction for film and television. Along with the claim that its aesthetic is not compromised by political actuality, Riefenstahl's *Olympia* is described by one writer as a 'hymn to the beauty of the human body in motion'.[45] Such language intimates transcendence, and mobilizes the term 'beauty' as

Olympia, Leni Riefenstahl

if it were self-evident. It insinuates eternal and universal values. But, in fact, the combination of beauty, body and motion – at this precise moment, at least – has a very particular meaning. Apparently infinite, this merger is actually about finitude, measurement, calipers and anatomization. This is dissection through cinema, indeed, but of a different quality and to a different end than that of Benjamin's benevolent, healing surgeon. As F.W. Taylor had found out, film, with its multiple frames per second, is the most excellent technology of time–motion analysis for industrial purposes – a machinery that spurs the mechanization of its subjects. This analytical use of film was not designed to reveal an 'optical-unconscious', a textured knowledge of the unseen of matter and motion – a goal that had perhaps motivated Muybridge's chronophotography[46] – but rather serviced the god of efficiency, and the already-known classical ideal.[47] The battle over beauty in the 1930s was a battle between the surreal and the ideal. The surrealists and Klee found beauty, new beauty, in cell life and deep-sea fish, a tentacle charm, an amoebic beauty of lower but disorderly life forms. Riefenstahl's life forms are barely alive. She imprisons the living body in standards inherited from an academic analysis of Greek statuary. The real body can only ever be an imperfect, failed imitation of the higher supermannish archetype. Futurism's vanguardist poetic chimera – the 'dreamed of metalization of the body' – hardens in the Taylorized factory into a prosaic instrumentalization of the body. The movies whose very basis is human movement mobilize movement without enlivening political movement, self-organized movement. Movies are used for disciplining and containing movement within a frame; dissecting and devivifying the living. When such a process is combined with myth and mist, analysis is not practicable. Such movies provide only an illusion of matter in motion. Formally, the apparent motion – the illusion of life – simulated by the filmstrip is twenty-four frames of stasis per second. These freeze-framed replicas of photographed reality evidence a semblance of life, the cavorting of flat ghosts, but if the machine falters, motion tends back to stasis, reversing the illusion formed by the final frames of Disney's film, as Snow White is reanimated by the prince's kiss, and reversing the animation of *Olympia*'s opening prologue as statues turn into athletes. These two films are about animation and stasis, and they both dramatize that interest in key scenes. And they both also seem to let on that the cult of the perfect body is a cult of death – the stone athletes, the dead princess – an idea that is made graphic and intensified in film's posthumous ontology. The sporting bodies of *Olympia*, less literally than Snow White in her suspended animation, awaiting the prince's kiss, but more profoundly, parade death, according to Adorno and Horkheimer, who note in response to the sporting body cults of the twentieth century:

> The body cannot be remade into a noble object: it remains the corpse, however vigorously it is trained and kept fit. The metamorphosis into death was simply part of that perennial process which turned nature into substance and matter.[48]

In the mid-1930s, while preparing 'The Work of Art in the Age of its Technical Reproducibility', Benjamin made the more precise, historical link between modern industrial methods and the Olympics. The Olympics is not a competition, but a representation of the human being tested – in seconds and centimetres – against the machine. Olympics are 'reactionary', Benjamin states bluntly, and continues, with reference to the 1924 Olympics in Paris, and the Finnish athlete Paavo Nurmi who won four medals and ran with his chronometer in his hand:

> Not for nothing is Nurmi said to be racing against the clock. Herewith is the contemporary position of sporting practice determined. It removes itself from the agonal to go down the road of the test. Nothing is more common to the test in its present form than measuring the human against an apparatus.[49]

The Olympics, and more concretely, representations of the Olympics, bolstered by micro-technology, re-present to watchers the industrial work process, wherein the body is an armature, a machine for work, the machine-pendant such as described by Marx, the automated node in a complexly divided process, as propagated by Ford.[50] But all this is renaturalized – paraded in the spectacle of the naked human body, aligned with classical antiquity.

The cultural industries, in Germany as in the USA, preside over a fantastic amassing of technological resources, and yet they pile these into the masking or counteracting of technological modernity. The spick and span gothic in Disney's *Snow White and the Seven Dwarfs* matches Riefenstahl's smoothly white Nordic classicism in *Olympia* – both are anxious reflections on modernization. Common also to the aesthetics of Disney and Riefenstahl is a negation of industrial modernity. This negation involves reasserting an idealist naturalism. This idealist naturalism cultivates a classicism that is contingent on modern technology – yet denies it. *Snow White and the Seven Dwarfs* uses modern technology to invoke a premodern world – European, feudal. The fantastic technology of animation and the technique of labour subdivision serves an archaic ideology of the pre-industrial. In *Olympia*, a cryptogrammic nature – a Nordic–Greek seascape, a now cruel, now gentle forest – is imagined as healthy contrast to society, and is thereby denatured.[51] Sport is celebrated as the ritual play of the superhuman, a serious play, preparation for war – the film's narration resounds with words of fight, conquest. *Olympia* twins technology and the anti-modern, sublating the divide in classicist modernity. Such a stance is anticipated in Hitler's phrase in *Mein Kampf*: 'Never was humanity closer to antiquity than today.'[52]

avant-garde/kitsch: germany

The Germano-romantic and the neoclassical are strangely united at this time in Germany. In the 1920s and 1930s significant historical schools strove to assert the Germanic roots of classical civilization, denying the Semitic (Phoenician) founts of ancient culture. Nordic-Greekism symbolizes this Romantic/neoclassical concoction: it found a newly militarist accent in Nazi Germany. As Dr Carl Diem, the sports official who had been charged with the task of 'renewing the Olympic Games',[53] wrote in 1942: 'How much of that which constitutes the new German ideology and German strength is an inheritance from ancient Sparta!' Diem was an athlete, a pioneer of physical education in Germany and an Olympic official. That the games were conceived militaristically is apparent from the following:

> Because they [the Games] served the fatherland in antiquity, as is shown so powerfully in the tale of Herodotos from the Persian Wars, because Couberten wanted to help his French fatherland in establishing the Games, because our athletics has national impulses – Jahn's impulse was Germany's servitude, the Dane Nachtigall's was the sacking of Copenhagen by the English fleet, the Swede Ling's was the defeat against Russia – that is why eternal value lodges in the Games, as long as people regard the fatherland as the highest thing. Such a love for the fatherland is also, as the games show, the best bridge to a healthy sense of humanity and a chivalrous friendship between peoples.[54]

The Nazi version of Nordic-Greekism improved upon original antiquity, however. Diem remembers his trip:

> I finished up in my homeland, after a glorious flight. For we must be led back to the homeland. No Greeking of the Germans! Rather the Greeks as our greatest spiritual antagonists: we will do justice to their legacy if we are as German as we can be. They looked up to eternal laws; we too will fulfil these on our part. The means to so do is a good disciplining of the body and a conscious schooling of the will.[55]

Nazi Germany was Sparta with added value for today. As Diem wrote in 1937 in *Olympische Reise* (*Olympic Journey*):

> Our new age is filled by a spirit that corresponds to the best age of Sparta, here too discipline, subordination, education into the community and toughness. State totality here as there! And yet we must bear in mind the warning, uttered by no less than Moltke, when he concerned himself with the question of mili-

tary training for youth: in the long run, the purely soldierly spirit destroyed Sparta. Care of the spirit and arts, properly united with soldierliness, gives duration to a people, and in such an educational plan sport has its ... role.[56]

In February 1934, Carl Diem persuaded Minister Heagard to submit a plan for a torch relay between Olympia and Berlin to the organizing committee of the 1936 Olympics. Diem had long been interested in the religious symbolic connotations of the flame and the torch. The torch relay was duly instituted at the 1936 Olympics. With the help of a concave mirror, sunrays lit the flame at ancient Olympia, and the relay route crossed twelve countries. It was as if a baton had been passed from the past to the present. The Nazi sculptors who provided a visualization of this fantasized antiquity, however, adjusted the features of their sculptures according to a mythological Aryan norm: thin lips, straight nose, square heads, high cheekbones, straight hair, no beards. In the turn to Sparta, well hyped by the event of the 1936 Olympic Games, Nazi Germany withdrew, apparently, from modernity.

The film of the games continued that work. Now was the time for German film to find a new form – the avant-garde, where it still existed, had to be rubbished – and Riefenstahl led the way. Greenberg, in his 1939 'Avant-Garde and Kitsch', referred to fascism's mission against the avant-garde – certain that the default culture of the masses everywhere was kitsch, the simple, emotional, immediate. Greenberg observed that the common man's resentment is silenced for as long as he is in awe of his leaders who patronize avant-garde art. Once political dissatisfaction develops, the common man feels able to criticize culture, because he resents it. This resentment towards culture is most often to be found where the dissatisfaction stoked is reactionary, expressed in revivalism and puritanism, 'and latest of all in fascism'. The Austrian house painter knows how to work it well: 'Here revolvers and torches begin to be mentioned in the same breath as culture. In the name of godliness or the blood's health, in the name of simple ways and solid virtues, the statue smashing commences.'[57] Even as a leftist, Greenberg was already disillusioned with the possibility of progressive mass politics, and particularly with the idea of pursuing politics through art. His disappointment was stoked by a Trotskyist-tinged distrust of Popular Front cultural policy, which bestowed legitimacy on Stalinist bureaucratic rule, and in artistic terms promoted middlebrow high culture, for purposes of 'art appreciation' and municipal folk culture, as a new kitsch. Greenberg could see the affinities between the Soviet Union and the Hitler regime because their art forms seemed so similar. And yet the industrially produced culture of the USA of anti-fascist 'radical America' provided no alternative, for it too was anti-art, enlisting the services, as James T. Farrell put it in 1939, of 'commercial writers, high-priced Hollywood scenarists, a motley assortment of mystery-plot mechanics, humorists, newspaper columnists, stripteasers, band leaders, glamour girls, actors, press agents, Broadway producers, aging wives with thwarted literary ambitions' – in short an anti-cultural 'frightened league of philistines'.[58] Greenberg's analysis of totalitarian kitsch dwelt on the vicious joy released by the Nazis' 1937 exhibition of degenerate art, where those who hated and resented modern artists could witness the staging of their vilification. Perhaps it was a premonition of what might happen in America too. For him, it justified the blasting of art out of any instrumental relation to politics into autonomy.

Olympia took on its form at a moment of particular significance for the politics of art in Germany.[59] In 1937 the German film industry was in the midst of a crisis caused by a boycott of German films abroad and the high costs of producing film in colour to a high technical level. The 'nationalization' of the film industry by the Propaganda Ministry and the Finance Ministry was decreed. A congress took place at the Reichsfilmkammer in March 1937, to look back over four years of National Socialist filmmaking. The president of the Reichsfilmkammer attacked profit-hungry filmmakers who had abandoned quality and were endangering the 'national cultural assets'.[60] Goebbels spoke at the congress, expounding on the meaning of 'German film art'. 'Artistic' value was promoted in the movies. The main feature was supplemented by non-cinematic entertainment. On the stage in front of the screen were performances by jugglers and ballet troupes, and sports displays. One bill, called 'With UFA into Fairyland', featured three Walt Disney films, some German-made Grimm films and a fairy-tale reading by Dora Stein. Film needed to be raised up into the canon of higher arts and disciplined, turned into cultured pageantry. The year 1937 saw the formulation of a purposiveness in Nazi art policy, with the official outlawing of German expressionism and the promotion of classical, heroic art, a process undertaken in conjunction with the highly publicized exhibition of 'Entartete Kunst' ('Degenerate Art'). The exhibition opened in July 1937 in Munich, and later embarked on a tour of Germany. Here, as Riefenstahl snipped away at her film, the artistic avant-garde was most publicly reviled. *Olympia* was waging a very specific war against the imagery most directly under attack in the exhibition – imagery of the body. In the catalogue for the Degenerate Art exhibition all the pictures but one were of human bodies and faces. The selectors were horrified by modernism's anti-idealist assaults on the body. At the core of revived classicism is the cult of the body. At the core of cult of the body is the cult of the integral body, auratic, reified, distanced, dead. The figures in *Olympia* mirror the figures of Nazi sculptors Breker, Albiker, Klimsch and Kolbe – or the numerous sculptures, bunkered in official buildings of the Reich, and called 'Party' or 'Army' or 'Torchbearer'. These sculptures were not for empathy but for intimidation; they erected impossible norms.[61] Breker in 1936 was allowed to view the entire male German Olympic team to choose the one he liked best. Gustav Stührk was duly chosen to be the model for fascistic 'Mann'. The Olympics was the prelude to the real blood-letting – so many beautiful bodies, about to be blasted apart on the battlefields. It was as if their wholeness had to be ecstatically affirmed, before being negated in actuality.

Riefenstahl was pirouetting on the grave of the avant-garde. Her mission, from *Triumph of the Will* (1934) onwards, was to prune documentary of its experimentalist, Weimar–Jewish cosmopolitan connotations. In *Hinter den Kulissen des Reichsparteitagfilms* (*Behind the Scenes of the Film of the Reich's Rally*), authored in 1935 either by Riefenstahl or on her behalf by Ernst Jäger, the Weimar genre of 'reportage' is rejected, because it lives only a speedy urban week and not a Nazi-tinged eternity. Riefenstahl's documentary had higher aims: 'to capture on film inner experience' ('Inneres Erleben filmisch festzuhalten'), whereby, countering the modernist revelation of the means of representation, the process of filmmaking becomes invisible. Significantly Riefenstahl refuses the avant-garde term 'montage' in favour of the seemingly organic term 'forming' (*Formung*).[62] Film was formed as a total work of art for a totalitarian society. Frank Maraun, in his article 'Triumph des Dokumentarfilms' ('Triumph of the Documentary Film'), a contribution to *Der deutsche Film* in May 1938, wrote of *Olympia* as a film that lifted the 1936 Olympics out of the sphere of a mere sports report for the creatively reproductive camera, in order to reveal the idea which animates and illuminates. He continues:

> This is not only an action of the film, it is a result of National Socialism, which is penetrating the total life of the nation into its most detailed ramifications, with its idea-based directional force and which has accustomed us to see reality and idea together. Only in the ideological structure of National Socialism could this great documentary film have come into being as an artistic achievement. Indeed it had never existed previously.[63]

There are unsupported rumours that experimental animator and new objectivist documentary filmmaker Walter Ruttmann worked on *Olympia*. In 1934 Ruttmann did film a frame story for Riefenstahl's *Triumph of the Will*, and he directed a number of studio scenes. From a left-modernist perspective, this collaboration marks the collapse of the avant-garde in Germany. While Ruttmann's animations had broken the mythic frames of high art and his new objectivist work had engaged with actuality, the Riefenstahl collaboration bowdlerized montage to promote political myth. Ruttmann, the former documentarist, filmed scenes of the pre-*Machtergreifung* for which no documentary footage existed. He entered the realm of mythic history. He did not cut it though, and his work was rejected. His prologue was deemed too 'Soviet'. But he did get reinvented in the Reich. He became a documentary filmmaker whose work had only ever glorified the fatherland. His work included such titles as *Blut und Boden* (*Blood and Soil*) (1933), *Altgermanisches Bauernkultur* (*Old-Germanic Peasant Culture*) (1934), *Deutsche Waffenschmieden* (*German Weapon Forging*) (1940), *Deutsche Panzer* (*German Tanks*) (1940). His early work – the abstract animations – was determinedly forgotten.

After *Olympia* Riefenstahl turned to her dramatic project, *Tiefland*, which was filmed from the mid 1930s and completed by 1944. *Tiefland* was a continuation of themes from Riefenstahl's directorial debut, the mountain film *Das blaue Licht* (1932). *The Blue Light* was a film of nature mysticism. *Tiefland* – lowlands, deep lands – told a story about the corruption of civilization in the village, set against the purity of nature and the mountains. Civilization's great export, war, impeded filming. The German invasion of France made filming in Spain impossible, and so the team had to return to the homeland, to film in the German Karwendel mountains. Gypsies were enlisted to play Spanish peasants. After the war, it was said that they had been taken from a concentration camp. In her memoirs, Riefenstahl denied this, but it was the case, at least, that their village later became a concentration camp.

The Nazi regime suppressed any idea of class as cleavage within society, insisting, in its stead, that the fundamental division between peoples was some sense of nationhood or an even vaguer sense of race. Propagandist Alfred Rosenberg articulated this idea, insisting that the conflict of the future occurs between blood and blood, race and race, people and people. Art circulated this fantasy of the Aryan German race. Through art, ideal types and ideal bodies, new human types, with their biology founded on racial principles, were designed and promoted. Sport was another mode of pitching race-people against race-people. Aestheticized sport fused the two: the art of the ideal plus the contest of races. Racially based concepts and eugenic ideas were not confined to Nazi Germany. They were naturalized in countless Hollywood films too, as was the taboo on miscegenation.

avant-garde/kitsch: usa

From the 1930s onwards the Disney studio had been taming the cartoon, displacing its original avant-gardish anarchy and formal inconstancy. By the mid-1930s, Disney was advancing a cartoon version of movie-style *mise-en-scène* and acting. Abstract modernist styles were not completely vilified at the studio. In the late 1930s Disney animators could attend lectures by Jean Charlot on the history of art and ways in which they might appropriate the modern styles of futurism, cubism, surrealism and abstraction, but realism was where the focus lay. The creation of this realist style had been aided by advances in depth-of-field generation, and the use of the multiplane camera. The multiplane system could set the animation, the background paintings, the overlay paintings on up to six levels with the different layers mounted on sheets of glass a foot or so apart. The camera tracks through these layers and different levels come into focus in imitation of a live-action camera. This movie-style technique negates flat space and the self-referentiality of the drawn cartoon and substitutes a deep cartoon space. It was the definitive reversal of modernist revelation of materials. If the modernists used the illusion of depth it was to investigate the illusion. The modernist return to zero, stripping away all the clutter and effects of culture, was reversed in the refurbishing of the screen with objects stretching into every corner.

In 1934, an animation of the classical myth of Persephone, titled *The Goddess of Spring*, had presented the Disney studio's first attempts to draw realistic movement, for an elevating neoclassical theme. This was further developed in *Snow White and the Seven Dwarfs*. Using techniques such as rotoscoping, the Disney studio strove after an increased knowledge of organic structure and a more acute sense of timing, breaking down movements in order to build them up mechanically. As so often, the Fleischers had beaten Disney to it. *Popeye the Sailor meets Sinbad the Sailor*, a two-reeler from 1936, was publicized as the first two-reel, full-colour, three-dimensional animation.[64] But this film wobbled between two dimensions and three dimensions. The Disney product eradicated such discontinuity. Max Fleischer's rotoscope was set to most striking use in *Snow White and the Seven Dwarfs*, although the strange dimensions of Snow White, five heads high instead of eight, caused some problems. Disney produced an animated imitation of realist cinema, in terms of content and form – romantically realistic, an idealized real.

Snow White and the Seven Dwarfs was also the first film to make extensive use of dialogue to define the personalities and show how the characters thought – fully rounded flat cartoon characters were born. *The Flying Mouse*, from 1934, was reputed to have been the first cartoon to move an audience to tears.[65] Cartoons, it was shown, could now provoke pathos. *Snow White and the Seven Dwarfs* milked this emotive aspect. Snow White's scenes were increased as the story took shape – she became the point of identification, rather than the curious dwarfs (and when she is immobilized in her glass coffin, it is as if animation itself is suspended). At the same time, the soundtrack was now being used to supply and interpret feelings and sensations, as well as conveying dialogue. In addition the feature-lengths tendered Disney's accomplished sell-out of the quintessence of cartoons: their modernistic dissolution of conventional reality. From *Snow White and the Seven Dwarfs* onwards the laws of perspective and gravity are reinstituted, flatness is repelled and the films no longer explode the world with the surrealistic and analytical cinematic dynamite of the optical unconscious that had been developed in 1920s' cartooning. The reinstitution of physical laws was most evident in the animators' dilemma when designing a scene that showed Snow White falling. They worried about the height of the drop and whether it could lead to her death.

By the mid 1930s, Disney was employing twelve story and gag men, forty animators, forty-five assistant animators, thirty inkers and painters, and a twenty-four-piece orchestra, plus other technicians. All these resources were deployed to re-create in perfected form the real. Disney was now on a quest to make his cartoons look 3-D real, perspectivally faithful, with lifelike movements and skin tone, and unobtrusive muted earthy backgrounds. This move towards the illusion of life was a critical success.

Cyprus Leroy Baldridge, a movie reviewer for the Birmingham News-Age Herald, saw Disney's *Snow White and the Seven Dwarfs* as a 'successful compromise between realism and abstraction'.[66] And many others said the same. Robert Feild was rather more reflective about the implications of this illusioning. He contemplated the implications of the multiplane camera:

> Its one outstanding purpose, as we have already indicated in this book, is to create a greater illusion of the third dimension than has hitherto been possible. That in itself opens up metaphysical problems of such magnitude that one would hesitate before expressing an opinion. Even in the eyes of the studio it is considered an instrument so loaded with artistic dynamite that, if not properly handled, it may blast the animate sound picture completely off its course. Walt, however, is never too concerned by such academic problems as the relation between realism and abstraction.[67]

Disney animator Hamilton Luske pushed hard for greater observation of the real world to find its place in cartooning. On 31 December 1935 he issued a 'General Outline of Animation Theory and Practice', which insisted that a story be told as clearly as possible in drawings. But he noted that the old style symbolism should be abandoned. Thinking was hitherto shown by a question mark above a character's head.[68] Now that internal life should be visible in facial expression, in the movement of an eyebrow or a mouth. On 30 September 1938, Luske made some statements on character handling, and how what he termed the 'illusion of life' has been sustained in Disney characters. He identified four constituents: drawing simple characters that can be duplicated by any of the many artists that have to handle them; making every part of their bodies round and animatable, so that they can be squashed and stretched and turned softly and without flaws; the use of a cutting technique of short scenes, clipped speeches and offstage dialogue; and the invention of moving holds (which means continual movement of all characters' body parts) – a substitute for the necessary pauses in good acting.[69] The recipe for success would appear to be standardization, smoothness, sophisticated montage and realism, as was at work in Hollywood film, now that, notably, much of the cartoon industry had quit New York to huddle in Hollywood.

At the beginning of Disney's *Snow White and the Seven Dwarfs* a white book opens and the audience enters the fairy-tale world through layers of background. It is a world where darkness and light fight for dominance. When the white light wins, we know that the bloodless idealism has won out – in moral fantasy, as in art. Here is not the world of the avant-garde, a world where modern art asserts the blackness of critique, as it defers happiness. Nor is it the world of young Mickey Mouse where an Al Jolson-based polyglot of vulgar motifs mocks authority, machinery and reality itself. Disney was clear about his hopes for *Snow White and the Seven Dwarfs*: to appeal to that 'kind, clean, unspoilt spot deep down in all of us'. If Disney product was still for adults, it was for the adult who still had the child within; like Snow White herself, both and yet neither, adult and child. There was this spot, Disney was sure, implying that it was well hidden and difficult to access, smothered in layers of dirt and perversion. Disney's phrase echoed Hitler's railings against 'hybridized and negrified culture' in which 'all conceptions of the humanly beautiful and sublime, as well as an idealized future for our mankind, would be lost forever.'[70] Something needed to be accessed, something preserved.

'Who is the fairest of them all?' asks the evil witch-queen of her magic mirror in *Snow White and the Seven Dwarfs*. Why, one whose skin is white as snow. And evil – as embodied in the witch and the vultures, of course –

is always dark, hooked-nosed and ugly. Beauty and evil manifest themselves on the body – as the witch cackles, while preparing her magic poisoned apple: 'on the skin the symbol of what lies within'. While class emerges in the image of the friendly but imbecilic and dirty dwarf-workers, Snow White, the temporarily fallen princess, possesses a white skin that is emblematic of her inner purity. Some are born to rule: it shows on their very bodies. The poets Stefan George and Hans Blüher and other fin-de-siècle esoterics had asserted the association of white skin and moral purity most forcefully. The ideas of the esoterics were enthusiastically taken up in the Third Reich.[71] One popular book, *Nordic Beauty* (1937) by Paul Schultze-Naumburg, explicated the theory of racial body types and moral substance, avouching a racist version of the pseudo-science of physiognomy. This proposed the idea that the soul is racially determined and its characteristics manifest themselves on the body. Schultze-Naumburg's examples were, in fact, a collage of ideal forms from artworks of the past. The author claims that Nordic bodies exhibit the Nordic virtues of logical clarity and truthful thoughtfulness. A good body has clear borderlines and separate parts. Nordic peoples are tall, slim, fine-limbed with narrow hips and narrow faces. The Nordic female breast has chiselled contours and is small and upright, unlike the rapid maturation of fleshy oriental breasts, or the mammoth, formless, spongy breasts of mongoloids – racial types who are deemed inferior, illogical and dissembling.[72] Snow White – as asexual as a Nazi sculpture of virtuous naked Germanic womanhood – and each of the seven dwarfs are all such clearly demarcated types, their bodies, their names, their souls all in unity. These might have had much to say to a 'Nazi' audience.

epilogue

Roy Disney visited Germany in March 1938 to seal a deal on *Snow White and the Seven Dwarfs*. But in the autumn of 1938 there was a controversy in Germany about whether or not the film would be shown in the Reich. Due to currency difficulties, the film was very expensive. Furthermore, embarrassingly for the Nazis, it was technically very advanced compared to German animation at the time. And anyway, certainly after *Kristallnacht* in

November, international reservations were growing about trade with Germany. After the production in Hollywood of a number of anti-Nazi films, the Propaganda Ministry put pressure on critics to express anti-American sentiments. In 1938 the Propaganda Ministry made possible the purchase of fifty American movies, including *Snow White and the Seven Dwarfs*. But critics were beginning to voice frustration at American domination of the silver screen. In *Licht–Bild–Bühne*, one critic bemoaned the fact that even though *Snow White and the Seven Dwarfs* was not going to be seen in Germany, at a conservative estimate at least two hundred pages of text and image about the film had appeared in the German press. In comparison the 'top film' *Heimat*, which was to be shown in America, had not even garnered fifteen pages of publicity in the American press.[73] In September 1939 a report in *Film-Kurier* attacked 'Bolshevik Machinations in Film America', and revealed details of the Dies committee's investigation into communist supporters amongst the Hollywood film community. The report stated that, with the exception of Snow White, almost every actor in Hollywood was helping the Reds.[74] By 1939 a little war had been declared in the press – on the Anti-Nazi League and the '56 Hollywood stars' who had signed a petition against Germany. The author of the *Film-Kurier* article claimed that a lack of artistic capability made the stars resort to 'atrocity propaganda' against Germany, or else they were forced to sign the petition under threat of violence. Those who attacked the Germans 'out of hatred or stupidity or cowardice' could surely not complain if they were refused appearance on German cinema screens. Despite this, in that year twenty new Hollywood movies were shown in the Greater German Reich. However, such sentiments in the film press made the purchase of *Snow White and the Seven Dwarfs* for German distribution very difficult. American films were banned from German premiere film theatres. And yet an exception was to be made for *Snow White and the Seven Dwarfs*. This was a film of high artistic quality, claimed the film experts; the gentlemen from the Propaganda Ministry agreed.[75] The same excuse had not been made for *Felix the Cat*, banned since 1935. The Nazis were inventive in finding ways around the ban on American product. That Disney enjoyed approval in the highest echelons of the Reich – even if for the German masses the product was vilified – could be seen by Goebbels's diary entry of 20 December 1937.

I gave the Führer 30 top films of the last four years and 18 Mickey Mouse films
… for Christmas. He was very pleased with this. Is very happy with this treasure
that will hopefully afford him much joy and relief.[76]

Goebbels also took the opportunity to show his children Mickey Mouse
films in his private cinema. And in 1938 Hitler arranged for a copy of *Snow
White and the Seven Dwarfs* to be taken to his private cinema at Übersalzberg.
He thought it one of the greatest films ever.[77] Powerful forces wanted to
preserve the Disney–Hitler axis. Some Nazi film historians tried to prove
that Disney's lineage was German. Another fictionalized biography put out
by the Reichspropagandaministerium claimed that Disney was born on 15
December 1901 in Mojácar in Almería in Spain. His original name was said
to be José Luis Guirao Zamora. In 1903 the family migrated to America,
where they found work on a farm owned by a Mr Disney. The parents
died young and so the Disneys adopted the child, rechristened him Walt
and sent him to art school in Chicago.[78] Correspondence between Günther
Schwarz of the Reichsfilmkammer and Dr Hans Cürlis in May 1941 revealed how important Disney's origin was for the Nazis. Cürlis had told
Schwarz at a showing of *Snow White and the Seven Dwarfs* that Disney was
a German, but Schwarz had read in a Spanish newspaper that Disney was
of Spanish origin. Cürlis reports in his letter that he had heard some years
before that Disney was German, used to be called Walter Distler, and had
once worked in Germany. This German origin had made sense to him
given Disney's use of German fairy-tales, but given the Spanish article that
Schwarz had included he was no longer so sure.[79] This troubled him and
others as they struggled to invent an Aryan past for the great filmmaker.[80]

Things were not going well on the home-grown animation front. Kurt
Stordel competed for a similar market to Disney. Between 1935 and 1938
he animated fairy-tales. In 1938 he wrote an autobiographical sketch in
Deutsche Filmwelt, as if he were his gnome character Purzel, who appeared
in two films in 1939 and 1942: 'In his films my father Kurt Stordel looks
intentionally for an atmosphere, and not merely for the grotesque; contrary to the Americans, he prefers watercolours to contoured drawing.'
Relationships between Disney's American distributors RKO and Germany
became strained after the Anti-Nazi League activity. RKO were producing
anti-Nazi films. Nevertheless, in the middle of 1939, despite the bans on

American films and the cost of obtaining the film, a German premiere of *Snow White and the Seven Dwarfs* was still being planned. The German version had already been synchronized. But then negotiations were broken off, following pressure from the American union of producers. It was only then that Schonger got the go-ahead to begin filming his German 'Snow White' film. Though this film had already been planned for some time, the European success of the American version had meant deferral.[81] It appeared in October 1939, featuring real dwarfs. *Film-Kurier* saw it as another facet of the long-running German debate on how to film a fairy-tale.

> The Germans in particular have thought a great deal about the fairy-tale film – since the fairy-tale is a matter of sensibility and poetry; in the meanwhile others decided to make fairy-tale films in their own ways. And only a few small producers here, with courage and with few means, have attempted to satisfy as well as they could the great need amongst youth. Here much work still needs to be done: the care of the German fairy-tale and its transposition into the filmic realm is a matter for German culture; it will cost us something, just as does the care of museums – which also do not 'bring anything in' in the usual sense. (And who says that a well-made, great German fairy-tale film is not able to do such good 'business' as Disney's 'Snow White'?)[82]

The film was dull and badly made, but Goebbels commissioned Schonger to produce several more live-action and animated fairy-tales. The Nazis needed something to show. On 2 February 1940 the trade relationship between Disney and Germany was dissolved. Despite Disney's own anti-Semitic prejudices Donald Duck went on, famously, to fight the Nazis. Curiously the Allies were keen to emphasize connections between the Nazi cabinet members and the Disney mouse – if only for the purposes of mockery. Sinclair Lewis had noted in 1936 that Dr Goebbels was privately known throughout Germany as 'Wotan's Mickey Mouse'. An edition of the wartime propaganda newsreel *Worker and War-Front* (no. 3), issued by the British Ministry of Information, included a little cartoon strip titled 'the gallery of beauty', showing the Nazi leaders as caricatures. Goering is a tiny little Mickey Mouse standing on a stool. According to the commentary he is saying, 'The true Aryan is always tall, I repeat upright, blue-eyed, fair-haired and with a high forehead.' Curiously, though, at this time, it was British children who most resembled Mickey Mouse: their gas masks imitated mouseketeer headdresses, a ploy suggested by the gas mask design and exploited in order to assuage children's fears.

With the cartoon world at war with its world, Germany had to produce its own animation. The leaders set the remaining artists on the task. In May 1941 the ministry decreed that a strong German animation industry be brought into existence. Hans Fischerkoesen was forced to relocate from Leipzig to Potsdam to be on call for the film studios at Neubabelsburg. Fischerkoesen, who had built his reputation in the 1920s, appropriated multiplane and stereo-optical technology in the 1940s. Goebbels insisted on the development of this aspect. He wanted three-dimensional effects that could compete with the Fleischers' stereo-optics and Disney's multiplane. There followed folkloric films by the Diehl brothers and, in 1940, a cartoon by Hans Held about the weaker animals in the forest combining together with good military strategy to drive out the nasty 'trouble-making' fox. Fischerkoesen was in subtle dialogue with the Nazi world of do's and don'ts. His film *Verwitterte Melodie* (*Weather-beaten Melody*) of 1942 followed a bee through layers of sky, grass and flowers until it comes across a broken-down phonograph abandoned in a meadow. The bee uses its sting – and, less successfully, a hedgehog uses a needle – to draw out sound from a swing hit on the turntable. It rings out 'the week would not be worthwhile were it not for the weekend when we can get away to enjoy nature'. In 1942 Goebbels encouraged the founding of 'Deutsche Zeichenfilm GmbH'. But the company's sole product was 1943's *Der arme Hansi* by Frank Leberecht, wherein a canary is subjected to distressing levels of gratuitous violence.

All this was on offer, but its charms were insufficient for the bigwigs. And luckily for them, despite the dissolution of the Disney–Germany axis, those in the inner circle were allowed to view any Disney films that the Reichsfilm Archive could get its hands on – for 'purposes of study'. In this way the chosen few saw *Snow White and the Seven Dwarfs*, *Pinocchio*, *Fantasia*, *Dumbo* and *Bambi*.[83] And they enjoyed the films, as did the rest of the cinema-going world. They might even have found extra titbits to relish, such as the hints of anti-Semitism and anti-gypsy attitude evident in the portrayal of Stromboli in *Pinocchio*, a film replete with Alpine village scenes and echoes of Rothenburg ob der Taube. It has Germanic influences in the carved workshop, and Geppetto is voiced by a German actor who was a Nazi sympathizer.[84] And if they felt offended by the German accent of the sadistic ringmaster in *Dumbo*, they might have been proud of the Austro-German origins of *Bambi*, a popular book by Felix Salten, published in 1923.[85] Or they might have responded to the images of centralized authority in *Fantasia* – the conductor, the sorcerer, both exerting control over their minions, reinstalling order where chaos might rule. Indicating that with the dissolution of the trade relationship nothing too ideological was at stake – at least from the point of view of the Nazi echelon – on 12 February 1940 Goebbels noted in his diary that he had enjoyed immensely his private viewing of *Snow White and the Seven Dwarfs*: 'A great artistic creation. A fairy-tale for grown-ups, thought through to the smallest detail and made with great love of humans and nature.' However, the official Reichsfilm Archive label, written out for the inner circle of Nazis who had access to the archive, stated: 'The Grimm fairy-tale has been transformed according to the American mentality.'[86]

On 11 December 1941 Germany declared war on America. Five days later the *Film-Kurier* said goodbye to Disney:

> In a Jewish film theatre in Zurich a new Walt Disney film called *Fantasia* has appeared. It is about a kitschification of sublime German cultural assets, such as Bach, Beethoven, Schubert, of which probably only the North American mental attitude is capable in this grotesque form. Disney seeks to execute the breadth of thought and feeling of the greatest German musicians in colour-animated drawings of the thinnest substance. Never have his drawing means worked as limitedly as in the interpretation of the unlimitedness of this music. It is quite a monstrous undertaking to illustrate a Bach fugue with red waves and violin bows, stars and clouds undulating around each other. With Beethoven's 'Pastoral Symphony' not even the appearance of a serious interpretation in images is provided. Here earthly centaurettes are offered with violet hair, pedicuring their hooves and allowing themselves to have roses plaited into their manes by cupids. Apart from this tasteless drawing the film is filled up with yet more kitsch, which spreads into the frame stories. Mickey Mouse, who plays Goethe's 'Sorcerer's Apprentice', runs over to a podium after the end of the story's portrayal in order to be thanked by the conductor of the Philadelphia Symphony Orchestra, who appears illuminated by Bengal lights. The musicians who appear in naturalistic takes do not tune their instruments in the intermission but play a hot jazz number between Tchaikovsky and Beethoven. This assassination of European culture seems to have got on the nerves of even the

Swiss press, who normally cannot praise American films highly enough. The Swiss radio-journal writes of a heinous crime, 'that building up pure music of a Bach and a Beethoven lathers it up with the brightly coloured foam of a subversive imagination. The cleavage between its serious power and the poverty (not to speak of the wretchedness) of the kitsch pictures afford the music lover bodily pain'. 'Disney profanes the metaphysical. It would be only a little leap to show the holy lord as a roller skater.' Not without a certain *Schadenfreude* do we hear these Swiss voices. 'The spirits that they call up…' This analogy from the sorcerer's apprentice, which is even exemplified in *Fantasia* by Mickey Mouse, has gained only an all too direct relation to the Swiss *Biedermänner*.[87] Germany quite punctually defended itself against such cultural imports from the USA, even before war broke out. If now students at high schools in Zurich protest against *Fantasia*, may they thank the Swiss film Jews for this gift.[88]

The Nazi film critics echoed Greenberg's vocabulary when they denounced Disney as kitsch, but they did not speak in the name of the aesthetic autonomy – or indeed social autonomy – that motivated Greenberg. The *Volk* would not get the chance to make up its own mind about the merits and demerits of avant-garde art and kitsch and 'Great German Art' and Hollywood film. Only the upper echelons of the Nazi party would have the opportunity to see this film.

eye-candy and adorno's silly symphonies

to grow up just like donald duck

In October 1935 a Disney Silly Symphony called *Music Land* was released. The story features a Saxophone boy who is in love with a Violin girl. This young prince, son of the King of the Isle of Jazz, has been discovered courting the princess-daughter of the Queen of the Land of Symphony. The prince is thrown into jail. When word reaches the prince's father jazz instruments turn into guns and a battle is fought. The prince and the princess are nearly drowned in the Sea of Discord, but a cease-fire is announced. The cartoon concludes with a double wedding and the uniting of the two kingdoms by the Bridge of Harmony. High culture and popular modernism smack up against each other. *Music Land* aims at a synthesis of high and low, a redefinition of culture. The popular, that which needs bringing up – but not too sharply – is represented by jazz. Classical music is for highbrows. They need to loosen up a little. And the swingers need more culture.

This was no surprise. Disney had been operating for some time with one foot in the mass entertainment camp and the other in a rather more salubrious place. The Disney studios had been the first animation outfit to run its own art school. From 1931 animators attended evening classes at the Chouinard Art Institute in Los Angeles, but at the end of 1932 a Disney art school was set up at the Hyperion studio. Two years later the art school provided a strict training programme and tested out hopeful animators. Such attention to detail – effectively the creation and management of a house style – paid off and earned Disney personal accolades.

The individual Disney and the studio are frequently conflated in this way, a mistake encouraged by the Walt Disney signature looming large on the cartoons and paraphernalia.

In July 1933, enthusiastic about Disney's successful exploitation of the Technicolor process the previous year, Dorothy Grafly, art critic for the *Philadelphia Enquirer*, wrote: 'Walt Disney has at last given the world what should have come through established art channels – the creative exploit of the animated cartoon in color, probably the first genuinely American art since that of the indigenous Indian.'[1] Such tributes continued in the next decade. David Low, for example, branded him 'Leonardo da Disney' in January 1942 in the *New Republic*, and noted his 'artistry and extension of range' and his 'understanding of the meaning of observed movement'. And art critic Emily Genauer applauded the comprehension of modern abstract art displayed in *Fantasia* where some of the animated segments recall Kandinsky and some Miró. 'And the opening night audience – many of whom, doubtless, raise up their hands in horror at abstract paintings – loved it.'[2] Genauer presented some proof of Walter Benjamin's thesis, which hinged on the advent of mechanically reproduced mass-spectator culture: 'The backward attitude toward a Picasso painting, for example, turns into the progressive reaction toward, for example, a Chaplin movie.' And the obverse: 'Although paintings began to be publicly exhibited in galleries and salons, there was no way for the masses to organize and control themselves in their reception. Thus the same public which responds in a progressive manner toward a grotesque film is bound to react in a backward manner to surrealism.'[3] Perhaps Kendall O'Connor, the layout artist for the 'Dance of the Hours' sequence in *Fantasia*, confirmed this later:

> In case the complex witchery of other *Fantasia* sequences may lead you to feel that your dance of the hours has the subtlety of a barn door, let me assure you that this is the art that conceals art. In fact, we concealed the art from almost a graphic league of nations. We concealed the art of France in the form of a flat pattern à la Matisse, and Picassine color; and from Japan, architectural space division and block prints. From Africa we brought masks and weird proportions which we concealed along with the primitive instinct to dance. America and Greece contributed when a rash of dynamic symmetry broke out in the layout room.... From Russia, Eisenstein's symphonic principles of handling graphic

forms threatened to turn our pencils into batons until this tendency was concealed by crass considerations such as the need for our audience to know what
was going on.[4]

Disney artists were expected to know some art history, and were con-
fidently working an eclectic range of influences into the new feature-length
productions. Their visual language might occasionally draw on modernist
experiment as part of the palette of styles. Disney hoped that he was
raising the cultural level of the masses through his worthy artistic product.
This was the meaning of *Fantasia*, the classical music extravaganza. Once
he had decided to extend the Silly Symphonies principle into a feature-
length classical music animation, Disney was compelled to reflect on the
meaning of 'culture'. The impulse behind 'such a radically different type
of entertainment' as *Fantasia* was Walt's 'faith in the discrimination of the
average person'. Feild quoted the following thoughts from Disney in 1942:

> We simply figured that if ordinary folks like ourselves could find entertainment
> in these visualizations of so-called classical music, so would the average audi-
> ence. I believe that you will find this spontaneous reaching out for the fine and
> the beautiful in all mankind; it is man's indestructible and godlike quality, and
> the guarantee of his future. All men want to be better than they are. And once
> a man's tasted freedom, he will never be content to be a slave.[5]

That year the question of culture must have been playing on Disney's
mind, for he voiced similar thoughts on the radio on 1 March 1942, in a
lecture titled 'Our American Culture', broadcast during the intermission of
a performance at New York Metropolitan Opera. There he noted that
Dopey was as well qualified as he to discuss culture in America, for culture
belongs 'equally' to all of us.

> As a matter of fact, at times I have caught myself viewing the word 'culture'
> with suspicion – it seemed to have an un-American look to me, sort of snobbish
> and affected, as if it thought it was better than the next fellow. Actually, as I
> understand it, culture isn't that kind of snooty word at all. As I see it, a person's
> culture represents his appraisal of the things that make up life. And a fellow
> becomes cultured, I believe, by selecting that which is fine and beautiful in life,
> and throwing aside that which is mediocre and phoney. Sort of a series of free,
> very personal choices, you might say. If this is true, then I think it follows that
> 'freedom' is the most precious word to culture. Freedom to believe what you
> choose – and [to] read, think, say, and be what you choose. In America, we are

guaranteed those freedoms. It is the constitutional privilege of every American to become cultured or to just grow up like Donald Duck. I believe that this spiritual and intellectual freedom which we Americans enjoy is our greatest cultural blessing. Therefore it seems to me that the first duty of culture is to defend freedom and resist all tyranny.[6]

The freedom to choose to be Donald Duck or the freedom to reject refinement defines Disney's notion of a cultured society. But Donald Duck could go quite far with his rejection of culture. His nihilism was quite stunning, for example in *Mickey's Amateurs* (1937), where Donald Duck gives an inspirational recitation of his favourite poem, only to be hooted off stage by the audience for forgetting lines. Worked up by the audience's taunting, he rushes out and returns clutching a machine-gun. He fires several rounds into the audience while reciting 'Twinkle Twinkle Little Star'.

The development of the Silly Symphonies with their locking of musical beats to film speed, and the development of the multiplane camera, pioneered in 1937 in *The Old Mill*, were pushing things in a more sophisticated direction – away from cheap nihilism into a realm where realist depth and the foregrounding of musical excellence were to play pivotal roles. The extravagant *Fantasia* began as a Silly Symphony proposal. Paul Dukas's musical piece *The Sorcerer's Apprentice* was to be animated with Mickey Mouse in the leading role. Then other sequences were added and the project grew into something to be called *Concert Feature*. Some would say that this development, in line with Disney's definition of culture, was quintessentially 'middlebrow', and was setting film on a course fit for the new age of 'book of the month' clubs and the like. *Fantasia* was completed in November 1940. In October 1937 Disney had begun to plan the first section, the 'Sorcerer's Apprentice' sequence, and its rough continuity was ready by early November. In the middle of November all seven hundred members of the Disney workforce received a synopsis of Goethe's ballad. Psychological colour effects were emphasized in the sequence, and Freddy Moore's modelling sheets gave Mickey Mouse's eyes irises and pupils, in order to increase his range of expression. In a reference to German expressionist techniques, shadow play is used. In the opening scenes of the 'Sorcerer's Apprentice' sequence, Mickey Mouse's shadow stretches across the cave's wall; the shadows of his hands stretch out to bring the broom to life. He dances into shadow and the broom's shadow darkens his face. When he attacks the overeager broom, snapping it in two, the act is shown as shadow play, just as in a Fritz Lang or a Murnau film. This is grotesque horror, the intensification of effect so manipulated in *The Cabinet of Dr. Caligari* or *M: A City Seeks a Murderer*, but it is also a hilarious – ironic – realism as drawn objects without any substance produce befitting shadows where they block light. This same light makes the substance of cinema.

When *Fantasia* was first released, it was restricted to only a few theatres, suggesting that its audience was quite circumscribed. The most prominent music critics were invited to its premiere in New York. Most of them vilified the film. For them, the music was submerged in the images and so was lost, or they thought that the images imposed too rigid a deciphering of the music's evocations. They noted how the cinema audience fidgeted too much. The music critics did not feel at ease. Panovsky registered this sense of critical unease in the 1947 revisions to his essay 'Style and Medium in the Motion Pictures', first written in 1934. Early Disney films and some sequences in the later ones represent, within their self-imposed limitations, a chemically pure distillation of cinematic possibilities. But the critic Panovsky felt obliged to catalogue a 'fall from grace' that occurred 'when *Snow White* introduced the human figure and when *Fantasia* attempted to picturalize The World's Great Music'.

> The very virtue of the animated cartoon is to animate, that is to say endow lifeless things with life, or living things with a different kind of life. It effects a metamorphosis, and such a metamorphosis is wonderfully present in Disney's animals, plants, thunderclouds and railroad trains. Whereas his dwarfs, glamourized princesses, hillbillies, baseball players, rouged centaurs and *amigos* from South America are not transformations but caricatures at best, and fakes or vulgarities at worst. Concerning music, however, it should be borne in mind that its cinematic use is no less predicated upon the principle of coexpressability than is the cinematic use of the spoken word. There is music permitting or even requiring the accompaniment of visible action (such as dances, ballet music and any kind of operatic compositions) and music of which the opposite is true; and this is, again, not a question of quality (most of us rightly prefer a waltz by Johann Strauss to a symphony by Sibelius) but one of intention. In *Fantasia* the hippopotamus ballet was wonderful, and the Pastoral Symphony and 'Ave Maria' sequences were deplorable, not because the cartooning in the first case was infinitely better than in the two others, and certainly not because Beethoven and

Schubert are too sacred for picturalization, but simply because Ponchielli's 'Dance of the Hours' is coexpressible while the Pastoral Symphony and the 'Ave Maria' are not.[7]

Middlebrowness was plain for everyone to see, not just the critics but also the assistant entomologist from Horley in England who responded to a 1943 mass-observation questionnaire:

Fantasia, fantasia, fantasia, fantasia, fantasia and fantasia. Has there been another film without any propaganda in it worth spending 10d on during the last 12 months? (NB I exclude propaganda, because like excretion, it is not meant to be entertainment.) *Fantasia* is very nearly art.[8]

Very nearly art, then, as agreed the architect in the Pioneer Corps who remarked that he saw in 'parts of it a great work of art'. The musician–journalist–author from Brighton noticed how 'desperately tasteless' it was in part.

Perhaps Disney's interest in raising the cultural *niveau* of animation was merely a response to the enhanced cultural capital of Hollywood. For now there were many exiled European intellectuals in Los Angeles: artists, writers and critics who had fled Nazi Germany or the Soviet Union and hoped to find a living or a handout in California with its thriving culture industries. Adorno and Horkheimer moved to Santa Monica, from New York, in 1941 because Horkheimer's bad health required a warmer climate. Hanns Eisler went there in 1942. The European Film Fund was arranging work for distinguished émigrés to justify their stay. Schoenberg was there. Brecht was around. There were many others and they all came across each other at 'salons'. Eisler ran into his former tutor Schoenberg and resumed a friendship broken off for political reasons in 1925. Brecht met Schoenberg and Chaplin at Salka Viertel's salons. William Dieterle, Fritz Lang, Otto Klemperer, Dimitri Tiomkin, Billy Wilder, Adorno, Stravinsky, Max Reinhardt and countless others dropped in on the Santa Monica house.[9] Disney was able to draw on this job-seeking horde, instigating at Burbank numerous encounters of European high culture and American popular modernism. Some of them dropped into the studios. Thomas Mann dropped by and looked at the storyboards for the 'Sorcerer's Apprentice' sequence, and it was he who informed Disney that Paul Dukas's music was based on Goethe's poem *Der Zauberlehrling*. Perhaps he told his neighbour Adorno about his visit later, for the two men were in contact in the exile years when Mann drew on Adorno's music theory for his novel *Doktor Faustus*. Prokofiev visited Disney at the studio in February 1938. Stravinsky came to the studios in December 1939. He was checking up on the progress of the animation of *The Rite of Spring*. Disney had first heard it on 13 September 1938, when he exclaimed: 'This is marvellous! It would be perfect for prehistoric animals'.[10] Disney risked the possibility of a creation-ist boycott, and turned his flash of inspiration into a sequence of *Fantasia*.

Eric Walter White's 1931 study for the Bloomsbury set had already drawn links between Stravinsky and animation. He had noted how formal and stylized animated cartoons were.

> In construction they somewhat resemble the artificial French music of the eight-eenth century; but in spirit and technique they are nearer to the music Stravinsky wrote at Morges about 1917 – the groups of Russian Songs, the easy piano duets, the pianola study that was orchestrated later and forms the piece known as *Madrid* in the *Four Studies*, and parts of *Les Noces* and *The Soldier's Tale*. In these compositions Stravinsky deliberately set himself the problem of utilising only the simplest materials. He confined his tunes to a series of changes rung on a mere handful of notes, and he chose his accompaniments for their rigidity, their capacity for infinite repetition and the 'shot colour' effects he could obtain from them by merely shifting the musical stress.

It was this rigidity, the repetition compulsion, that Adorno attacked in Stravinsky's music, so much so that his *Philosophie der neuen Musik* (*Philosophy of Modern Music*), written through the 1940s, pitched Schoenberg directly against Stravinsky.[11] Stravinsky's composition *The Rite of Spring* is said to have come to the composer in a dream, when he tapped some unconscious folk memory, and imagined a scene of pagan ritual in which a sacrificial virgin danced herself to death. Its origin was almost involun-tary, its connections primitivist. Debussy, one of the first to hear it, fixed its primitivism in the remark: 'c'est une musique nègre'.[12] Adorno censured *The Rite of Spring* for playing 'the familiar aesthetic game with barbarism', and evacuating all 'culture' from the work – that is, abolishing all that is humanly eloquent. When culture peels away, it reveals barbarism. *The Rite of Spring* roused 'only bodily animation instead of offering meaning'.[13] The music precludes empathy, allowing an objectification of the dramatic figures.

Stravinsky, jibes Adorno, is driven by the 'adolescent' desire to become a proven 'classicist' rather than a 'mere modernist'.[14] *The Rite of Spring* is secretly a conservative work, part of a fashionable vogue for African sculpture that reveals 'an anti-humanist sacrifice to the collective – sacrifice without tragedy, made not in the name of a renewed image of man, but only in the blind affirmation of a situation recognized by the victim.'[15] Stravinsky's primitivism is an attempt to invoke the pre-individual, pre-dialectical disposition by conjuring up the totem clan. Atrocity is presented without mitigation: 'The aesthetic nerves tremble with the desire to regress to the Stone Age.'[16] The attack on the individual ego reveals an anti-civilizational drive.

But at the same time, Stravinsky hoped to gain control over regression by offering an image of it. His primeval chaos is the effect of immense selection and stylization. There is violence in the music, in its hyper-rhythmicity. The rhythm hits the listener as shocks. To this extent Stravinsky is as much an expressionist as Schoenberg and other shock-emitting modernists. Through such shocks 'the individual becomes conscious of his nothingness in the face of the gigantic machine of the entire system'.[17] Stravinsky's work is sado-masochistic. In *The Rite of Spring* the listener is assaulted by compulsive blows and shocks that come from nowhere, and are not prepared by an anticipatory build-up:

> The musical subject makes no attempt to assert itself, and contents itself with the reflexive absorption of the blows. The subject behaves literally like a critically injured victim of an accident which he cannot absorb and which, therefore, he repeats in the hopeless tension of dreams.[18]

In essence, in the sounds of *The Rite of Spring* can be heard the submission of the individual to the collective, in a system that uses sacrifice as mode of domination. The 'ideological trick' of *The Rite of Spring* is to render this domination without antagonism. Stravinsky's work is infantilist, worn-out and ruined, as threatening as the worst nightmares. It represents a dance of the lifeless with mechanized movements. Stravinsky's music was not a critical practice. For Adorno, in its mechanistic assertiveness, its celebratory submission of the subject to the collective, its sadism, its emphasis of the static, the rhythmic and the spatial, it resembled its contemporary, jazz. *The*

Rite of Spring indeed made use of jazz syncopation and technique. The jazz subject, lonesome, quarantined, and yet plunged psychologically into the fake collectivity of a music that, notwithstanding the seeming freedom of its improvised solos, is scarcely able to conceal its reliance on the military march, mirrors Stravinsky's subject. Both musics were, for Adorno's ears, uncritical. Critical art had to be mimetic, mapping the objectification and alienation of the social world, but that mimesis needed to be torn from a natural immediacy through the integration of a constructively rational moment. Expression, vivid mimeticism, is shot through with self-conscious moments of reflection, as in the work of Schoenberg and Klee, and in Picasso's *Guernica*. From Adorno's perspective, it made sense that Disney would use Stravinsky. Bold, brash, colourful and affirmative, modernism had become spectacle, its critical edge blunted.

For Adorno, jazz as such is kitsch, but he defended Alban Berg's trans-formation of jazz against the kitsch deployment of jazzy themes. An essay on Berg notes Berg's struggles with the saxophone. Jazz has to be the music that represents the commercial world.[19] But for Adorno jazz, a 'phantasmagoria of modernity', is illusory, a counterfeit freedom. Jazz is the music of counterfeit integration of impotent subjectivity and inhuman objectivity. Jazz follows the law of the pseudo-metre, and peculiar to it is the way that it uses a basic sustained metre that appears to be fashioned from differing metres. Thus, while an illusion of freedom is maintained, the rigid authority of the metre persists. Berg has to use and abuse it – turning the unfreedom of its law into expression. Berg's 'Der Wein', with its 'tango-kitsch', embraces what it criticizes and, like a boa constrictor, squeezes life from it: 'the tango peers out of the music as with the empty eyes of a skull'.

> Kitsch, not tastefully dismissed but rather extended by its own laws, is, under these compositional hands, transformed into style; thus the banal stands re-vealed as the phenomenon of the commodity and thus as the prevailing societal premise: but at the same time as the cipher of its downfall.[20]

Stravinsky's music, in contrast, can perhaps become the kitsch that Disney makes of it because it has not sealed itself against that process. In *Time* magazine, in 1940, Stravinsky confessed that Disney's palaeontological cataclysm was what he had in mind all along in *The Rite of Spring*.[21] Perhaps the agreement was simply politic, or conformist. In later years it was said that Stravinsky had been critical of the Disney version of *The Rite of Spring*, but even if that were so he had sold Disney an option on three more pieces. In 1946, in an article in *Musical Digest*, Stravinsky turned on Disney. The terms, however, in which he wrote – the recourse to the pretechnologized individual listener, possessor of a sensitive 'soul' – might still not palliate, for Adorno, the charges levelled.

> When Walt Disney used *Le sacre du printemps* for *Fantasia*, he told me: 'Think of the numbers of people who will now be able to hear your music.' Well, the numbers of people who consume music is of interest to somebody like Mr. Hurok, but it is of no interest to me. The mass adds nothing to art. It cannot raise the level, and the artist who aims consciously at mass appeal can do so only by lowering his own level. The soul of each individual who listens to my music is important to me, not the mass feeling of a group. Music cannot be helped by means of an increase in the quantity of listeners, be this increase effected by the film or by any other medium. It can be helped only by an increase in the quality of listening, the quality of the individual soul.[22]

Stravinsky makes his own assault on the mass machinations of figures such as Disney and Sol Hurok, the Ukrainian émigré who introduced American audiences to ballet and expressive dance in the shape of Pavlova, Isadora Duncan and the like. Stravinsky is an 'artist', in pursuit of quality not quantity.[23]

The challenge of mass culture loomed simultaneously with the success of the Disney enterprise. In 1937 Mortimer J. Adler wrote *Art and Prudence*, a defence of the artistic value of film, measured, ahistorically, in Aristotelian terms as exemplar of the essence of art: 'imitation that combines the greatest similarity of form with the greatest difference of content'.[24] For Adler great art must be popular at one time or over time, and must satisfy all tastes. Adler brandishes Disney's cartoons as a great contribution to artistic heritage. Disney attains such perfection in his field, outclassing our best critical capacity to analyse while also delighting children and simple folk. Max Horkheimer composed a fierce retort in 1941 in a review written for the *Zeitschrift für Sozialforschung*. Adler believes in popularity and the market, and, in positivist fashion, esteems forms of popular entertainment that are but 'demands evoked, manipulated and by implication deteriorated by the cultural industries', notes Horkheimer, setting in circulation the trademark phrase of Frankfurt School critique.[25] Adler's static way of thinking levels everything: he confuses Raphael's and Disney's scenic backgrounds, and muddles up the Hays Office with the guardians of the Platonic Republic, exalting the former in the process.[26] He hopes to cut art free of history, measuring art's worth by its breadth of dissemination.

> While undertaking to raise art above history and keep it pure he betrays it to the contemptible trash of the day. Elements of culture isolated and disseemered from the historical process may appear as similar as drops of water; yet they are as different as Heaven and Hell. For a long time now, Raphael's blue horizons have been quite properly a part of Disney's landscapes, in which *amoretti* frolic more unrestrainedly than they ever did at the feet of the Sistine Madonna. The sunbeams almost beg to have the name of a soap or a toothpaste emblazoned on them; they have no meaning except as a background for such advertising. Disney and his audiences, as well as Adler, unswervingly stand for the purity of the blue horizon, but perfect loyalty to principles isolated from the concrete situation makes them turn into their very opposite and finally results in perfect relativism.[27]

Disney's azure skies may be a duplication of Raphael's heavens but, for Horkheimer, social change – the spread of commodity capitalism, the swelling of a mass market – has meant that they have more to do with the commercial world than the art world. Horkheimer perceives an invisible writing traced on their very form. Disney and his audiences cannot help but be implicated in the commodity swindle. And Horkheimer must have known that the characterization of Walt Disney as adman was truer in Disney's case than any other creator before him. Disney was a pioneer of cultural merchandising and advertising. Mickey Mouse had not only appeared as a toy, but had also endorsed coffee, detergent, stockings, firecrackers, shoes and much more. Of course, at first many of these appearances were illegal, unlicensed, but Disney soon put a stop to that and consolidated the licensing to the benefit of the business. Horkheimer's analysis of the degradation of Raphael in Disney contradicted Jean Prévost's comparison, neatly clipped from *Vendredi* by Walter Benjamin in 1938.

> It seems to me that a large number of painters and draughtsmen, those who richly imagine the beautiful subject, those who the great American critic Berenson calls illustrators, and whose great master is Raphael, have not been treated

according to their value by modern painting, which is too jealously plastic. If the animated drawings have a glorious future, they rescue this part of art, which is wilting at this moment; they rediscover its true role, which is to guide the imagination. Raphael taught humanity about classical antiquity. The art of Disney simply shows us once more the fairy-tale, and already we know with what force it teaches us to see the marvellous.[28]

Horkheimer sets out his analysis of the historical circumstances of culture. The private realm that is the realm of true art, of inner life, is increasingly under threat, because of the decline of the family. In place of the family as a socializing influence, mass culture steps in to manipulate the child.[29] The substance of the individual remains locked up in himself, though a world of technical omnipotence, increasing independence of production from its location, the transformation of the family and the socialization of existence could be the basis for an abolition of current miseries. The same process that liberated the slave and put an end to serfdom breaks the individual into two. One part is socialized, one part is free. The free part is burdened with a mortgage, its 'freedom' then construed in one particular way. Free to own, which means free to owe, and certainly not free to think, for popular judgement is directed from above, while public opinion surveys reveal only a mechanism not the human essence. In a bureaucratically organized society, where the mass is produced and reproduced as much as are their opinions of what is popular, there is no possibility of imagining a world different from the one in which we live. Social pressure produces conformity, and Adler mistakes conformity for self-willed choice. 'There are times when faith in the future of mankind can be kept alive only through absolute resistance to the prevailing responses of men. Such a time is the present.'[30]

Horkheimer rebukes Adler's praise of film's imitation of the real. For Horkheimer film's realism just affirms what is: the bad reality of the present. There is no negation in its blank naturalism, unlike *Guernica* or Joyce's prose. Both of these break with the code of realism to provide an alternative perspective, even if it only be one of isolation, loss of community and despair. Modern art has a consciousness cut off from society and 'forced into queer, discordant forms', for a time 'when the happy countenance has assumed the face of frenzy and only the melancholy faces of the frenzied remain a sign of hope'.[31] Horkheimer announces that the only outcome of opinion surveys is to discover that all people know themselves to be wicked and treacherous. They reveal themselves as the evil cunning beings that the demagogues know so well how to handle.[32] Horkheimer insists that such evil as exists is produced by society's violence directed at a human nature striving to develop into new forms.[33] And new cultural forms, he argues, accustom those masses to a brutality that is actuality, but passes it off on them sweetly by making it so amusing.

> The generation that allowed Hitler to become great takes its adequate pleasure in the convulsions which the animated cartoon imposes upon its helpless characters, not in Picasso, who offers no recreation and cannot be 'enjoyed' anyhow. Misanthropic, spiteful creatures, who secretly know themselves as such, like to be taken for the pure, childish souls who applaud with innocent approval when Donald Duck gets a cuffing.[34]

Horkheimer's essay was clearly a pre-study for the notorious chapter in *Dialectic of Enlightenment* titled 'The Culture Industry: Enlightenment as Mass Deception'. That book, co-authored with Adorno, was written between 1941 and 1944. It was an anguished cry against standardization in culture. In Nazi Germany *Gleichschaltung* ruled, and Hollywood was standardized. These two circumstances mirrored each other. Adorno and Horkheimer shift effortlessly between the two scenes. Mass culture and fascism both draw on psychological dependency and social conformism. Hollywood, however, dominates the competition in producing uniform product and acquiescent constituencies. Hollywood is Nazi Germany's liberal face, but its teeth are whiter. In Hollywood studios are associated with certain genres and stars. It appears as a calculated front of diversity in a rationalized commercial system: 'for culture now impresses the same stamp on everything'. 'Films, radio and magazines make up a system which is uniform as a whole and in every part.'[35] This was an extraordinary thing to write at a time when America presented itself as the saviour of the world from fascism, and when all sane and cultured types were supposed to be united in a common cultural front against the fascist enemy, producing through mass forms, such as Hollywood films or citified folk music or cartoons, an anti-fascist popular culture.

Cartoons came to figure as a key vehicle in the analysis of the industrialization of culture. A study of their historical development reveals the increasing rationalization of low cultural products. Over time, cartoons come to train the human subject to march to a new rhythm, one that is related to an inexorable unfolding of fate. Donald Duck's function is seen to turn in on the audience – rather than simply an excuse for sadistic pleasure, the cartoons become a training in masochistic behaviour.

> Cartoons were once exponents of fantasy as opposed to rationalism. They ensured that justice was done to the creatures and objects they electrified, by giving the maimed species a second life. All they do today is to confirm the victory of technological reason over truth. A few years ago they had a consistent plot which only broke up in the final moments in a crazy chase, and thus resembled the old slapstick comedy. Now, however, time relations have shifted. In the very first sequence a motive is stated so that in the course of the action destruction can get to work on it: with the audience in pursuit, the protagonist becomes the worthless object of general violence. The quantity of organized amusement changes into the quality of organized cruelty. The self-elected censors of the film industry (with whom it enjoys a close relationship) watch over the unfolding of the crime, which is as drawn out as a hunt. Fun replaces the pleasure which the sight of an embrace would allegedly afford, and postpones satisfaction to the day of the pogrom. In so far as cartoons do any more than accustom the senses to the new tempo, they hammer into every brain the old lesson that continuous friction, the breaking down of all individual resistance, is the condition of life in this society. Donald Duck in the cartoons and the unfortunate in real life get their thrashing so that the audience can learn to take their own punishment.[36]

Cartoons teach a lesson, not in the make up of actuality, but in social conformism, and the inevitability of violence if the subject acquiesces too slowly to submission.[37] Clowning around has been marshalled for a sinister purpose. The cartoons do not just promote the butchery of others; they make audiences accede to their own persecution, be it in a democracy or in a fascist state. Cartoonists themselves testified to the importance of the violence and, as much as some characters were allowed to develop into fully rounded human types, others were essentially dehumanized. Ollie Johnston reminisced that in the shorts, as Mickey Mouse became more humanoid, Goofy and Donald became more preposterous and inhuman. It was not necessary that anyone believe in the characters as sincere entities, only that the beating taken was real.[38] Sincerity was reserved for Mickey Mouse alone, and his sincerity was cloying, too sickly sweet to be true. The animators knew that Donald Duck and Goofy had only 'personality'. 'Personality' is an externalized selfhood, and bears little relationship to subjectivity. Ghastly things befall Donald Duck and Goofy: they plunge two thousand feet, get electrocuted, detonated, dissected, ignited, squashed, drowned, frozen in a block of ice. Through it all their personality remains unaltered. Camera tricks develop to convey the experience of violence. When the first film footage of military engagement was shown in America in the early 1940s, it revealed that the camera vibrated with the force of explosions nearby. The cartoon camera took to jarring when Goofy walked into a wall (the pegs were moved back and forth for a brief moment). Accompanying the audience's willingness to view punishment is the vision of the charismatic leader who demands sacrifice. *Fantasia* flaunted fixation on a centralized point of power, in recurrent images of a man looking down, perhaps from a dais, such as the conductor's podium or the music commentator at his music-stand looking down on his audience or the figure of Mickey Mouse on the mountain-top, conducting the elements and the sorcerer at the top of the staircase restoring order. The power wielded by the legitimate sorcerer is tremendous – that is, effective – but that of his apprentice is not, for he is unable to control the forces that he has evoked without sanction. Jean Prévost asked whether perhaps America was the sorcerer's apprentice of the modern world. What forces had it unleashed in the field of culture? Disney seemed to be suggesting that the little people, all the Mr Americas, should leave well alone. Power is for the professionals. But that is not to say that Disney could screen out ideas that were far from his own. Given the European source of the story, it echoed back the echoes of before. Marx had noted in *The Communist Manifesto* that capitalist society has conjured up such gigantic means of production like 'the sorcerer who is no longer able to control the powers of the nether world whom he has called up by his spells'. This was a description for the anarchy of production and the tendency to overproduction. Perhaps, too, the fantastic powers summoned up in the *Fantasia* version of the story were those of capital, particularly in its Fordist form, and the multiplying brooms were an image of overproduction. For Marx, crises were brought about by the 'revolt of modern productive forces against modern conditions of production, against the property relations

Popeye, the sailor man

Walter Ruttmann, *Opus 1*, 1921

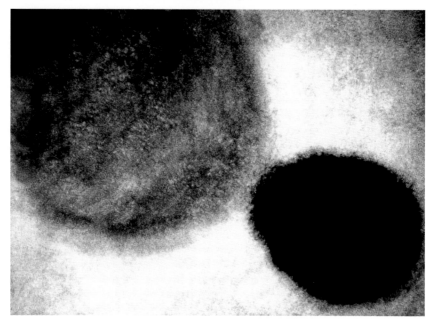

Walter Ruttmann, *Opus 2*, 1921

Walter Ruttmann, *Opus 3*, 1924

Walter Ruttmann, *Opus 3*, 1924

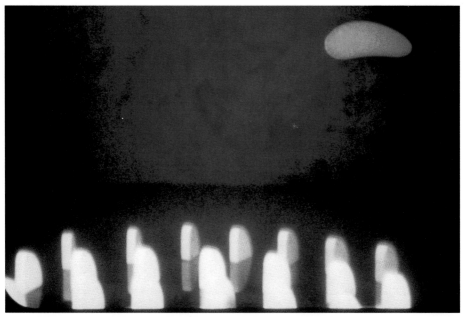

Oskar Fischinger, *Komposition in Blau*, 1935

Oskar Fischinger, *Kreise*, 1933

Oskar Fischinger, *R-1, Ein Formspiel*, 1927

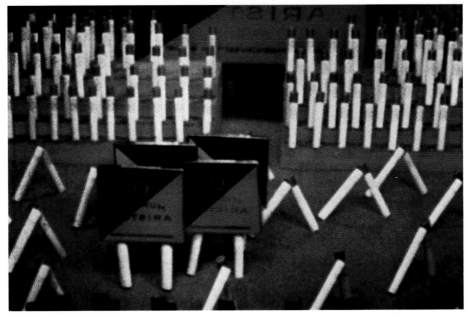

Oskar Fischinger, *Muratti Greift Ein*, 1934

A woodcut of Goethe's right eye as seen in a mirror,
with prism and magnifying glass, 1791

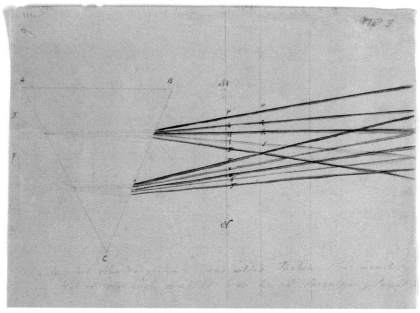

Goethe's polemical drawing against Newton's optics.
Two pencils of rays pass through a prism and exit as diverging bundles of five differently
coloured rays. Goethe wrote an epigram on the drawing: 'Newton made white out of all the
colours. He has made you believe many a thing to which your century gives credence.'

Disney's *Fantasia*, 1940

A cel setup on a preliminary background for
Disney's *Snow White and the Seven Dwarfs*, 1937

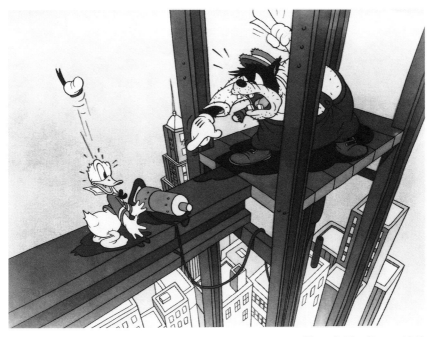

Disney's *The Riveter*, 1940

that are the conditions for the existence of the bourgeoisie and of its rule'. Those productive forces themselves could get animated and fight back.[39] They could strike back, or they could succumb again to the hand of authority, as seemed to happen again and again.

Addiction to the spectacle of punishment is evidence of the masses' acquiescence to a morality that is imposed on them. Confined by capialist production, body and soul, the workers uphold the ideology that ties them down, assert Adorno and Horkheimer:

> As naturally as the ruled always took the morality imposed upon them more seriously than did the rulers themselves, the deceived masses are today captivated by the myth of success even more than the successful are. Immovably, they insist on the very ideology which enslaves them. The misplaced love of the common people for the wrong which is done them is a greater force than the

cunning of the authorities. It is stronger even than the rigorism of the Hayes Office, just as in certain great times in history it has inflamed greater forces that were turned against it, namely the terror of the tribunals. It calls for Mickey Rooney in preference to the tragic Garbo, for Donald Duck instead of Betty Boop.[40]

This masochistic love for their rulers is the reason why the masses choose Donald Duck over Adorno's preference, the sexualized and immoral Betty Boop. The kitsch preferred is prudish and yet vicious. Adorno and Horkheimer, two men not totally opposed to low pleasures, reveal an interest in Betty Boop, the Fleischer studio missy. Here was a big-eyed chick with a short black dress, a garter and high heels, her story lines improvised in a studio that lacked a story department until the mid 1930s, allowing animators to unfold things gag by gag and unchecked. There were no directors to oversee the raunchy deployment of quick-fire gags. Through the 1930s Betty Boop's features, along with those of her dog Bimbo, were freezing into place on a model sheet. Then in 1935, following complaints from small town audiences, a makeover gave her wholesome clothing and her attention was turned to domestic tasks and loving animals. Instead of hip-swaying her way through impossible encounters in space and with dinosaurs, she became a 'rational' adult. Her vital juices squeezed out, she disappeared from screens in 1939. Adorno and Horkheimer might have witnessed this sanitizing process and seen how her pursuit of purity led to her demise.[41] It was a futile surrender to 'taste' – footsoldiered by the Hays Office Production Code Administration and the National Legion of Decency. This was the same procession of taste that insisted cow udders in Disney shorts be covered by little dresses.

> The industry submits to the vote which it has itself inspired. What is a loss for the firm which cannot fully exploit a contract with a declining star is a legitimate expense for the system as a whole. By craftily sanctioning the demand for rubbish it inaugurates total harmony. The connoisseur and expert are despised for their pretentious claim to know better than the others, even though culture is democratic and dispenses its privileges to all. In view of the ideological truce, the conformism of the buyers and the effrontery of the producers who supply them prevail. The result is a constant reproduction of the same thing.[42]

Popeye, the sailor man, underwent a similar process of refinement, after his cinematic debut in 1933. Cantankerous, bawdy, proletarian, a year after his birth he was succumbing to the Disney effect: nuggets of sentimentality and balletic moments merged in with the original grotesqueries. The problem, as Adorno sees it, is that low culture is not low enough – 'the eccentricity of the circus, peepshow, and brothel is as embarrassing to it as that of Schoenberg and Karl Kraus'. It expunges 'vulgarity, stupidity, and lack of polish', all things that might have been some sign of life.[43] The most successful players in the industry called the tune, and they were triumphant not because they truly delivered the most fancied goods, but because they fathered the audiences to fit the commodities, playing on the audience's socially induced infantilism, sense of worthlessness and self-hatred. Relentlessly the same point is hammered home by the culture industry: conform, and enjoy the spectacle of your own submission. The industry invades the psyche, squeezing inner nature to the smallest 'negative residue of freedom' as primal id, a spirit distorted by social contradictions. Drives are socially mediated. Culture is concerned with disciplining.

Betty Boop

> Culture has always played its part in taming revolutionary and barbaric instincts. Industrial culture adds its contribution. It shows the condition under which this merciless life can be lived at all. The individual who is thoroughly weary must use his weariness as energy for his surrender to the collective power which wears him out. In films, those permanently desperate situations which crush the spectator in ordinary life somehow become a promise that one can go on living. One has only to become aware of one's own nothingness, only to recognize defeat and one is one with it all.[44]

Adorno's objections to the public's opting for Donald Duck, and so its surrender to a masochism that made punishment – indeed genocide – imaginable, firmed up a complaint that he had levelled at Walter

Popeye, with Bluto and Olive Oyl

Benjamin in a letter in March 1936.[45] Part of this letter responded to Benjamin's claims about the effects of Disney and the funnies in 'The Work of Art in the Age of its Technical Reproducibility'. The highest culture and the lowest culture bear the stigmata of capitalism and elements of change, insists Adorno, against Benjamin's apparent disrespect for high art. Both have to remain in play – one cannot be sacrificed to the other. Indeed it is only the middlebrow – the quality film, for example – that should be discontinued.[46] Adorno agreed with Benjamin's critique of Franz Werfel. In his study of mass reproducible art, Benjamin had mocked Werfel for praising Max Reinhardt's film version of *A Midsummer Night's Dream*. Werfel regarded this filming of Shakespeare as film's deliverance from the sterile imitation of the external world with its streets, interiors, railway stations, restaurants, cars and beaches. All this mirroring, remarks Werfel, had stood in the way of film's rise to the realm of art. Film's true potentialities consist in its unique capacity for expressing the realm of the fairy-tale, the miraculous and the supernatural with natural means and incomparable convincing power.[47] Such comments went directly against

Benjamin's idea that it was precisely these prosaic urban zones that must be represented in film – and hardly as sterile imitations, but burst apart by filmic trickery. All those actual imprisoning interiors are blown apart by film's stretching of the laws of physics and geography. Space and time and movements through space and time are made elastic. The possibility of transformation is represented graphically on screen, though metaphorically. To insist that film linger in the supernatural, so that it may become art, is a double crime: fetishizing the hidebound 'auratic' entity called art and denying film's appropriate and democratic ability to represent and analyse the everyday.[48] Benjamin's dig at Werfel pleased Adorno, but it seemed to point to a contradiction in Benjamin's thought: 'But if you take Mickey Mouse instead, things are far more complicated, and the serious question arises as to whether the reproduction of every person really constitutes that *a priori* of the film which you claim it to be, or whether instead this reproduction belongs precisely to that "naïve realism", a registration of surface, whose bourgeois nature we so thoroughly agreed upon in Paris.' Adorno's comments on Mickey Mouse stop here, and maybe the cartoon mouse is mentioned only to represent mass culture in general, or is it a comment about the drawn status of Mickey Mouse, which shows up non-drawn film as just another type of surface registration, rather than an engagement with an actuality that has imprinted its details on film?[49] In any case, the lower sphere, he claims, can easily win a victory over poor high art. It could conceivably be more technically advanced than a hackneyed painterly or poetic effort, or more anarchic, or unconventional. But Adorno does not dwell on that. He wants to move quickly away from dubious modern art and the complications of low culture, to defend his favoured patch: Kafka and Schoenberg, the autonomous avant-garde. Benjamin's Brechtian hooliganism overlooks the 'technicality' of autonomous art, and overestimates the 'technicality' of mass culture, which tends in fact towards infantile mimeticism, and appeals to a dulled consciousness. Benjamin, notes Adorno, needs to abandon any hopes for the actual consciousness of workers because they 'bear all the marks of mutilation of the typical bourgeois character'. It was this mutilated audience of mass culture that Adorno was to spend so much time analysing. His critique of Benjamin homes in on the minds that are receptive to mass culture. He accuses Benjamin of inoculating himself against the horror of mass culture by overvaluing precisely what it is that makes it so dreadful: the laughter of the audience at a cinema. Such laughter is not therapeutic, good, liberatory, non-conformist, but is a manifestation of the 'worst bourgeois sadism'. Adorno thinks that he knows exactly what is happening when the audience splits its sides at the movies. He does not express it in the letter, but the theme of laughter occupies him in many of his subsequent writings.

Laughter is bound up with fear. Laughter 'is the echo of power as something inescapable'. Fun, a degraded form of pleasure, is 'a medicinal bath', which the pleasure industry never fails to prescribe.[50] Laughter is 'a fraud practised on happiness'. A 'laughing audience is a parody of humanity'.[51] This 'false' laughter is the signature tune of a barbaric life. For Adorno and Horkheimer, laughter signals the renunciation of childhood knowledge and ambition, and denotes the surrender to conformity and fitting in to the limits of socially sanctioned existence. The laughter of the culture industry banks on identification with the adult power of conformity, not childlike mirth at outfoxing that power. Later, in *The Authoritarian Personality*, Adorno propounds the argument that responses to propaganda are determined by earlier experiences in intimate family life. When Adorno and Horkheimer hear laughter, they hear either the terrible laughter of the apathetic spectator, or the barbaric laughter of the anti-Semite who tells jokes at Jewish expense. Kracauer sees, in *From Caligari to Hitler* (1947), German expressionist horror films as foretellings of the dictatorship to come, but Adorno and Horkheimer argue that the comedies are premonitions too: 'In Germany the graveyard stillness of the dictatorship already hung over the gayest films of the democratic era.'[52] Laughter is an escapism that provides no escape from the all-powerful injunction to have fun within the terms dictated. Culture-industry product works by setting up audience anticipation of the surprise that is in fact predictable, and so not really surprising.

> Banal though elaborate surprise interrupts the story-line. The tendency mischievously to fall back on pure nonsense, which was a legitimate part of popular art, farce and clowning, right up to Chaplin and the Marx Brothers, is most obvious in the unpretentious kinds. This tendency has completely asserted itself in the text of the novelty song, in the thriller movie, and in cartoons...[53]

The surprise is not the only predictable thing. Later, in 1964, Adorno describes Chaplin's brilliance in words that echo an earlier artistic excitement with cartoons.

> The Rastelli of mime, he plays with the countless balls of pure possibility, and fixes their restless circling into a fabric that has barely more in common with the causal world than Cloud Cuckoo Land has with the gravity of Newtonian physics. Incessant and spontaneous change: in Chaplin, this is the utopia of an existence that would be free of the burden of being one's self.[54]

The culture industry is all this is not: lacking spontaneity, closed to possibility, fixed. It asserts individual selfhood, personality, but this is individuality modelled on Yale keys, a pseudo-individualism. In short, the culture industry is boring. The record provides a way of imagining boredom. Pleasure must be effortless and so 'moves rigorously in the worn grooves of association'. Those worn grooves of the record are real. Music makes possible the boring into the psyche of culture industry values. That is what Adorno argues in the book that appeared three years after *Dialectic of Enlightenment – Composing for the Films*, written with Hanns Eisler.

quasi una fantasia

Eisler had worked on film music. He wrote some music for Ruttmann's *Opus III* in 1927, played by a chamber orchestra – two clarinets, a trumpet and a string trio, first live and then recorded using the Tri-Ergon process. Carl Robert Blum's chronometer invention allowed absolute synchronization between image and sound, a precision that underlined the geometrical shape of the abstract film. In 1931 Eisler worked on *Kuhle Wampe* with Brecht and Slatan Dudow, composing agitated music and music that was set in contrast to the screen activity. These experiments in counterpoising and synchronizing sound and image, carried out in the Weimar Republic, gave Eisler a context for criticizing Hollywood soundtracks. The contrapuntal use of sound had been advocated by film theorists, such as Paul Rotha, in 1928, when the Statement on Sound, authored by Eisenstein, Pudovkin and Alexandrov, raised fears about a loss of the culture of montage when sound weighs down the cutting up of actuality: 'Only the contrapuntal use of sound vis-à-vis the visual fragment of the montage will open up new possibilities for the development and perfection of montage. *The first experiments in sound must aim at a sharp discord with the visual images.*[55] In contrast, Eisler and Adorno argued, Hollywood film sound had brought about vulgarization and enchantment through sound. Music was the vanguard of this process of making audiences immature and dependent. In 1936 Adorno had written a rebuff to Benjamin's more positive thoughts on culture and mechanical reproduction, titled 'On the Fetish Character of Music and the Regression of Listening'. The article reflected on the exigencies of recorded music. The black disc is the commodity. Recorded music is heard differently. It is heard in parts, not as a totality. Through mass music's technique of the 'hook', its lulling into de-concentrated listening, and its ubiquity, because of an extensive machinery of distribution, listeners are remoulded as acquiescent purchasers, and kept retarded as children. The vicious circle spins, like a long-playing record. These easy listeners demand again and again the same dish, the one they know, the only one they get to hear, without making the effort that they have forgotten might be exertable. In *Composing for the Films*, Adorno and Eisler suggest that this effect is redoubled in film music soundtracks. The recording procedures 'neutralize' the music, flattening it out, losing its colour intensity and spatial depth. Then, added to this, when the music plays, as sound illustration to the film narrative – 'a running thread' that is more 'a picture of music' than music itself – it slips even further into the background, is further neutralized, and even the most advanced music is 'divested of its aggressiveness'.[56]

Adorno and Eisler shared a fundamental suspicion of music and how it works on people, especially in the context of film. In *Composing for the Films*, Trivas's *Niemandsland*, a pacifist film from 1930, is cited approvingly as a film that unveils music as the drug that it is in reality. Eisler had worked on the music for this film, producing 'closed, constructive pieces of music'. In it, he claims, music's intoxicating and harmfully irrational function becomes transparent. Music de-realizes.[57] Mostly the audience is not made aware of this function. It is simply subjected to it. Music lends the cinematic vision a veneer of humanity, thus obscuring its actual loss. Music is the antidote to the ghostliness of the picture. In the days of silent film, music backed the spectral silhouettes on the screen that mimicked our threatened muteness.[58] When sound film came, the music stayed, for the talking picture too is mute, peopled with speaking two-dimensional effigies, whose words are superimposed.[59] Music stayed to exorcize the fear that we are just as lifeless as the figures on screen. It hoped to sweeten the projected truth that we are but shadows of our former selves. It hoped to mask the whirr of the projector in the background that is the proof that we exist under the sway of mechanization.

But movie music is also the vehicle that clears the path for total commercialization. Echoing Horkheimer's comment on how in Disney cartoons the sunbeams almost beg to have the name of a brand of soap or toothpaste emblazoned on them, they claim:

> The whole form language of current cinema music derives from advertising. The motif is the slogan; the instrumentation the standardized picturesque; the accompaniments to animated cartoons are advertising jokes; and sometimes it is as though the music replaced the names of the commercial articles that the motion pictures do not yet dare mention directly.[61]

The introduction to *Composing for the Films* asserts a powerful relationship between the economic productive base and the cultural superstructure:

> In this advanced industrial age, the masses are compelled to seek relaxation and rest, in order to restore the labor power that has been spent in the alienated process of labor; and this need is the mass basis of mass culture. On it there has arisen the powerful amusement industry, which constantly produces, satisfies, and reproduces new needs.[60]

This cultural industry, monopolized and organized, mass-produces a new type of culture to service the needs of this large audience. Film is a perfect vehicle for the new culture. It consists of an amalgamation of bits of old autonomous art and entertainment forms, ideas and techniques from novels, drama, operetta, pulp fiction, revues. It is indiscriminate. The machine needs material. It sucks everything in.

> The old distinction between serious and popular art, between low-grade and refined autonomous art, no longer applies. All art, as a means of filling out leisure time, has become entertainment, although it absorbs materials and forms of traditional autonomous art as part of the so-called 'cultural heritage'.[62]

Adorno and Eisler are not dead set against popular, mass culture. Technology, they note, has opened up opportunities for art, and 'even in the poorest motion pictures there are moments when such opportunities are strikingly apparent'.[63] But technology also ties these films to big business, and that stamps a certain ideological character on the productions. Still, here is an objective contradiction. Here is the opportunity for critique. And the lowest culture escapes the middlebrow compromises of many culture industry products. Genre pictures, such as 'westerns', gangster films or horror films are easily superior to 'pretentious grade-A films'.[64] What offends is the aspiration to be 'unique' when the production is in fact so standardized. Music is a transmission belt of standardization. In another piece, 'Film Music – Work in Progress', probably written in 1941, Eisler's polemic is directed at the 'false associations' that music so readily conjures up. Traditional film music practice tended to select musical material because of its conventional resonances, and so its ability to express is further degraded. Eisler notes how symphonies come to sound like music for main and title credits – and he invokes a nightmarish vision of a man travelling in the jungle, meeting a lion that roars. After the roar 'the mystic words' 'MGM presents' flash up on the sky.[65] Again and again the same strings are plucked in order to achieve the desired affect. Except that the clichés may be too worn out to work any more.

> Such musical conventions are all the more dubious because their material is usually taken from the most recently bygone phase of autonomous music, which still passes as 'modern' in motion pictures. Forty years ago, when musical impressionism and exoticism were at their height, the whole-tone scale was regarded as a particularly stimulating, unfamiliar, and 'colorful' musical device. Today the whole-tone scale is stuffed into the introduction of every popular hit, yet in motion pictures it continues to be used as if it had just seen the light of day. Thus the means employed and the effects achieved are completely disproportionate. Such a disproportion can have a certain charm when, as in animated cartoons, it serves to stress the absurdity of something impossible, for instance, Pluto galloping over the ice to the ride of the Walkyries. But the whole-tone scale so overworked in the amusement industry can no longer cause anyone really to shudder.[66]

The cliché only works when it is deployed against itself. It has long stopped being effective in eliciting genuine reactions. Low culture might, with its less guarded attitude, hit on something truly shocking.

The horrors of sensational literary and cinematic trash lay bare part of the barbaric foundation of civilization. To the extent that the motion picture in its sensationalism is the heir of the popular horror story and dime novel and remains below the established standards of middle-class art, it is in a position to shatter those standards, precisely through the use of sensation, and to gain access to collective energies that are inaccessible to sophisticated literature and painting. It is this very perspective that cannot be reached with the means of traditional music. But modern music is suitable to it.[67]

Schoenberg's imaginary film music *Begeleitmusik zu einer Lichtspielszene*, with its sense of fear, is one example of soundtrack disrupting the soothing actions of music.[68] Its horror far outbids the terrible scenes of disaster in the Hollywood disaster movies *San Francisco* and *King Kong*. Adorno and Eisler recommend that modernist music combine forces with sensationalist cinema. The highest and the lowest together, but not compromising each other. Eisler carried this through in practice in his *Chamber Symphony op. 69*, the film music for *White Flood*. The film was made in 1940, by the filmmakers' cooperative Frontier Films; it was an educational film dealing with the formation of glaciers and the influence of the ice age – it even speculates on a new ice age yet to come. Its footage from Alaska and the Alps is accompanied by a musical score that tries to attain the precision of an animated cartoon in its synchronized treatment of each particular visual element. Huge lumps of ice break off from the edge of a glacier and tumble crashingly into the sea. To accompany them, some sonic Mickey Mousing – an overilluminating, hyper-explicit reference – was attempted.

Some way into the book Adorno and Eisler turn to the question of cinema aesthetics, a question that they claim has been addressed seriously by only one film director, Sergei Eisenstein. Films' contents have never been worthy of consideration, and so the aesthetics of cinema has largely been a formalistic enterprise, concerned with questions of colour or laws of movement and rhythm. Aesthetic consideration is anathema, for film, like recorded music, develops according to technological exigencies, not artistic concerns.[69] Adorno and Eisler reserve particular contempt for the film theorists who have derived insights from the perspective of the psychology of perception, the synaestheticists. The synaesthete's thought leads at best only to the 'ornamental applied-art duplicate of the "abstract" picture'. 'Arbitrarily established rules for playing with the kaleidoscope are not criteria of art', they protest.[70] Film experiments in synaesthetic music had gone quite far with the project of drawing shapes for sounds. Norman McClaren's *Synchrony*, in 1933, attempted to create synthetic octaves, correlations of image and noise. Moholy-Nagy carried out a similar experiment in *Tönendes ABC*, where the letters of the alphabet, silhouettes and fingerprints produced noise on the soundtrack. The soundtrack was then rephotographed so that the images could be seen and heard. Oskar Fischinger and Pfenninger carried out comparable experiments. A direct correlation was established between graphic image and sound. The experimenters were trying to create soundtracks directly from visual patterns. And there were also the more imagined synaesthetic relationships. From the late 1920s Fischinger had made abstract animations in which visual patterns were tightly synchronized to the music on disc, to make a total synaesthetic film experience. But all this is part of a past era, say Adorno and Eisler. Modern music has broken with the auratic identity thinking of the synaestheticists, and is 'working with might and main at the dialectical task of becoming unromantic while preserving its character of music'.[71]

Eisenstein had attacked the synaestheticists too, in *The Film Sense*, for asserting the existence of 'absolute' sound–colour equivalents, for even if they exist in nature that does not make them in themselves worthy elements of 'art'. Adorno, Eisler and Eisenstein agree that there is no benefit in redoubling an effect in two different media simultaneously. Eisenstein is also critical of the attempt to achieve unity between picture and music, 'by the addition of pictorial equivalents to the expressive associations of single musical themes or whole pieces'.[72] But Adorno and Eisler are not satisfied that Eisenstein's theory is free of formalist notions. The example cited is the use of the Barcarolle from *Tales of Hoffmann*, which inspired one film director to show two lovers embracing against a background of Venetian scenery. Eisenstein is disappointed with the predictability, and suggests that a Venetian motif might have been differently deployed: the ebb and flow of the water in the canals combined with the twitching reflections of light takes the interpretation of the music away from the illustrative and closer to the sensed inner movement of a barcarolle, a Venetian boat song, imitating the rhythm of a gondola. Adorno and Horkheimer regard this suggestion as simply an abstracted version of what the other film director had done. The motion of the water and the play of light coincide with the supposed undular character of the music. They turn to Eisenstein's support of Disney in *The Film Sense* (1942) to hammer home their criticism of Eisenstein's formalism.[73]

> In the Silly Symphony *Birds of a Feather* [1931],[74] Walt Disney related that piece to 'a Peacock whose tail shimmers "musically" and who looks into the pool to find there the identical contours of its opalescent tail feathers, shimmering upside down. All the approachings, recedings, ripples, reflections and opalescence that came to mind as a suitable essence to be drawn from the Venetian scenes, have been preserved by Disney in the same relation to the music's movement: the spreading tail and its reflection approach each other and recede according to the nearness of the flourished tail to the pool – the tail feathers are themselves wavering and shimmering – and so on.' However Disney's pretty idea does not imply the direct transformation of one medium into another. The transformation is indirect, literary in character, based on the generally accepted premise that this popular piece is associated with water, gondolas, and therefore with Venetian opalescent effects. The intention here is to show by the interpolation of a concept that the colors of a bird can symbolize Venice. The idea of the playful interchangeability of different elements of reality as well as subtle irony with regard to Venice, which is likened, in its picturesqueness, to a peacock, are ingredients inseparable from the effect of Disney's interpretation. This effect is certainly legitimate, but the doctrine of inner movement does not even begin to account for it. It is a highly sophisticated effect and Eisenstein's purely formal, literal interpretation misses the point. – This example shows the inadequacy of formal-aesthetic discussions of even highly stylized, non-realistic pictures; with regard to more realistic films, this inadequacy is even more flagrant.[75]

Adorno and Eisler complain that Eisenstein misunderstood how Disney's image works. It is not an abstracted representation of the inner movement, but actually a more complex metaphorical representation of Venice, using connotations that push beyond formal mirroring into questions of association and interpretation. They read the use of the peacock somewhat in the way that Eisenstein had already taught them to in *October*, where Alexander Kerensky features in a montage sequence, substituted by a crafted gold peacock, one of the precious *objets d'art* that cluttered the Winter Palace. Later Kerensky stands pompously in front of the tsar's bedchamber, his gloves and boots gleam like the gold leaf of the peacock figurine, and his movements imitate its clockwork jolts. The simile is made literal – 'this man is proud as a peacock' – but at the same time the vanity and inanity of Kerensky, whom the audience knows will soon fall, is ridiculed. Indeed, Adorno and Eisler go on to demand for film a montage principle, 'so emphatically advocated by Eisenstein'.[76] This montage principle must govern the relationship between picture and sound, and it is one, not of similarity, but of question and answer, affirmation and negation, appearance and essence. Music must never force identifications between it and the images with which it appears simultaneously. Music and film are two different media. They cannot express identical things. The sound-film, they state, interjecting a defamiliarization of forms and technologies, is 'an aesthetically accidental form'. Aesthetic models of genuine motion-picture music are found in the topical songs and production numbers written for musical comedies. The songs may be of little musical merit, but they have

> never served to create the illusion of a unity of the two media or to camouflage the illusionary character of the whole, but functioned as stimulants because they were foreign elements, which interrupted the dramatic context, or tended to raise this context from the realm of literal immediacy into that of meaning. They have never helped the spectator to identify himself with the heroes of the drama, and have been an obstacle to any form of aesthetic empathy.[77]

Adorno and Eisler always return to the material basis of film. For them it never stops being a soundtrack synchronized to an image-track, and a series of still photographs rapidly following in a sequence that imitates reality and so imitates movement. We realize that 'the frozen replica of external reality has suddenly been endowed with the spontaneity that it was deprived of by its fixation, and that something petrified is manifesting a kind of life of its own'.[78] Here music intervenes to supply momentum and energy, a stimulus to motion, against the deadliness of screen images. But it should be the tune that calls movement into being, not a reduplication of motion, an identity of intent.

It may not be a surprise that the ultimate film and music extravaganza, Disney's *Fantasia*, is given very short shrift in *Composing for the Films*. Of course, all the music pre-existed. None of it was really composed for the films, though Stravinsky's consent for his music to be used indicated some sort of complicity. *Fantasia* is described by Adorno and Eisler as an 'otherwise questionable film', but notable for its use of extraordinary technical resources in the form of 'fantasy-sound'.[79] Fantasound was the system developed to improve sound quality for this most soundful of films. Ub Iwerks patented the invention. For Fantasound the music was recorded on multiple microphones and reproduced on an equal number of loudspeakers. Fantasound installations at the cinemas where *Fantasia* played from 1940 cost thousands of dollars per unit. The outlay was extremely high, and the installation came at a time when government defence needs meant electronic equipment was difficult to obtain. Widescreen and Fantasound were to make the experience of *Fantasia* extraordinary, just as colour and sound had enhanced Mickey Mouse's antics. These sound capabilities had attracted the conductor of the Philadelphia Orchestra, Leopold Stokowski, to Disney's project. The recording abilities of the Disney studios amazed Stokowski, who was very keen to explore the new exigencies set off by recording. In early November 1937 Stokowski sent a delighted letter to Disney, stating that he would love to conduct for him. Stokowski suggested that Disney could give the animation treatment to Bach's *Toccata and Fugue in D Minor*.[80] They listened to the composition and they saw the music, in a synaesthetic experiment. Disney, after all, had seen a colour organ demonstration back in 1928 and Stokowski had used the Clavilux colour organ to perform Rimsky-Korsakov's *Scheherazade* and Skriabin's *Prometheus*. A loud crescendo appeared to Disney as 'like coming out of a dark tunnel and a big splash of light coming in on you'.[81] One passage suggested orange to Walt, but Stokowski saw purple. A woodwind section gave Disney the image of a hot kettle with spaghetti floating in it, and so on.

But there was another strand in the story of how Disney came to imagine the full-length film *Fantasia*. The German animator Oskar Fischinger had first contacted Stokowski about the possibility of a film based on Bach's *Toccata and Fugue*. And Stokowski then suggested the project to Disney. This meant that the full-length film had a direct link to German abstraction, though Disney claimed an interest in abstract film since seeing Len Lye's *A Colour Box* (1936) in the 1930s.[82] And the idea was in the ether – for example, when Disney was in Paris in 1935 Swiss abstractionist Charles Blanc-Gatti suggested to him the idea of making a synaesthetic film but was rebuffed. Fischinger had made fourteen animated studies between 1928 and 1932 in Germany. All were short films in which he set particular pieces of animation to music, all types of music, from jazz to Brahms to fandango. He wanted to concoct a new art form, called *Colour Rhythm*. This was what he saw as film's necessary direction. In the Berlin *Film-Kurier* in February 1931 he declares that 'the abstract film corresponds most closely to the true essence of film'. He continues: 'The narrative film will probably remain the daily bread of the masses but the layers of people who demand the true film, the abstract film, will grow permanently.'[83]

For his eighth study, completed in 1931, Fischinger decided to make a filmstrip to play along with Dukas's *The Sorcerer's Apprentice*. Unlike Disney, he did not choose to tell Goethe's story, but rather tried to translate the textures and movements of the sounds, synaesthetically, into shapes and colours. Rectangles steal across the screen, splitting, warping, shifting. *Study no. 8* was not made with music, in the end. With the advent of sound film, copyright laws changed. Before then any music could be used for film accompaniment, but now rights had to be obtained. The sum that the rights owner of Dukas's composition wanted was too high for Fischinger. He bought the rights to one side of the record, but had to leave the flipside, hoping to complete it at a later date.

Fischinger's films were quite successful, and he employed a small staff. But when the Nazis came to power, many of his friends, such as the activist Kurt Hiller and the sexologist Magnus Hirschfeld were attacked. He continued to work in Germany for a while. He imagined that Hitler might ride a wave that peaked and then dipped, sending the Führer into nothingness, out of the picture, like one of his abstract film figures. He helped to develop a colour film process that set off his films such as *Kreise* (1933) and *Komposition in Blau* (1935) to stunning effect.[84] And he worked on creating synthetic sound, designing images that produced sound once they were transferred to the optical soundtrack area of the filmstrip. At the third 'colour and sound' congress in Hamburg in October 1933 Fischinger's films were shown, alongside the colour organ of 'musical' painter Charles Blanc-Gatti. A little fringe meeting of anti-Nazis was called, and Fischinger attended. A speech by Georg Anschütz detailed the Nazi threats to abstract art and 'colour-music'. He asked all present to keep up abstract filmmaking, even if they had to use names such as 'ornamental' or had to maintain that abstract art was indeed part of the 'German essence'. Eventually, Fischinger was arrested for minor offences – for not hanging a flag from the window, for mocking *Völkischer Beobachter* headlines in public, and so on. The intercession of an influential film friend helped him out, until that film friend himself fell from grace. Fischinger's absolute films were deemed not to 'correspond to the *Zeitgeist*'.[85] And there were some critics who thought that concepts such as 'Opus' and 'Sinfonie', so beloved of the music-filmmakers, stank of intellectuality and art snobbism and went against the sensibility of the *Volk*. Devious means ensured that some absolute films were shown, and some press was garnered here and there. *Film-Kurier* in its New Year issue in 1935 published seasonal greetings from the remains of the avant-garde in Germany: Fischinger, Reiniger, Frank Wysbar, Wilfried Basse.[86] Oskar Fischinger said:

> I wish for 1935 the first, great, feature-length colour-film work – an *absolute* colour-work, born quite of music, *comprehensible to all people on earth* – and bringing massive amounts of currency into the country! That is what I wish with all my heart![87]

Fischinger's films, like all non-representational art works, had been labelled degenerate in 1935, even though the same year a film critic fan of Fischinger's claimed that 'ornament-art' was part of an old German tradition which included decorative motifs on clothes and books, architecture and landscape. In addition, said the critic, Fischinger had an international reputation and was as significant as Lotte Reiniger or Walt Disney.[88] But Fischinger's international standing was not high enough. At the Venice Film Festival that year the German film that aroused interest was Leni Riefenstahl's *Triumph of the Will*, and the colour sensations were Mamoulian's Technicolor *Becky Sharp* and Disney's *The Band Concert*. Fischinger had indeed tried to escape the ban imposed by Goebbels in 1935 by calling his films 'ornamental' or 'decorative'. He had written a long letter to Goebbels in December 1935, demanding respect, finance and distribution for his work. Nothing came of it. He tried to evade the ban by passing his films off as advertisements or logos. But, since the first aim had been the pursuit of truth in art, such strategies were another sort of death.

Fischinger's advertising work for Muratti cigarettes in April 1934 ran for more than a year, and it made him famous in Hollywood, where advertisements speak. The animation traded off the Olympics fever that descended on Germany in 1935 in preparation for the Winter Games in Garmisch Partenkirchen (where Alpine skiing was introduced) and the Summer Games in Berlin. The cigarettes were placed in a stadium performing a kind of skiing. Fischinger's previous adverts for the Social Democrats did not garner so much attention, luckily for him presumably. Universal Studios wanted to send an agent to Germany to lure him, but Paramount heard of this plan and beat their rivals to it. They helped him and his films to get out, with a pile of modernist canvases, just before the exhibition of 'Cultural Documents of Bolshevism and Jewish Work of Decay: Degenerate Art' opened in Munich in 1937. By then, Fischinger was heading for an apartment on Sunset Boulevard, with a thousand dollars a month in his pocket. Paramount had no real use for him though, and he sat in an office with little to do – but, at least, not doing anything for Paramount's competitors. Eventually he persuaded his bosses to let him make a film, but colour and art were not what they wanted to shell out for. The film came out in black and white and recognizable images were superimposed on Fischinger's abstractions, such as three singers at a microphone, a trumpet or a radio mast, hammering home the fact that the film was about music. Furious, Fischinger left the studio, a place whose regimentation he could not abide. Bad experiences at MGM followed. And then there was Disney. The European Film Fund secured for him a position at Disney's studios. He did not want to take it up, but he had already been in contact with Stokowski, back in the Berlin days, and later when they had discussed collaborating on an animation film. Fischinger was employed by the studio from November 1938 to October 1939 – as a 'drawn animation specialist', for sixty dollars a week. He animated the sparkle of the blue fairy's wand in *Pinocchio*.[89] He designed four varying, simultaneous movements for *Toccata and Fugue*, the project he had first suggested to Stokowski, who had taken it to Disney. Disney reduced it to one, a series of alternating undulating forms. Fischinger animated twenty seconds' worth of film and then left. Disney's other staff made the shapes more figurative, turning them into what they assumed would be more readily accepted by audiences. Where Fischinger had drafted an abstract wave, Disney demanded a crest of foam along the top edge. Abstract points had wings stuck on them. Only one figure would move at once. Clouds appear against a sky. Disney was concerned that the colours were too extreme, and so altered them.[90] Though Fischinger's synaesthetic idea of visualizing the soundtrack of the film remains, no trace of Fischinger remains in the credits. That was Fischinger's decision. In a letter reflecting on his time at Disney, he noted:

> The film *Toccata and Fugue by Bach* is really not my work, though my work may be present at some points; rather it is the most inartistic product of a factory. Many people worked on it, and whenever I put out an idea or suggestion for this film, it was immediately cut to pieces and killed.[91]

Fischinger thought that he would be more famous than Disney in the long run. He blamed American 'Kunstfeindlichkeit' ('hostility to art'), and he might have wondered what difference there was between the anti-art of the Americans and the work prohibition that had propelled him out of Germany. (But it was worse in Germany. His brother Hans made abstract animations too, and the showing of his *Tanz der Farben* (*Dance of Colours*) in 1939 at the Waterloo Theatre in Hamburg led to the revoking of the theatre's permit.) Oskar Fischinger tried to find backers in New York. He hoped to animate a full-length version of Dvorak's *New World Symphony*. In 1941 he bought back the rights of the Paramount film with money from the Guggenheim Foundation, remade it and called it *Allegretto*. But he never made any money.

Disney did not have it all his own way either. The labour disputes that would dog the studios in the following years were starting up. These concerned the rights to handle the installation of Fantasound equipment. Disney was being squeezed from below, while at the same time the money men at RKO were jumpy, given the war and its equipment needs. There was also a fear that *Fantasia* might flop. RKO wanted to put *Fantasia* into general release in shortened form. The producers were unconvinced that the American public was ready for such a confection. *Fantasia* broke with the realist aspirations of *Snow White and the Seven Dwarfs*. Walt Disney was moving on, generating new optical delights beyond photo-sketches endowed with mobility. And he did hope that all senses might be mobilized. Advanced sound systems were to allow discernible movement of music, for example, in the final, transcendent 'Ave Maria' sequence where the sound was to emerge from different parts of the cathedral. Also, Disney hoped to find a way of releasing scents and the odour of flowers and incense. But these advanced experiments in sense stimulation were not concluded. In 1942 Margaret Kennedy wrote of the essentially optical conception of Disney's films. Even in the sound-films the emphasis is still visual rather than aural, she insisted. But Disney had tried to create a duet of sight and sound

> by dint of the extreme simplification of cartoon drawing, which makes a comparatively small demand upon the eye. But, even so, many people found that the simultaneous demands upon eye and ear were too much for them – that if they looked they could not listen and if they listened they could not look. It may be that the public will catch up with Disney; the human race may, in a year or two, develop new faculties of coordinated attention. Or perhaps Disney may experiment upon lines of still greater simplification until he has discovered how much the average human being can see and hear simultaneously.[92]

Was Disney beyond his public with his twofold figures, people that are mushrooms, fish that double as harem girls? He certainly appeared to have left his German fan base behind, even before the film had been completed. In *Licht–Bild–Bühne* on 21 December 1938, the following indignant report appeared:

> 'I demand cultural protection for the classics!' The parody of Goethe's 'Werther' by an émigré clique in France has already been energetically rejected. Now Walt Disney from the USA is letting his intention to film Goethe's 'Sorcerer's Apprentice' be known. The bending of the Snow White fairy-tale into an American animation-revue lets one fear only the worst for Goethe's poem. The turning of German classics into kitsch in American entertainment films can be evidenced by dozens of examples. Create cultural protection of the classics of literature and music.[93]

The archive of the Reichsfilmkammer got hold of a black-and-white copy of *Fantasia* and a long catalogue entry was written in 1940. What Disney had made of Beethoven's Sixth Symphony enticed the otherwise descriptive film reviewer to voice objections:

> Disney presents a Hollywood-style, mythologized world made cute, with black-and-white Pegasuses with their children, centaurettes with make-up pencils and powder puffs, with little cupids and Bacchus, Zeus, Morpheus and the moon

goddess Artemis. (The German viewer may not understand the fusion of a Beethoven Symphony with Hollywood slapstick comedy and sweetness.)[94]

Officially the Nazi party railed against *Fantasia* as a 'degradation of German culture', but Goebbels, a secret admirer of Disney, organized private screenings of *Fantasia* for party bigwigs. Some German movie theatres showed Disney films after the ban on the importation of foreign films, but the war was a big blow for Disney. Within only a few months he lost almost the entire European market. He was in trouble. The trouble for some Europeans was that they found themselves in America.

adorno the clown

Where the stork brings babies from. – For every person there is an original in a fairy-tale, one need only look long enough. A beauty asks the mirror whether she is the fairest of all, like the Queen in Snow-White. She who is fretful and fastidious even unto death was created after the goat which repeats the verse: 'I've had enough, can't eat the stuff, bleat, bleat.' A care-worn but unembittered man is like the little bent old lady gathering wood, who meets the Good Lord without recognizing him, and is blessed with all her own, because she helped Him. Another went out into the world as a lad to seek his fortune, got the better of numerous giants, but had to die all the same in New York. A girl braves the wilderness of the city like Little Red Riding Hood to bring her grandmother a piece of cake and a bottle of wine, yet another undresses for love-making with the same childlike immodesty as the girl with the starry silver pieces. The clever man finds out he has a strong animal spirit, dislikes the idea of meeting a bad end with his friends, forms the group of Bremen city musicians, leads them to the robbers' cave, outwits the swindlers there, but then wants to go back home. With yearning eyes the Frog King, an incorrigible snob, looks up to the Princess and cannot leave off hoping that she will set him free. (Adorno, *Minima Moralia*)

Adorno and Horkheimer lampoon the imbecility of the culture industry. And it would be laughable were it not so sinister, were it not that powerful modes of mental manipulation had come in to play. Adorno and Eisler insist that motion picture music be absurd. There has to be something to set against this, an art that holds on to the promise of social bliss and reconciliation. It is not simply high culture, for that too, like the lowest, bears the scars of capitalism as well as elements of change. And Adorno was suspicious of the self-seriousness of high art.[95] In *Aesthetic Theory*, the 'quintessence' of his thought,[96] Adorno posits that there can be something different from the 'calculated "fun"' dished up by the culture industry and the pompousness of high art. It is genuine silliness – *Albernheit*.[97] Silliness in art is set against organized fun. Adorno insists on a silly moment in art – a moment that art anyway cannot escape, even if it tries. Silliness in art figures as an indictment of the self-proclaimed rationality of the system. It is an aspect of art's different logic. And silliness is a mimetic residue in art, a residue of 'amorphous, crude barbarity', an original moment. For art to be true to its essence, then, silliness must be served up, though not in a stupid way, not in an unreflexive way as done by the culture industry. Silliness is a moment devoid of intention, and so marks a place for truth.[98] Silliness takes humanity back to the animal world, providing the 'clownlike element of art' – that is, a 'cheerful reminder of the fact that art has its roots in the animal world'.[99] Adorno observes how apes in the zoo enact scenes that seem to be taken right out of clowns' acts. Children, he notes, are attracted to clowns and to art, for the same reasons. Both kinds of attraction are expunged by the world of adults, along with a third attraction: that to animals. Such likeness to animals, indicated by attraction, is a human characteristic that can never be entirely repressed by consciousness.

> The language of little children and of animals seems to be the same. The similarity between man and ape is thrown into sharp relief by the animal-likeness of clowns. The constellation of animal, fool and clown constitutes one of the most basic dimensions of art.[100]

The animal, the fool, the clown exist in us as traces – and form the true basis of art. This was the basis of the respect for Chaplin. Chaplin, 'using mimetic behaviour', causes 'purposeful grown-up life to recede, and indeed the principle of reason itself', Adorno notes.[101]

In the 'Second Manifesto of Surrealism' (1929) André Breton celebrated the 'truly harrowing poetry and philosophy' of Hegel and Feuerbach through to Jarry, Trotsky and Chaplin.[102] And three times Walter Benjamin jotted down notes on Chaplin in the late 1920s and again in 1934. Mature Chaplin was still analysable. In 1928 or 1929 Benjamin wrote about seeing *The Circus* (1928) and decided that Chaplin does not allow the audience to smile, but only to react extremely, doubling up with laughter or become deadly sad. Chaplin is an object, other than himself. The first thing that Benjamin notes is that, when Chaplin raises his bowler hat to greet people, it looks like the lid of the pot rising when the water boils over. Benjamin also comments on how Chaplin's mask of non-involvement turns him into a fairground marionette. Chaplin, he decides, is 'his own walking trade-mark, just like the company trademark seen at the end of other films'. Benjamin expands these thoughts for *Die literarische Welt* in February 1929, noting that Philippe Soupault has attempted 'the first definition of Chaplin as a historical phenomenon'. Soupault values Chaplin films because they are 'imbued with a poetry that everyone encounters in his life, admittedly without being conscious of it always'. Chaplin, he says, is a director of his films, not an actor. He makes his films as compositions, not as action movies or suspense stories. But the secret of his immense success, insists Benjamin, is that the films appeal to the most international and the most revolutionary emotion of the masses: their laughter. '"Admittedly", Soupault says, "Chaplin merely makes people laugh. But aside from the fact that this is the hardest thing to do, it is socially also the most important."'[103]

This power to evoke laughter, this revolutionary force, is asserted again. When Benjamin reflects again on Chaplin in August 1934, he is compared with another star, Hitler. Hitler's inferior masculinity is compared with the feminine taint of the immiserated tramp as represented by Chaplin. Hitler's following is compared with Chaplin's public. Chaplin is the ploughshare who tills the masses; laughter loosens them up. But the soil of the Third Reich is stamped right down and no grass grows there. The fascist dictators are a ridiculous anti-parody of this thing that has preceded them, and they know it. That is why marionettes are banned in Italy, and why Chaplin films are banned in the Third Reich, for every marionette can do Mussolini's chin, every inch of Chaplin can do the Führer.

> The poor devil wants to be taken seriously and at the same time he must summon up all of hell.
> Chaplin's generosity is visible to all, Hitler's is visible only to his task masters.
> Chaplin shows up the comedy of Hitler's seriousness; when he acts the well-bred man then we know how things stand with the Führer. Chaplin has become the greatest comic because he has incorporated into himself the deepest fears of his contemporaries.

Laughter and horror are deeply enmeshed. Chaplin works on the cusp, to particular effect for a German viewer. And Hitler's own modernity is an issue for Benjamin. Hitler does not adopt the trappings of feudal authority – military clothing or the rest – but the garb of a gentleman in casual wear. Here Chaplin shadows him, 'in order to take the master caste at its word', but reveals more:

> His cane is the rod around which the parasite creeps (the vagabond is no less a parasite than the gent), and his bowler hat, which no longer sits so securely on his head, betrays the fact that the rule of the bourgeoisie is tottering.[104]

Chaplin can reveal the truth of Hitler – something Chaplin must have perceived when he made *The Great Dictator* in 1940. But for Benjamin it is more than that. Chaplin dramatizes the whole decay of a bourgeois class that needs Hitler to do its dirty work in casual dress, asserting itself through an effeminate ordinariness. Chaplin, for Benjamin, was an example of reflexiveness.

In 1964 Adorno recounted his meeting with Chaplin at a Malibu villa in the years of exile – and he proudly told an anecdote involving an embarrassing shock experience of attempted hand-shaking with a handless actor, which Chaplin imitated to great effect. The anecdote is a theory of humour in miniature, and shows how close together Adorno believed laughter and cruelty, domination and mimesis, to be.[105]

Truth in art casts into relief the degradation and the potential of human interchange with nature. This might be done by dramatizing the world of overlively things or by doing that old circus trick – bringing on the animals. Adorno enjoyed Kafka because he let the animals talk, and in so doing questioned humanness. In some notes on Kafka, he demonstrates how out of control Kafka's characters were – and this constitutes their interest.

> The boundary between what is human and the world of things becomes blurred. This forms the basis of the frequently noted affinity with Klee. Kafka called his writing 'scribbling'. The thinglike becomes a graphic sign; his spellbound figures do not determine their actions but rather behave as if each had fallen into a magnetic field.[106]

Kafka is a realist – he shows agency as myth and humanness as lie. Chaplin, Kafka, Klee shared with Disney an assault on adult rationality. They turned to the animal and the childlike. Children know that they

desire a reconciliation with animals – that is, with nature. This reconciliation must be genuine. Despite his love of Chaplin, Adorno criticized the
wind-rustled cornfields at the end of *The Great Dictator*, for they give the
lie to the anti-fascist plea for freedom: 'They are like the blond hair of the
German girl whose camp life is photographed by the Nazi film company
in the summer breeze.'[107] Just as do the Nazis, their opponents view nature
as a healthy contrast to society and so denature it. Nature is a refuge for
Nazi thought – and false anti-Nazi thought – where nature is set in
opposition to the social world and imagined as the realm of innocence.
This is not the nature that Adorno wants. Rather this nature is more like
that of the fairy-tale image of children talking with animals, an indication
of children's affinity to the mimetic, which shows that the mimetic impulse, part of our originary self, is an impulse that has lost its object –
nature – inasmuch as we have been severed from nature socially. Adults
never forget this desire, this former part of their world, and memory of
it cracks apart the polished bauble of consumer entertainment or the
priggishness of high art, both of which never suffice for they both only
hammer home the separation of human from nature. In *Aesthetic Theory*
Adorno provides a tableau of this, demonstrating how art might reserve
a place for utopia. He quotes a poem by Eduard Mörike titled *Mouse-Trap
Rhyme.*

> The child goes three times round the trap speaking these words:
> Little guests, little house
> Dear Mrs. or Mr. Mouse
> Just dare to introduce yourself
> Tonight in the moonlight!
> But make sure to close the door behind you,
> You hear?
> And watch your tail as you do it!
> After dinner we are singing
> After dinner we are jumping
> We'll do a little dance:
> Witt woo!
> My old cat will probably dance too.[108]

Adorno interprets the poem as a utopian attempt to re-fuse with nature.
The child's spiteful last line need not be read as sadistic. The mouse need

not be a parasite. Perhaps, states Adorno, the poem does not end with an image of humans and the cat pouncing on the trapped mouse. Perhaps the final image is of all three participants in the dance, animals and humans, standing upright and dancing together. This is an image of reconciliation. In seemingly conforming to the socially sanctioned rite of torturing mice, the poem transcends that act. It lays it bare – but with a critical moment, a possibility of acting differently, audible in the tone of indignation. Artistic mimesis of the mouse's demise assembles an afterimage of liberty. The sadistic tenor is cancelled in the act of forming into art. Art is infinite. The image of the dancing mouse – in defiance of socially approved persecution – cancels out the crumpled figure of Donald Duck with blows thundering down on him. Sadistic art, the construction of extremity, breaks the spell that conjures quiescence. This is the service offered by the 'black writers of the bourgeoisie', the 'dark chroniclers' of rationalism turned insane – who know that 'only exaggeration is true', such as the truly sadistic Marquis de Sade.[109] Reality outbids even his fantasies.[110] As Adorno writes in *Negative Dialectics*:

> A child, fond of an innkeeper named Adam, watched him club the rats pouring out of holes in the courtyard; it was in his image that the child made its own image of the first man. That this has been forgotten, that we no longer know what we used to feel before the dogcatcher's van, is both the triumph of culture and its failure. Culture, which keeps emulating the old Adam, cannot bear to be reminded of that zone, and precisely this is not to be reconciled with the conception that culture has of itself. It abhors stench because it stinks – because, as Brecht put it in a magnificent line, its mansion is built of dogshit. Years after that line was written, Auschwitz demonstrated irrefutably that culture has failed.[111]

As Adorno remarks in *Aesthetic Theory*, the circus, habitat of animals and clowns, is the first form of anti-art, for it enacts an opposition to empirical life. Adorno states that every work of art alien to alienation is like the circus.[112] And yet, the silliness, in so far as it is a residue of amorphous, crude barbarity, threatens to turn culture into a disempowered infantilism and a model of calculated fun.[113] Except, says Adorno, when it is reflexive. When the image reflects on its own production, we are returned to Emile Cohl and the artist's hands refusing the illusion. When the technological apparatus that makes the cartoon come to life finds representation there, the mechanisms are laid bare. Violence appears here not as an issue in representation, but as a possibility of violation against the machine. Benjamin, indicating the Nazi use of sophisticated technologies to re-inforce cultish values, submits the feasibility of a rape of the machine.[114] He argues that by redirecting the technical apparatus to the production of cult values, fascism displaces the 'drive' to revolutionize relations of production and property relations. This is backed up by an ideological discourse that promotes flattery of the existing economic order by ahistorically insisting on its eternal features. Fascist art and politics demonstrate the re-entry of cult values, the re-entry of semblance into representation, and a repression of playful production and reception. Disney was no fascist party member, though he had his sympathies, but he did become a corporate type, striving after respectability, and in the process violated his early avant-gardism and produced the illusion that is now known as Disney magic, where everything sparkles with Disneydust.[115] But when animation finds its own form, and not a borrowed form, when it concedes flatness not the fakery of depth, it really gets deep into actuality, its own and ours.

siegfried kracauer, dumbo and class struggle

kracauer's flattened hopes

In December 1941 Siegfried Kracauer wrote a review of *Dumbo* for the Swiss newspaper *Neue Zürchner Zeitung*. He is critical of the film. The Disney vision has taken a bad turn. He thinks that, despite some wonderful episodes, Disney is continuing in a direction that has been present since *Snow White and the Seven Dwarfs*. Cartoons are no longer gag opportunities where technique is wittily foregrounded. Slapstick is no longer an element. Instead the films now seek to propagate conservative messages. For Kracauer there is a connection between this ideological turn and the move of cartoons away from slapstick and gags to feature-length productions. In the slapstick comedies the focus is on the weak creatures as heroes who struggle to maintain themselves against the evil forces of the world. Full-length features necessitate, in contrast, an 'interfering plot', leaving less room for 'such wonderful inventions as the uninhibited bunch of crows or the champagne pearl game'. The subservience of these elements to plot necessitates a change in the character of the heroes. No longer are they enmeshed gag for gag in an overly lively world. Rather, they develop emotional lives in realist settings. The consequence is conformism:

> They subordinate themselves in terms of content submissively to social convention; their fable tends to discredit the gags. Characteristic of this are some of the songs or also the conclusion of *Dumbo*: instead of flying with his mother to an unknown paradise, Dumbo ends up as a highly paid star for the same circus director who beat his mother.[1]

A little boy at the circus ridicules Dumbo's large ears. He sparks a near-riot. The disturbance is blamed on Dumbo's mother, who is then locked in a cage. The circus bosses force Dumbo to play a humiliating role in the clowns' act. He is made to plunge into a vat of plaster, a nightmare act that reduces him to tears. But once Dumbo discovers that his quirk – those freakish oversized ears – is actually his winning and bankable asset, he becomes a highly paid star. His mother, reinstated in her job, gapes at his success from the sidelines. The circus, Adorno's home of anti-art, is turned into the sadistic arena where power parades its ability to buy off dissent, and injustice rules. There is no escape from the system, only conformity and the hope of triumphing within its terms. In 1932 Kracauer wrote a piece titled 'Akrobat – schöön' for the *Frankfurter Zeitung*. It was a paean to the Spanish circus act, Andreu-Rivel. The act is a collection of chances, barely held together into a unity, and so is an image of the disintegration that always figures modern life in Kracauer's world. The act is a demonstration of practical dialectics, in which all that is unnecessary, everything that deviates, is more important than the main task – in this case building a bridge. The bridge is built, but the detours, the unintentional effects, along the way are more significant. For Kracauer, this reversal of priorities is clownery's indication that world relations should be upended too. Chaplin knows it too: 'the usual order is trivialized and the apparently trivial is pushed centre-stage'.[2] The hierarchy of values of the everyday is reversed, or set in question. Anything that claims to be self-evident is disputed. Proportion is lost, as the unimportant looms large, and thereby these clowns, ideal children, gesture towards the ambiguity that inhabits our action, and enact a 'politics of non-fulfilment', which constitutes a refusal to follow the path straight ahead, in favour of the inadvertent inventiveness of ideas. These clowns pursue the logic of the child's game and the fairy-tale, to induce a reality that is not identical to ours, in the sense that fairy-tales and dreams are not identical to ours. It is the logic of daydreams, half-conscious and less purposive than the logic of adults. This is not the clownery on display in the Disney big tent.

Dumbo, notes Kracauer, has betrayed the anarchic essence of the cartoon. Kracauer relies on a truth-to-materials modernism, and he claims that, once upon a time, Disney did too. In the beginning, Disney insisted that every artistic genre in harmony with its particular means has to perform a specific function. The function of cartoons is to mock photographable reality. Minnie Mouse uses her bloomers as a parachute; a skeleton uses a thighbone to play a ribcage as a xylophone. Nature and its laws come under attack. This attack is led by the possibilities of the means of production.

> All these metamorphoses result from relations between forms or movements, and the more they destroy conventional contexts the more correct they are, the more expressly they reveal the artist's power of disposal over his material.[3]

Cartoons have their form, a necessity. Early Disney exemplified it. In *Plane Crazy* simply through the power of the pencil a child's car turns into an aeroplane, flown by Mickey. In *Dumbo* a similar miracle occurs: the earthbound elephant begins to flap its oversized ears as wings and floats through the air 'like a Pegasus or a bomber'. But here the new Disney style introduces a crucial difference. This airborne aberration is not a result of the cartoon's capabilities, but is traced back to the psychological mechanism of a 'magic feather', which Dumbo's friend, the tiny mouse, tricks out of the mob of crows.[4] The cartoonist does not rely on the lunacy of connection made possible by drawing and montage, but rather conjures up enchanting princes, witches and magical feathers, all legitimating devices. This is the rationalization of the irrational.

A lunatic, preposterous and contradictory world is banished, and a cause-and-effect logic is introduced. At the same time, *Dumbo* imitates photographable reality. It tends towards conformity to the physical laws of the universe. In the early short films Disney created a world 'that had as little to do with ours as Mickey had to do with a living mouse'.[5] That cartoon cosmos was as capricious as the cosmos in which Emile Cohl's figures moved, homeless, destabilized, in a space ruled by the pencil, its dimensions expanding and shrinking without reason. 'It is only consequential that in this cosmos gravity is abolished, perspective rules are not valid and any distance can be covered at the speed of thought.'[6] In *Dumbo* unreal objects are invoked but they are treated like real ones. And they operate in a world of people and things that, Kracauer reckons, could just as easily have been photographed. In so doing Disney threatens the true interests of the cartoon in a double sense:

> On the one hand, the cartoon, as his best examples prove, strives not after the fixing but the dissolution of conventional reality. On the other hand, it certainly does not have the function of visualizing a reality for whose representation cartoon is not at all necessary.[7]

The cartoon was arguing itself out of existence. This process was graphically represented in *Pinocchio* (1940). The story of *Pinocchio* seems to mirror the story of the studio's desire to magic up reality. Pinocchio is a wooden puppet come to life, and desirous of being 'a normal little boy'. But of course he can never quite be that. Disney so wanted to reproduce the real in cartoon form. *Pinocchio* was the most expensive Disney film to date; it was more intricate than all the others. Disney declared in *The News of the World* in March 1940: 'We've tried in various ways to give the characters the feeling of more depth and roundness – or more of a three-dimensional quality.'[8] But the studio did not just chase the illusive real; animators also bowed down before nature, abandoning utopia and rebellion. In the late 1930s the critic and author Alexander Woollcott visited the studio and expressed wonderment at the rough pencil tests he was shown. The cobwebs of lines that roughly formed the characters' motile shapes were more vital and creative than the finished, smooth product. Disney said he liked that febrile energy of the rough animation too, and flirted with using it in combination with live action as inner ideas or dreams or as fantasies, visions, half-formed notions.[9] But that sort of experimentation disappeared. Disney confirmed the turn to nature's templates. In an article in *National Geographic*, August 1963, Robert de Roos reported Disney's comment that, 'In *Snow White*, we had cute little animals, more on the fantasy side. In *Bambi* we had to get closer to nature. So we had to train our artists in animal locomotion and anatomy.' De Roos continues:

> Walt introduced live animals into the studio, deer and rabbits and skunks. 'But they were no good,' he says. 'They were just pets. So we sent the artists out to zoos, and all we got were animals in captivity. Finally, I sent out some naturalist cameramen to photograph the animals in their natural environment.'[10]

Such fidelity to the natural world countered the core of Kracauer's film aesthetics. First, Kracauer did not believe fidelity could be achieved in any meaningful way. In a piece on the aesthetics of colour film, an article for

Diagonal Symphony,
Viking Eggeling

Das Werk of September 1937,[11] Kracauer notes how colour – supposed to be a move towards increased naturalism – has been working like dead ballast, and in fact intensifies the bad artifice of film. The blue of the distant mountain range on the screen surface awakens the fatal idea that nature has been painted blue, and the Sahara with the red sun above appears as an oil painting. Black and white films, maintains Kracauer, could better capture the subtleties of colour, because from the start it fulfilled film's artistic law – independence from the surface appearance of objects. The exclusion of colour in black-and-white films worked to film's advantage in forcing a certain independence from the object. Art, including film art, is perceived as a parallel system, a remaking of the world, not its mirroring. Colour film strives to attain a 'trivial concept of nature' as copy. It is an art of illusion. It loves cliché, enslaving objects to their hackneyed forms: 'The fewer connections to the surface the less the effort needed to abstract in order to montage elements.'

But colour has a place if it is understood. The correct use of colour, according to Kracauer, is demonstrated in a Disney cartoon. He writes of a Disney cartoon in which a rocket firework is fired. Such a lively play of colours in movement, he notes, had never been visualized before, but Disney stages it.

> A colourful spray of rain fizzes across the surface, generating unsuspected sensations. In another trick film whose hero is a little dog, colour constructs the change of circumstances in the tightest formula. The little dog wanders by mistakes onto a glacier and he takes on a green tone as sign of his exhaustion. However, as soon as a helpful St Bernard has poured some brandy into him, he immediately turns back to a cheerful red.[12]

Kracauer was referring to Disney's 1936 cartoon *Alpine Climbers*, where Pluto and his saviour, a St Bernard dog, strike up a friendship well oiled by drink. In his judging of film aesthetics Kracauer was measuring the possibilities of film against the achievements of avant-garde filmmakers. In March 1928, reviewing the experimenters' films on show in Paris, Kracauer had written enthusiastically that the Berliners had now formed an organization to treat film as film. The avant-gardists militate against translations of literary stuff into the silent language of optics. Instead they produce optical processes that cannot be translated into any other language.[13] Eggeling's *Diagonal Symphony*, with its strips of light and geometrical fragments, made certain works by Picasso come to life. Man Ray's *Emak Bakia* was less true to form for it allowed guesswork on the proper objects behind the abstract motifs – water reflections and stand-up collars. Man Ray's film creates light effects from glass that turns slowly and reflecting mirrors. The sensation of speed is analysed as the film dashes through Paris by metro and steamboat.[14] The films are analyses of material:

> Indeed unlocked in them is a new world, unsuspected until now, of spatial configurations. Optical achievements of great style are not only those film fragments in which a rigid ornamentation is released to perform extraordinary gymnastic exercises, but also all image series in which, whether it be because of the choice of viewpoint, or through isolating parts of objects, motifs are pushed forward from the world of things so familiar to us and are varied so that they no longer correspond to the known.[15]

Such experimentation must not be an end in itself, Kracauer adds. It is the expansion of inventories of things and sensations. It is the gathering of material, of data about vision and perception and the real. But

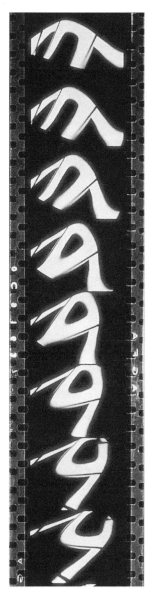

Emak Bakia, Man Ray

there are avant-garde films that are too systematically designed, films that 'turn material falsely into content and become hollow and mannered'.[16] Such films perceive themselves to be 'compositions', representations of a process that is complete in itself. They are nothing but stylized collections of expressive elements, 'devoid of precisely that reference to reality that alone would lend them meaning'.[17] In order really to use the new perceptions of space that this abstract filmmaking makes possible, all self-sufficiency, any value-in-itself, must be renounced. Isolation as a special genre has to be traded in for a relationship to 'reality film' – in order to secure a fuller reality. New optics must help to make the life of people and things more present, rather than cutting itself off from life. The new spatial motifs should penetrate 'reality film', not form a special genre in opposition in order to 'bequeath it with a fuller reality'. Only then can the 'signs' carry content and meaning. Popular film might already be in advance of all this. Invoking the star who garnered so much intellectual approval in the inter-war years, Kracauer notes: 'What are all the abstract compositions in comparison with a single one of Chaplin's grimaces? Their elements could serve his humanness.'[18]

In his 1937 article on the aesthetics of colour film, Kracauer alludes to Pudovkin's theory of film direction of 1928. Pudovkin notes there that film is not an imitation of the world but its construction through montage. Film's apparent positivism, its 'childlike pleasure in what can be achieved technically', tempts filmmakers to look at an image of a landscape from a postcard-like, conventional and banal point of view, while imagining that no point of view is involved. The magic of the postcard view is not an illusion designed to amuse the foolish, but rather a realistic rendition of the world as seen from a particular perspective. Kracauer emphasizes the role of the perceiving subject (here a banalizer) who synthesizes the image: 'Postcards do not falsify the world. It really is a postcard album when seen from a banal point of view.'[19] Such a view is 'blind' to the 'content of phenomena', and registers only a confused mass of coincidences that signify nothing. Against this, Pudovkin, and Kracauer, want to rip things from their superficial contexts. Familiar everyday images need to be exploded so that images can be montaged from their fragments. It is in the fragments that meaning resides. Montage, he states clearly, is the opposite of a 'trivial' imitation of nature. It does not seek 'similarity with so-called objects' but rather destroys 'irrelevant similarities and constructs from the elements derived from destruction images that are anything other than copies in the usual sense'.[20] But *Dumbo*, in contrast, appeared to resubmit film to natural laws.

This reneging happened at just that moment when the Disney studios faced a crisis in labour relations. *Dumbo* was begun just before the strike at the Disney Burbank studios in 1941. It was completed before the strike was over, and was ready for release in October 1941. Did the strike pervade the film? Rumour was that the nasty clowns who sing the song 'We're Gonna Hit the Big Boss for a Raise' were caricatures of the striking Disney cartoonists.[21] The scabs thereby wreaked revenge on the picket-liners, who led their own comic battle with picket-line placards that read 'Are we mice or men?' and 'One genius and 700 dwarfs'. 'I'd rather be a dog than a scab' declared an image of Pluto, while Jiminy Cricket announced ''Taint cricket to pass a picket'. Class politics were brought to light out of Disney raw material. The strike was a facet of an increasing labour militancy, on the rise since 1940. The Wagner Act of 1935 had been upheld by the Supreme Court in April 1937, spurring employees to take seriously the right to organize and to protect themselves against unfair labour practices. In Hollywood many of the salaried workers were unionized, except cartoonists. There were some areas left to win, and not only in Hollywood. Significantly, the important defeat at Ford in the spring of 1937 was revoked when in the spring of 1941 Ford signed a union contract with the United Auto Workers.

strike!

The Disney corporation was in trouble. The costs of producing the feature-length cartoons were high, and the European war had cut off sources of revenue. Some countries were not importing films, and others had outlawed the transfer of cash back to the USA. The new studio at Burbank cost $3 million, and a thousand-odd employees were now on the payroll. The employees thought the wage agreements capricious, ranging from a weekly $500 for a top animator to $12 for a painter, and the working conditions were factory-like. Disney, it was thought by some employees, rewarded only his friends. The Disney brothers' issuance of non-voting stock in April 1940 brought in $3.5 million. Despite this, *Dumbo* was made at a cheaper cost than the other feature films. RKO complained that it was a few minutes too short to count as a full-length feature, but Disney refused to stump up the rest of the money to extend it. He knew the cost of those extra minutes and felt the studio was in no position to be profligate. Money worries were being voiced. But the workers refused to accept the argument that the bosses and the workers were all part of one organism, when only a few of the people involved were taking the credit. Battered by the Depression, they now wanted security. With the outbreak of war, rumours of mass layoffs were doing the rounds. Some thought that women from the Paint and Ink department were to be upgraded, replacing experienced animators at lower costs. They were also frustrated at the lack of screen credits, as Disney did not believe that the public needed to know who did what.[22] Workers were antipathetic to Walt Disney's paternalist style of management, particularly given that in such a large factory-like organization he could be fatherly to only a few. As the rumours undermined harmony in the workplace, the market value of shares began to fall. Employees, worried about their financial situation, began to sell stock.[23]

The animation industry had exacting conditions. A six-day working week was standard. Time clocks were common. Electric bells announced when coffee breaks could begin and when they were over. The first labour conflict of the animation industry, organized by the Commercial Artists and Designers Union (AFL) had won a five-month-long strike at the Fleischers' studio in New York in 1937. The strike was in response to poor wages and unhealthy working conditions. Just before the strike a speed-up in the production of *Popeye* cartoons had been ordered. Pickets carried banners that read 'We can't get much spinach on salaries as low as $15.00 a week', while they sang 'I'm Popeye the Union Man'.[24] Schlesinger-Warner Studios had a six-day lockout in 1941, which ended when Schlesinger signed with the Screen Cartoonists' Guild. Now Disney was the target. In January 1941 Disney and other studios conceded a forty-hour week to try and head off a unionization drive. But the activists were busily organizing. Herb Sorrell recruited staff to the cause and handed in the required number of signature cards to gain recognition of the Screen Cartoonists' Guild in accordance with the labour laws established by the Wagner Act. Disney claimed that the cards were signed under duress or falsely. He wanted dealings only with the Federation of Screen Cartoonists, a 'company union'. In February 1941 he called a meeting to address the 'real crisis we are facing'. Tellingly he revealed his homespun thoughts to the hundreds of workers present in the Burbank theatre:

> Everything you are going to hear is entirely from me. There was no gag meeting or anything to write this thing. It's all me, and that will probably account for some of the poor grammatical construction and the numerous two-syllable words.[25]

Then came the Disney story, the years of fighting the prejudices of the industry, persuading the bosses that animation is more than filler, more than a novelty; the hungry years, the mortgages, the reinvestment of profits. He spoke of the way in which he would like to know all the employees and be friendly but now the organization was too big and if he knew only a few that would be toadying. He finished by citing his memo to staff:

> The Company recognizes the right of employees to organize and to join in any labor organization of their choosing, and the Company does not intend to interfere with this right. HOWEVER, the law clearly provides that matters of this sort should be done off the employer's premises and on the employees' own time, and in such a manner as not to interfere with production...[26]

The homilies did not impress the entire workforce. The Disney story was too cute. Strike agitation continued. A picket line appeared in front of the studio on 29 May 1941. Disney's interview with the FBI, during the strike, noted that the curtailment of performance of his pictures abroad led to the lay-off of nineteen men. As a result of this, the men put about rumours that about two hundred were to lose their jobs. A whispering campaign took off, and it was this that led to a general strike. 'A picket line was maintained at the gates of the studio, and a "goon squad" of about 15 men was organized to prevent any trucks from entering the plant.'[27] A flyer aimed at the public was distributed. It showed Donald Duck pounding the floor in fury, screaming 'This makes me mad! I've been making you folks laugh for years and years, but now something has happened that ISN'T FUNNY AT ALL.' Illustrated with Goofy holding a placard that read 'Even I got wise' and Dopey, Grumpy, Pinocchio, Mickey Mouse and Pluto, the flyer put the workers' case, from Donald Duck's point of view:

> Every major cartoon studio in Hollywood has signed a contract with the cartoonists. But, when the artists at the Disney Studio, people who were directly responsible for Mickey and me, asked the management to discuss collective bargaining with them — the Studio said 'TOO BUSY'. The management not only refused to talk with the cartoonists, but also fired 10 members, including the President, the treasurer, and 4 stewards. All the cartoonists wanted was:
>
> 1. Recognition by the company.
> 2. Reinstatement of discharged members.
>
> They make less than house painters. The girls are the lowest paid in the entire cartoon industry. (They earn from $16 to $20 a week, with very few earning as high as $22.50) The much-publicized bonuses didn't even compensate the artists for the two years of overtime they spent on SNOW WHITE, Pinocchio and FANTASIA. (Snow White grossed more than $10.000.000.00). The NLRB dissolved a fake union organized by the Studio. The company then organized another one with the same officers. It failed! Now they are attempting to organize a *third*! 450 out of 580 artists at the Disney Studio belong to the Cartoonists. This is a clear majority! The Screen Cartoonists demand that Disney recognize this majority.[28]

The flyer asked audiences to refuse to patronize theatres showing Disney pictures, and to tell the manager why. It pleaded for donations to help feed the 450 strikers, and called on all to join the picket line. Sorrell called a secondary boycott of Technicolor, to stem the flow of film into the studio. In the second week of July, Technicolor Corporation gave support to the strikers and announced its refusal to process any Disney film until the right of the SCG to exist was recognized. Williams and Pathé too suspended the processing of Disney films. Sixteen AFL unions came out in support of the strikers. Disney proposed a settlement that offered reinstatement, union recognition, a closed shop, back pay for time on strike, increased wages and paid leave, but it was knocked back. His response was to take out full-page advertisements in *Variety* and *Hollywood Reporter* on 2 July 1941:

> I am positively convinced that Communistic agitation, leadership and activities have brought about this strike, and have persuaded you to reject this fair and equitable settlement.

Leaflets appeared all over Hollywood, put out by the Committee of Twenty-One. The leaflets, presented as 'exposés', branded the union activists Babbitt, Sorrell and Hilberman communists. It reported that the 'subversive red spiders' were duping 'American courage' with their 'paralyzing poisons'.[29] All strikers were asked to pose this question: Am I a loyal American or a dupe? But while Disney fretted about Moscow gold, it was he who was able to produce the most dazzling propaganda. The studio had just finished a part live action, part cartoon film titled *The Reluctant Dragon*, a docu-fiction on the workings of the Disney studio. The humorist Robert Benchley travels to the studio to pitch an idea, and finds himself stumbling from department to department in search of Uncle Walt. The film presents Burbank as a workers' paradise, a fun factory of Fordist proportions, efficient at generating laughs but fuelled by imagination. This was Disney trademark style – a real-looking world presented in ideal terms. But the film was a tool in the strike too. Its live action portions were seen as a threat to the animators' craft skills and a possible future direction for Disney movie-making. When *The Reluctant Dragon* premiered in Hollywood, strikers angry at the portrayal of such deluxe working conditions picketed the event. They carried a large cut-out dragon with Disney's glowering face and the word 'unfair' on the body.[30] Emotions ran high. Disney had to be got out of the way, in order that a settlement could be reached. He was ranting more and more about the communist motivation of the strike. In a letter to friend and newspaper columnist Westbrook Pegler, sent just before he left on the South American Goodwill Tour, he mentioned that front organizations and groupings, The People's World, The American Peace Mobilization and 'every known Communistic outfit in the country' had been the first to put him on their 'unfair list'.[31] He called Sorrell 'dirty, sneaky, and as foul as they come', and wrote of how he was convinced that the leader of the strike was 'a tool of the Communist group'.[32]

On 18 August 1941 Walt Disney Productions closed down the studio for several weeks while arbitration took place. Disney and his entourage had left for Latin America the day before for a two-month tour. The State Department and Nelson Rockefeller had requested the tour, for they had thought that, given the popularity of the Disney cartoon characters in the region, Disney would be a perfect envoy for the newly established Office of the Coordinator of Inter-American Affairs. This Office aimed to counter-act the penetration of pro-Nazi influence in the area, in the interest of forming a defensive super-bloc. Disney was to spread goodwill like Disney-dust. Back home, with Uncle Walt out of the way, the government and brother Roy settled the strike with a deal that rehired all cartoonists sacked as a result of union activities, recognized the Screen Cartoonists' Guild with no further votes, equalized pay among staffers, granted employees vacations with pay, and instituted regular grievance procedures. Manage-ment also accepted the union's closed shop. It was a victory for labour, as basic pay shot up and screen credits were guaranteed. However, in November 1941 massive layoffs were pushed through.[33] One point of contention was how many of those nominated on the redundancy lists would be workers who had participated in the strike.

America's entry into the Second World War saved the studio from financial difficulty. A day after the bombing of Pearl Harbor, on 8 December 1941, US military personnel moved in on the studio, restricting free movement. The studio was commandeered as a primary defence station to guard the Lockheed plant. The US government commissioned Disney to produce a series of educational war films. These taught troops how to identify enemy aircraft or how to strip and reassemble a gun. Then there were films for the home front, encouraging the purchase of war bonds and the like. There were propaganda films, bringing the war into the American housewife's everyday life. *Out of the Frying Pan into the Firing Line* was a lesson for Minnie Mouse and Pluto and anyone else who was keeping the home fires burning while Mickey fought. Frying fat could be turned into bombs and Pluto should renounce his selfish urge to lap it up. Donald Duck joined the anti-Nazi fight too, starring in *The Fuehrer's Face*, which won an Oscar in 1942 for best short film. The fairy-tale – its Germanic associations productively enlisted – was used too. In *Education for Death* (1943), an exposé of the Nazi indoctrination of youth, Germania (a cari-cature of Goering) appears as an obese Sleeping Beauty. A knight in shining armour rescues her. It is Hitler – in the same shiny tin guise as he adopts in Hubert Lanzinger's glorifying portrait *Hitler – Der Bannerträger* (*Hitler – The Standard Bearer*)[34] – and he can barely lift his enchantress. The war and its impact on daily life found its way obliquely into other cartoons, such as *Chicken Little*, from 1943, a moral tale provoking wariness against agitators and scaremongers. Everyone was pulling together now. The Communist Party of the USA was no longer advocating a neutral stance towards the war since the German invasion of the Soviet Union in June 1941. Communists and government embraced each other for a brief while in the interests of 'national unity', and, when not Nazi-bashing, they set their combined sights on a new enemy – the Trotskyists, many of whom were arrested in 1941 under the statutes of the Smith Act for 'advocating the overthrow of the US government' through their denunciation of imperialist war aims.

Bambi was released in August 1942. A small group of animators had worked on the naturalist tale about virtue and pluck since 1937. But Disney was inspired by his brush with government. He wanted to be involved in something more consequential, and altogether more grown up. He made an animation plus live-action film, *Victory Through Air Power*, which was released in the late summer of 1943. Based on a book by Major Alexander De Seversky, it attempted to influence military policy.[35] The film re-commended that long-range bombers form an essential part of military strategy. Battleships were not effective, argued the major, against official US policy. He advocated instead a policy of mass aerial bombing. In an animated history of aeroplanes, the early days of aviation segue into the uses of aeroplanes for mass destruction. Seversky, born in Russia in 1894, had been a thirteen-kill pilot in the First World War. He became an American citizen in 1927. In 1931 he founded the Seversky Aircraft Corporation: he had a particular investment – economic – in the success of air power. He argued that this technological solution to modern warfare would cost less than the maintenance of huge land armies. The film did not give any hint of death; indeed James Agee worried that it presented a 'victory-in-a-vacuum', a techno-vision of war as machine-eat-machine, without blood-shed.[36] The *Daily Worker* condemned Disney's film version of Seversky's book for being an 'Arabian Nights fantasy', and it noted that Major de Seversky's ideas should be treated with suspicion for he was an anti-Soviet reactionary.[37] The anti-Nazi films were quite different to Disney's standard entertainment fare. Effective modes for relaying information forced an inventiveness that diverged from the usual presentation of nature through a proscenium arch. Symbolism (for example, the American eagle fighting a Japanese octopus, or the Axis power as a huge iron wheel struck by allied hammers), maps, graphs, diagrams, dissolves, two-dimensional limited animation: all the images were vivid and brash in order to broadcast the necessarily unambiguous messages.

It was not just the overt policy-drang of *Victory Through Air Power* that annoyed the communists. The look of the cartoon world was also a matter for discussion. Communist artists were devising more general theories of culture, society and aesthetics at the time. The war had saved Disney's bacon, but it also bucked up the left organizations in the Californian Popular Front, after their knock-back in the years of the Red Scare from 1940 to 1941.[38] Communist cartoonists who were involved in a popular-front artists' grouping were formulating proposals for cartoon aesthetics. There were arguments about the applicability of social realism. For some animators, realism was Disney's business. The new animators were inspired by modernist artists such as Picasso, Dufy, Matisse. Exposed to Soviet cartoons, with modern music, flat backgrounds and highly stylized characters, they pushed for a flattened out, childlike and stylized design, away from Disney's archaic watercolour sentimentalism. In the autumn of 1943 some radical animators presented their ideas at a UCLA Writers' Congress, organized by the Hollywood Writers' Mobilization. John Hubley – who had left Disney in the wake of the strike – delivered a speech on 'The Writer and the Cartoon'. He insisted on the importance of social responsibility. The cartoon had to be an observation on real daily life. The radical cartoonist, in Hubley's view, was opposed to gags, and longed to remould cartoons as a commentary on the epoch and the difficulties of ordinary life. While Disney had achieved a formal and technical advance, his cartoons refused any social role. The gags all derived from 'pure', single-action situations, such as Pluto all stuck up in flypaper, or sundry characters fighting mechanical props or natural forces. And *Fantasia* Hubley considered to be pure formalism. Against it, Hubley proposed Chaplin. He 'utilized essentially the same abstract symbolism that cartoons have continually used', but his stories have been written 'in terms of human behaviour and broad social caricature'.[39] The popular-front animators held Chaplin up against Disney, measuring the social observation and critical animus of *Modern Times* and *The Great Dictator* against the frivolity and escapism of *Snow White and the Seven Dwarfs* and *Fantasia*. Chaplin was all things to all men.

The Californian popular-frontist verdict did not concur with Kracauer's 1941 commentaries on Disney. Kracauer judged *Fantasia* more positively, precisely because of its formal inventiveness. The more it was a formalist spectacular, the less plot-bound it was. Imagination, anti-realism and contingency take their place in the full-length feature. Kracauer faults *Fantasia* instead for its problematic 'illustration of absolute music'.[40] And he brought Disney into a constellation with Chaplin. Like Chaplin, Disney avoids bringing fairy-tales into alignment with the conventional everyday, electing instead to reveal everyday stories as fairy-tales, in Disney's case, via the medium of cartoon film. This makes possible the transformation of real and imaginary things alike, in order to lift both into a new sphere. Jean Prévost's 'Walt Disney, the Man Who Never Had a Childhood' emphasized that Charlie Chaplin was Mickey Mouse's predecessor.[41] Chaplin was a semaphore, with a limpidity of gesture. This is what Disney had copied. It may have been true. But by 1947 Disney had dissolved any sentimental bond between himself and Chaplin when a journalist for the *New York Times* reported, in a piece titled 'That Million Dollar Mouse': 'Walt wouldn't tell me about Mickey's politics, except to say that they do not resemble Chaplin's.' But Disney found it hard to believe that Chaplin was truly a radical.[42] He thought he could tell. He thought that he had a nose for it. Whoever was a radical, Disney wanted to sniff them out. In February 1944 the Motion Picture Alliance for the Preservation of American Ideals (MPA) was formed. Its members were mainly studio executives, largely from Metro–Goldwyn–Mayer. Disney was its first vice-president. An FBI memorandum dated 22 March 1944 noted:

> The MPA originally was organized to combat 'a rising tide of communism, fascism, and kindred beliefs that seek by subversive means to undermine and change this way of life.' Specifically, however, the organization was concerned with combating communism.[43]

'Communists, crackpots and radicals' were the targets.[44] The MPA passed names to the Joint Fact-finding Committee on Un-American Activities of the California State Legislature and the Committee On Un-American Affairs of the US House of Representatives. The film industry magazine *Variety* took umbrage in an editorial on 15 March 1944.[45] The MPA had written to the chairman of the House Committee on Un-American Activities with claims that 'Motion Picture Industrialists of Hollywood have been coddling Communists and co-operating with so-called intellectual superiors they have helped to import from Europe and Asia'. *Variety* insisted that they name the communists and the intellectual superiors. And they should name the groups characterized as 'totalitarian-minded'. Despite fear of this 'rising tide of communism, fascism and kindred beliefs that seek by subversive means to undermine and change this way of life', the FBI report noted that virtually all speakers directed their remarks solely at communism.[46] Some of the communists saw the formation of the MPA as part of an anti-Roosevelt move – 'by defeatist forces' who want to 'clamp down on the production of win-the-war films and to prepare a reactionary Republican attack on President Roosevelt'.[47] The investigations into communist influence in Hollywood lasted several years. Disney did not stop at MPA support. He was involved as a 'friendly witness', along with Gary Cooper, Ronald Reagan, Sam Wood, Robert Montgomery and Adolphe Menjou, in the interrogations in 1947 of writers, directors and actors called before the House Committee for Un-American Activities. Brecht and Chaplin were among the forty-three names subpoenaed to testify to the Hearings Regarding the Communist Infiltration of the Motion Picture Industry – and though charges against Chaplin were dropped, eventually he would be exiled from the Land of the Brave and the Free. The same report announcing the 'Movie Witch-Hunt' in the US *Daily Worker* noted that a postponement of the investigation – in order for some listed to return from Europe – would not delay the hearings on the case of Hanns Eisler.[48] This attention directed at Eisler had caused Adorno to withdraw his name from their jointly authored book on film music composition. Paranoia and justified fear reigned in the Golden State.

Disney gave testimony before the House Committee on Un-American Activities on 24 October 1947.[49] Asked by H.A. Smith where the Disney studio films were distributed, Disney answered 'All over the world'. Smith queried: 'In all countries of the world?' Disney replied 'Well, except the Russian countries.' Asked why not, he responded: 'Well, we can't do business with them.' According to Disney, the Russians, in the 1930s, had decided the films 'didn't suit their purposes'. The interrogator turned to the question of propaganda. Had Disney made propaganda films? Yes, replied Disney, during the war for government agencies, and one for the Treasury on taxes, and four anti-Hitler films. Then the interrogator cut to the point: 'From those pictures that you made, have you any opinion as to whether or not the films can be used effectively to disseminate propaganda?' Disney said yes. And he observed that a Gallup poll had found that people had been influenced by the Treasury film to pay their taxes early. But apart from those films no other propaganda films had been made at the studio, assured Disney.

Disney overlooked his recently premiered products from the vacation in South America, when the Disney entourage had been off sketching local flora and fauna, collecting stories and noting customs, chatting to people, listening to music, and keeping Disney away from the studio's fraught labour relations. All this material was utilized in two features, *Saludos Amigos* (1943) and *The Three Caballeros* (1945). Disney sold the films as advertisements for good neighbourliness and peaceful coexistence: 'While half the world is being forced to shout "Heil Hitler", our answer is to say "Saludos Amigos"', he proclaimed in a radio broadcast.[50] Salvador Dalí, one of Disney's favourite artists, was supposed to be involved in the project – his realist improbability fitted well with Disney's current magic realism. *The Three Caballeros* mixed live action and animation in the same scene. But the live action took place on theatrical sets that had been designed with flat surfaces and elementary shapes so that they fitted in with the animated drawings. The live world in the film was a prototype of the world of Disneyland simulacra to come, full of props and fake-perspective structures.

Were there any people at the present time at the studio who Disney believed to be communist or fascist? the interrogator continued. 'No,' Disney replies, 'at the present time I feel that everybody in my studio is one-hundred-percent American.' But in the past, he declared, there were some people that he was sure were communists. The strike was addressed. Disney named Herbert Sorrell as a communist who had tried to take over his artists. Disney recounted his side of the story. He spoke of how Sorrell claimed to have 'all the tools of the trade sharpened'. He told of the threats to turn the plant into a dustbowl, and his responsibility to 'his boys' who did not want to be 'sold down the river' to Sorrell's gang. He recounted the smear from the 'Commie fronts'. The communists 'distorted everything, they lied; there was no way that you could ever counteract anything that they did; they formed picket lines in front of the theatres, and, well, they called my plant a sweat-shop, and that is not true, and anybody in Hollywood could prove otherwise.' The chairman intervened at this point: 'In other words, Mr. Disney, Communists out there smeared you because you wouldn't knuckle under?' Disney named another communist, David Hilberman: 'I looked into his record and I found that, number 1, that he had no religion and, number 2, that he had spent considerable time at the Moscow Art Theatre studying art direction, or something.' He also named William Pomerance and Maurice Howard, but noted these were only suspicions as 'No one has any way of proving those things'. Smith asked Disney what his personal opinion of the Communist Party was. Disney replied:

> Well, I don't believe it is a political party. I believe it is an un-American thing. The thing that I resent the most is that they are able to get into these unions, take them over, and represent to the world that a group of people in my plant, that I know are good, one-hundred-percent Americans, are trapped by this group, and they are represented to the world as supporting all of those ideologies, and it is not so, and I feel that they really ought to be smoked out and shown up for what they are, so that all of the good, free causes in this country, all the liberalisms that are really American, can go out without the taint of communism.

Disney agreed that if the Communist Party could be 'proven un-American' it ought to be outlawed. But this should be done without interfering with the rights of the people. Somehow the communists had to be got out of the unions and the unions had to be kept clean. But by now Disney had had enough of the Hollywood film industry. Television was grabbing his attention. With the end of war came the end of aluminium rationing and the relaunch of television set production in 1946. Television was the future. A decade after set production had begun again 38 million sets had been sold in the USA. This was a new world for Disney to conquer.

eisenstein shakes mickey's hand in hollywood

elastic eisenstein and the line

Sergei Eisenstein was a fan of Walt Disney. They met in 1930. In 1929 Eisenstein had set off on a tour. Avoidance of Stalin and his censors was one motivating factor. Investigation of new sound technologies was another. Eisenstein declared that Walt Disney was the only man working in the United States who could use sound film properly.[1] Eisenstein visited Berlin first and then Switzerland, in order to attend the First International Congress of Independent Cinematography. There he mucked around on celluloid with Hans Richter, who showcased his 'absolute' films *Inflation*, *Ghosts Before Breakfast* and *Film Study*. Eisenstein watched abstract films by Eggeling and saw Walter Ruttmann's *Berlin: Symphony of a City*. He participated in the conference discussions, which, eventually, despite differences of opinion, agreed 'as an absolute principle the difference in practice and spirit between the independent cinema and the commercial cinema in any shape or form'.[2] He returned to Berlin to talk with artist-intellectuals, filmmakers and theorists, including Bertolt Brecht, George Grosz, G.W. Pabst, Fritz Lang and Magnus Hirschfeld. After this, he journeyed to Paris for art-historical research and discussions with Marinetti, Léger, Cocteau, and with James Joyce, who said to a friend that if *Ulysses* were ever to be filmed, the director must be Eisenstein or Walter Ruttmann.[3] Then Eisenstein visited London to deliver a lecture to Ivor Montagu's London Film Society, and once again met up with Hans Richter. They made a film, in which Eisenstein played a London policeman. Montagu left for America to arrange Eisenstein's visit, while Eisenstein travelled between France and England.

Despite the discussions in support of independent cinema, Eisenstein was longing for and waiting for a Hollywood contract. Paramount came up with a proposal: six months' work and the option to return to Sovkino afterwards. Eisenstein sailed from France on 8 May 1930 on the *Europa*. The European avant-gardist delight in Americanism, expressed in the manifestos from the Eccentrics, the Futurists and the like, was still alive. Installed with entourage in Hollywood's Beverly Hills, he met Disney – the entourage visited the studios and all came away with signed photographs[4] – and the two directors began a correspondence. Eisenstein's closest friend there was Charlie Chaplin.[5] Eisenstein had written about Chaplin in 1922 in his first published article (with Sergei Yutkevich), which, in typical Americanist style, praised Eccentrism, detective stories and Chaplin.[6] The deal with Paramount fell through. Eisenstein's film ideas were too complicated – and the US State Department refused him a work permit. He returned to the Soviet Union after a while, and there, on the walls of the library of his home at Potylika, on the outskirts of Moscow, he placed his signed photographs from Chaplin and Disney, amongst others.[7] These were the celluloid memories of a curious encounter between filmists. There were photographs, too, of Eisenstein and Disney outside the Disney studio, entwined and sharing the frame with a cut-out Mickey Mouse, arm outstretched, thumbs up to the two of them. And there was a comic-strip-frame postcard from Walt Disney to 'my friend Serge Eisenstein', with a terrified Mickey Mouse and some hysterical jungle animals hurtling, hell for leather, up a dirt track.[8] The lines of speed, the puffs of smoking acceleration plotted their course, and oversized beads of sweat sprang off their wide-eyed bonces. It was when this static image

Hans Richter, *Film Study*, 1925/26

Eisenstein shakes Mickey's
hand in Hollywood, 1930

was set in motion through repetition that Eisenstein swooned. In addition
to Disney's talent for sound, Eisenstein admired the drawings, or rather
the moving outlines, as they danced in conjunction with the sounds.

As a child Eisenstein loved to draw. His drawings often showed animals
as humans and humans as animals. The themes of the sketches were
frequently transformation, metaphor and metamorphosis. Eisenstein
regarded drawing and dancing as two actions formed of the same impulse.
Drawing always tends to movement. When he was older, Eisenstein submitted cartoons to satirical magazines. These too often outlined fantastic
transformations. He stopped drawing for a while, from 1923, in order to
make films. But he began again around 1931 and continued until the late

1940s. In Hollywood in September 1930 he had bought an album of drawings by the Mexican artist Miguel Covarrubias; the collection was called *Negro Drawings*.[9] Covarrubias's drawings showed bendy-limbed dancers with huge hands and feet. These images, once they had mingled with musings on 'snake dancers' in New York nightclubs, squirming in abstract, silken robes, impelled Eisenstein to draw again. He made thousands of drawings. He hoped to capture a particular figure, the boneless human snake. And recourse to caricature injected the twin elements of transformation and humour. Daumier was an influence, alongside Grandville. Eisenstein collected the metamorphic images of these caricaturists. A photograph of him taken in Alma-Ata, his evacuation home in 1941, has caught on camera an illustrated edition of Lewis Carroll's works. These were the drawings that he prized and about which he wrote. He studied the Swiss experimenter Rodolphe Töpffer, who is reputed to have invented the genre of *bandes dessinées* in the mid-nineteenth century. Töpffer produced little albums of continuous strips, with characters in whimsical, nonsensical plots. Sometimes his strips plotted transformations of an object, for example a face. Lortac in France animated Töpffer's first printed story strip from 1827 called *Monsieur Vieux-Bois*, about a man who is beaten repeatedly and always begins anew simply by changing his undergarments. Töpffer travelled in various Hollywood exiles' suitcases. The European animators of Disney's *Snow White and the Seven Dwarfs* used Töpffer-like variations in the shot of the dwarfs at the end of Snow White's bed, their noses drooped over the bedstead, each face a little different from the others.

Eisenstein jotted down some notes on drawing in 1932. He wondered why his drawings were disturbing for viewers, despite the fact that they were not imitative. He decided that their potent effect stemmed from their 'protoplasmic' form, the fact that they captured something primal. By primal Eisenstein meant that they were able to address the development of the human being from blob to limbed entity. The drawings evoke the beginnings of it all, of us all. The drawings in the Mickey Mouse films, Eisenstein asserts, share this quality of primal 'plasmation', with their stretching shapes, swaying trees and disintegration, 'like quicksilver scattering and rolling back into a cohesive little ball'.[10] Such assault on coherent form, with its intimations of primitivism, was obvious in Picasso's work and Dalí's too, he believed – for example, Dalí's drooping watches in *The Persistence of Memory* (1931). All these personify, though only slightly, plasma. It could be taken much further than this. Eisenstein declared of his own drawings: 'Arms and legs in my drawings are always ... pseudopods of the primal plasma-amoeba.'[11] And, in addition to this barely formed plasmatic mass, the figures hover above the ground, like primal forms suspended in the originary liquid, the fluid whence our species emerged as well as the liquid that buffers us inside the uterus.

After his American adventure, Eisenstein visited Mexico. There he drew everything he could – and came home with bundles of bullfight sketches and pornographic drawings. His drawing style had changed. Now he drew with a closed line, an unbroken line – he regarded it as a sort of pure drawing. This closed line had a dynamic effect on the cellular, plasmatic shapes that it formed.[12] Drawing was a form of magic for Eisenstein. But his films were not composed of drawings. There were others in the Soviet Union who played that game. Mayakovsky, for one, had attempted to animate political manifestoes. And Dziga Vertov inserted animated passages in his *Kino-Pravda* documentary newsreel. And in 1922, in a treatise titled 'We: A Version of a Manifesto', Vertov revealed the graphic potentials of film:

> We must have graphic signs for movement so that we can represent a dynamic exercise on a sheet of paper.
> WE *are searching for cine-scales.*
> WE fall and rise with the rhythm of movements that have been slowed down and speeded up,
> rushing from us, past us, towards us,
> in circles, straight lines, ellipses,
> to the right and the left, with plus and minus signs;
> movements curve, straighten out, divide, split, multiply again and again, soundlessly shooting through space.
> The cinema is also the *art of inventing the movement* of objects in space responding to the demands of science, the incarnation of the inventor's dream, whether he is a scientist, an artist, an engineer or a carpenter, the realisation by the Cine-Eye of what cannot be realised in life.
> Drawings in motion. Blueprints in motion. Projects for the future. The theory of relativity on the screen.[13]

Only through the animation of geometry could film be understood in its most appropriate form – the art of inventing movement. Long live dynamic geometry, the race of points, lines, planes and volumes, cries Vertov. Film must broadcast that which cannot be realized in life, and this will allow the analytical, scientific attitude, the dissection of reality. And it will allow an opening onto the future, the possibilities of the new world, on the bases of the science and technique of the present. All this is in a spirit akin to the universal language project of Eggeling and Richter.

In 1924 Alexei Gan reported on Vertov and the cine-eye movement for a journal. He noted that number 18 of the *Kino-Pravda* reels included two Soviet animations, *Humoresques* and *Soviet Toys*. While the films may be technically weak, and certainly not as well made as those in the West, he notes that their themes are at least pertinent and they demonstrate a 'complete immersion in our reality'.[14] The same filmmakers, Aleksandr Ivanov and Aleksandr Buskin, and camera operator Ivan Beljakov also made *In the Face of the Second International* and *McDonald's Career*. These short films appeared to have a future, for Lunacharsky in his 'Revolutionary Ideology and Cinema – Theses', of March 1924, accented the propagandistic importance of film caricature, what he called *agitki* or living posters of five to ten minutes in which the political tendency could dominate but which must remain witty and absorbing.[15] These living posters were envisaged as one part of a programme of events. In 1925 Vertov proposed a variety of film genres and types on a single cinema bill in 'Cine-Pravda and Radio-Pravda'. There he argued that 'cinemas that show full-length films are the most conservative'.[16] Mixed programming was Vertov's slogan – and it would deliver ideally a three-reel newsreel of the Cine-Eye type, a one-reel cartoon, a one- or two-reel scientific film or travelogue, a two-reel drama or comedy. Not as accompaniment to but as component of the newsreel *Kino-Pravda* number 21 of 1925 is a cartoon that depicts Lenin being wounded by an arrow shot at his head.

Vertov was addressing what he hoped would prove to be the future of cinema – mixed programming and multi-genre – but he was also returning to cinema's origins as a variety programme of attractions, and sloughing off what seemed to be the bourgeois-theatrical institution of the feature film. His specific interest in the cartoon as documentary also reanimated the past, for Eric Walter White observed that the cartoon film probably originated in the topical newsreel, when a lightning cartoon sketcher would dash off his speedy drawings in front of the camera, as interlude between the unveiling of a new memorial and the latest fashions from Paris. White remarks that in the updated version the cartoonist is done away with, but the cartoon remains.[17] Indeed what had happened was the removal of the illusionist from the frame. Now the illusionist was behind the camera or was the drawer, one of many perhaps. Perhaps the maker of the illusion was anonymous, just one of a number strewn out along a production line, working in combination with others. Such segmentation of labour modified the whole cinema industry. Recognition of this division of labour within the cinematic industry led Eisenstein to develop a bitterly critical stance towards 'bourgeois' filmmaking and film theorists. In 1926, he wrote an attack on these, titled 'Béla Forgets the Scissors'. There had been some discussion in the Soviet Union on the question of European avant-garde film. Ilya Ehrenburg brought clips to Moscow in 1926 from films by Abel Gance, René Clair and Jean Renoir and he used them to accompany a lecture on 'The New French Cinema'. This lecture was widely discussed in the press, and the following year Ehrenburg published a pamphlet titled 'The Materialization of the Fantastic'. Eisenstein hated the films:

> These are sheer *enfantillages* – 'children's playthings' – based on the photographic possibilities of the photographic apparatus. I am not exaggerating when I say that: if we have these 'children's playthings' today, tomorrow they will be used to refurbish the formal methods of a whole branch of art (for instance, the 'absolute': the plotless film of Picabia, Léger or Chomette).
>
> We are taking our conviction that light can come only from the West to the point of absurdity.[18]

The French films were formalist trinkets, turning a mechanical and reality-sampling optics back into 'art'. But Eisenstein's key point concerns the labour involved in making a film. His criticism is directed at the critics. Film is a collective effort, yet the industry and its supporters regard the camera operator as just a mechanic. They are fixated on the 'star'. This mirrors the individualism of the West – Béla Balázs's novelty was apparently to have suddenly discovered the cameraman as star, instead of the director. But Eisenstein was not convinced. None of Balázs's ideas betoken a recognition that film is a collective effort. And in addition, he complains, Balázs has forgotten the importance of editing in film; expression through juxtaposition, sequence, relationships. Film is an aggregate and assemblage process, insists Eisenstein. That this could not be recognized is indicative of a wider ideological crisis in bourgeois cultural production. Eisenstein notes that the large Berlin film studio UFA is situated on a corner where 'swastika-wearers' constantly throng, distributing their propaganda. UFA, he warns, will follow suit.[19] Balázs, working in Weimar cinema at this time, was exposed to such influences, though it is unlikely that he would be drawn in. More pressing on him is the influence of a German art cinema, conceived perhaps as the worthy alternative to the commercial sphere. In submitting to this influence, the temptation is to be dragged back into bourgeois approaches to art works as the output of inspired individuals and possessing everlasting value. This was clearly exposed in Balázs's writing style:

> His terminology is unpleasant. Different from ours. 'Art', 'creativity', 'eternity', 'greatness' and so on. Although some prominent Marxists write in the same dialect and this counts as dialectics. It looks as if this style has become acceptable.[20]

In his opposition to such terminology Eisenstein anticipates Walter Benjamin's objections in 'The Work of Art in the Age of its Technical Reproducibility' (1935–39). Benjamin complains that art works are envisioned by critics and artists in terms of outmoded concepts, such as creativity and genius, eternal value and mystery, 'concepts whose uncontrolled (and at present almost uncontrollable) application would lead to a processing of data in the Fascist sense'.[21]

Towards the end of the 1920s Soviet production of animation increased, but much of this larger quantity of material was not innovative. Socialist realism had kicked into this realm, sanctioning the adaptation of classical texts and popular traditions, often for children's entertainment and edification. The rounded, cuter forms that were ever more present in American animation also crop up in the productions of Sojuzdetmultfilm. Gan had suggested in 1924 that much Soviet animation was ideologically correct but technically weak. However, in 1935 avant-gardist Moholy-Nagy, in

'Supplementary Remarks on the Sound and Color Film', was prepared to praise as 'perhaps the most important project realized so far' the synthetic sound scripts of Humphries, Pfenniger, and a series of Russians: Avramov, Janovski, Vojnov and Scholpo. These occupied the same universe of experiment as the sound tricks in films by Harold Lloyd and Walt Disney, where speech speed-ups and reversal of sounds are exploited for their comic potential.[22] Experiments with 'drawn sound' had been an area of research in Russia from the 1910s onwards. Experimenters worked on the shape of sounds, in imitation of the visualizations of futurist Velemir Chlebnikov, who had conceived sonics physically, mathematically and graphically. In 1917 Avramov, Scholpo and Dijanim founded the Leonardo Da Vinci Society in order to investigate the generation of artificial sound and to understand sound scientifically and technically. Scholpo signed a contract with Lenfilm, which made it possible for him to build an apparatus to generate sounds. Avramov put his energies into creating an 'international balalaika' which could play all the melodies of the world in a combined world-tonal system. International, internationalist music of the future was to be created, until a full stop was put to so much of this experimentation by Stalinist diktat. But sound in general was the future of film. There was international interest in reproduced sound – if at the same time the coming of language cinema reinforced national boundaries, or linguistic boundaries, for film. The painter and book illustrator Mikhail Tsekhanovsky directed *Post Office* (1929). This description of world mail carriers was re-edited in 1930 for a sound version and shown all over the world. Frank Lloyd Wright showed it to Disney as an example of thought-provoking animation. Even sound film – presumed by some to be so nationally, linguistically bound – could be in a worldwide dialogue. Walter Benjamin notes in his essay on the art work in the age of technical reproducibility that, at first, sound film was a setback to international distribution of cinema, because of linguistic barriers. However, he notes, this was soon overcome by refined dubbing techniques. Benjamin was more interested in the relationship between the coming of sound film and the coming of fascism. Both are attributed to the Depression. Fascism was capitalism's rescue package. Sound was cinema's hook to ensnare greater audiences, more box-office receipts. It also brought in extra sources of capital from the electrical industry. Benjamin's closing verdict is that sound film promoted national interests, but it also helped to internationalize film production on a greater scale than before.[23]

eisenstein, animation and the universal

Indeed, film was a central element of a world culture, as the many film festivals and award ceremonies testified. Disney animation was showcased at the First Moscow International Film Festival in 1935. Eisenstein was a member of the jury, and he insisted that the first prize should go to Disney's *Three Little Pigs*, a Silly Symphony from 1933. He lost the vote (though the film received a special prize) and the first prize went instead jointly to Lenfilm for *Chapayev*, and *The Youth of Maxim* and Ermler's *Peasants*; the second prize went to René Clair's *Le dernier milliardaire*; while Disney took third prize for his contribution to animation. At this time, Eisenstein was tumbling from grace. In 1934 he wrote an attack on Soviet film titled 'Eh! On the Purity of Film Language!'[24] He attacked Soviet film's artistic conservatism and its theatrical use of sound and actors. This was an unfavourable time to make such negative statements. Consolidation of socialist realist tendencies in art was manifested in the cultural conferences where speakers, party men loyal and true, turned again and again on the misdemeanours of the avant-garde. A keynote conference was the First Congress of Soviet Writers in August 1934. There Andrei Zhdanov laid down the guidelines for the approved art policies of socialist realism and revolutionary romanticism, and Karl Radek thrashed James Joyce for his indiscriminate and cinematographic reproduction of internal life, replete with its hallucinations and uncensored thoughts: 'A heap of dung, crawling with worms, photographed by a cinema apparatus through a microscope – such is Joyce's work.'[25] But film was to be further assailed in its own specially convened congress. In January 1935 there was the All-Union Creative Conference of Workers in Soviet Cinema, where Eisenstein, Kuleshov, Vertov and Dovzhenko were rebuked in the name of a new filmmaking that would be closer to the people. Eisenstein spoke at this conference. He addressed the dialectical unity in tension of form and content in art, through which he hoped to reconcile his interest in pre-logical sensuous appeal with the demands for intellectual attention. That same year Eisenstein acknowledged the shortcomings of the old-guard avant-garde of Soviet filmmaking, nominating, in a film journal poll, *Three Little Pigs* as the year's major achievement in the advancement of film art.[26] Eisenstein and co. were on the way down, but his favoured Disney was doing well enough in the Soviet Union to attract the scorn of Nazi film critics in Germany. A news report in a *Film-Kurier* of 1936 laughed at the idea of Mickey Mouse as a social reformer and mocked the fact that, at a showing in Moscow, Disney's *The Band Concert*, *Three Little Pigs* and *Peculiar Penguins* enjoyed enthusiastic applause from the public. The report noted that Soviet reviewers greet Walt Disney as a genius and attribute social meaning to Mickey Mouse. Enthusiastic critics make the patently absurd claim that 'Disney shows us, in actuality, the people of the capitalist world disguised as pigs, mice and penguins!'[27]

Thought and double-thought on Disney's meanings might only have encouraged Eisenstein in his own analyses of Disney product. Eisenstein began to jot down notes for an article on Disney at the end of 1940. It was to be one of three articles on film masters. The other two were to be on Charlie Chaplin and David Wark Griffith. Disney films were praised as the work of a man who achieves 'absolute perfection in what he does'. And indeed it was clear to Eisenstein that here indeed, in Disney films, the capitalist world was indicted, though not through obvious branding or preaching or exposure of its crimes, but through the release of the viewer out of this world of suffering and separation into an oblivion that is not the escapism of 'happy-ends' but a return to something essential and true.[28] Eisenstein took Disney extremely seriously. He was aware that his own mode of filmmaking was not so removed from Disney's mode, even if it might seem to some a world apart. Both used storyboards, for example. Eisenstein used storyboards because he conceived of film shot by shot and focused on the relations between parts. Walt Disney and his staff developed an animation storyboard system in 1928. For the full animation that Disney desired, an enormous number of drawings needed to be produced. In order to make selections from these many drawings, the animators had to pin their drawings up on the studio walls. That same year Eisenstein was stalled in his practical activities and turned his attention to developing theories of montage. He first considered montage principles through the ideograms of Japanese writing and kabuki theatre's decomposition of the coherence of reality, where sounds and visual data fall apart and are recombined. Disney animation's basis in drawing meant that Eisenstein could relate all he saw to his wide knowledge of drawing and art history, and he could cross-reference its evolution with developments in his montage theory. Animated drawing's reference to nature was the aspect that most concerned him. Animation is thoroughly in tune with nature, with its dynamic, its dialectic and its motility. This is nature understood without preconception and without convention, such that nature becomes freedom rather than necessity. Nature becomes non-nature, anti-nature, something in movement. The category of nature implodes. In the introduction to his unfinished article on Disney, written in Alma-Ata in 1941, Eisenstein reflects that Disney 'creates somewhere in the realm of the very purest and most primal depths. There, where we are all children of nature.'[29] Disney's own self-understanding was not so far removed. Asked once about the secret of the universal charm of *Snow White and the Seven Dwarfs*, Disney replied:

> Over at our place we're sure of just one thing. Everybody in the world was once a child. Planning a new picture we don't think of grown-ups or children but just of that kind, clean unspoiled spot down deep in every one of us that the world has maybe made us forget and maybe our pictures can help recall.[30]

Such nostalgia for a lost childhood meant, for Eisenstein, that Disney 'creates on the conceptual level of man not yet shackled by logic, reason or experience'. Eisenstein and Adorno were quite opposed on this point: what Adorno saw as the reactionary mythics of late Disney, a fetishistically organized expression of an originary infantilism, becomes in Eisenstein a progressive vitalism. For Eisenstein, Disney creates a captivating current of interflowing images, just as is the celluloid strip. But this access to the flow of pre-logical creativity is not special to film. It is there in Hans Christian Andersen's fairy-tales, in Lewis Carroll's *Alice*, in E.T.A. Hoffmann's fantastic tales. But Disney is a master, as Eisenstein's notes declare in November 1941:

> One of Disney's most amazing films is his *Merbabies*. What purity and clarity of soul is needed to make such a thing! To what depths of untouched nature is it

necessary to dive with bubbles and bubblelike children in order to reach such absolute freedom from all categories, all conventions. In order to be like children.[31]

Eisenstein distinguishes this from nostalgia for a childhood that can never be had again, a Paradise Lost, the clash of childhood and adult reality, which appears to compose the tragic tone of Chaplin's films. Disney allows for a better, socialist future – not least because he draws and redraws the world, conjuring up a 'complete return to a world of complete freedom (not accidentally fictitious), freed from the necessity of another primal extinction'.[32] This world is epitomized in the figure of an octopus with four legs, a fifth as a tail, and a sixth as a trunk. This is a reconstruction of the world, based on it but also freely reimagining it according to fantasy and will. 'Omnipotence' appeals to Eisenstein: something of the director is coming through here, in his desire to reshape the world. After all, the drawing is so much easier to manipulate than actors and props: 'You tell a mountain: move, and it moves. You tell an octopus: be an elephant, and the octopus becomes an elephant. You tell the sun: "Stop!" – and it stops.'[33]

This fantastic mastery is envisioned for a society in which nature has been completely enslaved, for America. Most strongly it magnetizes those who live in such a rationalized country. The little man lives in the grey grey grey of city blocks and prison cells, and he suffers the division of the soul like pig carcasses in Chicago slaughterhouses or cars on Ford's conveyor belt. Against this grey, Disney's films are ablaze with colour. This colour, this mutability, this vitality is a 'drop of comfort'.[34] The anxiety of the little man in America is alleviated for a few moments by the magic of animation. The violence does not hurt and the daily destruction is magically reversed. The cartoon dazzles with brilliant tones and mutable forms. Its flexibility is shared by music, which changes constantly, and by that inexhaustible object of fascination, fire – a dialectical form, as Lenin notes via Hegel[35] – with its endlessly changing contours and tones.[36] The fantastic mastery of animation seems both to reinforce nature's subjugation by the creator – thus engaging pleasing feelings of omnipotence – and to allow nature to speak, to come alive, to elasticate and bend the laws of physics and convention, the 'fetters of form', appealing then to revolutionary and dynamic sensibility. Eisenstein marvels at stretched body parts, at nature distended. It is attractive; although, he admits, it is a strange fact that such elasticity is attractive. Disney's work is 'the most omni-appealing': 'It's justifiable to suppose that *this* work has *most* or all the traits of pre-logical attractiveness.'[37] It entices because of its rejection of the 'metaphysical immobility'[38] of once-and-forever allotted form. It proposes freedom from ossification, and the ability dynamically to assume any form.[39] Eisenstein adulates the transformations – for example, the striped fish in the cage which turns into a tiger and roars like a lion or a panther. At the centre of this pliant world stands the human, who is attracted to this reshaping because none of it is arbitrary. Rather, this is the species recapitulating its whole development, all the stages as mapped out by Darwin, notes Eisenstein in November 1940.[40] Beings are presented which behave like the 'primal protoplasm', not possessing yet a stable form, but dashing up and down the 'rungs of the evolutionary ladder'.[41] Disney's nature made sense of Engels's dialectics of nature. Evolutionary biology offered Eisenstein ways of conceiving natural development in terms of ontogenesis and phylogenesis. As Engels put it:

> For, just as the development history of the human embryo in the mother's womb is only an abbreviated repetition of the history, extending over millions of years, of the bodily evolution of our animal ancestors, starting from the worm, so the mental development of the human child is only a still more abbreviated repetition of the intellectual development of these same ancestors, at least of the later ones.[42]

Archaic, plasmatic nature reinventing itself, while retaining links through histories of form, excited Eisenstein. If the archaic is in any sense 'eternal', this 'eternal' is different to the bourgeois notion of 'eternal value' in art works. There the eternal, imagined as unchanging, correlates actually to a term for a limited period of human development (rooted in antiquity). Eisenstein's eternal is always transforming, and would appear to stretch back endlessly to the beginning of our species, or other species, or life, or time, or even the cosmos. Protoplasm was the beginning of life – it might be simple and structureless or moulded by evolutionary forces or industrial needs. 'Plasma' is Eisenstein's master-term, and for Engels it is the protein that 'contains potentially within itself all other forms of protein', because of its absence of specificity.[43] Rather than concentrating on the DNA code, a copyrightable word of life that capitalist research tracked down in the post-war era, dialectical evolutionism looks into the staggering potential of protein as life-making material, the manner in which different series of nucleic acids in one dimension produce endless complexities once realized in three dimensions and allowed to interact over time with other molecules. As against the penalizing survival-of-the-fittest ultra-Darwinists, who turn evolution into an internecine affair of extermination and genocide, progressive biology accentuates the stunning potential of protein as material ('a modest protein, with molecular weight of some 34,000 and containing combinations of only 12 of the naturally occurring amino acids, could exist in 10^{300} possible forms, and if only one molecule of each existed the total mass would be around 10^{280} grams – compare this with the mass of the entire universe, which one estimate puts at "only" 10^{55} grams!'[44]). Eisenstein's excitement with the potential of protein is consistent with the anti-Platonic materialism of progressive biologists from Engels onwards. Eisenstein's thoughts on plasmation from 1932 develop into a grander theory of 'plasmaticness'. This concept was designed to defy social miseries justified in terms of science, objectivity and atomic fact.

The potential that Eisenstein spies in life forms is dramatized in the mouldable forms of the cartoon universe. Plasmaticness understands the 'poly-formic capabilities of an object'.[45] Elasticity attracts – for it provides a palette of all possible forms for us. Eisenstein does not think it very possible that an archaic memory resides within us (though he is won over to intracellular memory), but he does insist that there exists a universal feeling for a multiplicity of forms. Each human responds to the charm of that potentiality. This feeling can only be more intense in a mercilessly standardized country, where existence dances to the rhythm of the machine and life is squeezed out of existence. It is a case of abandoning the stiff corsets and collars of high society and the strictions of the workplace, in favour of spinelessness, bonelessness, nudity, the flowing line. The line is liberated – liberated even from the slavish tracing of correct, naturalistic, containing contours. The line is unrepressed. The shapes of life as multiple and dynamic combine with the sense of a universe in which anything can mutate, thus suggesting the limits of our concepts of natural and social existence. Eisenstein wanted to go further with this promotion of flexibility. He craved a screen that could change shape.[46]

But there remains the question of content. Disney outdoes himself when the assertion of inconstancy, the embrace of the pre-logical and the rejection of discipline and control become subject matter, such as when Donald Duck smashes up the radio that had been lecturing him on behaviour in *Self-Control* (1938), or when Mickey Mouse and friends in *Lonesome Ghosts* (1937) exterminate ghosts. Eisenstein is on the side of the spooks.

> The 'Ghost Exterminating Company' – isn't this actually a symbol of formal logic which drives out everything living, mobile, fantastic? Its failures and losses in the war with a handful of ghosts, with the fantastic which lurks in the nature of every night table, of every soup bowl, behind every door and in every wall![47]

The moral of the tale is that freedom from logic's fetters and political subjugation can be secured only after having united with the fantastic, the alogical, the sensuous order. Duped by the ghosts, the ghostbusters fall into a blob of dough and turn into white shadows. They become ghosts, and terrify the real ghosts, who take off from the creepy 'haunted house'. Identifications shift, the real and the fantastic swap places. The cartoon offers a moment's freedom, a quick break for the psyche. And it most often does this by offering displaced identification, mostly animals in place of people, or animals substituting for other animals. The turn to the animalistic is occasioned by the 'lack of humaneness in systems of social government or philosophy'. This enables Eisenstein to draw analogies between Fordist America and the French Enlightenment of the seventeenth century with its mathematical abstractions, systematized metaphysics and reason disassociated from bodies, and against which the matterism of the eighteenth century struggled. Rational ahumanism bore as antidote the animal fables of La Fontaine, which rediscovered nature and defended it against Descartes' vivisection and Versailles gardeners' geometricizing clippers. But La Fontaine's rediscovery of nature is not asocial. Eisenstein compares his sensitivity to that of caricaturist Grandville. Grandville humanizes, his animal images are endowed with human nature, suggested by their look – the frogs' round and vacant eyes making them appear stupid, the ant's narrow waist and black colour suggesting a thrifty house-keeper.[48] Disney casts nature just as successfully. And that there were confusions between animal nature and human nature was evidenced not just in the behaviour and personalities of the Disney characters but also in the look, such as when Bambi animator Marc Davis transposed the shape of a baby's head to his drawing of the fawn. At the end of December 1943, Eisenstein praised *Bambi*. In its deer as human – or rather human as deer – it images evolutionary pre-history.[49] This is totemism. *Bambi* enacts a return to pure totemism. Transpositions do not conceal animal nature, Eisenstein insists, but cast it into relief. It is poetry and so it expresses something truer than mere slavish imitation. But most important of all is that Disney's cartoons enframe the unexpected rebirth of universal animism: 'The animated drawing is the most direct manifestation of … animism!'[50] Eisenstein copied out the definition of animal from *Webster's Dictionary*, for the English made clear the connections that he wished to tease out:

> *Animal* … – Lat. *anima* – breath, soul … akin to Lat. *animus* – soul, mind. Greek *anemos* – breath, wind. Sanskrit *an* – to breathe, to live … To supply with life, to enliven; as how the soul *animates* the body … An *animated picture. Animism* – from Lat. *anima*: soul … The belief that all objects possess a natural life or vital force or that they are endowed with an indwelling spirit. The term is usually used to designate the most primitive and superstitious forms of religion.[51]

Eisenstein was excited by the links in this polyglot, multi-meaning word complex. Breath, soul, mind, liveliness, mobility, atavism – all present in the most modern, flat, trivial and mass form of entertainment; and present in multiple ways. Cartoon drawings were animated – that is, they were mobile, they had life – indeed so much so that their bodies stretched and popped and twisted. The objects drawn were again animated in the sense that they were endowed with traits and emotions that were generally human – they were endowed with soul. This animation then operated at a physical and a spiritual level. But further, the magic of primitivism imbued the whole event of the cartoon, with its audio-visual synthesis and its meta-morphic storylines. In 1944 Eisenstein explained the magical aspect of

Gesamtkunstwerk synthesis, which 'returns' the viewer to non-differentiated, primordially sensuous perception.[52] For the viewer, Mr Little American, all this amounts to an ecstatic experience – that is to say, a non-static experience of self-immersion (i.e. self-obliteration) in nature and animals, out of which nothingness 'everything can arise'.[53] The little man is taken out of himself in order to enter far more deeply into inner and past selves as protoplasm, as beast, as unformed potentiality.

Eisenstein compares Disney's humanization of animals to the totemic beliefs of the Indians of the Bororo tribe. The Bororos imagine the red parrot of Brazil to be a manifestation of their selves. They have a simultaneous identity. And so too in Disney, the peacock, parrot, nightstand and dancing flame are at one and the same time animal/object and human.[54] And, at one and the same time, we know that they are drawings and not living beings and that they are projections, and yet we sense them as alive, moving and even thinking. Animation provides readmission to the stages of human development in relation to nature over the course of time. In the earliest years of our species I and nature were 'one and the same'. As time has passed I and nature have undergone a process of separation, according to Eisenstein. They were 'identical' and then they were 'alike', and, later still, they became 'different' from each other. However, that original one-and-the-sameness of I and nature still lingers as a trace somewhere in the deepest recesses of the mind or in ourselves as children. This primordial mode of empathy accounts for the transfer of mobility to the immobile. It is rooted in perception. The eye moves as it sees. It runs along the contours of the objects in the eye's sightline. This eye movement, notes Eisenstein, is then attributed to the object seen – and is the basis of metaphorical language – an art of transfer.[55] The road stretches, the rainbow skips, the mountain creeps. Disney visualizes this process in the elastic play of contours of his images. These repeat the movements of the looking eye, making subject and object as one. And the drawings demonstrate this in curious ways. When a character trembles, its body quivers and, in addition, the line that forms its contour also crinkles and wobbles. When the contours of Disney's horses, cows, goats, ostriches and monkeys dash forwards, they leave themselves behind. Humour derives from the combination of image, the representation, and lines that form the image, the graphic marks. These two elements, whose linkage should normally be indissoluble and invisible, may contradict each other, or play with each other's dominion.[56] Essence and form, the unity of an object and its form of representation, are severed, and the viewer finds this shocking and amusing because the viewer knows that they should be in contact. Here is a further level of animation: the line itself takes on a life of its own, independent of what it represents. Organic unity is broken up. Eisenstein seems to be accounting for the existence of modernist formalism, aspects of which had emphasized a fascination with primitivism (Picasso, for one) and the drawings of the insane (Max Ernst, Paul Klee and so on).

> For periods of collapse, i.e. a regressive return to primitive patterns, there is characteristically the very same collapse of the unity of form and content, as for periods standing on the threshold of their future merger. Construction becomes an end in itself. Composition – the sole content of the thing.[57]

Ecstasy is the aim. The self must be taken out, taken in, led astray and led back. The object must be drawn out. Shape and line must be set in tension. He speaks of swelling. It is a sexualized language that hopes to address analogically the political – going beyond what is – as much as the anthropological – that we can become more than what we are now, perhaps by recognizing what we have been when we were still open to possibility.[58] These thoughts flowed into a more general theory of representation. Eisenstein valued the pushing out of limits. In *Non-Indifferent Nature* he traces the points of transition in art, the dialectical moments of leaping from one quality into another. In the ecstatic and erotic milk separator sequence in *The General Line*, he reveals, a perspective-distorting lens and modes of editing were some of the factors that instilled 'pathos' and enabled objects to 'go beyond themselves, beyond their natural bounds of volume and form'.[59] Human plasticity, object plasticity, is on display. Object and human are equally animated.

animal magic

Discussion of animism – in the context of dialectics – was taking place in another corner of the revolutionary ménage. Leon Trotsky – who, like Eisenstein, sought refuge under a Mexican sun – was needled into breathless disbelief by statements on the part of the American Marxist editor of *The Masses* (who was also his translator). Max Eastman was pronouncing on the necessary, and calamitous, connection of dialectics and animism.[60] Eastman wrote a study of Marx and Lenin and the 'science of revolution' in 1926. In it he attacked the very idea of dialectical thought. He decreed it a form of animism.

> In primitive culture it is possible to distinguish two quite different kinds of thinking – animistic thinking, in which one tries to adjust oneself to the external world as to a person, and the ordinary practical thinking by which the daily arts of life are carried on. Animistic thinking consists essentially in trying by some sort of hocus-pocus to transfer your own wishes into the external world, and so get them realized. It is emotional and ceremonial and soon becomes institutionalized in the religious festivals, the Mysteries, the Priests, the Church. And because of its emotional hold upon men, it is taken in charge by the ruling and exploiting classes, and becomes the guardian of custom and 'good morals', and the chief cultural instrument for the maintenance of the *status quo*. It is aristocratic thinking, and makes up in elaboration and social standing what it lacks in its convincing force.[61]

Against such thinking is the plain materialism of Practical Man, another one in the family of Mr Little American. Practical Man's matter-of-fact convincing explanations of how the world is put together must be refuted by those in power. The refutation comes in the form of mystification. It is the invention of 'Philosophy', blusters Eastman the pragmatist. The philosopher's task is 'to preserve animism at all costs', a metaphysics that contradicts the scientific viewpoint.[62]

> German philosophy is the ultimate grandiose convulsion of animistic thought, expiring under the encroachments of the scientific point of view. And the philosophy of Hegel is the ultimate flower of German philosophy, the most adequately bold and all-comprehending and all-obscuring, the most sublimely animistic and the most beautiful.[63]

Hegel placed at the centre of his world-view a material world in perpetual process and development. Natural scientists were reaching similar conclusions at the same time and so animism found its way into the heart of science in the nineteenth century. The animistic attitude also influenced the young Marx and Engels. It came too soon and too forcefully ever to be fully overcome. Animism lurks in the laws of dialectical materialism, in the idea of communism as the automatic progress of a world spirit. Trotsky was appalled by Eastman's rejection of dialectics.[64] He found it impossible to reconcile a non-dialectical approach with a revolutionary attitude. In response to Eastman's views he began to jot notes in a notebook. Eastman called on Freud as an authority to back up his claim that dialectics was a form of animistic thought. Freud had examined animism in *Totem and Taboo*, pointing out that anthropomorphism was the first form of spirituality and also that it still persisted in contemporary language, belief systems and philosophies. Freud thought that the past ruled over the present. Feelings of uncannyness, for example, as he had written in 1919 in a reflection on E.T.A. Hoffmann's *The Sandman*, a fairy-tale about an automaton, were evidence of the persistence of primitive beliefs in modern life. Here he would have agreed with Eisenstein, though Freud found that grip of the old to be unsettling and evocative of death, not the plenipotentiality of life. Archaic beliefs persisted in modern life. To that extent, he was no 'modernist', even if the modernists were Freudians.

In 1935 Trotsky reflected critically on Eastman's ideas once more in his diary written in exile. He alleged the absurdity of the theories of Eastman and others who thought that revolutionaries were 'engineers' building the new social order out of the materials at hand. Trotsky insists on 'the autonomous rhythm of the vital processes'. The language is organic. History, movements, are inert or they are active. Or they are somewhere in between the two, the point being that where there is change, there is the right moment. There is a social body, unpredictable, ripe, then unripe, not a machine, regular as clockwork and mechanical.[65] At that moment, the Marxist struggles against the grain. The automatic road of history trudged by the Marxist party is not for Trotsky. Dialectics is not reduced to a set of pre-determined laws of history. Indeed, he states, it is the bureaucracy of the Communist Party that pretends that it is marching along the road of history to universal liberation, when in fact it gratifies only its own interests. This privileged caste flows in a stagnant stream.

> In general it is impossible for people to come out of the woods on to the main road of history without the conscious participation of the 'sectarians', i.e., the Marxist minority, which today is pushed aside. But it must be a question of participation in an *organic* process. One must know its laws, as a doctor must know the 'healing power of nature'.[66]

The laws of nature cannot be ignored. The revolutionary movement is an organic one, not a mechanical one. Trotsky appealed to Darwin. He spent much time examining the theory of evolution, and this for him was inextricably bound up with dialectics. Evolutionary theory mapped the alterations in species-being. These changes could be dramatic and the result of environmental crisis goading laws of natural selection to take effect. This might result in sudden leaps in nature. Trotsky slid such revolutionary–evolutionary theory sideways to account for the process of social change. 'Only the inner tie of Marxism and Darwinism permits us to understand the living current of being and its primal tie with inorganic nature.'[67]

Climatic crisis and civil war, disruptions of equilibrium, the storm that always follows the lull, catalyse the transition of quantity into quality. In his *History of the Russian Revolution*, or, to be precise, in Max Eastman's translation of the volume, Trotsky writes:

> Physical analogies with revolution come so naturally that some of them have become worn-out metaphors: 'volcanic eruption', 'birth of a new society', 'boiling point'.… Under the simple literary image there is concealed here an intuitive grasp of the laws of dialectic – that is, the logic of evolution.
>
> Armed insurrection stands in the same relation to revolution that revolution as a whole does to evolution, it is the critical point when accumulating quantity turns with an explosion into quality. But insurrection itself again is not a homogeneous and indivisible act: it too has its critical points, its inner crises and accelerations.
>
> An extraordinary importance both political and theoretical attaches to that short period immediately preceding the 'boiling point' – the eve, that is, of the insurrection. Physics teaches that the steady increase of temperature suddenly comes to a stop; the liquid remains for a time at the same temperature, and boils only after absorbing an additional quantity of heat. Everyday language also comes to our aid here, designating this condition of pseudo-tranquil concentration preceding an explosion as 'the lull before the storm'.
>
> When an unqualified majority of the workers and soldiers of Petrograd had come over to the Bolsheviks, the boiling temperature, it seemed, was reached. It was then that Lenin proclaimed the necessity of immediate insurrection. But it is striking to observe that something was still lacking to the insurrection. The workers, and especially the soldiers, had to absorb some additional revolutionary energy.[68]

Trotsky cautioned against social Darwinism, but he was committed to an organic, dynamic, energy-laden vision of the development of the human race. In the ecstatic climax of *Literature and Revolution* he outlines a techno-logically enhanced leap in the quality of existence. Communist life is not formed blindly, like coral islands, he states, but consciously, through intelli-gence and processes of correction. Shells of life burst apart through techno-logical and cultural change. Artificial selection and psycho-physical training, which is 'entirely in accord with evolution', will enhance capabilities and bring about a much-desired harmonization of the self, its organs, its be-haviour, its abilities, its intellect. The nature of man, 'hidden in the deepest and darkest corner of the subconscious, of the elemental, of the sub-soil' will be illumined. Evolution becomes a process of conscious will and science.[69] Organicism, primal energies and animation are the watchwords.

Trotsky was criticized for his anthropomorphism from another quarter. A sympathizer, the surrealist André Breton, recalled in 1942, in 'Prolegom-ena to a Third Surrealist Manifesto or Not', a visit to Trotsky's Mexican exile home. Under Breton's gaze, Trotsky turned into Mickey Mouse, the boy who has always at his side his faithful but dumb hound, who is more than a hound, and is his friend – Pluto. Walking on the patio, Trotsky stopped to pat and pet a dog. He began to speak of the love of animals, the love for animals, the love that comes from animals. Breton retorted in unsentimentalizing fashion that animals cannot have feelings of friend-ship. Trotsky for his part *insisted* that they could share those feelings in every sense of the word. This anthropomorphic view of the animal world evidences, says Breton, 'a regrettable and facile way of thinking', though it is also poignant because it betrays – or even confirms for Breton – the weakness of this man who is by the time of Breton's memoir-writing the casualty of 'a tragic fate'.[70] But is it not touching that Trotsky should hold out such hope for dogs, the very delegates of faithfulness, of fidelity, condemned as he is to exist in a world of agents, spies and betrayers?

John Berger, in 'Why Look At Animals', registers the historical nature of the man–pet affiliation.[71] It is, he claims, a fraught relationship, anchored firmly in the industrial epoch. In a sweeping survey of human–animal relations across time, Berger notes how animals, once resident at the centre of the human world, subjected but also worshipped, endowed with magical significance and anthropomorphized, 'disappear' during the process of urban industrialization in the nineteenth century. Later they resurface, first as machines and later still as raw materials – meat, leather and horn. Exotic animals become inmates of public zoos. Used up or caged in, animals' special and equal relation to humans vanishes. A chasm opens up between man and nature, which is really a gulf within nature, would man but acknowledge it. However, simultaneously, the 'marginalization' of animals is revoked by the invention of the household pet. Pets, asserts Berger, are nothing other than animals reduced and drained, 'mementoes from the outside world', lodging in the hermetic family home, along with pot plants and romantic landscape paintings.[72] The owner's relationship to the pet is corrupt, because the animal is corrupted. Pets resemble their owners for they live lives like them, but inasmuch as they do this, they lose their animality and autonomy. In such a filiation, nature, lost to urban man, is regained in compromised form. Since the nineteenth century, children have been surrounded daily by likenesses of animals in toys, pictures and cartoons. These animal icons are frequently cute and often humanized. It is a peculiarity of the industrialized world and it ensconces early on in life the fantasy that to be at one with animals is to inhabit a lost paradise.

Images of reconciliation rescind recollection of an ongoing instrumental violation of animals, as initiated by Descartes, who conceived animals as soulless machines. In order to prove that animals have no soul Descartes nailed his wife's dog by its four paws to a board and dissected it alive, thereby instating a common practice for scientific researchers at London's Royal Society. Marx observed 'incidentally', in a footnote in Volume 1 of *Capital*, the materialist basis of Descartes' view. Descartes, in defining animals as mere machines, saw with eyes of the manufacturing period, while to eyes of the middle ages animals were assistants to man.[73] Descartes was just slightly prophetic. Live animals flayed and dissected appeared to the vivisectionists to be like watch or clock mechanisms. Ostensibly activated by wheels, ratchets, springs, gears and weights, they were conceived as automatons. It is here that the cuddly toy and the faithful pet and the cartoon animal submit their counter-claim, voiding the justification for cruelty and overriding its actuality. In a radio lecture for children, titled *True Stories about Dogs* (1930), Walter Benjamin notes that the dog is the only animal (with the possible exception of the horse) with which man has been able to establish a bond of intimacy.[74] Benjamin attributes this familiarity to the victory of humans over animals, secured long ago, when animals were tamed and became dependent on man. Not for Benjamin Berger's idea of a pre-industrial golden age of animal–human relations, when humans depended upon animals, and so had to respect them. For thousands of years, Benjamin insists, dog has been slave and man master. But man's victory is not absolute, and dogs retain traces of their untamed and self-sufficient origin. Caught between wolfish past and devotion to humans, the dog straddles the line between nature (animality) and culture (humankind). The dog is dialectical – so perhaps Trotsky and Breton are both correct, each just in part. But Breton's hard-boiled humanism – so curious a rationalism for a surrealist – did not prevent him from speculating further about other intelligences, other sentient beings. He qualifies his anti-animism immediately afterwards in a cursive reflection on 'The Great Transparent Ones'. There he says that man may not be the centre, and conjectures that there may be something above him 'on the animal scale, beings whose behaviour is as strange to him as his may be to the mayfly or the whale'.[75] Breton is with Novalis, the Romantic thinker who exclaimed that, 'In reality we live in an animal whose parasites we are. The constitution of this animal determines ours and vice versa.'[76]

Eisenstein approached the affinity of man and animal from a different direction from both Trotsky and Breton, his imagination grounded in evolutionary science rather than philosophical speculation or dog-loving. These animals dwell in us. These animals live in us as our past – as species and as embryo – though also as our unfurled possibilities. It was a whale who made this clear to him. In July 1946 Eisenstein received a copy of *Life* magazine. He studied the stills from *Make Mine Music*, a sequel to *Fantasia*, which had been 'an experiment in the realization of *synthesis* through *syncretism*'.[77] Even from the static reproduced drawings Eisenstein could exclaim that 'The Whale Who Wanted to Sing at the Met' was working in the same realm as his own *Ivan the Terrible*. He was tickled to discover their junction; for example, that both Disney and he used Prokofiev in their films.[78] The Disney cartoon opens with a 'kick', the jolt into the realm of the subconscious. Eisenstein was developing theories of prenatal memory, a memory that was intra-uterine and forged at the stage of pre-individual being. Where Disney, until this point, had intimated this subconscious zone formally, in 'plasma appeal', in bendiness and stretching, as well as in the rapid transformations between species, now the object itself – Willie the whale – possesses something, his voice, that contains infinite variability. It is no longer a question of forms that shift their shape, but of a character attribute that possesses the ability to recapitulate all potential voices. Willie the whale is a vast sea animal, into whose mouth we peer as his tonsils wobble, sliding up and down the range through tenor, baritone and bass. The tale is tragic. Willie the whale is pierced by a harpoon at the close, after his dream of treading the boards in the USA as a famous opera singer and appearing on the covers of *Life* and *Time* magazines. Infinite possibility of variation is displaced, the voice-over relates, to 'whatever heaven is preserved for creatures of the deep still singing in a hundred voices, each more golden than before…'

human, all too human

When Eisenstein first investigated Disney's methods it was the use of sound that caught his attention. Sound was the most significant develop-ment for cinema, argued Eisenstein in a statement on sound issued jointly with Vsevolod Pudovkin and Grigori Alexandrov in 1928. There they speak of the 'insignificance of colour and stereoscopic cinema in compari-son with the great significance of sound'.[79] Sound overcomes the blind alley of the inter-title, which has proven unintegratable as a montage element and the blind alley of the long shots, explanatory sequences that impede the rhythm of the film. Sound – as Adorno and Eisler will later stress in *Composing for the Films* (1947)[80] – must be used contrapuntally, in 'sharp discord with the visual images'. Disney was so interesting because his métier was sound and moving drawing, together, apart, in dialogue and conflict. But recognition of the importance of colour soon found a place in Eisenstein's montage theories. It was another element that needed to be theorized so that it could take its place in the montage armoury. Eisenstein addressed the question of colour in 1929 in an essay titled 'The Drama-turgy of Film Form (The Dialectical Approach to Film Form)'. Here he speaks of colour in the context of counterpoint and conflict. Colour is conceived 'purely physiologically'. He tells us that a colour shade 'conveys a particular rhythm of vibration to our vision', because 'colours are distinguished from one another by the frequency of their light vibrations'.[81] Colour is a physical, material property, insists Eisenstein. It appears in conflict and contrast with the colours or shades that surround it, and so dynamism is introduced into the picture surface. Colour is drawn into montage theory. Eisenstein hoped that Disney would show the way with colour, just as he had shown the way with sound. But colour turned out to be Disney's downfall. In 1947, Eisenstein lectured to the Faculty of Direction at the Film School on the correspondence between music and depiction, in terms of metre, rhythm and melody. Disney, he notes, is a 'unique master of the cartoon film' with regard to melody: 'Nobody else has managed to make the movement of a drawing's outline conform to the melody. In this Disney is inimitable.'[82] However, on the question of how to use colour in film, Eisenstein reckoned that Disney had blundered:

> But when he made the transition to colour, it seemed he could not make it 'work' musically, even in *Bambi*. True, I have not studied his *Fantasia* in this sense. But in other works he failed to make a 'colour melody' to ensure that there was not only an emotional correspondence between the colour and the music, but a precisely formulated musical correspondence. But that is the second stage, when colour is connected not so much to the melody as to the orchestral hues.[83]

The webwork of connections across the filmic product had disintegrated. Correspondences – the thickening of filmic texture by reinforcement and commentary on mood, tone, polemic – were lacking. No attention was paid to colour's musicality, whereby Eisenstein meant, as did the synaesthetists before him, that colours each possess a musical tone, a sound. This means that from shot to shot small symphonies sing visually in the play of colour. This is just one element that needs to be mobilized. Eisenstein compares direction to a military campaign:

> When you handle this whole range, when you make a colour film, it is as complex as hell. You have to handle extraordinarily large numbers of correspondences. But why should it be any easier for you than for the general who has to deploy infantry, artillery, tanks and transport? The most brilliant and intelligent strategy is built on a combination of different weaponry, on the

relationship between the various types of forces in action. Which is why any respectable director must also know how to be a 'general'.[84]

The reference to war was apt. Eisenstein's experiments in colour orchestration in scenes in *Ivan the Terrible* were possible only because of the confiscation by the Red Army of Agfacolor film stock from German film studios and laboratories in the closing weeks of the war. Military success opened a small space for necessary experimentation. Colour needed yet to find an expressive language. Contemporary directors were failing, but this was cinema's urgent task. Colour was the field to be mastered. Eisenstein lectured the film students on how to make colour break free from the task of representation, in order to express meaning, independent emotional values in connection with precise ideas. He reflected on how colours had social and cultural connotations (red and revolution mediated through countless festivals and demonstrations), but also psychological meanings (such as the negativity of blackness or the warmth of yellow and gold). These specific meanings can never be worked with, for differing social, cultural and psychological meanings adhere to colours; and yet Eisenstein maintains that it is possible to have 'a sense of the colour as a whole' and this must then be handled as music is handled in combination with image – as independent elements in creative relationships. The independence of colour is, of course, more difficult to achieve than that of film, for colour is contained in the object, and yet still the demand is raised: 'take apart an existing link, and creatively try out various combinations'.[85] Only cartoons could make Eisenstein's colour theory clear.

Cartoons. To take the problem to its extreme, you have to make a cartoon. When I began considering what had been done with colour in cartoons, I thought that to resolve it correctly, you could find the very nature of the principle there.

In my dacha I have got some Vyatka dolls. They are on a shelf upstairs. I lie and think: if I am to pursue work in cartoons, I would of course avoid the mice and pigs of Disney and follow Russian folklore. The models of folklore construction – Vyatka dolls. I began to look at them closely: what could be done with the colour? The first thing I thought was: you have a horse with little red and green circles on it; in the cartoon, the spots would come away from the horse and begin to lead a life of their own.

The second doll is a nurse. And now these red and green spots transfer themselves to the nurse, and the performance begins. The check on her skirt seems to exist purely for this. Then it goes further. The spots come away and run off. A spring landscape. An old man sitting beneath a bare tree. Red apples suddenly appear on its branches. Then these green circles become red, the apples ripen. The circles then fall off at a crossroads, on to a traffic light. A red light shines where there should be a green one – the red spots jumped up there, and all hell breaks loose.

Or this would not be a bad idea: a girl and a young man sit on bench. She suddenly turns green, then he leaves and she turns red.[86]

Colour should be differentiated from its object, severed from what lies beneath it, in order to become itself a player in the drama. It is an element of the montage, an element to be montaged. It has to be drawn out 'into a general feeling' and this general feeling is made into a subject. Here Disney was lacking – he had only begun to address the use of colour. And *Bambi* demonstrated these failings. *Snow White and the Seven Dwarfs* was saccharine. *Bambi* was worse, however, because not only was the colour wrong – and out of synchronization with the music – but also the shading and the drawing style were inappropriate, too harsh and bald, and not lyrical enough for the depiction of nature. In *Bambi* what is important is lyricism. And yet, on the plus side, line and sound still jived together.

Eisenstein addresses the weaknesses of *Bambi* once more, in *Non-Indifferent Nature*. His planned article on Disney had been abandoned by now, but he formulated thoughts here and there on animation in this large study of 'film and the structure of things'. Nature is a particular concern in this late work. The depiction of nature allows the evocation of those primal urges that Eisenstein found so quintessential. Nature is least burdened with 'servile narrative tasks' and could express mood. Nature represented bears pathos, for it is the image of a mutual immersion of man and nature, mutual interpenetration of man and nature. Here Disney fails – and it is the use of colour that makes this clear. Eisenstein speaks of colour catastrophes, citing two examples: *Bambi*, 'by my friend Disney' and *Chopin* by Columbia Pictures (1944). Eisenstein registered his particular disappointment with the first film: 'it was so bad in the unmusicality of its *landscape* and *color*'.

> Disney – is the brilliant master and unsurpassed genius in the creation of audiovisual equivalents in music of *the independent movement of lines* and a graphic interpretation of the inner flow of the music (more of the melody than of the rhythm!). He is surprising when it is a question of the structure of the comically exaggerated movement of the human characters, the masklike figures of the common animals, but this same Disney is amazingly blind when it comes to *landscape* – to the *musicality of landscape* and at the same time to the *musicality of color and tone*.[87]

It is not just a question of colour, but also one of drawing. The early works of Disney disturbed Eisenstein because of their stylistic rupture between the foreground, with its brilliantly moving figures, and the background, childishly and weakly drawn (despite this rupture, he thought the early animations Disney's best). For example, in *The Skeleton Dance* the background is naturalistically shaded, dead and 'extremely ugly'. The *Mickey Mouse* series – especially the black-and-white ones – is a little better, for its landscapes were composed mostly of linear graphics with concise black washes, a technique that was also applied to the drawing of Mickey and Minnie.[88] There is a unity of parts and style. But in *Bambi* the failure is vast, and responsibility must be placed quite unambiguously at Disney's door. For in animation the landscape is entirely shaped by the pen. There Disney has an advantage over other filmmakers, who have to select from nature's palette. But more than that, the medium in which he works precisely allows the animation of all its parts. Nature animated could 'live and pulsate in the tone and emotions of corresponding action'.[89] But, instead, *Bambi* uses only meaningless panoramic shots or a tracking camera over crude naturalistic dabs of background. Nature has died. Nature has become an effect, not a (formal) principle of the film – its mobility. And there is no consistency of style across the image – the figures of the foreground are flat but occupy conventional volume, whereas the setting acquires a '*false three dimensionality*', which is 'painted with all the care of a bad oleographic print'.[90] The environment presented is too emphatic. There is no attempt to convey mood. It is not nuanced in its presentation. The animators had reverted to the old-style Disney drawing, with 'sharply confined linear contour and the continuous *outlining*' of coloured areas.[91] This was inappropriate:

Sergei Eisenstein and Walt
Disney at the Disney
Studio, 1930

In Disney's earlier works this type of drawing corresponded completely to Mickey's paradoxical charm, which consisted in the very fact that Disney, within the self-contained, concrete representational form, subjected it to an immaterial free play of free lines and surfaces. This is one of the basic springs of the comic effect of his works. In *Bambi* it is just the reverse.[92]

In *Bambi* there is no comic effect. The overall mood is supposed to be lyrical. Eisenstein compares *Bambi* unfavourably to Chinese landscape and animal painting that uses fluffy strokes and soft spots of colour with indistinct edges. Sadly the sketches for Bambi had used this downiness and it had not been retained – Eisenstein had seen preparatory sketches in Robert Feild's *The Art of Walt Disney*.[93] The fluidity of the image and the merging of figures and landscape were blocked in the reversion to the old drawing style. A lack of graphic and painterly method, an absence of unity of setting and figures, presents a most melancholy spectacle. The 'ecstasy' of *Bambi*, its serious, eternal, purely totemic theme of '*the repeating circles of life*', praised by Eisenstein in 1943, now motivates only frustration and anger.

Perhaps it was really the war and then the propaganda that Disney produced that forced Eisenstein eventually to articulate the break. The war forced Disney to grow up. The result was educational films, government-friendly propaganda and polemics on war policy. The trouble with *Fantasia* and *Bambi* and the instructional films begins when they attempt to be mature, serious, worthy. And the live-action/animation spectaculars are simply trash because they have no uniting principle. They introduce the human, via mechanical means, to interact with the subhuman cartoon characters. Everything falls apart. The 'incorrect Disney' is beating the 'correct Disney'. For Eisenstein, in his jottings on Disney in July 1946, there is too much of man in a medium that belongs to the 'subhuman'.[94] This man is severed from his inorganic and organic predecessors by a return of the bad old metaphysic – the notion of human essence as divine or immaterial. Mickey's outstretched hand is ungrasped. Man is winning. Man will distinguish himself. Man is divided from nature, from others and in himself. He is disconnected. His spine is straightening and stiffening. Man is walking upright.

techne-colour

My heart leaps up when I behold
A rainbow in the sky
William Wordsworth, 1802[1]

'die farben sind taten des lichtes, taten und leiden'

Walt Disney's weekly television show began in 1954 as ABC's *Disneyland*.
It was broadcast in colour from September 1961, transmitted on the NBC
network and renamed *Walt Disney's Wonderful World of Color*. Unlike other
networks, the NBC network was promoting colour because its parent
company, RCA, manufactured colour television sets. Colour, delivered to
the lounges of millions of Americans, was to remake Disney fortunes in
the post-war period. Colour and television sold the theme parks as dream
destination. Television entered right into Disney's vocabulary, as evidenced
in a Disney television film on perception made for the Bell Telephone
Company. A cross-section of a human head is depicted with various chambers, and in the optical chamber a tiny man sits watching a television
screen, connected to the eyes.[2] Disney's idea of vision was that of the
passive, mediatized experience of the 'couch potato'. Vision collapses into
television – the new medium for all; latest and most hefty blow for the
power of the visual image (in league with sound) against the written word.
Television was seen to counteract the active participation of the audience.
It came as testimony a century later to the rightness in tone of the alarm
raised by William Wordsworth, who in 1846 wrote this sonnet titled
'Illustrated Books and Newspapers':

Discourse was deemed Man's noblest attribute,
And written words the glory of his hand;
Then followed Printing with enlarged command
For thought – dominion vast and absolute
For spreading truth, and making love expand.
Now prose and verse sunk into disrepute
Must lacquey a dumb Art that best can suit
The taste of this once-intellectual Land.
A backward movement surely have we here,
From manhood – back to childhood; for the age –
Back towards caverned life's first rude career.
Avaunt this vile abuse of pictured page!
Must eyes be all in all, the tongue and ear
Nothing? Heaven keep us from a lower stage![3]

Here Wordsworth rages against engraved plates of text and image, perhaps the first offprints of a mass-produced culture. Wordsworth resisted the tyrannical power of the visual, preferring instead, in 1835, to call the ear the 'organ of vision'. Sound was preferred – or words at least, if written they must be. But the image appears to have something regressive about it. The battle between the audiophiles and the iconophiles did not subside, but it found some sort of compromise in synaesthetics, a sphere that opened up as the century closed. Synaesthesia was also known as 'coloured hearing', and colour was often its most striking cloak. Colour investigation was not novel. The late eighteenth and early nineteenth centuries had seen intense experimentation into questions of colour, but it was only in the next century that experiment's fruits ripened in the new technologies of vision.

In 1959 Edwin Land's 'astonishing new theory of colour' caused a sensation in the international press. The procedures were said, by their initiator, the founder of the Polaroid Corporation, to be drawn from Johann Wolfgang von Goethe's colour theory and built on Goethe's studies of coloured shadows. Goethe had carried out various experiments in different types of light in order to observe this phenomenon. For example, when an opaque object is lit up by a coloured light and a white light, one shadow cast appears in the colour diametrically opposite on the colour wheel that Goethe was devising. Varying the chromatic illuminant allows one shadow to appear in complementary hues from across the whole spectrum. Land drew on such experiments to demonstrate a coloured photographic image, and managed to make a black-and-white photograph of a young woman appear in full colour with 'blonde hair, pale blue eyes, red coat, blue-green collar and strikingly natural flesh tones'. The demonstration made evident that the colours were not there as such in the photograph or the illuminants, but were colour illusions. It was supposed to show that rays in themselves are not colour-making, but are rather the conveyers of information used by the eye to assign appropriate colours to objects in an image.

Goethe began his investigations into colour and theories of colour in 1786. His colour doctrine had its origins in a survey of the optical effects achieved by artists' use of colour. He intended to examine the properties of cool and warm colours, and to see why natural affinities and contrasts seemed to exist between colours. A journey to Italy disclosed to him that artists theorized all aspects of painting except for colour. And the scientific theory of colour had little to offer artists. The historical section of his *Farbenlehre* (*Theory of Colour*) (1795–1810) alleged that Isaac Newton's optical theory was not of use to technicians and artists. Goethe hoped to span art, science and technology to provide something that would speak to all. His colour theory relied on extensive experimentation. Experiment, testing the world, touching the world and observing it, is, he is sure, how knowledge is won. Genuine knowledge is not wrested from the imposition of categories and the invocation of numbers. Experimentation is not meant to be the testing out of propositions, but about observing how one phenomenon or hypothesis connects to another without too quickly generalizing. In the preface to the first edition of the *Farbenlehre* Goethe insists that with every attentive glance into the world we already theorize.[4] With this approach, a cherishing of experience, he set out to counter Newton's claims. The experiments are to reproduce the experience. All the experiments are to be seen as variants of a larger experiment comprising 'manifold perspectives'. Goethe's 'tender empiricism' hoped to crack rudely Newton's mechanical laws. Goethe was too gigantic a figure to let his arithmetic deficiencies hold him back in the fight against a man who had made his proofs as difficult as possible to follow in order 'to avoid being baited by little smatterers in mathematics'.[5] Goethe presented his findings to Louisa, Duchess of Saxe-Weimar and Eisenach, in lecture form. These lectures were intended no doubt to suggest pixilated amusements for the assembled, who could then test out his claims about the fugitive nature of colour, light's optical tricks and pranks, through observation and play in the gardens of the court.

From his experiments Goethe discerned that light and colour are in tension. Tension produces colour, and submission produces greyness. This vision was won of a morphological view of nature. Goethe criticized the static conception of nature, promoted by Linnaeus and Newton, who both perceived the world correspondingly as simply divisible. In his *Zur Morphologie* (*On Morphology*) of 1807 Goethe presents all of nature in permanent flux. Plasticity and animation are the watchwords. The concept of nature as alive and mutable was energized by experiments with electricity and magnetism at the end of the eighteenth century. These stimulated ideas of deep sources of energy infusing the world of matter. Perhaps, it was thought, these founts of energy animate the responses of living creatures. Electricity might bring life. Poets snatched at this idea. Frankenstein was spawned in 1818 of mesmerism, the theory of animal electricity and Luigi Galvani's experiments in 1789 with sparks that stimulated muscular spasms in frogs' legs. In Goethe's universe light struggles against darkness. Colour is not contained in light, but emerges in the interaction of light and darkness. Goethe's emphasis on deeds and suffering is set against Newton's cause and effect. The principles of striving and activity are witnessed in colour's emergence from the polarity of light and dark. Newton had once shut himself in a dark room, with only a tiny hole that admitted light focused to pass through a prism and then hit a white surface. Newton recorded the continuous spectrum of red, orange, yellow, green, blue, indigo and violet on the white screen and concluded that the colours of the spectrum are hidden in white light. Reminiscing in *Confession des Verfassers* (*The Author's Confession*) (1810), Goethe tells how, in the 1790s, he borrowed a prism, and turned his room into a camera obscura by covering the window with a sheet of metal pierced by a small hole. He wanted to reproduce Newton's experiments.[6] Before he got the chance, however, his friend requested the return of the prism. He looked through it for a last time, in a room that was completely white. He expected to see an array of colours cast on the white wall, but there was none. Only where dark areas were in the room – for example, the bars of the window – did determinate colours appear. This was the beginning of Goethe's realization that the mode of experimentation – a series of necessary conditions including the arrangement of the prism and the hole – manufactured the particular results received. If the hole is enlarged or narrowed the colour effects change. And, crucially, he realized that light and dark played their roles in producing colour too.[7]

The incongruent results of Goethe and Newton were due in part to the differing viewpoints of the observers, in two senses.[8] Each stood in a different place and recorded results from a different perspective. In another sense, Goethe's *Vorstellungsart*,[9] his mode of imagining the question, took up this difference of perspective into the method. Goethe brought the observing eye into the puzzle. Newton left the observer to one side. The Newtonian system appears to decipher light and colour in terms of mechanical laws that are oblivious to human sensation, and it seems to refuse human response any bearing on the physical event. Where Newton saw the prismatic image as complete and unchanging, Goethe saw 'something only ever in becoming, and always amendable'.

Not only was the liveliness of the human included in the analysis. Nature too, the physical world, was brought to life. Contra Newton, Goethe insisted on the inaccuracy of concluding that all colours were contained in white. Colour emerges from the shading of light into darkness. And just as colour is an effect of struggle, so the eye too is animated, battling to produce effects as much as be affected. Goethe experimented by staring at a coloured square against a white board and then removing it to see another colour. This second colour, he says, leaps from an image that belongs to the eye. For Goethe the organ of reception must already possess the qualities it discovers in the world. Nature is alive. We eavesdrop on nature. Just as do humans, the universe feels tension, intensity and resolution. In his preface to his *Theory of Colours* he writes:

> The colours are acts of light; its active and passive modifications: thus considered we may expect from them some explanation respecting light itself. Colours and light, it is true, stand in the most intimate relation to each other, but we should think of both as belonging to nature as a whole, for it is nature as a

whole which manifests itself by their means in an especial manner to the sense of sight. The completeness of nature displays itself to another sense in a similar way. Let the eye be closed, let the sense of hearing be excited, and from the lightest breath to the wildest din, from the simplest sound to the highest harmony, from the most vehement and impassioned cry to the gentlest word of reason, still it is Nature that speaks and manifests her presence, her power, her pervading life and the vastness of her relations; so that a blind man to whom the infinite visible is denied, can still comprehend an infinite vitality by means of another organ.[10]

Goethe was less interested in an analysis of the seen than in the process of seeing and the modulations of colour as it appears to the eye. He delineated different types of colour and grouped them according to the activity of the eye in their generation. He found physical colours, which were prismatic and fugitive and arose through mediation, such as the several bands of colour that are engendered either side of a candle flame when it is observed with a thin wire held before the eye. He found colours that came as a sort of interference – a mixture of reflected rays glancing off surfaces of varying thickness – such as the colours of oil on water, in soap bubbles and in mica schist. These are all subjective–objective, which is to say that they are produced as much by the viewing eye as by the object. He also analysed chemical colours, found in the shimmer of a bird feather, or the iridescence on an insect. These were objective colours, but they too might suffer permanent revision, altered by different intensities of light or by a movement of the eye. And he identified physiological and psychological colours, subjective colours, produced by the eye. Such colours include the colours of afterimages, positive images that are aroused by dazzling light, and negative afterimages in which rich colours are excited by fixing on their contraries.

Charles Eastlake, who in 1840 translated Goethe's *Farbenlehre* into English, hoped to persuade artists to use Goethe's teachings. In his preface Goethe compared Newton's theory of colours to a ruined, 'uninhabitable' castle, many times patched up after attack, but now 'abandoned'. Goethe claims that his own theory is the 'free space' new vista that opens up after the demolition of the 'Bastille'.[11] The English art academy was more open to Goethe's teaching than was the scientific establishment. Scientists did not welcome his investigations. Even those who were devising the new optical technologies of amusement – such as David Brewster, inventor of the kaleidoscope in 1816 – resisted his attribution of psychological effects to colour perception. Brewster was suspicious of the emphasis on perception's mediation, on the possibility of the eye being deceived. The positivists could not countenance his consideration of imagination as a shaping modality, nor his talk of 'transient concrescence'. Goethe's science called for a critique of the senses. It was an aesthetic science. It was fascinated by perception. This aesthetic science was certain that nature speaks to humanity through its senses – however the capacity to see is learnt. Goethe thought that the eyes detect more as the intellect becomes alert to the process of seeing. Aesthetic response to colour and colour combinations is secured as the eye learns how to see. Seeing belongs to the eye as organ. The eye is not a mirroring surface. There is no passive viewer equipped with aperture reviewing a parade of thing-images on the wall of the world outside it, but a subject with such an aperture that lets burn onto the retina an impression from which the subject can never cut itself loose, even with the eyes closed. Light and colour dwell in the nerves. Goethe's colour theories were worked into his fictions. In *Faust* God is light, and Mephistopheles is darkness. Humanity inhabits the refractive middle ground of colour. It delights them, as Faust and Mephistopheles confirm when they let loose some fiery illusions before the emperor, and promise him further the beauties of the deep sea with its waves light-green and purple edged, and gold-scaled colourful dragons and sharks (ll. 5989 ff.).[12] Colour symbolism pervades the play: the colours nearest to white – yellow, red – are positive, and evoke motion and action, and those nearest to black – blue and violet – are negative, inducing torpor. Red is the *Urfarbe*. Goethe's colour circle places purple-magenta red at the top, striving up towards heaven. It is the kindling power of dawn (ll. 3913–31). In the opening scene of *Faust*, part two, Faust wakes to life's pulses beating fresh vitality, as colour upon colour emerges in the dell. At the close of the scene, colour has adopted its highest form. Against the torrent of the waterfall, the rainbow forms its changed–unchanging arc, and twinkles now clear, now evanescent. Faust celebrates the rainbow for its animating power. The rainbow is a symbol of striving and in its many-hued reflection is life (l. 4727). To renounce the *Wechseldauer*, the change in permanence, is to relinquish life's vitality.[13] Newton had pitched his science at the rainbow. For Newton the rainbow provided the proof of his theory that white contains all colours and when white is fractionated it produces the rainbow array. Scientists retraced the geometric arc in the sky, in order to understand it and to investigate what it could tell further about light and colour.[14] But some poets preferred to retain the mystery. Friedrich Schlegel's 'On the Limits of the Beautiful' (1794) perceived the divine at work in the rainbow: 'the friendly rainbow with which the infinite, as it were, spans the heavens'.[15] Schlegel was a magnetist and he too carried out experiments on colour inversion and afterimages, but he also investigated colour symbolism, such as that which emerged in Countess Lesniowska's trance accounts. Drawing on the ideas of Jakob Boehme, whose *Aurora* (1612) correlated light and divinity, the early German Romantics advocated a colour symbolism. Novalis wrote of a blue flower in his novel *Heinrich von Ofterdingen*. This was one instance of his obsession with blue, the colour of highest activity, the colour of the soul. Red, he claimed, is the colour of fading energy, of colour subsiding into the body.[16] Such was romantic colour theory.

In his attempt to fuse the scientific and the poetic, Goethe's theory edged towards the practical. He thought the eye could be trained to see. That the eye could be trained was an important lesson of Goethe's *Farbenlehre*. It is an instruction manual for investigations into aspects of perception. Goethe distinguishes the healthy eye from the unhealthy eye or mind, in which can appear all manner of morbid phenomena.[17] These optical effects, such as sparks, flashes, tubes and bubbles, may be organically caused or a result of mental instability or moral weakness. However, they might also be the result of a heightened perception or receptivity to phenomena, such as is possessed by artists. The eye could be educated to summon up fugitive images such as afterimages. Or at least educated people could perfect their ability to summon up colour effects. Goethe's *Faust*, part one, published in 1808, showed an encounter between the educated eye of the genius Faust and the untutored eye of his assistant Wagner. Wagner is unable to discern the afterimage of the black poodle's spiral. To Faust's eye, however, it appears as a swirl of fire.

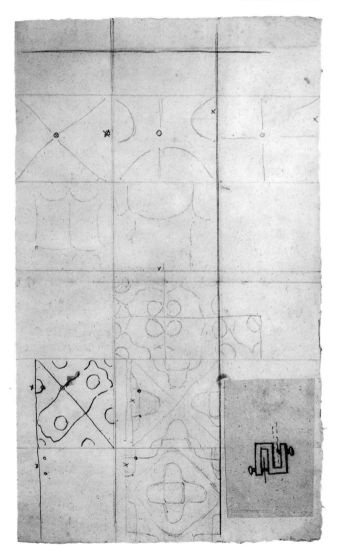

Goethe's drawings of Chladni sound figures stuck onto the back cover of his copy of Chladni's 1789 book on the theory of sound. Goethe includes a drawing of his screw clamp used to secure a glass plate or tin sheet on his desk

Faust	Do you see the black dog scour the grain that sprouts from the stubble?
Wagner	I saw it long ago, but thought it unimportant.
Faust	Observe it well! What do you think the creature is?
Wagner	A poodle that in the usual way goes to the trouble of tracking its master!
Faust	Do you notice how it races around us in a great spiral, getting closer and closer? And unless I'm mistaken, an eddy of fire follows closely wherever it goes.
Wagner	A mere black poodle is what I see – you, I suspect, some optical illusion. (ll. 1147–57)

Faust is the striving soul who is addicted to chimeras (though Goethe forbade the scientific use of the term 'optical illusion'). His excessive will to creativity allows him to be bewitched. Mephistopheles and Faust perceive things differently, and this forms the matter of their discussion, as for example in the Walpurgisnacht witches' kitchen scene, which closes with the phantom image of Gretchen, a deathly-pale lovely girl, her feet in fetters (ll. 4184–209). It is an optical illusion. Goethe relates his own ability to capture flower-shapes in the middle of his visual organ. In a darkened room he would orchestrate these patterns, turning the eye into a kaleidoscope. For Goethe, Faust's susceptibility to visions and his own ability to conjure up patterns on his closed eyelids was a sign of poetic genius. The scientist Purkinje carried out further experiments with retinal images. Goethe reviewed his book *Sight from a Subjective Standpoint* (1824), and discussed his own retinal amusements:

> When I closed my eyes and lowered my head, I could imagine a flower in the centre of my visual sense. Its original form never stayed for a moment; it unfolded, and from within it new flowers continuously developed with coloured petals or green leaves. These were no natural flowers; they were fantasy flowers, but as regular as rosettes carved by a sculptor.... Here the appearance of an afterimage, memory, creative imagination, concept and idea all work simultaneously, revealing themselves through the unique vitality of the visual organ in complete freedom and without intention or direction.[18]

Purkinje had parted company with Goethe, for he was not convinced that artists possess an exceptional sensitivity to afterimages, writing in 1819 that those in heightened states – those who are intoxicated with alcohol or narcotics, feverish or brain-damaged – were more susceptible

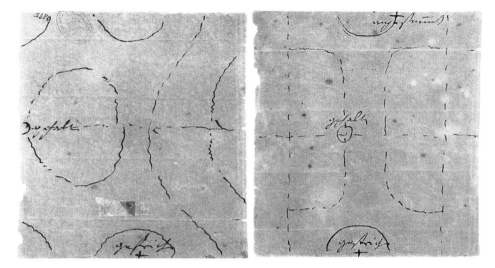

Tone patterns by Goethe

to perceive their delusions as objective.[19] Purkinje's first experiments involved turning towards the sun, and waving splayed fingers before closed eyes. Various patterns appeared on the screen of the inside eye. Patterns could also be summoned by putting pressure on the eyeball or by applying electrodes to the conjunctiva. Purkinje's *Druckfiguren* drawings were named analogously to Chladni's *Klangfiguren*, the patterns manifested by sand on a plate brought to vibration by soundwaves. Goethe asked K.A. Schwerdegeburth to repeat Purkinje's experiment and engrave onto copper plates the retinal images that appeared. And so the subjective images took on an objective form.[20]

In building the camera obscura, in using the wall as a white surface for light projection, and in carrying out the retinal experiments that turned the inside of the eyelid into a sort of screen, Goethe turned his body and his immediate surroundings into a projection zone. He wanted to see new things, to see things anew, and to see seeing newly.

Goethe's *Farbenlehre* came back into vogue at the end of the nineteenth century. Ewald Hering's colour research pushed many physiologists towards Goethe's psychological and physiological colour theory. Hering had noted distinct patterns to colour afterimages and subjective colour combinations that were not accounted for in Helmholtz's trichromacy theory of colour vision. With the beginning of the new physics, and the theories of Ernst Mach and others, curiosity intensified. Optical illusions, the meaning of sensation, were still to be defined. The debate on perception was reopened by Neo-Kantians such as Ernst Marcus, who researched the optic and the haptic in his 1918 book *Das Problem der exzentrischen Empfindung und seine Lösung*. Artists took up Goethe's theory. Kandinsky, for one, considered Goethe's colour theory in his influential *Concerning the Spiritual in Art*. Prolonging the symbolist legacy of synaesthesia, Kandinsky held a 'colour seminar' at the Bauhaus in 1922 and 1923. He carried out inquiries into connections between colours and shapes. The triangle, he discovered, was yellow, the square red and the circle blue. Alexander Laszlo, author in 1925 of *Coloured Light Music*, devised a colour organ, like the one that Skriabin proposed for his *Prometheus* in 1910. Its keys issued not sounds but strongly coloured light, red for the note C, orange-pink for G, and so on. The painter and composer Matyushin investigated the conditions of colour conception in connection with a widening of the angle of vision, under the influence of sounds, in movement, and so on. In 1927 Malevich brought charts to Germany that illustrated these experiments. In 1930 he carried out his own experiments in order to determine the relation between colour and form in painting, believing that geometric shapes evoke particular colours. Henri Bergson's philosophical science was also a stimulus for research into perception. Bergson's *Matter and Memory*, first written in 1908 and updated through various editions and translations, affirmed the reality of spirit and the reality of matter, and attempted to determine the relation between the two by looking at memory. Here, envisioning the brain as a central telephonic exchange,[21] Bergson maligned the commonly held notion of perception as a kind of photographic view of things, taken from a fixed point by that special apparatus which is called an organ of perception. This photograph is then seen to be developed in the brain-matter by some unknown chemical and psychical process of elaboration. But, inquires Bergson, is it not obvious that the photograph, if photograph there be, is already taken, already developed in the very heart of things and at all the points of space? No metaphysics, no physics even, can escape this conclusion.[22]

disneydust in benjamin's eyes

> I remember a satanic phase. The red of the walls became the determining factor for me. My smile took on satanic features: even if it assumed rather more the expression of satanic knowledge, satanic satisfaction, satanic repose than the satanic destructive effect. The involvement of those present in the room intensified: the room became more velvety, more flaming, darker. I named it Delacroix.
> (Walter Benjamin, 'Hashish Protocol', 15 January 1928)

At the beginning of the 1920s, Walter Benjamin collated a bundle of notes on colour. These supplemented other writings on colour that he had worked on since 1914. Many of his earliest writings on colour were repeated in later reviews. For over ten years colour – understood as an aspect of fantasy – played on his mind. He intended to write a book on colour and children's literature. It was to have been a study that spanned anthropological thought and art theory. In 1927 he planned to write a documentary work on 'phantasy', the outline of which he showed to a children's book collector in Moscow.[23] As part of these interests he compiled a bibliography on the theme of colour.[24] The bibliography included a book by the editor of Goethe's scientific archive, Rudolf Steiner, on Goethe's colour theory, and Portal's *Couleurs symboliques*.[25] Reading Rudolf Steiner would have brought Benjamin into the orbit of Madame Blavatsky and the theosophists with their blend of Eastern exoticism, occultism, Schilleresque and Goethean speculations. Here Kandinsky found a spiritual home, as did Mondrian and Klee, though he denied any adherence to the creed. Benjamin read Kandinsky's *Concerning the Spiritual in Art* around 1919. Another reference was to an article from a journal of psychology and physiology of the sense organs, written by Richard Müller-Freienfels and titled 'Tones of Feeling in Colour Sensation'. Of this Benjamin noted that he needed to incorporate elements of its suppositions in his own work, which meant that he intended to complete a study of colour and fantasy. His notes on the article by Müller-Freienfels prompted him to recall a poem from Goethe's *Westöstlichen Divan* on God:

> Da erschuf er Morgenröte,
> Die erbarmte sich der Qual;
> Sie entwickelte dem Trüben
> Ein erklingend Farbenspiel,

Und nun konnte wieder lieben
Was erst auseinander fiel.

(Then he made the pink of dawn,
it poured pity on the pain,
So inventing for the dark,
Of hues and harmonies a game,
And everything that fell apart
Now could fall in love again.)

And he notes of it that the unifying element, the dawn, transition between light and dark, is a harmonic resounding play of colours and is just like the colours of fantasy. He adds that the same power of reconciliation appears in the rainbow, the symbol of peace.[26]

The 'colours of fantasy' had been a theme for a while, since the first traces of Goethe's colour romanticism emerged in early writings such as 'Reflection in Art and in Colour' (1914–15), where colour is presented as the highest concentration of seeing, or 'The Rainbow' (1915–16). 'The Rainbow' is a series of reflections on colour and painting in the form of a dialogue between Georg and Margarethe, namesake of Goethe's *ewig-weiblich* heroine in *Faust*. Margarethe tells Georg her dream before it fades. It is a dream of a landscape that glowed with colours never before seen. And seeing saw only colours. Georg is a painter and he tells Margarethe that he knows these colours. They are the colours of fantasy. Painting cannot re-create them, for painting is an art of surface not of colour. Painterly colour is a reflection of fantasy. Painting sets out from form. Colour appears in painting as an inscription on a surface. Pure colour is infinite, but only its reflection appears in painting, for here colour appears as an inscription on a surface. Painting is beholden to the rule of inscription, the contrast between light and shade. It cannot be infinite, as absolute colour must be. Colour has no substance, so it cannot be form. Chromatic infinity proposes infinite contrasts between all colours, a play in infinite nuance. Colour, it transpires, is pure seeing, object and organ at the same time. 'Our eye is coloured'.[27] Most open to the pure sensation of colour are artists and children, claims Margarethe. Both live in the world of colour. Children's connection to colour is achieved through their imagination and their innocence, and the proof of their connection is shown by their blushing, a sinking into the realm of colour. Benjamin notes of children in 1920–21 in a fragment titled 'Blushing in Anger and Shame', 'That they so often feel ashamed, evidenced by the redness of their faces, is connected to the fact that they have so much fantasy, especially in their earliest years.'[28] Margarethe evokes the colours of her childhood: the beautiful strange colours of old picture books, with their rainbow games, the colours always floating over things, soap bubbles, the damp colours of magic lanterns, indian inks, decals. The colours were always blurred, without shading. Georg points out that pure colour is the colour of nature, of mountains, trees, streams, flowers, butterflies, sea and clouds. Its highest form is the rainbow, pure colour without form. The rainbow lends spirit and animation to nature, and shows it to be the silent *Urbild* of art. In 'Fantasy' (1920–21) Benjamin writes of how the world is caught up in the process of unending dissolution, eternal ephemerality – 'die Welt in unendlicher Auflösung', the world in ceaseless dissolution. 'On Fantasy', from around the same time, presents deep coloration as a connection to the passing away of earthly life. The rainbow colours of phosphorescence in rotting meat are proof of this connection between colour and transition. Becoming takes on forms – young buds – while passing takes on colours. The paling of people in death, and of nature in winter, is a passing into the finality of death and the zone of the *überirdisch*, the supernatural, the celestial. It leaves behind unending dissolution, and so it leaves behind colour.

'A Child's View of Colour' (1914–15) contains similar ideas. For children, colour is not superimposed on matter. Adults abstract from colour, regarding it as a deceptive cloak for individual objects existing in time and space. Where colour provides the contours, objects are not reduced to things but are constituted by an order consisting of an infinite range of nuances. Children delight in colour's shimmering in subtle, shifting nuances – for example they are enchanted by soap bubbles – or they like to see definite explicit changes in intensity as in oleographs, paintings and pictures produced by decals and magic lanterns. Their eyes are not concerned with three-dimensionality, for this they perceive through touch.[29] Pure seeing is the seeing of colour, unsubstantial and paradisiacal. Colour is perhaps a medium of intuition prior to the Kantian gridwork of space and time.

Benjamin's interest in children's response to colour continued in the completion of several studies of the children's books that he collected. 'On the Surface of the Uncoloured Picturebook', of 1919, dismisses the idea that children recognize real things in the imaged things, or that through pictured things children are led into the realm of real things and made familiar with them. The true meaning of these simple graphic children's books with their naturalistic drawings lies far away from the dead, dull explicitness for which rationalist pedagogy recommends them. Children only make the images their own – comprehend their existence in the world – when they ask for the word. Images that work call words to life. The images are the location for an endless condensation. These surfaces are not like those of art works – with their *noli me tangere* – but the site of a poetic, creative script, a hieroglyphics. 'In the world of these colourless images the child awakes, just as in the world of coloured ones it dreams its dreams, which are full of memories.'[30] This idea is repeated in 1924 in 'Old Forgotten Children's Books'. To children's way of seeing, a whole new world opens up in black-and-white woodcuts. The original value of these woodcuts is equal to that of the coloured prints; they are in fact their polar complement. The coloured picture immerses the childish imagination in a dream state. The black-and-white woodcut, the plain, prosaic illustration, draws the child out. The compelling invitation to describe, which is implicit in such pictures, awakens the word in the child. And describing these pictures in words, he or she also describes them by enactment. The child inhabits them. Their surface, unlike that of coloured pictures, is not a *noli me tangere* – either in itself or in the mind of the child. On the contrary, it seems incomplete, and so can readily be filled out. Children fill the images with poetry of their own. This is how it comes about that children 'inscribe' and 'describe' (*beschreiben*) the pictures with their ideas in a more literal sense: they scribble on them. As they learn language, they also learn how to write: they learn hieroglyphics.[31]

In 'Old Forgotten Children's Books' Benjamin comments on children's books by establishing a history of coloration. The Biedermeier epoch presents a 'self-sufficient resplendent world of colours' where colours are independent of the graphics and the imagination has free rein. Again he states that the purpose of these books is not to bring children into the world, recognizing its objects in the representations; rather, it is to find what children already possess within themselves.

> The inwardness of this way of seeing is located in colour, and in its medium objects lead their dreamy life in the minds of children. They learn from bright colouring. For nowhere is sensuous, nostalgia-free contemplation as much at home as in colour.[32]

Late Biedermeier works, such as the collaboration between Grimm and Johann Peter Lyser, use a pale careworn coloration, in accord with their threadbare figures, and it is not without an ironic, satanic streak. At the same time, sensationalism enters children's lithographs, as evidenced in the multiple versions of *The Thousand and One Nights*, with its hodgepodge of fairy-tale, saga, local legend and horror story.

A doubled focus emerges. Children's literature appeals to an untethered imagination and so is fantastic and to be cherished. But at the same time, Benjamin's interest in children's books is part of an analysis of where value is to be found in a devalued culture. He notes that at the end of the Biedermeier period, in the 1840s, the growth of technical civilization and the levelling of culture connected to it meant that the 'finest and noblest substances often sank to the bottom'.[33] The astute observer may be more likely to rediscover them in the lower reaches of printed and graphic publications, such as children's books, than in the official documents of culture.

'View into Children's Books' of 1926 opens with a line by C.F. Heinle, Benjamin's boyhood friend who killed himself in August 1914: 'A green shimmer in the evening red.'[34] Green against red is the fundamental colour pairing. Later-nineteenth-century sensualists knew it well. Heinle's words echo Verlaine: 'flakes of crimson or emerald rain'. In his colour theory, Goethe had revealed how deeply that particular pairing could burn itself into the eye and the mind's eye. He tells of a flesh-and-blood Snow White:

> I had entered an inn towards evening, and, as a well-favoured girl, with a brilliantly fair complexion, black hair and a scarlet bodice, came into the room, I looked attentively at her as she stood before me at some distance in half shadow. As she presently afterwards turned away, I saw on the white wall, which was now before me, a black face surrounded with a bright light, while the dress of the perfectly distinct figure appeared of a beautiful sea green.[35]

Red is the real, the hot body of passion; green the fantastic, colour of longing. Together they evoke desire, and they leave unforgettable, almost indelible, impressions.

The nineteenth century was a colour-saturated century of optical toys and marketed optical illusions. Across its course, Goethe's visual stimulations developed into myriad devices: panoramas, dioramas, cosmoramas, diaphanoramas, fantoscopes, fantasma-parastasias, phantasmagorias, phanoramas, cykloramas, and so on.[36] Many of these found a home in the arcades. In his notes on the Paris arcades Benjamin points out how red and green are so frequently the colours of places of amusement. He interprets this colour scheming as a modish appearance which corresponds darkly to the wisdom revealed by Ernst Bloch in his *Spirit of Utopia* that the chamber of memory is lined in green with evening-red curtains.[37] And purplish-red and bile-green are the colours of posters in the arcades, where false colours are possible. Green and red – polarities of colour – are the colours of myth, memory and desire revamped in modern guise.

> Falser colours are possible in the arcades: no one is surprised that combs are red and green. Snow White's stepmother had such a one, and when the comb did not do its work, there was the pretty apple that did its bit, half-red, half-poisonous green, just like the cheap combs.[38]

Benjamin explains once more his theory of colour in 'View into Children's Books'. Colour is a fantasy. Seeing colours, the intuitions of fantasy, is seeing an *ur*-phenomenon. All form, each outline, that humans can perceive corresponds to something inside the human that makes reproduction possible; dance and drawing are forms that the body can produce. They are active forms, movements of the body in creative production. But the human body cannot produce colour. It can only receive colour, 'through the shimmering colours of the eye'.[39] Sight is a sense on the cusp, for it can perceive form and colour. Colour relates to sight as a passive sense, along with smell and taste. And so colour inhabits the 'pure medium of fantasy'. Benjamin turns to Goethe's *Farbenlehre*, pointing to colour's '*sinnlich–sittliche Wirkung*', its 'sensuous, moral effect'. For Goethe, this means that colour participates in aesthetic perception sensuously and ethically. Like beauty itself, it cannot be measured in numbers. Benjamin quotes Goethe's 'supplement' to the *Theory of Colours*:

In their illumination and their obscurity, the transparent colours are limitless, and fire and water can be regarded as their zenith and nadir.... The relation of light to transparent colour is, if one immerses oneself in it, infinitely stimulating, and the kindling of colours and their merging into one another, arising anew and vanishing, are like taking breath in great pauses from one eternity to the next, from the greatest light down to the solitary and eternal silence in the deepest tones. The opaque colours, in contrast, are like flowers that do not dare to compete with the sky, yet are concerned with weakness (that is to say, white) on the one side, and with evil (that is to say, black) on the other side. It is these, however, that are able ... to produce such pleasing variations and such natural effects that ... ultimately the transparent colours end up as no more than spirits playing above them and serve only to enhance them.[40]

With these words, notes Benjamin, Goethe's supplement to the colour theory reveals what is the essence of children's games, games of pure contemplation in fantasy: soap bubbles, the damp colours of magic lanterns, indian ink and decals. In all of these phenomena colour hovers above its objects, and the magic comes from a coloured glow, a coloured brilliance. Benjamin evokes a perfect image from a children's book: a poet rests against a sky-blue goddess, a muse who whispers details that a winged child then translates into drawings. There is a harp, a lute, and dwarfs toot and fiddle in the depths of the mountain while the sun sets. Colour and childhood, colour and fantasy: these were the watchwords of Benjamin's anthropological art theory, and also he read these connections out of his own childhood experience. In a reflection on colour in *A Berlin Childhood Around 1900*, he writes:

In our garden there was an abandoned, rotten pavilion. I loved it because of its colourful windows. As I passed inside from pane to pane, I transformed; I was coloured like the landscape framed in the window, now tawny, now dusty, now smouldering and now luxuriant. It was just as with painting in Indian ink, when the things opened up their very laps to me, once I smothered them in a damp cloud. It was a similar case with soap bubbles. I darted amongst them in the room, mingling with the coloured play of domes until they burst.[41]

The child is the rule-breaker, for the child does not yet know the rules. Children, pre-socialized, have not yet sanctioned the socially necessary knowledge of self and other, of substance and surface, of public and private – that is, property relations – and of subject and object. They inhabit a utopia of similarities without differences. It might be the experience of the *flâneur* too. Later, in 1939, in 'Some Motifs in Baudelaire', Benjamin notes the poet's reference to a man who dives into the crowd as into a reservoir of electrical energy. Baudelaire calls this man 'a kaleidoscope equipped with consciousness'.[42] The experience is the experience of colour, shifting, flickering, unfixed and immersive, as the impressionists had realised in their riotous daubs of colour.[43] Benjamin's ideas came straight from Baudelaire. In 'L'Art romantique' (1868) Baudelaire writes:

> The child sees everything in a state of newness; he is always *drunk*. Nothing more resembles what we call inspiration than the delight with which a child absorbs form and colour ... Genius is nothing more nor less than *childhood recovered* at will, a childhood now equipped for self-expression with manhood's capacities and a power of analysis which enables it to order the mass of raw material which it has involuntarily accumulated.[44]

Many of Benjamin's first short skits on colour and its relation to fantasy were chunks of a larger study of natural science and Romantic art. This found expression in a short piece of *Kant-Kritik* titled 'On the Coming Philosophy', written in 1918, and it found academic form in his doctorate on the concept of art criticism in German Romanticism (1919). In these writings Benjamin sets Goethe against Kant, but also draws on Ludwig Klages. Kant's thought, Benjamin notes, is entangled in the matrices of Euclidean geometry and Newtonian physics. Newton's physics, cradle of Kant's certainty, is 'a low, perhaps the lowest order', notes Benjamin, 'an experience virtually reduced to a nadir, to a minimum of significance'. (Of course all this obscures the 'secret', 'unpublished' Newton, the one who was obsessed with Jakob Boehme, alchemy, the occult, the cabbala and hieroglyphs, and the divine plan in nature and history.) The Newton–Kant axis rules out an immediacy of knowing. It rules out other types of knowledge and experience:

> We know of primitive peoples of the so-called pre-animistic stage who identify themselves with sacred animals and plants and name themselves after them; we know of insane people who likewise identify themselves in part with objects of their perception, which are thus no longer *objecta* standing opposed to them; we know of ill people who relate the sensations of their bodies not to themselves but rather to other creatures, and of clairvoyants who at least claim to be able to feel the sensations of others as their own.[45]

Following a comment on how for the Romantics 'to observe a thing means only to arouse it to self-recognition', a footnote in Benjamin's doctorate invokes Goethe's concept of *Empirie*:

> There is a tender empiricism that conforms intimately to its object and that, through identification with it, becomes its true and proper theory. Such heightening of the spiritual faculty belongs to a highly cultivated age.... This empiricism grasps what is essential in the object itself; therefore Goethe says: 'The highest thing would be to understand that everything factual is already theory. The blue of the sky reveals to us the fundamental law of chromatics. One must not look for anything behind the phenomena; they are themselves the doctrine.'[46]

Some of Benjamin's first fragments on method draw on Goethe's colour theory and scientific method in order to determine the relationship of knowledge and truth. A jotting from 1920 quotes Goethe's 'Materials on the History of the Theory of Colour':

> Since in knowledge, as in reflection, no totality can be created, because the first lacks the inner and the second the outer, we must necessarily think of science as art if we are to hope for totality of any kind from it.[47]

Benjamin's essay on Goethe's novel *Die Wahlverwandtschaften* (1921) quotes from the *Farbenlehre*. What interests Benjamin is how for the attentive spectator nature is 'never dead or mute. It has even provided a confidant for the rigid body of the earth, a metal whose least fragment tells us about what is taking place in the entire mass.'[48] Magnetic metal speaks from the interior of the earth. It is an *Urphänomen*, and, notes Goethe, it 'reveals itself', as 'even' scientists realize in their drive to construe external, visible, tangible parts as a whole. These are understood as indications of what is within, and so they attempt to master the whole in perception. Nature as animate was not a one-off insight in Benjamin's writings. Just as the ideas of colour, play and fantasy surface again and again, so the notion of affinities between inner earth, outer space and the human body is evident across Benjamin's work, in his theories of mimeticism and indexicality. Benjamin has a sense of the history of perception as a history of the body – perspective depends on how upright the gait is; the perceptual evaluation of distance depends on the amount of movement made, and so on.[49] In 1933 Benjamin

wrote two articles on the mimetic capability, 'Über das mimetische Vermögen' ('On the Mimetic Faculty') and 'Lehre vom Ähnlichen' ('Doctrine
of the Similar'), which describe the mimetic capacity as an adaptation to
the environment. The pieces consider nature as a realm that produces
similarities. This is evident, for example, in the phenomenon of mimicry.
Here Benjamin regards astrology as an ancient hangover of a link between
humanity and the position of the stars. And words, especially in the form
of onomatopoeics, are a type of similarity. The latest graphology is seen to
teach that handwritten words are picture puzzles that conceal the unconscious of the writer – Benjamin analysed the handwriting of the serial
killer Peter Kürten. Writing is, in this sense, already the writing on the
mystic writing-pad of Freud.[50] It reveals once it is subjected to interpretation. It samples the truth of things and gives that truth up when pressed.

Freud was interested in mimesis in connection with the comic and
laughter. He wrote of 'ideational mimetics' in *Jokes and their Relation to the
Unconscious*,[51] referring to the way in which pleasure is derived from automatic mental mimicry, which empathizes and distances at the same time.
This has a bodily component – for memories are thereby invoked of
previous nervous innervations: someone raises an arm, my arm stirs faintly
too; I yawn, you yawn. Benjamin's ideas of mimesis and body memory may
have been influenced by Freud, but also by Marcel Proust. Proust's *À la
recherche du temps perdu* evokes a memory held by limbs, individual body
parts, which causes them, with no urgings from the conscious mind, to
readopt positions that they had held at an earlier time, for example when
in bed. The body mimics itself. The mimetic impulse is a key element of
Benjamin's thought. For Benjamin, mimesis is the original impulse of all
creative activity, and as such has a special relationship to childhood.[52] The
memories that mimesis draws on are not individual but collective mnemic
systems that cut across time. A mimetic capability manifests itself in the
body's imitation, in social and cultural forms, of acts that have been essential to its survival. So dancing and pictorial activity emerge in their
particular forms because they relate to remembered practical activities. In
1936 Benjamin noted that stone-age man drew the elk so incomparably
because the hand that moved the drawing stick still remembered the arrow
with which the beast had been brought down.[53] Drawing emerges, then,

as a way of retracing the social activities crucial to survival. And these are embedded in memory – and passed on to the collective. Memory is thus a tracing pad that retains knowledge, recollections, histories, and not just for the individual but for the collective, and it passes them down through time. While preparing the writings on mimesis Benjamin took notes on Georg Lichtenberg, a physics lecturer who advised Goethe in his researches. Lichtenberg reads the book of the world and the book of nature, a social world and a natural world both alive and historical.[54]

> As the cuts on the surface of a tin plate relate the story of all meals in which it has participated, so too the form of each belt of land, the shape of its hills of sand and rock, tells the history of the earth, each smoothed pebble thrown out by the ocean would tell of a soul which was chained to it as ours is to our mind.[55]

Historical activity – including that of a cosmic dimension – imprints its scratches on the tin surface, just as photography is a chemical imprinting of a likeness, and just as the external world imprints its traces on the psyche, where they may or may not be read. The mechanisms of the photographic arts are now not an illustration for psyche but an analogue for the mind and the body, themselves receiving and preserving traces. In his memoirs Benjamin insists that traces of mimetic behaviour are to be found in children's pleasure at imitating things – windmills, trains – as much as in their aping other people and elements of nature. Benjamin's autobiographical reminiscences pull photography even deeper into mimetic and mnemic reflections. On being photographed as a child in a studio, with a painted alpine scene, or in the shadow of a small palm tree, clutching a straw hat, Benjamin recalls an inability to resemble himself and a desire to be identical with the embroidered cushion or the ball handed him as prop.[56] Photography, a chemically based art, is mimetic and mnemic. 'A Small History of Photography' (1931) accents the indexicality of the photograph, with its chemical connection to actuality that snatches a flash of variegated light and shade and exports it into the future. Just as the person imprints the world on the self by identification with its objects, so the photographic object imprints traces of the world.[57] The object speaks through its traces, its scratches, its imprints; of course, this script might be needful of decipherment. The photographic object imprints traces of the world.[58] As August Sander proclaimed, 'In photography there are no unexplained shadows!'. Everything that appears is indexical to the material world, and its derivation – that is, its existence – can be traced back through the process that brought it into being. Benjamin quotes Goethe in connection with August Sander's social typological images, gleaned 'from direct observation': 'There is a tender empiricism that so intimately involves itself with the object that it becomes true theory.'[59]

Benjamin's most tender empiricism, a period of intense experimentation and note-taking, was perhaps the stretch of time he spent investigating hashish. Under the casual supervision of the experimental psychopathologist Ernst Joel, Benjamin made himself a site of experimentation in 1927. This was one way of importing the *Rausch* into modern life, one way to regain the cosmic experience of pre-rationalized humanity. In his study of surrealism, Benjamin wrote of the importance of *Rausch*, a component of every revolutionary act. It is imperative to win its powers for the revolution, for it induces an intensified sense of the realities of this world in a 'profane illumination'.[60] Between 1927 and 1934 Benjamin, together with test subjects Ernst Bloch, Fritz Fränkel and Egon Wissing, wrote several protocols on their experiments with hashish, opium and mescaline.[61] Sensations experienced during the periods of intoxication were noted. For example, one of the things noted in Benjamin's 'Crock Notes' is the way that colours can exert an uncommonly powerful impression upon the smoker. Describing a corner of Jean Selz's room, he sees a pair of tumblers filled with flowers, sitting on a crate, which was draped by a lace scarf. In the scarf and the flowers various shades of red predominated. Some time into the party, Benjamin discovers that the constellation has an almost deafening effect upon him. His task was to discover the sense of colour in 'the laboratoire rouge'. During the various experiments the participants observed each other, jotting down the new words coined or the relayed impressions, when objects and people turn into other, impossible things. Test subjects jotted down their own impressions at the time or afterwards. The protocols are specific notes on each particular experience of *Rausch*. The protocols attempted to understand the mode of seeing and thought processes of a mind in an altered state. That Benjamin could take this insight up into his theoretical work meant he regarded the visions as significant. Knowledge was being accessed, a scientific understanding could be gained. While the drugs took effect the test subjects handed each other objects, or attempted to stimulate perceptions. Fritz Fränkel's protocol of May 1934 describes a series of Rorschach tests on Benjamin, who had received mescaline subcutaneously in the thigh. Poodles, woolly sheep and pelican-lambs appear.[62] Benjamin also conjured up his own images, behind closed eyes, and they were wrought of an ornamentation as fine as hair. The experiments and the theorizing of them resembled those carried out by Goethe and Purkinje. After an experiment in January 1928 Benjamin noted:

> It is known that when one closes one's eyes and gently presses against them ornamental figures appear whose form we cannot influence. The architectural and spatial configurations that one sees before one's eyes on hashish are related to them. When they appear and what they appear as is, first of all, involuntary, so lightning quick and unannounced do they show themselves. Then as soon as they are there, conscious playing fantasy comes in order to take certain liberties with them.[63]

Under the influence of the drugs all of the senses are intensified. Hearing, seeing, taste and touch become at points unbearably acute. In March 1930 Benjamin records his first experience of '*audition colorée*' when he was unable to understand the words his cousin spoke because he translated the sounds immediately into coloured, metallic spangles that fell into patterns.[64] The presentation of an innervated body revelling in *Rausch*, with senses so attuned that they merge and exchange properties, drew out ideas expressed in 1920 when Benjamin recorded in his general bibliography Kandinsky's *Concerning the Spiritual in Art*, a book which provided 'material for an artistic doctrine of painting, if not a philosophy of art'.[65] Benjamin puzzles over Kandinsky's idea of the discrepancy between art's contemporary value and its eternal value. Kandinsky had argued that after a time audiences come to see art works more clearly, for they are no longer dazzled by the 'contemporary value' of the work. What emerges into light is termed by Kandinsky 'eternal value'. Benjamin disagrees with the appellation. He agrees that there are properties in art works that emerge only after time, only after the art work is no longer modern. But he does not agree that what emerges is eternal value (as opposed to contemporary value). It needs further investigation, but it will not be a matter of 'values'. In any case, it will not be the creator who can learn, for Benjamin agrees with Kandinsky's idea of synaesthesia, in that, for the creator, the medium around an art work is so thick that the composer sees his music, the painter hears his image, the poet tastes his poem, when he approaches it.[66] Through synaesthesia, it can be seen that drugged intoxication has some similarity to artistic experience. The transferred sensations characteristic of synaesthetic experience feature in a drug-induced state where time lags exist between touching and feeling, and the nerve endings in limbs seem to be displaced. Benjamin takes seriously the data that emerges of these drug experiments and he finds analogues in other modern experiences. He insists that they are not just particular experiences, but possess more general validity for an inquest into contemporary perception. Some of the formulations in the protocols resurface in other writings. In the *Arcades Project* Benjamin repeats phrases first uttered in the experiments, such as the 'ambiguous winking from nirvana', or the recognition that 'things are just mannequins and even great historical moments are only costumes, and looks of complicity exchange with the nothingness, the low, the banal'. The room seen from the drugged eye is 'a thick, self-woven, self-spun spider's web in which world affairs hang strewn around like corpses of insects sucked dry'.[67] This becomes a description of selfhood in the nineteenth century, where the superficiality and suffocating nature of public events in bourgeois society are avouched. The cutting up of space and time, the *colportage* effect, in the hashish *Rausch* mirrors that of the filmic montage, as is evident in the 'Artwork Essay'. But more than that, the very types of perception accessed in the drug state are made analogous to the type of perception the camera affords. Benjamin argues in the first two versions of 'The Work of Art in the Age of its Technical Reproducibility':[68]

> For the manifold aspects that the recording apparatus can win off reality lie for the most part only outside a *normal* spectrum of sense perceptions. Many of the deformations and stereotypes, the transformations and catastrophes, open to detection by the world of optics in film, are actually found in psychosis, in hallucinations, in dreams. And so those methods of the camera are practices,

thanks to which collective perception appropriates the individual ways of seeing of the psychotic or dreamer.[69]

The strange visions of dreamers and psychotics – and drug-takers – are re-created in cinematic techniques. The segmenting, slicing, allegorizing effect of cinematic devices severs the natural appearance of the everyday landscape like a surgical instrument, counteracting film's tendency to imitate the surface. Camera operators and their apparatuses perforate deep into the material of reality, administering a technologizing of the look and an anatomizing of the 'total'. Translated into aesthetic terms, this signals the need to reject a simple reflection theory in favour of representing actuality in its multiple potential modalities. The image is 'a multiply fragmented thing, whose parts reassemble themselves according to new laws'.[70] These new laws can be understood only if the old laws governing the comprehension of perception are discarded.

Benjamin's *Kant-Kritik* and his drug experiments were both part of his research into perception. Film and photography suggested to Benjamin that modes of perception were historical and mutable, and that new technological forms mediated perception in important ways. Such ideas coalesced with theories of film emerging from Soviet Russia. Shortly after meeting Eisenstein, Malevich wrote two articles, 'And Images Triumph on the Screens' (1925), and 'The Artist and the Cinema' (1926). Malevich stresses the potential for continuity between easel art and film, whereas Benjamin asserts that it is this continuity that denies film its full modernist significance. Malevich demands an end to images and the illustration of everyday life, in favour of cinema 'as such', whereas Benjamin insists that images, properly treated, correctly smashed and rearranged, may be the proper stuff of montage. But both are insistent on the legitimacy of film as artform, its access to truth, and the need for cinema to explore its full technical possibilities, including adopting the most advanced compositional laws. Imitative cinema – as surface reflection – is the enemy. Malevich notes how artists have influenced the compositional law of cinematography, and he looks forward to the technical developments that will allow film to appear textured, with a 'special lining on the images of the colour ray (of light) of such quality as to arouse the viewer's emotions in the same way that, for example, painterly pictures in museums do.' Cinema has not broken with the way of representing nature, colour and light invented by the oil painting of Monet, Rubens, Polenov and the rest. Each filmmaker constructs the film of stills whose compositional techniques are inherited from painters. The painter-artist enters the cinema in order to play the part of a scenery painter or furniture arranger. But, Malevich notes, the painter-artist must overcome any prejudice against the 'dead objective' of the camera, and realize that 'rays of colour are projected through this dead objective and that with them one can in fact paint a *painterly* picture, complete with texture'. It is colour that provides the link between painting and cinema. Where once painting held the advantage over cinema – for it could conjure up a world of hues – now cinema fights back with a luminosity only dreamt of before. Malevich insists that the new cinema-artists use colour. He berates the 'artist-dynamicists, who are *innovators* in their new means but *reactionaries in their treatment* of and attitude towards light and the subject'. They eschew colour for white and cold steel-like colouring. He endorses the artist-painters who are 'probably waiting impatiently for a palette of colour rays in order to weave from them painterly planes of texture like Renoir, Degas, Millet etc.'[71] Only so can all the wisdom of art be put to cinema's use.

Malevich had experimented with colour, the results of which were noted in 1930 in 'An Attempt to Determine the Relation between Colour and Form in Painting'. The impact of colour on the perception of a room's size was observed. Differences were noted between town dwellers and country dwellers in their attraction to colour, thus establishing for Malevich a social basis to colour predilection. And artists were shown geometrical shapes and asked to observe the colour associations that they invoked. The responses were fairly consonant, and were supposed to prove that, in some way, form may have its own colour. Art, however, ignores and bends these rules, investigating and playing with the relationship between colour and form. Malevich is quick to note that 'the artist does not perceive the universe as a form for which he must select colour, but creates painting alone, *which cannot be resolved into colour and form*'.[72] The artist is an organism inside of which exists a rather precise laboratory, equipped for experiments in psychophysiology.

the wonderful world of cartoon colour

> Last night I was in the Kingdom of the Shadows. If one could only convey the strangeness of this world. A world without colour and sound. Everything here – the earth, water and air, the trees, the people – everything is made of a monotone grey. Grey rays of sunlight in a grey sky, grey eyes in a grey face, leaves as grey as cinder. Not life, but the shadows of life. Not life's movement, but a sort of mute spectre. (Maxim Gorky, 'The Lumière Cinematograph', 1896)

> I should like to warn you against the impoverishment that comes of taking the law too literally. I should not like you to misunderstand what I have been teaching you. Such a misunderstanding might lead you to end up with nothing but grey, on the ground that it is the centre of the whole and contains all the colours, blue, yellow and red. And black and white for that matter. The result would be to outlaw all colours, even black and white. Only grey would be permissible, and only the one median grey. And the result? Would the world be grey on grey? No, worse than that. It would be one single grey, one nothing. Yes, simplicity can be carried to such an absurdity, the ultimate impoverishment, the end of life. (Paul Klee, *The Thinking Eye*, 1922)

Attempts to join colour and film mechanically dated back to the turn of the century, but in the first twenty years of the twentieth century the process was, in the main, carried out by hand. The first colour films were artists' films. Arnaldo Ginni, for example, devised some, conceiving of painting directly onto film around 1908, for there was then no stop-frame camera.[73] In 1908 he painted *Neurasthenia*, said to be one of the first abstract paintings of European modernism.[74] He thought that just as a musical motif is formed by sounds changing in a time sequence, so in painting a chromatic motif emerges if cinematographic techniques present colours changing in time sequence. Ginni's music–colour analogy was a component of the synaesthetic idea. On its basis he performed, together with his brother Bruno Corra, several experiments with the spectrum, dividing it into octaves; they then translated these octaves into practice with coloured electric light bulbs corresponding to keys on a keyboard.

The idea of a parallelism between music and colour predated Symbolist synaesthesia. Newton had discerned a music–colour octave analogy, and colour organs were first proposed in the sixteenth century. These became popular in the late nineteenth century with the Light Organs of Bishop

Bainbridge and Wallace Rimington; after that Skriabin and others began to devise them.[75] In 1910 Skriabin scored *Prometheus* for piano, orchestra, organ, wordless chorus and a *clavier à lumières* with keys that were each primed to beam luxurious coloured light into the concert hall. The colour organ devised by Ginni and Corra was abandoned because its light intensity was too weak and the bulbs were discoloured by their own heat. Ginni and Corra turned to film. In 1910 Ginni attempted several abstract film paintings, a colour chord after a painting by Segantini, a study of the complementary colours, a chromatic rendering of Mendelssohn, and a visualization of a Mallarmé poem. There was also a film called *The Rainbow*, where the colours of the rainbow provided the dominant theme, appearing occasionally in different forms, increasingly intense until it explodes. The screen was grey for a while, slowly interrupted by radiant tremors in a struggle between cloudiness and colour, until the whirling spectrum was finally triumphant. The light potency of film was strong, and the single frame on the filmstrip could be their unit of colour. The films were lost, if they were ever truly completed, and all that remains is their description in Corra's article from 1912 'Abstract Film – Chromatic Music'.[76]

Léopold Survage was another artist who painted onto the filmstrip. Apollinaire wrote in 1914 about the plan of Léopold Sturzwage, who later changed his name to Survage, to set in motion a series of abstract paintings using animation: 'It's the thing of the future. It has to come if our art is to have any relation to this rhythmic moving cinematographic age of ours.' Survage was convinced of the imperative of mobility:

> Painting, having liberated itself from the conventional forms of the object in the exterior world, has conquered the terrain of abstract forms. It must get rid of its last and principal shackle – immobility – so as to become as supple and rich a means of expressing our emotions as music is. Everything that is accessible to us has its duration in time, which finds its strongest manifestation in rhythm, action and movement, real, arranged and unarranged. I will animate my painting. I will give it movement, I will introduce rhythm into the concrete action of my abstract painting, born of my interior life; my instrument will be the cinematographic film, this true symbol of accumulated movement. It will execute the 'scores' of my visions, corresponding to my state of mind in its successive phases. I am creating a new visual art in time, that of colored rhythm and of rhythmic color.[77]

In the *Paris Journal* of 15 July 1914, Apollinaire insisted on the specific logic of Survage's *Coloured Rhythm*. It is not analogical to music, but an independent art with infinitely varied resources of its own. It stems from 'fireworks, fountains, electric signs, and those fairy-tale palaces which at every amusement park accustom the eyes to enjoy kaleidoscopic changes in hue'.[78] Convinced that colour becomes the content, the very soul of abstract form, Survage had begun in 1912 a series of nearly two hundred abstract watercolours, but the work of bringing them to life was too much for him alone, and, finding no assistant, he abandoned the project. In 1913 Kandinsky, who wrote the first publication on Schoenberg, hoped to collaborate on a colour-film version of his *Die glückliche Hand*. This, too, never came to be.

A few years on Walter Ruttmann took up the challenge of producing coloured abstract film. He brought colour into his films by using chemical toners, so transforming a black-silver material into a coloured compound, blue, red, sepia and so on, or by printing the film on a colour nitrate base, or tinting prints with aniline colours. The colours were not intended to be naturalistic, for the images were abstract. Colour, too, was liberated from reference. *Lichtspiel Opus I* was hand-coloured. For the critic Diebold – a member of the audience at the first showing, together with his friend Fischinger – it rendered the synthesis of painting, dance, music and film that he had proposed in 1916. The invitation sent out by Ruttmann claimed: 'The symphony of the optical, perhaps till now only a speculation on the part of aestheticians, becomes a reality here.'[79] Ruttmann's colour-strip was shown while music specially composed by Max Butting played. Here, Ruttmann split away from common cause with Eggeling. Eggeling's idea of synaesthesia was so strict that he refused to have music accompanying the projection of his films. They were music in themselves. For Fischinger, a lover of Goethe, Ruttmann's shapely dance gave him a mind to do the same, but supplemented by prerecorded classical music.

The last piece of Ruttmann's writing to appear before his death in 1942 was an essay on colour film (1941).[80] Ruttmann observed that technicians and artists, on the one hand, and business figures, on the other, had an interest in the synthesis of colour and film. The former thought that by the addition of colour naturalism could be enhanced; the latter thought that colour would draw in more audiences. The European film industry, in particular, was longing for something to turn its failing black-and-white fortunes around in the face of Hollywood's winning formulas. But, warns Ruttmann, just as sound had not increased the value of film, so colour would count for nothing if it were deployed only as a naturalistic enhancement. Anyway, there are psychological reasons why natural colours are impossible. Each person perceives differently and there would seem to be no objective sense of colour. Ruttmann aimed for an artistic use of colour, not a naturalistic one. In fact, it seems that for him nature is unaesthetic, its colours random. The colours in film need to be ordered; they need *Gestaltung*. That is why, of course, animation is superior. Ruttmann bemoans the decline of colour in the modern age. In a language that appears to be burdened by the pseudo-depth of Nazi discourse – for he had by then been a documentarist in that regime for nearly a decade – he complains that the 'inner life-connectedness with colour' has been lost, the 'inner need' diminished.

> It must be supposed that seldom has there been a time that is more helpless than ours as regards colour. The 'sensuous, moral' effect of colour, which Goethe in his colour theory treats as generally self-evident, is no longer graspable by anyone. Even the simple registration of optical impressions takes place in consciousness quite without colour. The overwhelming majority of people do not dream in colour, but in black and white. Grey, black and white are the preferred tones of contemporary life. Colour is used almost exclusively decoratively.

Ruttmann demands that film artists return to the colour wheel and the ABC of colour, to relearn the basics in order to work intelligently with colour. Moholy-Nagy's reflections in 1939, 'Light: A New Medium of Expression', were more generous and utopian about the possibilities of practice. Like Ruttmann, Moholy-Nagy insisted that education was crucial: 'We must become familiar with colorimetry, wave lengths, purity, brightness, excitation of light, and with the manifold possibilities of the artificial light sources.' Optical illusions, surrounding effects of negative shapes, of hue, chroma and value must be further explored, alongside experiments with polished surfaces, transparencies and translucencies, shadows, refraction with prisms and grating, polarization and interference with light. These investigations are complemented by scientific research into the physiology of the eye and the physical properties of light, and our own permanent observations of light and colour offered in the daily routine of home and stage, street and laboratory. Moholy-Nagy's article is a study of the uses of painterly techniques of 'mixture by addition' and 'mixture by subtraction' for film colour. But he is keenly aware of the differences that arise with the addition of light. Colour is an art of light. He turns to Goethe and his 'anti-Newtonism theory of coloring in which he established that black through a "turbid" medium appears as blue and light gives us yellow-orange up to yellow-red'. The emphasis is on colour relations of complement and contrast. Newton, he remarks, only once mentioned a complementary colour pairing – gold–indigo. Each colour, insists Moholy-Nagy, is responded to in the eye with its complement. Our eyes react to red with green, to yellow with blue, and so on. The psychological and physiological experiences of colour, he laments, have not been integrated with the physical laws of light in the work of artists and publicity men. The experimenters that he praised were the colour-organists Castel, Hoffman, Rimington, Skriabin, Hirschfeld-Mack, Wilfred and Laszlo, and in the realm of film Eggeling. The synaesthetic dream was kept alive and he reiterated the emphasis on technical invention intrinsic to the early modernist avant-garde:

> it seems to me that we should direct all our efforts like the Dadaist Raoul Hausmann toward the creation of an optophonetic art which will one day allow us to see music and hear pictures simultaneously.[81]

Oskar Fischinger had been busy designing new technologies for film that would allow such multi-sensual perceptions. Even before the development of sound film he developed a technology that allowed records to play synchronously with film strips. In 1932, in *Studie no. 14*, he produced the first European colour film using Bela Gaspar's Gasparcolor, a three-layer colour process, like Kodacolor used later.[82] His first colour film was an advertisement called *Kreise*. Then the same year he made an advertisement with animated cigarettes called *Muratti greift ein*. Later, when Fischinger was disillusioned with the film industry because of the Hollywood studios' refusal to give him creative control, he hoped to strike gold by inventing a Lumigraph, a piano that projected colours onto a screen. He imagined that every good bourgeois home would like a Lumigraph next to the piano.

Technologies were moving on but they were not adopting the shapes that Fischinger imagined. In the late 1920s John Randolph Bray released the first animation on colour film, *The Debut of Thomas Cat*. But it was too expensive, and the film stock too brittle. Herbert Kalmus and friends at Technicolor had been working on colour processes since 1912, and had produced a two-colour additive system in 1917, whereby a conventional black-and-white print ran through a special projector with red and blue-green colour lenses adding the tints. Additive systems lose light when the black and white image is projected through colour filters. The experimenters at Technicolor moved quickly on to a subtractive two-colour system, for subtractive systems hold the colour information in the images. Technicolor's output was boosted from 1928 to 1930, and the company coped with the accommodation of sound on some of the film strips, but crisis hit in 1931 as the effects of the Great Depression took hold, and the restricted colour palettes of the two-colour processes could rarely tempt audiences to spend the little money they had. Kalmus worked on a three-strip Technicolor process using dye-transfer printing. The first camera was unveiled in 1932, and at a cost of $30,000 was remarkably expensive. Kalmus managed to persuade stockholders to invest despite studios' almost total abandonment of colour film production. It was far better suited to animation than to photographing live-action footage. Disney, a pioneer in the use of sound film in 1928, struck Kalmus as a fitting person to approach for try-outs. Kalmus asked Disney if he wanted to be the first to use the red–green–blue process. Disney agreed, trashed a partially completed film called *Flowers and Trees* and began it again in Technicolor. In *Flowers and Trees* a crabby tree stump disrupts a romance between two young trees, starting a fire that threatens the whole forest. Birds puncture clouds, causing rain to fall to drown the flames, destroying the stump and allowing the lovers to marry with a glow-worm for a wedding ring. The flowers celebrate the nuptials. The result impressed Disney's competitors as much as, if not more than, it struck audiences. But Disney had strung up Kalmus in an exclusive five-year contract (later cut to one year under protest from those competitors in other studios). Whether Technicolor boosted Disney's fortunes, or Disney boosted Technicolor's, is uncertain, but both, according to Kalmus, profited greatly from the deal.

Sequential photography was ideally suited to the frame-by-frame principle of animation. For the Disney cartoons a camera was made with a filter wheel in front of the lens; each frame was exposed three times, recording the blue, red and green elements in sequence. The processed negative was sent to the Technicolor laboratory to be step-printed to three individual matrix films, one for each colour record. From the gelatin relief maps of each original image complementary dyes were absorbed by the matrix films – blue turns to yellow, red goes cyan and green shines with magenta. These dyed matrices were then printed onto blank printing film with mordant chemicals to control the absorption of the dyes. These multiple processes of dye transfer and printing demanded incredible precision and a high level of quality control to create the most perfect little film frame with Technicolor's characteristic heavy colour saturation. But Technicolor had a code of colour. It endeavoured to promote the idea of Technicolor's truth to nature. Natalie Kalmus was the director of Technicolor's Advisory Service, and in 1935 she drafted stringent guidelines for the use of colour in live-action films. The Unified Technicolor System demanded that colour should look natural. Colour should follow established conventional standards of harmony, contrast and cultural connotations. And colour should be subordinated to narrative in order to add to the story without distracting the audience. Natalie Kalmus called for 'natural colours' which did not overload the eye, reckoning that: 'Even when Nature indulges in a riot of beautiful colours, there are subtle harmonies which justify those colours.'[83] Nature is always justified. Walt Disney had been rigorously imposing strict rules of colour harmony, colour balance, similarity of hue, and the use of sizeable areas with weak chroma in his Silly Symphonies, for which the studios won five Academy Awards. The first colour film with Mickey Mouse, *The Band Concert*, won the prize for best animation film at the Venice Film Festival of 1935. Disney had to train his animators and storywriters in colour theory to win these accolades for skilled use of colour.

Walter Ruttmann had worried about the problems of imitating nature's colour scheme, for he thought that nature's choices were not rightful, but rather random. The Disney colourists thought this too, in fact. Colour schemes were seen to match characters' personalities, and then the painted backgrounds blended harmoniously with figures in the foreground, and were never cluttered with distracting detail or lurid colours. Scene by scene, whole sections of *Fantasia* were colour-keyed. The colours in each shot harmonized with each other, and with the colours in the shots before and after. Colour harmony went beyond aesthetic stylization into the near ideological, as the centaurs and 'centaurettes' paired up in matching colour casts. All the colours were keyed psychologically, matching the changes in emotions being expressed by the actions. Robert Feild wrote in 1942:

> Before the narrative pattern was completed in any great detail, an overall colour scheme was worked out in sympathy with the general mood of the music and patterned to correspond with the development of the subject matter.[84]

Music and narrative are supported by the colour scheme. Despite the observation by Lewis Jacobs, who proclaimed in the *New York Times* in 1935 that 'Disney alone understands the problem of color on the screen',[85] and claimed that 'Disney was the first to realize that color in motion pictures need not bear any resemblance to color in real life, that objects on the screen could be endowed with any pigmentation dictated by the imagination', Disney revealed a more realist intent.[86] On 1 December 1936 he noted his thoughts on colour:

> We want to imagine it as rich as we can without splashing color all over the place. I saw Harman-Ising's cartoon about Spring … last night. They got colors everywhere and it looks cheap. There is nothing subtle about it at all. It's just poster-like. A lot of people think that's what a cartoon should have. I think we are trying to achieve something different here. We are not going after comic supplement coloring. We have to strive for a certain depth and realism … the subduing of the colours at the right time and for the right effect.[87]

Colour could be deployed to increase the longed-for illusion of depth, a component of filmic realism, by the use of contouring and variation in colour intensity. Different planes were generated through the use of the receding tendencies of cool colours and tints and the illusion of advance put out by warmer colours and shades. The colours lift off from anything strictly factual – and yet they reinforce a 'natural world'. These animations left nature quite inanimate, with muted colours. The Disney studios used Technicolor's capabilities in various ways. There was *Snow White and the*

Seven Dwarfs with its soft watercolour washes that were so reminiscent of old book illustrations, perhaps at best like those in the Brothers Grimm fairy-tale books or those of Johann Peter Lyser with their pale careworn hues that Benjamin admired. Greyed-down transparent casts doused the backgrounds. Such a subdued palette suited Technicolor's ability to best capture mid-range colours at that time.[88] But the real test of Technicolor was the 1940 extravaganza *Fantasia*. Its several sections each evoked a very different mood, according to the music that the images attempted to visualize.

The Disney colourists deployed colour in landscape to punctuate the personality of characters and influence the mood of the audience. Their standard semiosis – not unlike Goethe's in *Faust* – shows darkness aligned with evil and chaos, while light sketches goodness and harmony. For example, the closing sequences of *Fantasia* with Mussorgsky's 'Night on Bald Mountain' set in gloomy black and grey tones, followed by Schubert's 'Ave Maria' and dawn in a hazy forest that transforms into the pink hues of a cathedral interior. Ken Anderson, the art director who colour-keyed the storm in the 'Pastoral Symphony' section of *Fantasia*, devised a colour scheme chart to portray classical music in the 'classical world'. It was designed to show the painters responsible for backgrounds what colours might communicate Bacchus's fear as he is raided by Zeus's sportive light-ning bolts, or what colours could relate the relief of characters as they step out from their shelters once the storm has given way to the glorious sunlight. The sequence closes with a glut of colour, dripping from the rainbow into the water, saturating the rosy-bottomed cupids, and caressing the landscape. The 'Shepherd's Hymn of Thanksgiving' imagines it follows the colours of Beethoven's musical tones in the piece that was written just as Goethe completed his colour theory. The outcome answers Disney's eager cry on first seeing three-strip Technicolor back in 1932: 'At last! We can show a rainbow on the screen!'[89] The rainbow provided the greatest screen test of all. As Iris drags her cloak of many colours across the sky, its colours intensify. Nature's most unnatural-seeming trick shimmers out from the screen.

In 1938 Herbert Kalmus addressed the Society of Motion Picture Engineers on the topic of Technicolor and Disney. He wanted to prove that the wonders of colour were worth the financial investment. He touched on the rainbow in *Funny Little Bunnies*:

> You remember the huge rainbow circling across the screen to the ground and you remember the Funny Bunnies drawing the colour of the rainbow into their paint pails and splashing the Easter eggs. You will admit that it was marvelous entertainment. Now I will ask you how much more it cost Mr. Disney to produce that entertainment in color than it would have in black and white? The answer is, of course, that it could not be done at any cost in black and white.[90]

But one-time Disney fan Eisenstein did not agree with Kalmus's verdict on Disney's glorious techno-reproduction of nature. For him, Disney's were black-and-white cartoons coloured in. From his perspective, the studio undertook no serious research into colour, colour perception and colour effects, colour montage or synaesthetics. 'He has not progressed to the next stage', Eisenstein decreed in 1947.[91] But Disney was already moving on to another stage, a vast stage for 'a cast' of 'colourful characters'. Disney was giving up on the marshalling of the world in film and the struggle to re-create nature. He wanted to stylize reality itself – at Disneyland.

winding up: a flat ending

Disney realized his perfect 'real world' at Anaheim in California in 1955. The cartoon version persisted too, in a parallel world of fake perspectives. The feature-length cartoons furnished scale models for coming attractions at the three-dimensional park. Production of full-length animations had picked up again after the war, with *Cinderella* the first major release in 1950. *Cinderella* was chosen because it was a fairy-tale (the other feature-length that was being worked on was *Alice in Wonderland*), and it was hoped that its magic might reanimate the sense of marvel that had greeted *Snow White and the Seven Dwarfs* in the pre-war period. Production of *Cinderella* had begun before the war – though it had not gone past the stage of preparing storyboards – but had been suspended in wartime and picked up in earnest again in 1947.[1] The cartoon's Cinderella was pegged as 'the ideal American girl',[2] and she was as peachy as Snow White herself. That the cartoon made it to the screens and in such lavish form was taken as a sign that Disney had survived the war unscathed, noted one *Newsweek* contributor.[3] And so the American dream – with a European fairy tang – resumed transmission. In Europe, too, the post-war New World order had kicked off with a resumption of transmission: on 7 June 1946 BBC television broadcast from London's Alexandra Palace the rest of *Touchdown Mickey* (1932) – for it had been interrupted on 'Black Friday' 1939, at just that point where Mickey Mouse imitated Greta Garbo's line: 'Ah tink ah go home.'

Disney's finances were in bad shape, and one-third of the workforce had been shed. Much of *Cinderella* was shot using actors first, and was only afterwards translated into drawings. Animators were made to use photostatic frame enlargements to guide their drawings. They were restricted by the technological pre-vision. The grounds for this were economic – it 'helped Walt see what he was getting before he spent his money on it'[4] – but it was the drive to realism that made this a reasonable course of action. Cinderella was lavishly realistic. As Richard Schickel put it, writing on *Cinderella* and *Sleeping Beauty* (1959):

> detail was piled on detail, technical effect on technical effect, until the story was virtually buried under their weight. It was an art of limited – some would say nonexistent – sensibility, a style that labored to re-create the trifles of realistic movement, that fussed over decorative elements, that refused to consider the possibilities inherent in the dictum that less is more. The wonderful simplicity that Disney's graphic art naturally possessed in the beginning and that he might have distrusted as betraying its humble and primitive origins, disappeared. In the late films complexity of draftsmanship was used to demonstrate virtuosity and often became an end in itself, a way of demonstrating what was a kind of growth in technical resourcefulness but not, unfortunately, in artfulness.[5]

That was the Disney style – excessively detailed, pernickety realism, exuding 'magical radiance';[6] but there were other players in the cartoon world and these were sketching a new look, to match a new post-war America. In the early 1940s three ex-Disney employees, Dave Hilberman, Zachary Schwartz and Stephen Bosustow, began working on a cartoon on safety in the workplace. The United Auto Workers were sponsoring the campaign to get Roosevelt elected in the 1944 elections and the three ex-Disney animators offered their services for a pro-FDR film called *Hell Bent for Election*. Warner Brothers, a left-liberal studio, had turned it down, fearful of involvement in overt politicking. (In the 1950s the McCarthy witch-hunters would scrutinize Warner Brothers, for many of its employees appeared on the blacklist.) After more commissions – some industrial films, some government films – the company changed its name from Industrial Films and Poster Services to United Productions of America (UPA). From 1946, following a disagreement in the triumvirate, Bosustow took over the company and the other two quit to form an animation company, Zac–David, which became successful in the field of television animation. Bosustow's UPA dismantled the assembly-line system of animation, devolving work onto small spontaneous grouplets. UPA's look denied the flesh-and-blood realism of Disney's feature-length films. They – like other studios – abandoned the pursuit of the real. Stereoptical and multiplane technologies tended to be discontinued in the 1940s, as flat graphics came into vogue. Thin outlines stylized reality rather than imitating it. Even the Disney studios sometimes took on the style. *The Three Caballeros* (1945), *The Adventures of Ichabod and Mr Toad* (1949) and *Alice in Wonderland* (1951) used strong geometric patterning in the backgrounds, with foliage or buildings insinuated cursorily in limber linear designs drawn over fields of colour.

In the spring of 1945 the post-Trotskyist journal *Partisan Review* published an article by Barbara Deming. It was called 'The Artlessness of Walt Disney'.[7] Deming cites Wolcott Bibbs's verdict on Disney's Latin American fantasy *The Three Caballeros*: it is a product of 'awful taste', monstrous, lewd, and psychopathically chaotic. She agrees with Bibbs, but also traces the cartoon in relation to a Yeatsian reflection on 'the centre' that 'cannot hold', a content that turns and turns in the widening gyre where 'things fall apart'. *The Three Caballeros* shifts its styles repeatedly. There is a logic to this, argues Deming, in contrast to Eisenstein's condemnation of the loss of stylistic unity in later Disney.[8] The loss of unity is symptomatic; that is to say, it is true to the epoch. The film reflects the deep bewilderment of the time, a time of war. Disney comes yet again to be a symptom of the crisis of culture, and the crisis of the social world, yet this time negatively, without hope. Disney is absorbent of the prevailing energies. In a bright-faced and aggressive epoch, he invented Mickey Mouse. In a time of crisis, Disney improvises chaotically and without inhibition. The film demonstrates how things fall apart. It is about falling, or falling asunder. This is a world of nightmares, suffered in pursuit of a quest that always turns out to be a disappointment. The props are removed, all that is solid puffs into thin air. Disney, Donald Duck, and the malevolent aracuan bird stand on the periphery of the film and run through a panoply of tricks and styles in order to explode the cartoon world that is projected on a screen within a screen. The cartoon questions its own reality, interrupting its narration, breaking its frame. But that is only the first reel. Yet that opening forces reflection on the spectacle that unfolds.

After this first scene, Donald Duck enters the cartoon world, climbing into the pop-up book to act. Now the chaos begins, with 'techniques mixed incongruously', producing formlessness. This is a chaos that cannot be made accessible to meaning, thinks Deming. The representation of disintegration had its logic, but now another feature, inconsistency, takes over. Inconsistency has no logic, indeed is in itself an offence against logic. Deming criticizes the film's incoherent use of space and perspective. In-side the pop-up book, which has appeared to offer itself to us fully, suddenly corners and streets appear, 'without deference to the laws of physics'. And yet, periodically, the camera withdraws to give an overall glance at the pop-up book, so denying acknowledgement of where we have been. The purpose of the return to the over-all view is, Deming says, 'to assure us that there is no going so far afield that one cannot return'. Wings are clipped on these strange birds. The inconsistent geography has an ideological purpose – it seeks to comfort and contain. And yet the solid ground to which Donald Duck always returns is nowhere, notes Deming. It is a blank background, a coating of solid colour. For Deming this nowhere that appears on screen is evidence of emptiness, meaninglessness and a lack of control. It is echoed in the abstract shapes that burst into the frame, and is manifest in the blurred boundaries between Donald Duck's vision and the actuality that is represented in the cartoon.

The meaninglessness gives way to collapse and the centre falls apart – nihilistically – when a kaleidoscopic vortex opens up in the film's final scene. The audience is sucked into the cartoon from the inside, as Disney surrenders to the nightmarish whirl of colour, shape and spin. Here, it could be said that, for a moment, cartoon returns to Emile Cohl's vision, as Donald Duck, strung along by desire, kisses female faces, which always, at the moment of approach, mutate into flowers, and his head crashes through like a dog through a paper hoop, or they turn into mocking friends on ugly long necks. Or desire achieved collapses into whirl and blur, which forms a decorative pot, which turns back into Donald Duck, surrounded by cacti as phallic as that which Eisenstein straddled for a lewd photograph on his Latin American jaunt. But in this whirl of signi-fication and instability, Deming sees only horror, vacuity without conclusion. Only erupting fireworks can interrupt this nightmare, she notes. Deming did not foresee the possibility that were the world to right itself – that is to say, were America to become its stable point, its point of command and perspective, in the post-war scene – then the dreams might return and the nightmares fade. That appeared to be the promise of *Cinderella*, at least.

A stylized world of abstract shapes and thin lines had the advantage of being cheap. In the face of dwindling budgets, Warner Brothers, ever the spoofers of Disney's middlebrow seriousness (for example, in 1943 they presented *Coal Black and de Sebben Dwarfs*, and in 1946 *A Corny Concerto* mocked *Fantasia*), selected a sparse look for the backgrounds to their snappy, anarchic cartoons featuring Bugs Bunny, Daffy Duck, Elmer Fudd, Wile E. Coyote and Porky Pig. These were gleeful exercises in wise-guy formalism, constantly bursting through the fourth wall of the screen and using baring devices such as audience address and Brechtian placards. Tex Avery was a key figure of this 'vulgar modernist' style.[9] Avery developed his style at Warner Brothers and moved to MGM in 1942, where he cultivated his violent, erotic and surrealistic techniques. UPA cartoons, such as *Gerald McBoingboing* and *Mister Magoo*, emphasized the two-dimensional plane. In 1949 UPA made *The Ragtime Bear*, with the supporting character of Mr Magoo. It was the first example of UPA's limited animation style. Where Disney used one cel for each frame of film, UPA used one cel for every two or three frames of film. This was a matter of style as well as a question of cost, or at least a question of where the available money should be spent – on perfecting single frames or on drawing multiples. UPA animations used minimal, sketchy forms, oblongs and angular abstract shapes and large sections of dense colour. One of the UPA co-workers, John Hubley, ex-Disney striker and radical art theorist, had worked on *Bambi*, *Dumbo*, *Fantasia* and *Pinocchio*, and, in 1947, was art director on the film of Brecht's *Life of Galileo*, directed by Ruth Berlau and Joseph Losey, but flatness caught his imagination. Later, he was to continue to take flatness extremely seriously, when, in 1962, he joined the staff of Harvard as the first teacher of animation in the new Visual Arts Center, and floated the idea of making a film based on Edwin Abbott Abbott's 1880s' story of life in a two-dimensional world, *Flatland*.[10]

UPA's sensibility was often neurotic, restless, edgy, not luxuriant and lavish, while Warner Brothers' quickly drawn cartoons illustrated another

From *All in Line*,
Saul Steinberg

Freudian feature – repetition, frustrating, demeaning repetition, as in the Sisyphean endeavours of Road Runner. In both, the drawing was plain and expressive, stripped down and essential. This was an aesthetic reaffirmation of modernism, now located, in the main, in New York, the newly minted world cultural epicentre, crucible of the new art trends of abstract expressionism, colour field painting and gesture painting.[11] Jean Charlot's paradox in *Art from the Mayans to Disney* (1939) was once more affirmed. The animated film is 'whipped into form' by the pressures of the balance sheet, and yet where once it 'solved' the problems of cubism, now it addressed the turn to flatness that the latest art demanded. It captures the impersonality of the epoch – in its stripped-down look as much as in its communal and mechanical mode of production.[12] American-style, this was a popular modernism, a 'vulgar modernism'. John Hubley later acknowledged the debt to Saul Steinberg's spiky, sparse cartoon drawings for the *New Yorker*: 'we went for very flat stylized characters, instead of the global three-dimensional Disney characters. It was very influenced by Saul Steinberg and that sharp-nosed character he was doing at the time.'[13]

Eisenstein, too, was pleased by America's flat aesthetic as represented by Saul Steinberg. Eisenstein owned a copy of Steinberg's album *All in Line* (1945). He relished the fact that the drawing style reputedly came from Steinberg's play with a piece of wire. Steinberg's lines are few and the perspective awry. They often depict grotesque beasts, sometimes half-animal and half-human, operating beneath distorted skyscrapers. As the years passed, Steinberg's style became more abstract and his drawings began to fill up with letters and punctuation marks. One Steinberg cartoon that attracted Eisenstein in particular shows a figure in an economically gestured lounge bending wire coat hangers into dog shapes. So easily can the world be transformed. All forms are provisional – just temporary arrangements. Perhaps the young Ad Reinhardt, before he became a black-pigment-smearing abstract expressionist painter, knew the transformative force of the quick and simple line when he contributed his drawing skills to magazines such as *New Masses* and *Soviet Russia Today*, publications of the American Communist Party and its front organizations, in the shape of cartoons and comic strips.[14] Their lines followed the party line as it twisted and turned in the 1930s and 1940s. The economic line, the snappy joke, politics as an art, if not Art.

Disney lost any interest that he had in flatness as the decade progressed. Disneyland was ever rounder, and ever more stimulating to him. The sugar-sweet animations continued with *Peter Pan* (1953) and the painstakingly realist *Lady and the Tramp* (1955). Live-action films were made from 1950, beginning with *Treasure Island*. 1959 was the release year of the extremely lush animation of *Sleeping Beauty*. The backgrounds of this fairy-tale fare were deluxe and elaborate. The aesthetic reference was to medieval illustration and early Renaissance painting, such as Dürer and *Les Très Riches Heures du Duc de Bery*.[15] Details were abundant. The desired effect was deep focus. It was wide-screen Technirama and the sound was stereophonic. Animators were requested to study a full-length live action version, and Disney told his artists to make the characters 'as real as possible, near-flesh-and-blood'.[16] But he was losing interest in animation, for the theme park was absorbing all his attention now. At the theme park there was a real-life fake Sleeping Beauty castle, open since 1957. It looked a little like Ludwig II's pastiche of an early Gothic chateau from the 1860s, constructed on top of the ruins of a number of older castles on a mountain top in Hohenschwangau, south Germany. Mad Ludwig had wanted to climb high, to transcend. He wrote to Richard Wagner: 'The gods … will stay with us way up here, breathing the air of heaven.' But it was not high enough, and so he turned his mind to a final grand scheme, a castle at Falkenstein near Füssen, the highest castle in Germany. A clay maquette of the never-completed dream house had been on display since the 1920s at another castle at Herrenchiemsee. These were the treasures of Europe and no post-war touring American wanted to miss them. But Disney could reproduce them, and better and cleaner, under a kindly, predictable Californian sun.

The modernists and the mass culture purveyors part ways here in postwar America. The modernists refuse to purchase entry tickets to the new states of Adventureland, Tomorrowland, Fantasyland and Frontierland. Clement Greenberg, authoring a modernist tradition for the new art capital of the world, gives modernism the qualification 'high', and hopes to sever the links, for all that could emerge of a union would be the monstrous hybrid of 'midcult', which Milton Klonsky deems an 'aesthetic hippogriff', and is, according to Dwight Macdonald's article 'Masscult and Midcult', in *Partisan Review* in 1960, a bastard offspring of masscult's unnatural intercourse with High Culture.[17] To produce middlebrow culture, pleasure without pain, as in, for example, accessible versions of the bible or primers on poetic masters, is, for Macdonald, 'like taking apart Westminster Abbey to make Disneyland out of the fragments'.[18] The most terrifying thing for Macdonald is that it is lapsed avant-gardists who produce it, placing 'the modern idiom in the service of the banal'. The result is that 'Bauhaus modernism has seeped down, in a vulgarized form, into the design of our vacuum cleaners, pop-up toasters, supermarkets and cafeterias'. (It might be noted that some ex-Trotskyists, ex-comrades of the Partisans, were quite enthusiastically playing their part too, most notably Max Eastman, who from 1941 was roving editor for *Reader's Digest*, a most powerful motor of middlebrow culture and anti-communism.) Milton Klonsky hits at the heart of cartooning in his 1949 essay 'Along the Midway of Mass Culture', with its never-the-twain-shall-meet stance. High art and mass culture must never alloy, for their structuring principles are discrete: mass culture products always have a cinematic time sense and 'the glass they hold up to modern life is a mirror that focuses certain aspects sharply but reflects nothing in depth'.[19] This semi-reflection Klonsky terms its two-dimensionality.

Two-dimensionality was, however, enjoying a renaissance. The flatness of mass culture met Clement Greenberg's new art-for-art's-sake, abstract expressionism, where the canvas must reveal itself to be what it is, and nothing else: the site of pigment laid on a flat surface. This had always been the objective of modernism: to flatten out, to bring to the surface, in order to make the base show itself for what it is. When Cézanne painted his *Large Bathers* of 1904–06, it was its flatness that stunned the viewers. At just that moment Emile Cohl worked on his little animated screenplays of flatness and illusion, which transformed one thing through a few quick pen strokes into another. In Cohl's animations, a man turns into a bottle, or a clown turns into a lotus bloom. In Cézanne's *Large Bathers*, too, at least one figure is transitive. Flattened out and transforming, one set of marks at the edge of the painting could be either the shoulders of one woman or the buttocks of another. It is undecidable.[20] And then it was on to cubism, with its flat panes juddered into a self-baring illusion of space, wearing its means of representation on its canvas sleeve, or El Lissitzky's *Prouns*, made of black, white and grey bars and geometric shapes and words on plywood, analysing space and the 'technical materials' used for analysis' sake. Cartoons followed that road too, as Felix the Cat and Koko the Clown acknowledged the flatness of the surface over which they skimmed – one in which likewise words sprang out to emphasize the paper nature of it all and play was made of the fluidity of the inks that pretended to give them body. Always what is done in one place gets repeated in another – perhaps as joke, perhaps as middlebrow abomination, perhaps simply because artists and artisans, whoever they were, responded to the same world, the same problems, the same questions, wherever they were, and even if, sometimes, one group responded tragically and the other farcically. After a decade of abstract expressionism, Greenberg found that the work of chimpanzees was being praised and that any flat surface could serve as the support for a mediocre artistic event.[21] He moved on to colour as the place where advances could be made. There was a less pessimistic reading of ape art – though valid only in the context of utterly revolutionary hope. In 'One More Try if You Want to be Situationists: The S.I. in and against Decomposition' (1957), Guy Debord discusses an exhibition at London's Institute of Contemporary Art of 'paintings executed by chimpanzees, which bear comparison with respectable action painting'. They excite Debord as a naked expression of crisis, a manifestation of the decomposition of bourgeois culture.[22]

In the United States, highly cultured American citizens – including the leftist critics in Greenwich Village – turned their back on America's songs that made the whole world sing and its clowns that made the whole world laugh. It was as if, on leaving for Frankfurt, Adorno had left behind in the United States a germ, which the revolutionary Trotskyists around the Partisan group had picked up. Their Trotskyism was now less a conviction in the possibility of world revolution and more a pretext for an anti-Stalinism that coincided with US Cold War rhetoric. Like Adorno, they condemned the political instrumentalization of art that they saw at work in the Eastern bloc, and they scorned the commercial appropriation of culture in the West. This appropriation took the form of 'bad high culture', a curious formation, and mass trash, an industrial one, produced in the factories of distraction. The industrialization of culture was advancing rapidly. Less than half a century on and the Eccentrics' call was repulsed. In 1922 they had loudly, and rudely, proclaimed, 'YESTERDAY – the culture of Europe. TODAY – the technology of America. Industry, production under the Stars and Stripes. Either Americanization or the undertaker.'[23] The Eccentrics evoked a film and pulp-fiction world of the echoing footsteps of chases and tap dancers and policemen's truncheons, scandal

and newspaper vendors. And they enthused about 'the cult of the amusement park, the big wheel and the switchback, teaching the younger generation the BASIC TEMPO of the epoch'. Now, *sotto voce*, urbane Americans
repelled the association. Coney Island – home of 'heightened reality made
dramatic',[24] locale of Clement Greenberg's outcast tap dancers, Tin Pan
Alley music, commercial art and thrills without danger – was bad enough.
But even worse was the cleaned up version without the gamblers and the
prostitutes, that yeast of the original bohemian avant-garde, and without
the folks fucking on the beach – Disneyland.[25] The American dream was
too lucrative a nightmare for these intellectuals. They had to invent a new
story of modernism, to give it a new footing, a new origin and future, far
away from all this. They had to beat a path for American modernism, a
version that was seen to rekindle 'art for art's sake', art as poetry, art as
autonomous, art as 'free' – formal, abstract, detached – and on the path
of 'self-purification'.[26] Duchamp, the surrealists, the Dadaists had to be
excised, for perhaps they were to blame for the kitsch art that followed
in vulgar pop and beyond. 'Picassoid space' had to be left,[27] in order to
float colour on the surface, as Kandinsky had once done. The new
American painting had to continue the task of divesting painting of its
'expendable conventions', resuming the quest for 'utter abstractness'.[28]
'Our painting', a first time Great American Painting, was flattening the
surface, abolishing sculptural illusion. It was busy being painting, not politics
or fantasy figuration or universal critique. Greenberg's perspective was
coloured by his position as art critic in a new superpower. He might have
granted that aspects of his new aesthetic were contained in the American
trash he reviled. Dwight Macdonald had, after all, noted the trickle-down
effect of avant-garde art into domestic settings, and, in 1939, Greenberg
had defined kitsch as yesterday's avant-garde diluted.[29] But this was not
yesterday's avant-garde. Cartooning was the place where research into
flatness and illusion and abstraction was most conscientiously carried out.
Cartoon trash could cast the most curious and fantastic lights.

Adorno, by now in his safe European home, held on to the modernist
dream of an art that could illuminate life, a life distorted, yet recognizably
ours. He wanted an art that could transform life under its glare. He voiced
his dream in the language of another. He ventriloquized dead Walter

Benjamin's revolutionary dialect of redemption. As Adorno phrases it in his finale to *Minima Moralia: Reflections from Damaged Life*, in a section written in 1946 or 1947: philosophy must contemplate all things as they would present themselves from the standpoint of redemption. This modernist continues with the insistence that defamiliarization – the distortion of the distortion, negation of the negation – is the only hope for hope in the world. 'Perspectives must be fashioned that displace and estrange the world, reveal it to be, with its rifts and crevices, as indigent and distorted as it will appear one day in the messianic light.'[30] This was, Adorno noted, simultaneously the simplest task and an impossible task. It was simple because of the urgency of the need for the knowledge. This meant it was simply necessary. It was an impossible task because it demands distance from what is, and yet knowledge can only be wrested from what exists and is therefore imbricated in the 'distortion and indigence which it seeks to escape'. Indigence, distortion – this is how the world is and yet we do not see it yet. We need to mutilate it to see its mutilations. To see them we need further to be able to imagine the world – that is, ourselves – from the perspective of a future, liberated condition.[31] The ideology of naturalism, faithfulness to appearance (which is never really the real and may be only ever an 'appearance', after all), must be abandoned. Displacing glances, looks of estrangement, must show up the deformity that the world is or can appear to be to our future selves. Those energies of negativity, the displacing and estranging perspectives, might then be put to liberatory ends. Adorno would probably not have conceded that cartoons might customize the desired perspectives. But they might have done, once, and might do yet.

 **notes**

prelude

1. For further thoughts on intellectual attitudes towards mass and popular culture in the context of Frankfurt School and cultural studies approaches, see Esther Leslie, 'Space and West End Girls: Walter Benjamin versus Cultural Studies', in 'Hating Tradition Properly', *New Formations* 38, 1999, pp. 110–24.
2. There are a number of detailed histories of cartoon production and studio output. Some of those that I have found useful include: Michael Barrier, *Hollywood Cartoons: American Animation in its Golden Age*, Oxford University Press, Oxford 1999; Giannalberto Bendazzi; *Cartoons: One Hundred Years of Cinema Animation*, John Libbey, London 1994; Richard Schickel, *The Disney Version*, Pavilion Books, London 1986 (originally published in 1968); Frank Thomas and Ollie Johnston, *The Illusion of Life, Disney Animation*, Hyperion, New York 1981; Steven Watts, *The Magic Kingdom: Walt Disney and the American Way of Life*, Houghton Mifflin, New York 1997. A good guide to cartoon theory can be found in Norman M. Klein, *Seven Minutes: The Life and Death of the American Animated Cartoon*, Verso, London 1993.

preclusion

1. For details of *Fantasmagorie*, see Donald Crafton, *Emile Cohl, Caricature and Film*, Princeton University Press, Princeton 1990, pp. 257–8.
2. Guy Debord, *Society of the Spectacle*, Black and Red, Detroit 1983, no folio.
3. For a Marxist analysis of the shift from 'utopian' and 'scientific' uses of photography to artistic and status-quo affirming uses, see Walter Benjamin, 'Kleine Geschichte der Photographie' (1931), in *Gesammelte Schriften* (Collected Works; hereafter *GS*), 7 vols, edited by Rolf Tiedemann and Hermann Schweppenhäuser, Suhrkamp Verlag, Frankfurt am Main 1972–91, vol. II.1, p. 370. *One-Way Street and Other Writings*, New Left Books, London 1979, p. 242.
4. Marx's *Eighteenth Brumaire* also contains a reference to the optical gadget.
5. See Karl Marx, *Das Kapital*, Volume 1, *Marx–Engels Werke*, Dietz Verlag, Berlin 1969, p. 86. The standard English translation of 'die phantasmagorische Form'

substitutes the word 'fantastic' for 'phantasmagoric'. *Capital* Volume 1, Charles Kerr, New York 1904, p. 83.

6. Otto Rühle, paraphrasing Marx, quoted by Walter Benjamin, in *Das Passagen-Werk*, edited by Rolf Tiedemann, Suhrkamp Verlag, Frankfurt am Main 1982, p. 245. (The *Passagen-Werk* is volume 5 of the *Gesammelte Schriften*. It consists of numerous *Konvolute* or files.) English translation: *The Arcades Project*, trans Howard Eiland and Kevin McLaughlin, Belknap/Harvard University Press, Cambridge MA 1999, p. 182.

7. See Benjamin, *Passagen-Werk* 1, p. 260 (my translation); *Arcades Project*, p. 195.

8. See Benjamin, 1935 'Exposé', *Passagen-Werk* 1, p. 50; *Arcades Project*, p. 7.

9. Benjamin, *Passagen-Werk* 2, p. 1006; *Arcades Project*, p. 838.

10. Benjamin, *Passagen-Werk* 1, p. 51; *Arcades Project*, p. 8.

11. See Benjamin, *Passagen-Werk* 1, p. 249; *Arcades Project*, p. 186 (which translates *Zauberpriester* as 'tribal priest').

12. See Benjamin's citation of Pierre MacOrlan (1934), in *Passagen-Werk* 1, p. 121; *Arcades Project*, p. 72.

13. Hans Richter, *Der Kampf um den Film*, Fischer, Frankfurt am Main 1979, pp. 38–9; *The Struggle for the Film*, Scolar Press, Aldershot 1986, p. 54.

14. The sofa and footstool in *Thru the Mirror* (1936) were singled out in this regard.

15. Karl Marx, *The Eighteenth Brumaire of Louis Bonaparte*, Lawrence & Wishart, London 1984, p. 19.

16. See, for example, Friedrich Engels, 'The International in America', in *Marx and Engels Collected Works*, vol. 23, Lawrence & Wishart, London 1988, (originally published in *Der Volksstaat* 57, 17 July 1872, 'Spirit-rappers, spirit-rapping shakers' (pp. 179–80)).

17. Friedrich Engels, letter to Sorge, 29 November 1886, in *Marx and Engels Collected Works*, vol. 47, Lawrence & Wishart, London 1993, p. 533. In or around 1878 Engels wrote an article called 'Die Naturforschung in der Geisterwelt' ('Natural Science in the World of Ghosts'), exposing spiritualism as a fraud, in much the same way that Thomas Huxley argued. See *Marx–Engels Werke*, vol. 20, Dietz Verlag, Berlin 1962, pp. 337–47; 'Natural Science in the Spirit World', in Frederick Engels, *Dialectics of Nature*, Progress Publishers, Moscow 1976, pp. 50–61.

18. Like Walt Disney, Pat Sullivan was an incompetent drawer. Otto Messmer designed Felix the Cat and drew him for the first few years until Felix's popularity required the hiring of other drawers.

19. John Canemaker, *Felix: The Twisted Tale of the World's Most Famous Cat*, Da Capo Press, New York 1996, p. 102.

20. Benjamin, *GS*, vol. VI, p. 132.

21. Quoted in Richard Taylor and Ian Christie, eds, *The Film Factory: Russian and Soviet Cinema in Documents 1896–1939*, Harvard University Press, Cambridge MA 1988, pp. 58–9.

22. Quoted in ibid., p. 64.

23. See 'Eccentrism, in ibid., pp. 58–64.

24. See Sergei Eisenstein 'The Montage of Attractions', in ibid., p. 88.

25. Viktor Shklovsky, in ibid., p. 98.

26. Ibid., p. 99.

27. Ibid.

28. Rudolf Kuenzli, ed., *Dada and Surrealist Film*, Willis Locker & Owens, New York 1987, p. 5.

29. This was worked on by an American, Dudley Murphy, and dated back to 1920–21.

30. Huntly Carter, *The New Spirit in the Cinema: An Analysis and Interpretation of the Parallel Paths of the Cinema, which have led to the great Revolutionary Crisis forming a Study of the Cinema as an Instrument of Sociological Humanism*, Harold Shaylor, London 1930, pp. 29–30.

31. E.A. Abbott, *Flatland: A Romance of Many Dimensions*, Dover Publications, New York 1952, p. 4.

32. See Crafton, *Emile Cohl, Caricature and Film*, p. 209.

33. For a discussion of ideograms and logos, see Norman M. Klein, *Seven Minutes: The Life and Death of the American Animated Cartoon*, Verso, London 1993, pp. 6–8.

34. See *Hans Richter by Hans Richter*, edited by Cleve Gray, Thames & Hudson, London 1971, p. 187. Richter uses the word 'ragpicker' to describe Schwitters (p. 152).

35. Ibid., p. 155.

36. See Don Macpherson, ed., *Traditions of Independence: British Cinema in the Thirties*, BFI, London 1980, p. 105.

37. Eric Walter White, *Walking Shadows: An Essay on Lotte Reiniger's Silhouette Films*, Hogarth Press, London 1931, p. 30.

38. See Robert Feild, *The Art of Walt Disney*, Collins, London and Glasgow 1944, p. 14.

39. Ibid., p. 2n.

40. See Robert Heide and John Gilman, *Disneyana: Classic Collectibles 1928–1958*, Hyperion, New York 1995, p. 39.

41. See Michael Barrier, *Hollywood Cartoons: American Animation in its Golden Age*, Oxford University Press, Oxford 1999, pp. 89–90.

zeros, dots and dashes

1. Reprinted in Charles Harrison and Paul Wood, eds, *Art in Theory*, Blackwell, Oxford 1993, p. 272.

2. G.W.F. Hegel, *Logic*, edited by W. Wallace and J.N. Findlay, Oxford University Press, Oxford 1975, p. 17.

3. In Richard Huelsenbeck, *The Dada Almanac* (1920), English edition prepared by Malcolm Green, Atlas, London 1993, p. 56.

4. In English in *Hans Richter by Hans Richter*, edited by Cleve Gray, Thames & Hudson, London 1971, p. 96.

5. See *Moholy-Nagy: An Anthology*, edited by Richard Kostelanetz, Da Capo Press, New York 1991, p. 132.

6. Reprinted in Harrison and Wood, eds, *Art in Theory*, p. 166.

7. See Charles Harrison et al., *Primitivism, Cubism, Abstraction: Modern Art Practices and Debates*, Yale University Press and Open University Press, New Haven and Milton Keynes 1993, p. 238.

8. K.S. Malevich, *Essays on Art 1915–1933*, vol. 1, Rapp & Whiting, London 1971, pp. 224–5.

9. *Hans Richter by Hans Richter*, p. 34.
10. Ibid., p. 41.
11. *Film as Film: Formal Experiment in Film 1910–1975*, exhibition catalogue, Hayward Gallery, London 1979, p. 38.
12. This is the argument put forward by R. Kurtz in his chapter on 'Absolute Kunst', in *Expressionismus und Film*, Verlag der Lichtbildbühne, Berlin 1926.
13. See *Kazimir Malevich 1878–1935*, catalogue published by the Armand Hammer Museum of Art and Cultural Center, Los Angeles 1990, p. 18.
14. See Hans Richter, Werner Haftmann and Werner Hoffmann, *Kurt Kranz: Early Form Sequences 1927–1932*, MIT, Cambridge MA 1975, p. 40.
15. *Film as Film*, p. 82.
16. F.T. Marinetti, Bruno Corra, Emilio Settimelli, Arnaldo Ginna, Giacomo Balla and Remo Chiti, 'The Futurist Cinema 1916', in *Futurist Manifestos*, Thames & Hudson, London 1973, p. 207.
17. Ibid., p. 208.
18. Reprinted in Harrison and Wood, eds, *Art in Theory*, p. 226.
19. Marinetti et al., 'The Futurist Cinema 1916', p. 219.
20. Malevich, *Essays on Art 1915–1933*, vol. 1, p. 232.
21. Ibid., p. 233.
22. Ibid., p. 234.
23. Ibid., p. 238.
24. Walter Benjamin, *One-Way Street and Other Writings*, New Left Books, London 1979, pp. 55–6.
25. Ibid., p. 56.
26. Ibid., p. 96.
27. Karl Marx, *Capital* Volume II (1885), Penguin Books, New York 1992, pp. 201–3.
28. Karl Marx, *Capital* Volume III (1894), Penguin Books, New York 1991, pp. 798, 807–11, 878–81.
29. Guy Debord, *Society of the Spectacle*, Black and Red, Detroit 1983.
30. Malevich, 'To The New Image', in *Essays on Art 1915–1933*, vol. 1, p. 51.
31. *Hans Richter by Hans Richter*, p. 47.
32. Hans Richter, *Der Kampf um den Film*, Fischer, Frankfurt am Main 1979, p. 42; *The Struggle for the Film*, Scolar Press, Aldershot 1986, p. 59. The book was written through the 1920s and 1930s, but was revised again shortly before Richter died.
33. Hans Richter, *Filmgegner von Heute – Filmfreunde von Morgen* (1929), facsimile, Verlag Hans Rohr, Zurich 1968, p. 33.
34. See Jeanpaul Goergen, *Walter Ruttmann: Eine Dokumentation*, Freunde der deutschen Kinemathek, Berlin 1989, pp. 20–21.
35. Ibid., p. 21.
36. Quoted in ibid., p. 99.
37. Quoted in ibid., p. 98.
38. Quoted in ibid., p. 23.
39. Pinschewer projected animations where previously graphic slides had sufficed.
40. See Goergen, *Walter Ruttmann*, pp. 23 and 47.
41. Reprinted in ibid., p. 99.

42. Eric Walter White, *Walking Shadows: An Essay on Lotte Reiniger's Silhouette Films*, Hogarth Press, London 1931, p. 10.
43. Cited by Reiniger in Giannalberto Bendazzi, *Cartoons: One Hundred Years of Cinema Animation*, John Libbey, London 1994, p. 33.
44. White, *Walking Shadows*, p. 23. And, furthermore, White thought that the film predated Eisenstein's montage effects by speeding up the cutting rhythm as climaxes approach. See p. 25.
45. Reprinted in Ian Christie and David Elliott, *Eisenstein at Ninety*, Museum of Modern Art, Oxford 1988, p. 50.
46. See ibid., p. 51.
47. See *50 Years Bauhaus*, exhibition catalogue, Royal Academy of Arts, London 1968, p. 23.
48. Reprinted in Harrison and Wood, eds, *Art in Theory*, p. 349.
49. Reprinted in ibid., p. 348.
50. Reprinted in ibid., p. 285.
51. That was rather a polemical statement. Rodchenko did use thin brushes for fashioning his lines.
52. Written in Moscow, 23 May 1921. Reprinted in Peter Noever, ed., *Aleksandr M. Rodchenko and Vavara F. Stepanova: The Future is Our Only Goal*, Prestel Verlag, Munich 1991, p. 135.
53. According to Janco. See Louise O'Konor, *Viking Eggeling 1880–1925. Artist and Filmmaker: Life and Work*, Almquist & Wiksell, Stockholm 1971, pp. 39, 248.
54. Hans Richter, *Dada: Art and Anti-Art*, Thames & Hudson, London 1978, p. 63. The book appeared in German with the title *Dada – Kunst und Antikunst*; DuMont, Cologne 1964. The definitive edition is the third, 1973.
55. See Nadezhda Krupskaya, *Memories of Lenin*, Lawrence & Wishart, London 1942, p. 240.
56. V.I. Lenin, *Philosophical Notebooks*, in *Collected Works* vol. 38, Lawrence & Wishart, London 1972, p. 97 (written in Berne in 1914).
57. Ibid., p. 360.
58. Ibid., p. 362.
59. *Veshch* editorial, quoted in John Elderfield, *Kurt Schwitters*, Thames & Hudson, London 1987, p. 123.
60. Quoted in Elderfield, *Kurt Schwitters*, p. 124.
61. See statement from 1923 in *50 Years Bauhaus*, p. 117.
62. Benjamin, *One-Way Street and Other Writings*, p. 96.
63. See *50 Years Bauhaus*, p. 118.
64. See *Hans Richter by Hans Richter*, p. 21.
65. Ibid., p. 94.
66. See John E. Bowlt's article in *Kazimir Malevich 1878–1935*, p. 182.
67. *Film as Film*, p. 47.
68. Leon Trotsky, *Literature and Revolution*, Redwords, London 1991, p. 212.
69. Benjamin, *One-Way Street and Other Writings*, p. 62; *Einbahnstraße* was published by Ernst Rowohlt Verlag, Berlin 1928.
70. Walter Benjamin, *Gesammelte Schriften* (hereafter *GS*), 7 vols, edited by Rolf Tiedemann and Hermann Schweppenhäuser, Suhrkamp Verlag, Frankfurt am Main

1972–91, vol. II.2, p. 602.

71. Benjamin, *GS*, vol. II.3, p. 1412.
72. Benjamin, *GS*, vol. II.2, pp. 605–7.
73. Gershom Scholem, *Walter Benjamin: The Story of a Friendship*, Jewish Publication Society of America, Philadelphia, 1981, p. 61.
74. Benjamin, *GS*, vol. II.1, p. 213.
75. Benjamin, *GS*, vol. II.2, p. 606.
76. Walter Benjamin, *Briefe*, vol. 1, Suhrkamp Verlag, Frankfurt am Main 1978, p. 260.
77. Benjamin, *Briefe*, vol. 1, p. 154.
78. Theodor W. Adorno, *Noten zur Literatur*, Suhrkamp Verlag, Frankfurt am Main 1981, p. 430.
79. I follow Freud's affection for multilingual puns, for the original German title, 'Notiz über den "Wunderblock"', does not carry the sense of Freud writing his notes upon the surface of the 'Wunderblock' or 'Mystic Writing-Pad'.
80. Sigmund Freud, *Pelican Freud Library*, vol. 11, Penguin, Harmondsworth 1984, p. 430.
81. Ibid., p. 441.
82. Ibid., p. 440.
83. See 'Aus einer kleinen Rede über Proust, an meinem vierzigsten Geburtstag gehalten' ('From a small lecture on Proust delivered on my fortieth birthday') (1932), in *GS*, vol. II.3, p. 1064.
84. Walter Benjamin, *Das Passagen-Werk*, *GS*, vol. 5, p. 245; *The Arcades Project*, trans. Howard Eiland and Kevin McLaughlin, Belknap/Harvard University Press, Cambridge MA 1999, p. 476.
85. See *Berliner Chronik*, in *GS*, vol. VI, p. 519; 'A Berlin Chronicle', in *One-Way Street and Other Writings*, pp. 345–6.
86. Benjamin, *GS*, vol. II.2, p. 752.
87. Benjamin, 'Kleine Geschichte der Photographie', *GS*, vol. II.1, p. 371; 'A Small History of Photography", in *One-Way Street and Other Writings*, p. 243.
88. See Catherine Wilson, *The Invisible World: Early Modern Philosophy and the Invention of the Microscope*, Princeton University Press, Princeton 1995, p. 243.
89. V.I. Lenin, 'On the Question of Dialectics', in *Philosophical Notebooks*, in *Collected Works*, vol. 38, pp. 360–61.
90. For contemporary reviews of the film, see Goergen, *Walter Ruttmann*, pp. 130–32.
91. Richter, *Filmgegner von Heute – Filmfreunde von Morgen*, p. 146.
92. See Goergen, *Walter Ruttmann*, p. 131.
93. In ibid., pp. 117–18.
94. In ibid., pp. 118–21.
95. Boris Arvatov, *Kunst und Produktion*, Carl Hanser Verlag, Munich 1972, p. 27.
96. Alexander Rodchenko, 'Downright Ignorance or a Mean Trick?', in Christopher Phillips, ed., *Photography in the Modern Era*, Aperture, New York 1989, p. 247.
97. Stalin's doctrine of 'Socialism in One Country' was first formulated in November 1924, and was the arsis to Trotsky's concept of world revolution. It was a succinct locution for the political perspectives of the Soviet bureaucracy.
98. See Benjamin, *GS*, vol. VI, pp. 292–409; *Moscow Diary*, Harvard University Press, Cambridge MA and London 1986.

99. 'Moskau' was written for the journal *Kreatur*. See Benjamin, *GS*, vol. IV.1, pp. 316–48; 'Moscow', in *One-Way Street and Other Writings*, pp. 177–208.

100. See, for example, Benjamin, 'Moskau', pp. 325, 337–9; 'Moscow', pp. 185–6, 197–9.

101. See Benjamin, 'Moskau', p. 325; 'Moscow', pp. 185–6.

102. See Benjamin, 'Moskau', p. 316; 'Moscow', p. 177.

103. See Benjamin, 'Moskau', p. 317; 'Moscow', p. 178.

104. See Benjamin, 'Moskau', p. 318; 'Moscow', p. 178.

105. See Benjamin, 'Moskau', p. 319; 'Moscow', pp. 179–80.

106. See Benjamin, 'Moskau', p. 319; 'Moscow', pp. 179–80.

107. See Benjamin, 'Moskau', p. 317; 'Moscow', p. 178.

108. See Benjamin, 'Moskau', p. 330; 'Moscow', p. 190.

109. See Benjamin, 'Moskau', p. 320; 'Moscow', p. 180.

110. Siegfried Kracauer, *Kino*, Suhrkamp Verlag, Frankfurt am Main 1979, p. 89.

111. For discussion of the rather tense relationship between Ruttmann and Vertov, see the quotation from Vertov's letter from Berlin (18 July 1929), cited in Vlada Petric's *Constructivism in Film: The Man with a Movie Camera; A Cinematic Analysis*, Cambridge University Press, Cambridge 1993, pp. 79–80. There is further speculation on the relationship between the two in ibid., p. 152. For Vertov's critical verdict on Ruttmann, see his speech to the First All-Union Conference on Sound Cinema, August 1930, in Richard Taylor and Ian Christie, eds, *The Film Factory: Russian and Soviet Cinema in Documents 1896–1939*, Harvard University Press, Cambridge MA 1988, p. 301.

112. Kracauer, *Kino*, p. 90.

113. See Benjamin, *GS*, vol. I.2, p. 498; 'The Work of Art in the Age of Mechanical Reproduction', in *Illuminations*, Fontana, London 1992, p. 229. (The title of this essay is commonly translated as 'The Work of Art in the Age of Mechanical Reproduction', which is not a literal rendition of the original German title. For reflections on the implications of such paraphrasing, see Esther Leslie, *Walter Benjamin: Overpowering Conformism*, Pluto Press, London 2000, pp. 132ff.)

114. Benjamin, *Berliner Chronik*, in *GS*, vol. V.1, p. 464; *A Berlin Chronicle*, in *One-Way Street and Other Writings*, pp. 297, 299.

115. See Walter Benjamin, *Briefe*, vol. 2, Suhrkamp, Frankfurt am Main 1978, p. 562.

116. Siegfried Kracauer, 'Uber Arbeitsnachweise: Konstruktion eines Raums', in *Straßen in Berlin und Anderswo*, Das Arsenal, Berlin 1987, p. 52.

117. Siegfried Kracauer, 'Schrei auf der Straße', in *Straßen in Berlin und Anderswo*, pp. 21–32.

118. David Frisby, *Fragmente der Moderne*, Daedalus Verlag, Rheda-Wiedenbrück, 1989, p. 150.

119. See Siegfried Kracauer, 'Analyse eines Stadtplans', in *Straßen in Berlin und Anderswo*, p. 12; 'Analysis of a City Map', in *The Mass Ornament: Weimar Essays*, Harvard University Press, Cambridge MA 1995, p. 41. (Contradicting Zohler, Levin gives the date as 1926.) See Kracauer's 'Cult of Distraction' (1926) for a similar statement (in Kracauer, *The Mass Ornament*, pp. 323–8; original publication: 'Kult der Zerstreuung: Über die Berliner Lichtspielhäuser', *Frankfurter Zeitung* vol. 70, no. 167, 4 March 1926, pp. 1–2 (feuilleton).

120. See Kracauer's 'The Mass Ornament', in *The Mass Ornament*; original publication: *Das Ornament der Masse; Essays*, Suhrkamp Verlag, Frankfurt am Main 1977.
121. Siegfried Kracauer, 'Straße ohne Erinnerung', in *Straßen in Berlin und Anderswo*, pp. 15–18.

mickey mouse, utopia and benjamin

1. See Carsten Laqua, *Wie Micky unter die Nazis fiel: Walt Disney und Deutschland*, Rowohlt Verlag, Hamburg 1992, p. 35.
2. 'Mouse' is feminine in German and when Benjamin speaks of Mickey Mouse he uses the female gender. This emphasizes perhaps, above all, the character's ambiguous or non-gendered nature.
3. J.P. Storm and M. Dreßler, *Im Reiche der Micky-Maus: Walt Disney in Deutschland 1927–1945*, documentation of an exhibition in the Filmmuseum Potsdam, Henschel Verlag, Berlin 1991, p. 29.
4. See Walter Benjamin, *Gesammelte Schriften* (hereafter *GS*), 7 vols, edited by Rolf Tiedemann and Hermann Schweppenhäuser, Suhrkamp Verlag, Frankfurt am Main 1972–89, vol. II.1, p. 354.
5. Walter Benjamin, *One-Way Street and Other Writings*, New Left Books, London 1979, pp. 157–8.
6. Benjamin, 'Zu Micky-Maus', *GS*, vol. VI, p. 144.
7. Ibid., p. 145.
8. Benjamin, *GS*, vol. III, pp. 319–21.
9. Benjamin, 'Zu Micky-Maus', p. 144.
10. Ibid., p. 145.
11. Karl Marx, *Economic and Philosophical Manuscripts*, in *Early Writings*, Penguin/New Left Review, London 1977, pp. 326–7.
12. The Benjamin papers (now in the Adorno archive in Frankfurt) left behind in the Georges Bataille archive in Paris (to where Benjamin moved in 1933) include press clippings on Mickey Mouse and Walt Disney from French newspapers. Benjamin was following the Disney phenomenon as it developed.
13. Benjamin, 'Zu Micky-Maus', p. 144.
14. See Benjamin, 'Erfahrung und Armut' (1933), *GS*, vol. II.1, p. 214.
15. Ibid., p. 215.
16. Scholem introduced Benjamin to Scheerbart's writing in 1917.
17. Benjamin, 'Erfahrung und Armut', p. 216.
18. Benjamin, 'Erfahrungsarmut', *GS*, vol. II.3, p. 962.
19. Benjamin, 'Erfahrung und Armut', p. 218–19.
20. See *One-Way Street and Other Writings*, p. 190.
21. Walter Benjamin, *Passagen-Werk*, in *GS*, vol. V.1, p. 432; *The Arcades Project*, trans Howard Eiland and Kevin McLaughlin, Belknap/Harvard University Press, Cambridge MA 1999, p. 342.
22. Benjamin, 'Erfahrung und Armut', pp. 218–19.
23. See Benjamin, *GS*, vol. II.1, p. 219.
24. Amongst Benjamin's papers, left behind in Paris, was another piece by Eberhard

Schulz, from 30 September 1937, titled 'Screenplay and Drama'. Schulz seemed to be offering a film studies course via the *Frankfurter Zeitung*. In this piece Schulz notes that film has to show everything very blatantly. Schulz also points out the extent to which it is not only people that act in film; the camera acts as well. 'It is the actual main character, above the other figures, which is always present, indeed is so to speak the mechanized director of the play, that integrates itself in all scenes.' Perhaps it was Schulz's arguments that led Benjamin to shift his own thoughts on the relationship between actor and camera in the third version of 'The Work of Art in the Age of its Technical Reproducibility'. See Benjamin, *GS*, vol. I.2, p. 488; 'The Work of Art in the Age of Mechanical Reproduction', in *Illuminations*, Fontana, London 1992, p. 222. Compare with the earlier versions of the same part of the essay: that is, the conclusion of *GS*, vol. I.2, p. 450, paragraph 10, and *GS*, vol. VII.1, p. 365, paragraph X.

25. See Jean Charlot, *Art from the Mayans to Disney*, Sheed & Ward, New York and London 1939, pp. 278–9.
26. Benjamin, *Passagen-Werk* 1, pp. 465–6 (my translation); *Arcades Project*, p. 368.
27. See Benjamin, 1935 'Exposé', in *Passagen-Werk* 1, p. 47 (my translation); *Arcades Project*, p. 5. Benjamin, *Passagen-Werk* 2, pp. 785–6; *Arcades Project*, pp. 638–9.
28. Benjamin, *Passagen-Werk* 1, p. 466; *Arcades Project*, p. 368.
29. Benjamin, *Passagen-Werk* 1, p. 64; *Arcades Project*, p. 17.
30. Benjamin, *Passagen-Werk* 2, p. 777 (my translation); *Arcades Project*, p. 631.
31. Benjamin, *Passagen-Werk* 2, p. 781 (my translation); *Arcades Project*, p. 635. The reference to Marx is found in *Capital* Volume 1, chapter 10, in a discussion of Fourier's idea of labour.
32. See Benjamin, *Passagen-Werk* 1, p. 490; *Arcades Project*, p. 388.
33. See 'Über das Mimetische Vermögen' (1933), in Benjamin, *GS*, vol. II.1, p. 210.
34. Benjamin, 'Alte vergessene Kinderbücher', *GS*, vol. III, pp. 16–17. See also the section titled 'Baustelle'/'Construction Site', in *One-Way Street*.
35. See 'Alte vergessene Kinderbücher', pp. 14–22.
36. Ibid., p. 15.
37. See John E. Sadler's introduction to *Orbis Sensualium Pictus*, by Johann Amos Comenius, Oxford University Press, Oxford 1968, p. 20.
38. Ibid., p. 21.
39. Ibid., pp. 44–5.
40. Benjamin, 'Schränke', in *Berliner Kindheit um Neunzehnhundert*, *GS*, vol. IV.1, p. 286.
41. Ibid.
42. See Benjamin, 'Aussicht ins Kinderbuch', *GS*, vol. IV.2, p. 611. The *Oxford English Dictionary* notes that the word 'rebus' derives from the ablative of the Latin *res*, thing – as used in the phrase *de rebus quae geruntur*, meaning 'concerning things that are taking place'. This was the title given by the guild of lawyers' clerks of Picardy to satirical pieces containing riddles in picture form.
43. Benjamin, 'Eduard Fuchs, der Sammler und der Historiker' (1937), GS, vol. II.2, p. 483; 'Edward Fuchs, Collector and Historian', in *One-Way Street and Other Writings*, p. 365.
44. Benjamin, *Passagen-Werk* 2, p. 899; *Arcades Project*, p. 740.
45. Benjamin, *Passagen-Werk* 1, p. 246 (my translation); *Arcades Project*, p. 182.

46. Ibid. Benjamin quotes the passage from Marx in full on p. 262 of *Passagen-Werk*.

47. Benjamin, *Passagen-Werk* 1, p. 260 (my translation); *Arcades Project*, p. 195.

48. Benjamin, *Passagen-Werk* 1, pp. 257–8; *Arcades Project*, pp. 192–3.

49. Benjamin, *Passagen-Werk* 1, p. 66; *Arcades Project*, p. 18.

50. See Theodor W. Adorno and Max Horkheimer, *Dialectic of Enlightenment*, Verso, London 1995, pp. 74–5.

51. See Benjamin, *Passagen-Werk* 1, p. 215; *Arcades Project*, p. 153.

52. Benjamin, *Passagen-Werk* 1, p. 267 (my translation); *Arcades Project*, p. 200.

53. Benjamin, *Passagen-Werk* 1, p. 113; *Arcades Project*, p. 64.

54. Karl Marx, 'The Counter-Revolution in Berlin', in *The Revolutions of 1848*, trans. Rodney Livingstone, NLR/Penguin, Harmondsworth 1973, p. 179.

55. *Arts et métiers graphiques* 44, December 1934, pp. 19–25.

56. Ibid., pp. 22–3.

57. See Benjamin, *Passagen-Werk* 1, p. 501; *Arcades Project*, p. 396.

58. *Arts et métiers graphiques* 44, p. 24.

59. Benjamin, *Passagen-Werk* 1, p. 121; *Arcades Project*, p. 72

60. For a reference to the working title for the *Arcades Project*, 'Eine dialektische Feerie', see the letter to Gretel Adorno, 16 August 1935, in Walter Benjamin, *Briefe*, vol. 2, Suhrkamp Verlag, Frankfurt am Main 1978, p. 687.

61. See Benjamin, 1935 'Exposé', *Passagen-Werk* 1, pp. 46–7; *Arcades Project*, p. 4.

62. Benjamin, *Passagen-Werk* 1, p. 570; *Arcades Project*, p. 456.

63. See Benjamin, 'Pariser Passagen' ⟨1⟩, *Passagen-Werk* 2, p. 1033; *Arcades Project*, p. 863.

64. See Benjamin, 1935 'Exposé', *Passagen-Werk* 1, p. 47; *Arcades Project*, pp. 4–5. See also Notes for the 1935 'Exposé', *Passagen-Werk* 2, pp. 1224–5.

65. Benjamin, 1935 'Exposé', *Passagen-Werk* 1, pp. 46–7; *Arcades Project*, pp. 4–5.

66. Benjamin, *Passagen-Werk* 1, p. 432 (my translation); *Arcades Project*, p. 342.

67. There are three completed versions of 'The Work of Art in the Age of its Technical Reproducibility', written between 1935 and 1939. Each version differs substantially from the others at certain points.

68. See Michael O'Pray, *Eisenstein and Stokes on Disney: Film Animation and Omnipotence*, University of East London, School of Architecture, Art and Design Working Papers, London 1995.

69. Benjamin's library slips, conserved from the Bibliothèque Nationale de Paris, show that he was reading the new French literature on cinema. He borrowed Chareusol's *Panorama du Cinéma* (1930), Vellard's *Cinéma Sonoré* (1933), Pirandello's *On Tourne* (1925), and the journal *L'art cinématographique* II (1927).

70. Benjamin, *GS*, vol. I.2, p. 460; Benjamin, *GS*, vol. VII.1, p. 375.

71. For an account of the uses of lenses and microscopes in scientific investigation, see Steven Rose, *Lifelines: Biology, Freedom, Determinism*, Penguin, Harmondsworth 1998, pp. 58–61.

72. Benjamin, *GS*, vol. I.2, p. 461. Benjamin repeats sentences from his 1927 response to Oscar H. Schmitz.

73. Benjamin, *GS*, vol. I.2, pp. 461–2; Benjamin, *GS*, vol. VII.1, pp. 376–7.

74. Benjamin, 'Über einige Motive bei Baudelaire' (1939), *GS*, vol. I.2, pp. 646–8; Walter Benjamin, *Charles Baudelaire: A Lyric Poet in the Era of High Capitalism*, New Left Books, London 1973, pp. 148–9.

75. Benjamin, 'Über einige Motive bei Baudelaire', p. 610; *Charles Baudelaire*, p. 112.

76. *Trotsky's Notebooks, 1933–1935*, edited by Philip Pomper, Columbia University Press, New York 1986, p. 102.

77. David King's book *The Commissar Vanishes: The Falsification of Photographs and Art in Stalin's Russia* (Canongate Books, Edinburgh 1997) is a compendium of falsified images. Drawing on a vast collection of original and falsified photographs, King documents the lack of traces of Stalin in the early years of the revolutionary movement as well as the attempts to counter this embarrassing fact in subsequent years by faking, manipulating and fabricating images.

78. *Trotsky's Notebooks, 1933–1935*, p. 79.

79. Ibid., p. 82.

80. Ibid., pp. 97–8.

81. Lev Trotsky, 'Vodka, the Church and the Cinema', in *Problems of Life*, Methuen, London 1924, pp. 37–8.

82. Benjamin, *GS*, vol. I.2, p. 462.

83. Ibid.

84. See Wyndham Lewis, *Time and Western Man* (1927), Black Sparrow Press, Santa Rosa 1993, pp. 64–6.

85. Benjamin, 'Erwiderung an Oscar A. H. Schmitz', *GS*, vol. II.2, p. 752.

86. Ibid., p. 753.

87. Storm and Dreßler, *Im Reiche der Micky-Maus*, p. 29.

88. Benjamin, *GS*, vol. VII.2, p. 669.

89. Benjamin, 'Kleine Geschichte der Photographie', *GS*, vol. II.1, p. 379; 'A Small History of Photography', in *One-Way Street and Other Writings*, p. 251.

90. Ibid.

91. Benjamin, *GS*, vol. I.2, p. 451; Benjamin, *GS*, vol. VII.1, p. 369.

92. Benjamin, *GS*, vol. I.3, p. 986.

93. Ibid., pp. 986–7. The rather cloying tone of the letter acknowledges Adorno's great influence, then continues with Benjamin's expression of hopes about continued collaboration with the Institute of Social Research, now that Adorno is more closely involved.

94. Benjamin, *GS*, vol. IV.1, p. 515.

95. Benjamin, *GS*, vol. VII.2, p. 377.

96. Benjamin, *GS*, vol. VII.1, p. 377.

97. The French translation of the second version of the 'Work of Art' essay cuts the reference to fascism and the reference to pogroms – which is to say, it cut the reference to Jewish persecution. This version of the essay expunged all references to Marxism too and all topical political references and passages that confessed political positions. Horkheimer demanded the erasure of lines that betrayed 'political allegiance' or used a 'politically topical formulation'. At stake were good relations with the Institute of Social Research's hosts, the Americans. See Benjamin, *GS*, vol. I.2, p. 732.

98. Adorno and Horkheimer, *Dialectic of Enlightenment*, Verso, London 1989, p. 138.

99. Storm and Dreßler, *Im Reiche der Micky-Maus*, p. 93.

100. See Ernst Bloch et al., *Aesthetics and Politics*, Verso, London 1977, pp. 123–4.

101. Theodor W. Adorno, *In Search of Wagner*, New Left Books, London 1981, pp. 126–7.

102. Benjamin, *GS* II.2, p. 458; 'The Storyteller', in *Illuminations*, p. 101.

103. See Benjamin, *GS* II.2, p. 496; 'Edward Fuchs, Collector and Historian', in *One-way Street*, p. 378.

104. Benjamin, 'Über einige Motive bei Baudelaire', p. 645; *Charles Baudelaire*, p. 147.

105. See Benjamin, 'Über einige Motive bei Baudelaire', p. 630; *Charles Baudelaire*, p. 132. See also Benjamin's 1939 review of the *Encyclopédie Française*, in *GS*, vol. III, p. 583n.

106. See Benjamin, 'Zentralpark' (1938), *GS*, vol. I.2, p. 614.

107. Benjamin, 'Über einige Motive bei Baudelaire', p. 631; *Charles Baudelaire*, pp. 132–3.

108. See Benjamin, 'Über einige Motive bei Baudelaire', p. 632; *Charles Baudelaire*, p. 133.

109. Benjamin, 'Über einige Motive bei Baudelaire', p. 630; *Charles Baudelaire*, p. 132.

110. See Benjamin, 'Über einige Motive bei Baudelaire', p. 632; *Charles Baudelaire*, p. 133. See also Benjamin, 'Konvolut m; Müßigang', *Passagen-Werk* 2, p. 966; *Arcades Project*, p. 804.

111. James Hay labels *Snow White and the Seven Dwarfs* a 'fairy-tale for middle class audiences'. See James Hay, *Popular Film Culture in Fascist Italy: The Passing of the Rex*, Indiana University Press, Bloomington 1987, p. 83.

leni and walt

1. See Pierre de Coubertin's lecture, reprinted in *Le manifest olympique*, Les editions de grand pont, Paris 1994.

2. See Michael H. Kater, *Different Drummers: Jazz in the Culture of Nazi Germany*, Oxford University Press, Oxford 1992, p. 50.

3. See Leni Riefenstahl, *A Memoir*, St Martin's Press, New York 1992, p. 238. German edition: *Memoiren 1902–1945*, Verlag Ullstein, Frankfurt am Main 1987, p. 325. Riefenstahl represents Ford's political alignment as socialist.

4. Cited in Julian Stallabrass, *Gargantua*, Verso, London 1996, pp. 223–4. Ford's book was published in German in Leipzig in 1923.

5. The Anti-Nazi League in Hollywood was a popular frontist organization. After the Hitler–Stalin pact in August 1939, many CPUSA members jumped to the new line and became pro-German, leading to the organization's collapse.

6. See Riefenstahl, *A Memoir*, pp. 239–40; *Memoiren 1902–1945*, pp. 323–7.

7. J.P. Storm and M. Dreßler, *Im Reiche der Micky-Maus: Walt Disney in Deutschland 1927–1945*, documentation of an exhibition in the Filmmuseum Potsdam, Henschel Verlag, Berlin 1991, p. 128.

8. Ibid., p. 128.

9. Quoted by Ernst Jäger, 'How Leni Riefenstahl Became Hitler's Girlfriend', in 11 parts, *Hollywood Tribune*, 28 April–17 July 1939, part ix, p. 13, cited in Cooper C. Graham, *Leni Riefenstahl and Olympia*, Scarecrow Press, Metuchen NJ 1986, pp. 222–3. The importance of 'Snow White', derived from Grimms' German fairy-tales, in both their biographies is striking. As a boy Disney had seen a silent film version of 'Snow White', based on a nineteenth-century version. It apparently

stayed with him, and in a 1938 article he cited childhood memory as the sentimental reason behind his choice. Disney remembered seeing the 'play' (originally performed on Broadway in 1912) with money saved from his paper round, in its 1915 or 1916 silent film restaging, starring Marguerite Clark, projected on four screens in a huge auditorium. Riefenstahl says in her memoirs that 'Snow White' was the first play she ever saw, at the age of four or five, in Berlin. It spurred her, she said, to enter the world of entertainment.

10. This version is from *Grimms' Fairy Tales*, trans. L.L. Weedon, illustrated by Ada Dennis, E. Stuart Hardy and others, Ernest Nister, London 1898, pp. 9–20.

11. Storm and Dreßler, *Im Reiche der Micky-Maus*, p. 110.

12. Ibid., p. 117.

13. Ibid., p. 118.

14. Ibid., p. 119.

15. Ibid., pp. 121–3.

16. Ibid., p. 121.

17. Ibid., p. 90.

18. Bob Thomas, *Walt Disney: A Biography*, W.H. Allen, London 1976, p. 128.

19. Martin Krause and Linda Witkowski, *Walt Disney's Snow White and the Seven Dwarfs: An Art in the Making*, Indianapolis Museum of Art, Indianapolis 1994, p. 26.

20. For a detailed examination of European influences on Disney, see Robin Allan, *Walt Disney and Europe*, Indiana University Press, Bloomington 1999.

21. See Storm and Dreßler, *Im Reiche der Micky-Maus*, p. 121.

22. See the document reprinted in ibid., p. 121.

23. Storm and Dreßler, *Im Reiche der Micky-Maus*, p. 122.

24. Susan Sontag brings Disney and Riefenstahl together in her essay 'Fascinating Fascism' (1974). Here she attempts to define a fascist aesthetic. She delineates this aesthetic's preoccupation with situations of control, submissive behaviour, extravagant effort, massification, reification. She details how 'fascist dramaturgy centers on the orgiastic transactions between mighty forces and their puppets, uniformly garbed and shown in ever swelling numbers. Fascist art glorifies surrender, it exalts mindlessness, it glamorizes death.' And she indicates that such art is not confined to work labelled fascist, or produced under fascist governments. Walt Disney's *Fantasia* (1940) is cited as exemplary. (The article is reprinted in Brandon Taylor and Wilfried van der Will, eds, *The Nazification of Art*, Winchester Press, Winchester 1990; see p. 211.)

25. Clement Greenberg, 'Avant-Garde and Kitsch', in Charles Harrison and Paul Wood, eds, *Art in Theory*, Blackwell, Oxford, 1993, pp. 529–41.

26. Ibid., p. 537.

27. Ibid., p. 534.

28. Theodor W. Adorno and Max Horkheimer, *Dialectic of Enlightenment*, Verso, London 1989, p. 41.

29. Ibid., p. 121.

30. See Marc Eliot's muckraking biography *Walt Disney: Hollywood's Dark Prince*, Andre Deutsch, London 1994, p. 135. In April 1940 Disney visited Ford's model village in Michigan, Greenfield Village. Ford's town was a curious blend of historic buildings of interest to the founder and period replicas that housed favourite Ford

projects, such as schools for hand-picked pupils. The farmhouse that Ford grew up in was also there. It must have influenced Disney's vision of his own theme park, conceived in the late 1940s. Indeed, he visited it again in the summer of 1948, and sent designers there in the 1950s.

31. Commercial supremacy was, however, lost in the mid 1920s to General Motors.

32. See Ferruccio Gambino, 'A Critique of the Regulation School', *Common Sense* 19, June 1996, pp. 47–8.

33. American Ford has insisted that it had no management control over its German subsidiary in this period, but documents found recently show that, after the war, dividends were paid by the German firm to the American firm for the years 1940–43.

34. On 13 March 1933 the German film industry was made a part of the Reichs-ministerium für Volksaufklärung und Propaganda.

35. See Riefenstahl, *A Memoir*, pp. 200–202; *Memoiren 1902–1945*, p. 280.

36. Walter Benjamin, *Gesammelte Schriften* (hereafter *GS*), 7 vols, edited by Rolf Tiede-mann and Hermann Schweppenhäuser, Suhrkamp Verlag, Frankfurt am Main 1972–91, vol. I.2, pp. 459–96; *GS*, vol. VII.1, p. 374. 'The Work of Art in the Age of Mechanical Reproduction', in *Illuminations*, Fontana, London 1992, p. 227.

37. Benjamin, *GS*, vol. VII.1, p. 377.

38. See Benjamin, *GS*, vol. I.2, p. 506; 'The Work of Art', p. 234.

39. See Benjamin, *GS*, vol. I.2, pp. 467, 506; *GS*, vol. VII.1, p. 382. 'The Work of Art', pp. 243–4.

40. Benjamin, *GS*, vol. I.2, pp. 467, 506; *GS*, vol. VII.1, p. 382. 'The Work of Art', p. 244.

41. Benjamin, *GS*, vol. I.2, pp. 469, 508; *GS*, vol. VII.1, p. 383. 'The Work of Art', p. 235.

42. See Siegfried Kracauer, *The Mass Ornament: Weimar Essays*, Harvard University Press, Cambridge MA 1995, pp. 75–86.

43. Theodor W. Adorno, 'The Schema of Mass Culture', in T.W. Adorno, *The Culture Industry*, Routledge, London 1992, pp. 75–7.

44. Adorno and Horkheimer, 'Notes' to *Dialectic of Enlightenment*, p. 235.

45. See, for one example of this often repeated aestheticizing claim, specifically in relation to the men's highboard diving sequence, Taylor Downing, *Olympia*, BFI Film Classics, BFI, London 1992, p. 83.

46. Disney studied Muybridge as a young man, according to Bob Thomas; see *Walt Disney*, p. 44. Shamus Culhane, in *Animation: From Script to Screen*, Columbus Books, London 1989, testifies to the continuing importance of Muybridge for action analysis in the late twentieth century.

47. For the concept of the 'optical-unconscious', see Benjamin, 'Kleine Geschichte der Photographie', in *GS*, vol. II.1, p. 371; 'A Small History of Photography', in *One-Way Street and Other Writings*, New Left Books, London 1979, p. 243.

48. Adorno and Horkheimer, 'Notes' to *Dialectic of Enlightenment*, p. 234.

49. Benjamin, *GS*, vol. 1.3, p. 1039.

50. See Walter Benjamin, *Charles Baudelaire: A Lyric Poet in the Era of High Capitalism*, London, New Left Books, London 1973, pp. 132–3.

51. See Adorno and Horkheimer, *Dialectic of Enlightenment*, p. 149.

52. Quoted in Taylor, 'Post-Modernism in the Third Reich', in Taylor and Van der Will, eds, *The Nazification of Art*, p. 136.

53. See Carl Diem, *Olympische Reise*, Deutscher Schriftenverlag, Berlin 1937.

54. From ibid.

55. Ibid., p. 80.

56. Ibid., p. 41.

57. Clement Greenberg, 'Avant-Garde and Kitsch', p. 538.

58. Quoted in Michael Denning, *The Cultural Front*, Verso, London 1998, pp. 107–8.

59. Much of the literature locates the year 1937 as the moment when, as expressed by Brandon Taylor, 'relations between National Socialism and Modernism were finally fixed for all to see'. See Brandon Taylor, 'Post-Modernism in the Third Reich', in Taylor and Van der Will, eds, *The Nazification of Art*, p. 132.

60. Storm and Dreßler, *Im Reiche der Micky-Maus*, p. 96.

61. In a report in 1958 to the post-war Filmbewertungsstelle, which had refused a certificate for *Olympia*, Riefenstahl denies that 'men are stylized in the film', insisting that 'we see man as he is, not stylized or heroized' (quoted in Graham, *Leni Riefenstahl and Olympia*, p. 284). But what men? The selection was already made by the time of filming. Reality was made ideal by pre-digestion.

62. *Hinter den Kulissen des Reichsparteitagfilms*, Zentralverlag der NSDAP, Munich 1935, p. 28. In an interview in 1964 Riefenstahl related likewise that *Olympia* was conceived before shooting, and its law was architectural; it was formed not of montage, but rather as a *Gesamtkunstwerk*.

63. Quoted in Graham, *Leni Riefenstahl and Olympia*, pp. 257–8 (translation originally published in *Film Culture* 56/7, Spring 1973, p. 162).

64. There had been other attempts at achieving a three-dimensional look. Carl Lederer had a three-dimensional system in the 1910s, and Lotte Reiniger and Carl Koch had worked on one in the 1920s. Ub Iwerks invented one in 1934.

65. As reported in Frank Thomas and Ollie Johnston, *Too Funny For Words*, Abbeville, New York 1987.

66. Quoted in Steven Watts, 'Walt Disney's Art and Politics in the American Century', *Journal of American History*, June 1993, p. 95.

67. Robert Feild, *The Art of Walt Disney*, Collins, London and Glasgow 1944, p. 274.

68. Luske's 'General Outline of Animation Theory and Practice' was an internal studio publication. It was included in the *Studio Animation Handbook* (1936). Luske's 'General Outline' is reprinted in Frank Thomas and Ollie Johnston, *The Illusion of Life: Disney Animation*, Hyperion, New York 1981, pp. 545–7.

69. 'Character Handling', an internal studio document, reprinted in Thomas and Johnston, *The Illusion of Life*, p. 550.

70. Adolf Hitler, *Mein Kampf*, quoted in Taylor, 'Postmodernism in the Third Reich', in Taylor and Van der Will, eds, *The Nazification of Art*, p. 129.

71. The Stefan George circle, with its assertion of a moral basis to politics, did also produce the aristocratic resistance to Hitler, in the form of Claus von Stauffenberg and friends, who appropriated a line from George's 1907 poem 'Der Widerchrist' (The Antichrist) to describe Hitler: 'Der Fürst des Geziefers verbreitet sein Reich/ Kein Schatz der ihm mangelt/ Kein Glück das ihm weicht' ('The high Prince of Vermin extends his domain/ No treasure eludes him, no pleasure or gain.').

See Michael Baigent and Richard Leigh, *Secret Germany: Claus von Stauffenberg and the Mystical Crusade Against Hitler*, Jonathan Cape, London 1994, p. 10.

72. See Taylor and van der Will, eds, *The Nazification of Art*, pp. 66, 137.
73. Storm and Dreßler, *Im Reiche der Micky-Maus*, p. 122.
74. Ibid., p. 99.
75. Ibid., pp. 123–4.
76. Ibid., p. 11.
77. Ibid., p. 110.
78. Ibid., p. 124.
79. Ibid., p. 127.
80. Disney liked to trace his lineage back to France via England. Robin Allan assures us that Disney was of Irish, English and Canadian stock on his father's side, while his maternal grandmother was German. See Robin Allan, *Walt Disney and Europe*, Indiana University Press, Bloomington 1999, p. 2.
81. Storm and Dreßler, *Im Reiche der Micky-Maus*, p. 129.
82. Ibid., p. 130.
83. A captured print of *Snow White and the Seven Dwarfs* was probably also shown to filmmakers to help them in planning a rival German version.
84. See Allan, *Walt Disney and Europe*, p. 89.
85. Felix Salten was the arch-enemy of satirist Karl Kraus, who held him responsible for the journalistic degradation of language. Salten had been active in wartime propaganda for the *Neue Freie Presse* in the Great War.
86. Storm and Dreßler, *Im Reiche der Micky-Maus*, p. 134.
87. This word means 'petty bourgeoisie', but it also carries intimations of 'philistine'.
88. Storm and Dreßler, *Im Reiche der Micky-Maus*, pp. 104–5.

eye-candy and adorno's silly symphonies

1. Quoted in Martin Krause and Linda Witkowski, *Walt Disney's Snow White and the Seven Dwarfs: An Art in the Making*, Hyperion, New York 1994, p. 9.
2. In John Culhane, *Walt Disney's Fantasia*, Harry N. Abrams, New York 1987, p. 43.
3. Walter Benjamin, *Gesammelte Schriften* (hereafter *GS*), 7 vols, edited by Rolf Tiedemann and Hermann Schweppenhäuser, Suhrkamp Verlag, Frankfurt am Main 1972–89, vol. I.2, pp. 460, 498; *GS*, vol. VII.1, p. 375. 'The Work of Art in the Age of Mechanical Reproduction', in *Illuminations*, Fontana, London 1992, pp. 227–8.
4. Culhane, *Walt Disney's Fantasia*, pp. 168–70.
5. Robert Feild, *The Art of Walt Disney*, Collins, London and Glasgow 1944, pp. 283–4.
6. Quoted partially in Paul Wells, *Understanding Animation*, Routledge, London 1998, p. 231, and partially in Steven Watts, 'Walt Disney's Art and Politics in the American Century', *Journal of American History*, June 1993, pp. 101–2.
7. The essay is reprinted in Daniel Talbot, ed., *Film: An Anthology*, University of California Press, Berkeley and Los Angeles, 1966, p. 23.
8. Jeffrey Richards and Dorothy Sheridan, eds, *Mass-Observation at the Movies*, Routledge & Kegan Paul, London 1987, p. 222.

9. In 1964 Adorno recounted a meeting with the brilliant imitator Chaplin at a Malibu villa. See 'Chaplin in Malibu', reprinted together with a short piece on Chaplin and Kierkegaard from 1930 as 'Zweimal Chaplin', in Theodor W. Adorno, *Ohne Leitbild*, Suhrkamp Verlag, Frankfurt am Main 1969, pp. 89–93.
10. Culhane, *Walt Disney's Fantasia*, p. 108.
11. It was published in Germany in 1948.
12. See Igor Stravinsky and Robert Craft, *Expositions and Developments*, Faber & Faber, London 1962, p. 142.
13. Theodor W. Adorno, *Philosophy of Modern Music*, Sheed & Ward, London 1973, p. 140.
14. Ibid., p. 137.
15. Ibid., p. 145.
16. Ibid., p. 148.
17. Ibid., p. 156.
18. Ibid., pp. 156–7.
19. Theodor W. Adorno, 'Der Wein', in *Alban Berg*, Cambridge University Press, Cambridge 1994 (the book was written between 1937 and 1968).
20. Ibid., p. 117.
21. Culhane, *Walt Disney's Fantasia*, p. 120.
22. Cited in ibid., pp. 117–18.
23. Later, in the 1960s, in an interview with Robert Craft, Stravinsky made more critical comments on Disney, refusing any notion that Disney musicians' musical invention might have anything to do with 'art'. 'What about the "infinity of possibilities" in connection with the new art material of electronically produced sound? With few exceptions "infinite possibilities" has meant collages of organs burbling, rubber suction noises, machine-gunning, and other – this is curious – representational and associative noises more appropriate to Mr. Disney's musical mimicries. Not the fact of possibilities, of course, but choice is the beginning of art. But the sound lab is already part of the musical supermarket.' Igor Stravinsky and Robert Craft, *Dialogues*, Faber & Faber, London 1982, p. 126.
24. Quoted by Max Horkheimer, 'Art and Mass Culture' (1941), in *Zeitschrift für Sozialforschung*, Jahrgang 9 (reprint), Deutscher Taschenbuch Verlag, Munich 1980, p. 297.
25. Ibid., pp. 302–3.
26. Ibid., p. 302. Adler is mentioned in 'The Culture Industry' chapter in *Dialectic of Enlightenment* by Adorno and Horkheimer. Dwight Macdonald, the harsh critic of middlebrow culture, reveals in his 1952 *New Yorker* essay 'The Book-of-the-Millennium Club' that Adler runs the Institute for Philosophical Research, an enterprise largely funded by the Ford Foundation, and involved in bringing Great Culture and the 102 Great Ideas to the masses, through door-to-door salesmen. See Dwight Macdonald, *Against the American Grain: Essays on the Effects of Mass Culture*, Vintage, New York 1962, p. 243.
27. Horkheimer, 'Art and Mass Culture', pp. 296–7.
28. *Vendredi*, 17 June 1938 (from Benjamin papers in the T.W. Adorno archive).
29. The splicing of the neo-Thomist Adler and Disney continues: in 1998 Disney's online 'family' site was recommending one of Adler's many books as a guide to

methods of enlightening children about the world.

30. Horkheimer, 'Art and Mass Culture', p. 296.

31. Ibid., p. 294.

32. Ibid., p. 296.

33. Ibid., p. 293.

34. Ibid., p. 296.

35. Theodor W. Adorno and Max Horkheimer, *Dialectic of Enlightenment*, Verso, London 1989, p. 120.

36. Ibid., p. 138.

37. In this context, it is rather curious to note that the irascible Donald Duck replaced Mickey Mouse as the 'international symbol of Good Will' in 1935, following a declaration by the League of American Nations.

38. Frank Thomas and Ollie Johnston, *The Illusion of Life: Disney Animation*, Hyperion, New York 1981, p. 522.

39. In 1969 Adorno took to court one of his revolting students, Hans-Jürgen Krahl, who had led the occupation of his Institute for Social Research in Frankfurt, as part of a critique of capitalism, consumerism and war in Vietnam and elsewhere. The public prosecutor was unsympathetic to the critical theorist. He branded him a sorcerer's apprentice, for he had conjured up spirits that he could not control. See Esther Leslie, 'Introduction' to a letter exchange between Adorno and Marcuse, *New Left Review* 233, January–February 1999, p. 122.

40. Adorno and Horkheimer, *Dialectic of Enlightenment*, pp. 133–4.

41. She turned up on German screens in 1937, together with Popeye.

42. Adorno and Horkheimer, *Dialectic of Enlightenment*, p. 134.

43. Ibid., p. 136.

44. Ibid., pp. 152–3.

45. See Ernst Bloch et al., *Aesthetics and Politics*, Verso, London 1977, pp. 120–26.

46. Ibid., p. 123.

47. See Benjamin, *Illuminations*, p. 221.

48. Adorno and Eisler quote Benjamin's critical comments on Werfel favourably in their *Composing for the Films*. See Theodor W. Adorno and Hanns Eisler, *Composing for the Films*, Athlone Press, London 1994, pp. 72–3.

49. See letter of 18 March 1936 from Adorno to Benjamin in response to the 'Artwork essay', Benjamin, *GS*, vol. I.3, p. 1004; Bloch et al., *Aesthetics and Politics*, p. 124.

50. Adorno and Horkheimer, *Dialectic of Enlightenment*, p. 140.

51. Ibid., p. 141.

52. Ibid., p. 126.

53. Ibid., pp. 137–8.

54. T.W. Adorno, 'Chaplin in Malibu', reprinted together with a short piece on Chaplin and Kierkegaard from 1930 as 'Zweimal Chaplin', in *Ohne Leitbild*, Suhrkamp Verlag, Frankfurt am Main 1969, pp. 89–93.

55. Reprinted in Richard Taylor and Ian Christie, eds, *The Film Factory: Russian and Soviet Cinema in Documents 1896–1939*, Harvard University Press, Cambridge MA 1988, pp. 234–5.

56. Adorno and Eisler, *Composing for the Films*, p. 87.

57. Ibid., p. 24.
58. Ibid., p. 75.
59. Ibid., p. 76.
60. Ibid., p. 60.
61. Ibid., p. li.
62. Ibid., pp. li–lii.
63. Ibid., p. liii.
64. Ibid., p. 16.
65. See Hanns Eisler, 'Film Music – Work in Progress' (1941?), in *Hanns Eisler, Musik und Politik, Schriften, Addenda*, edited by Günter Mayer, Reklam, Leipzig 1983, p. 148.
66. Adorno and Eisler, *Composing for the Films*, p. 17.
67. Ibid., p. 36.
68. Ibid., pp. 36–7.
69. Ibid., pp. 62–3.
70. Ibid., p. 65.
71. Ibid., p. 73.
72. Ibid., p. 66.
73. Eisenstein analyses this Silly Symphony again in a lecture in 1947. He praises the musical–visual analogue but is critical of the tonal resolutions. He deems the pictorial form, the landscape, poor. However, the colours are good, 'very attractive, because they have the pallor of celluloid'. See Sergei M. Eisenstein, *The Eisenstein Reader*, edited by Richard Taylor, BFI, London 1998, p. 185.
74. The Athlone edition of the book gives the date incorrectly as 1921.
75. Adorno and Eisler, *Composing for the Films*, pp. 66–7.
76. Ibid., p. 70.
77. Ibid., pp. 73–4.
78. Ibid., p. 78.
79. Ibid., p. 111. The name is actually 'fantasound'.
80. See Bob Thomas, *Walt Disney: A Biography*, W.H. Allen, London 1981, p. 151.
81. Ibid., pp. 151–2.
82. Culhane, *Walt Disney's Fantasia*, p. 36.
83. *Film-Kurier*, February 1931. Cited in Jerzy Toeplitz, *Geschichte des Films, Band 2, 1928–1933*, Henschel, Berlin 1985, p. 334.
84. William Moritz notes that various texts and film catalogues misdate films such as *Komposition in Blau* or Reiniger's *Das gestohlene Herz* (1934) so that it appears they were produced prior to the Nazi regime.
85. William Moritz, 'Oskar Fischinger', in *Optische Poesie: Oskar Fischinger, Leben und Werk, Kinematograph* 9, 1993, Deutsches Filmmuseum, Frankfurt am Main, p. 40.
86. Reiniger and her husband Carl Koch attempted to emigrate in 1936 but found no country prepared to offer them permanent refuge. They made it to Italy eventually, but the retreating Nazi occupiers forced them back to Germany, and Reiniger was compelled to work on an animation film as Berlin fell violently to the Allies.
87. Moritz, 'Oskar Fischinger', p. 42.
88. Ibid., p. 43.
89. *Film as Film; Formal Experiment in Film 1910–1975*, exhibition catalogue, Hayward Gallery, London 1979, p. 78.

90. Moritz, 'Oskar Fischinger', p. 55.

91. Fischinger, quoted in Robin Allan, *Walt Disney and Europe*, Indiana University Press, Bloomington 1999, p. 113.

92. Quoted in Talbot, ed., *Film: An Anthology*, p. 92.

93. J.P. Storm and M. Dreßler, *Im Reiche der Micky-Maus: Walt Disney in Deustchland 1927–1945*, documentation of an exhibition in the Filmmuseum Potsdam, Henschel Verlag, Berlin 1991, p. 123.

94. Ibid., p. 136.

95. Theodor W. Adorno, *Aesthetic Theory*, Routledge & Kegan Paul, London 1986, p. 175.

96. Ibid., p. 493.

97. Ibid., p. 175.

98. Adorno adopted the notion of 'being devoid of intention' from Walter Benjamin's *The Origin of German Tragic Drama*.

99. Adorno, *Aesthetic Theory*, p. 175.

100. Ibid.

101. See Adorno, 'Chaplin in Malibu'.

102. Reprinted in Charles Harrison and Paul Wood, eds, *Art in Theory*, Blackwell, Oxford 1993, p. 448.

103. Benjamin, *GS*, vol. III, p. 158.

104. Benjamin, *GS*, vol. VI, pp. 103–4.

105. See Adorno, 'Chaplin in Malibu', pp. 89–93.

106. Theodor W. Adorno, 'Notes on Kafka', in *Prisms*, trans. Samuel and Shierry Weber, Neville Spearman, London 1967, p. 262.

107. Adorno and Horkheimer, *Dialectic of Enlightenment*, p. 149.

108. Adorno, *Aesthetic Theory*, pp. 180–81.

109. Adorno and Horkheimer, *Dialectic of Enlightenment*, pp. 117–18.

110. Ibid., p. 118.

111. Theodor W. Adorno, *Negative Dialectics*, Routledge & Kegan Paul, London 1973, p. 366.

112. See Adorno, *Aesthetic Theory*, p. 120.

113. Ibid., pp. 174–5.

114. For example: 'The rape of the masses, whom fascism, with its cult of the Führer, forces to their knees, has its counterpart in the rape of an apparatus that is pressed into the production of cult values'. Benjamin, *GS*, vol. I.2, p. 506; *Illuminations*, p. 234.

115. Richard Schickel, *The Disney Version*, Pavilion Books, London 1986, pp. 206–7.

kracauer, dumbo and class struggle

1. Siegfried Kracauer, 'Dumbo', in *Kino*, Suhrkamp, Frankfurt am Main 1979, p. 60.

2. Siegfried Kracauer, 'Akrobat – schöön', in *Schriften* 5:3, *Aufsätze 1932–1965*, Suhrkamp Verlag, Frankfurt am Main 1990, p. 128.

3. Kracauer, 'Dumbo', p. 58.

4. Ibid.

5. Ibid., p. 59.

6. Ibid.
7. Ibid.
8. Quoted in Robin Allan, *Walt Disney and Europe*, Indiana University Press, Bloomington 1999, p. 75.
9. Frank Thomas and Ollie Johnston, *The Illusion of Life: Disney Animation*, Hyperion, New York 1981, p. 531.
10. Robert de Roos 'The Magic Worlds of Disney', in Eric Smoodin, ed., *Disney Discourse: Producing the Magic Kingdom*, American Film Institute, Routledge, London 1994, p. 56.
11. Siegfried Kracauer, 'Zur Ästhetik des Farbenfilms', in *Kino*, pp. 48–53. The galley proofs of this essay were among Walter Benjamin's Paris possessions.
12. Ibid., p. 52.
13. Kracauer, 'Abstrakter Film', in *Kino*, p. 45.
14. Ibid., p. 46.
15. Ibid.
16. Ibid.
17. Ibid., p. 47.
18. Ibid.
19. Kracauer, 'Zur Ästhetik des Farbenfilms', p. 51.
20. Ibid., p. 50.
21. The rumour is repeated in Michael Denning, *The Cultural Front*, Verso, London 1998, p. 403.
22. See Karl F. Cohen, *Forbidden Animation: Censored Cartoons and Blacklisted Animators in America*, McFarland, North Carolina 1997, p. 160.
23. An account of the strike, in the context of union politics and popular-front policy, can be found in Denning, *The Cultural Front*, pp. 403–22. Cohen's *Forbidden Animation* provides good detail too.
24. See Cohen, *Forbidden Animation*, p. 159.
25. Quoted in Bob Thomas, *Walt Disney: A Biography*, W.H. Allen, London 1976, p. 168.
26. Ibid., p. 170. See also Steven Watts, *The Magic Kingdom: Walt Disney and the American Way of Life*, Houghton Mifflin, New York 1997, p. 221.
27. See Richard L. Trethewey, ed., *Walt Disney: The FBI Files*, Rainbo Animation Art, Pacifica CA 1994, p. 18. This comprises materials from heavily censored FBI files, including internal memos, telegrams, correspondence, newspaper articles and clippings relating to Walt Disney's political life. A transcript of Disney's 1947 HUAC hearing on communist infiltration of the motion-picture industry is included.
28. See the illustration in Watts, *The Magic Kingdom*, first illustrated section.
29. See Marc Eliot, *Walt Disney: Hollywood's Dark Prince*, André Deutsch, London 1994, p. 140. See also Watts, *The Magic Kingdom*, p. 211.
30. See the description in Michael Barrier, *Hollywood Cartoons: American Animation in its Golden Age*, Oxford University Press, Oxford 1999, p. 307.
31. Quoted in Bob Thomas, *Walt Disney: A Biography*, W.H. Allen, London 1976, pp. 172–3.
32. See Watts, *The Magic Kingdom*, pp. 225–6.
33. See Cohen, *Forbidden Animation*, pp. 162–3. There are other details in Barrier,

Hollywood Cartoons, pp. 308–9. For the claim that the atmosphere at the Disney studios and, consequently, the types of films made there were changed decisively as a result of the strike, see Watts, *The Magic Kingdom*, pp. 226–7.

34. This was the only self-portrait chosen by Hitler for the 1938 Great Exhibition of German Art. It later hung over Speer's office desk, and copies and reproductions were widespread in the Third Reich.

35. Churchill and Roosevelt watched the cartoon at a conference on the Allied Invasion of France.

36. See Richard Schickel, *The Disney Version*, Pavilion Books, London 1986, p. 275.

37. See Watts, *The Magic Kingdom*, p. 236.

38. See Denning, *The Cultural Front*, p. 416.

39. See ibid., p. 417.

40. Kracauer, 'Dumbo', p. 60.

41. *Vendredi*, 17 June 1938, among Walter Benjamin's possessions.

42. See Watts, *The Magic Kingdom*, p. 239.

43. See Cohen, *Forbidden Animation*, p. 169.

44. Trethewey, ed., *Walt Disney*, p. 55.

45. Ibid., p. 46.

46. Ibid., p. 44.

47. Ibid., p. 52.

48. Ibid., p. 70.

49. The transcript is reproduced in ibid., pp. 39–42.

50. See Watts, *The Magic Kingdom*, p. 246.

eisenstein shakes mickey's hand in hollywood

1. Ivor Montagu, *With Eisenstein in Hollywood*, Seven Seas Books, Berlin 1968, p. 82.

2. Yon Barna, *Eisenstein*, Secker & Warburg, London 1973, p. 140.

3. Ibid., p. 143.

4. Montagu, *With Eisenstein in Hollywood*, p. 82.

5. Barna, *Eisenstein*, p. 155. For Eisenstein's account of their relationship, see the piece from 1939 titled 'Charlie Chaplin', in Sergej M. Eisenstein, *Yo – Ich Selbst*, Fischer Verlag, Frankfurt am Main 1988, pp. 393–6.

6. See the introduction to Sergei M. Eisenstein, *The Eisenstein Reader*, edited by Richard Taylor, BFI, London 1998, p. 3.

7. Barna, *Eisenstein*, p. 16.

8. This card is reproduced in Norman M. Klein, *Seven Minutes: The Life and Death of the American Animated Cartoon*, Verso, London 1993, p. 55.

9. Sergei M. Eisenstein, *Eisenstein on Disney*, Methuen, London 1988, p. 89.

10. Ibid., p. 69.

11. Ibid., p. 70.

12. Ibid., p. 84.

13. Quoted in Richard Taylor and Ian Christie, eds, *The Film Factory: Russian and Soviet Cinema in Documents 1896–1939*, Harvard University Press, Cambridge MA 1988, p. 72.

14. Quoted in ibid., p. 105.

15. Quoted in ibid., p. 109. Lunarcharsky lost his government post in 1929.
16. Quoted in ibid., p. 130.
17. See Eric Walter White, *Walking Shadows: An Essay on Lotte Reiniger's Silhouette Films*, Hogarth Press, London 1931, pp. 9–10.
18. 'Béla Forgets the Scissors' (1926), in *The Eisenstein Reader*, p. 67.
19. Ibid., p. 68.
20. Ibid., p. 72.
21. Walter Benjamin, *Gesammelte Schriften* (hereafter *GS*), 7 vols, edited by Rolf Tiedemann and Hermann Schweppenhäuser, Suhrkamp Verlag, Frankfurt am Main 1972–91, vol. I.2, pp. 435–73; *GS*, vol. VII.1, p. 350. 'The Work of Art in the Age of Mechanical Reproduction', in *Illuminations*, Fontana, London 1992, p. 212. Benjamin had reservations about Balázs too. He provided an exasperated write-up of a discussion with Balázs in 1929, wherein he condemned Balázs's 'banal language mysticism', setting against it the intentionality of poetry, conqueror of the word's originary magic and myth. Walter Benjamin, 'Notes on a Conversation with Béla Balázs (end of 1929)', in *Selected Writings*, volume 2, Belknap/Harvard University Press, Cambridge MA 1999, pp. 276–7.
22. See *Moholy-Nagy: An Anthology*, edited by Richard Kostelanetz, Da Capo, New York 1991, p. 139.
23. See Benjamin, *GS*, vol. I.2, pp. 443, 481–2; *GS*, vol. VII.1, p. 357. 'The Work of Art', p. 237.
24. Reprinted in *The Eisenstein Reader*, pp. 124–32.
25. Maxim Gorky et al., *Soviet Writers' Congress 1934: The Debate on Socialist Realism and Modernism in the Soviet Union*, Lawrence & Wishart, London 1977, p. 153.
26. Eisenstein, *Eisenstein on Disney*, p. 91.
27. See J.P. Storm and M. Dreßler, *Im Reiche der Micky-Maus: Walt Disney in Deustchland 1927–1945*, documentation of an exhibition in the Filmmuseum Potsdam, Henschel Verlag, Berlin 1991, p. 91.
28. Eisenstein, *Eisenstein on Disney*, p. 8–10.
29. Ibid., p. 2.
30. Cited on 'The Making of Snow White and the Seven Dwarfs', included on the *Snow White and the Seven Dwarfs* video, Walt Disney Classics, Buena Vista Home Video (D215242).
31. Eisenstein, *Eisenstein on Disney*, p. 2.
32. Ibid., p. 3.
33. Ibid.
34. Ibid., pp. 3, 6.
35. Ibid., pp. 45, 47.
36. Ibid., pp. 26–7. Eisenstein drafted a section on plasmation and fire in October 1940.
37. Ibid., p. 41.
38. Ibid., p. 33.
39. Ibid., p. 21.
40. Ibid., p. 10.
41. Ibid., p. 21.
42. Frederick Engels, 'The Part Played by Labour in the Transition from Ape to Man',

in *Dialectics of Nature*, Progress Publishers, Moscow 1976, p. 178.

43. Engels, *Dialectics of Nature*, p. 256.

44. Steven Rose, *Lifelines: Biology, Freedom, Determinism*, Penguin, Harmondsworth 1998, p. 255.

45. Eisenstein, *Eisenstein on Disney*, p. 41.

46. Montagu, *With Eisenstein in Hollywood*, p. 82.

47. Eisenstein, *Eisenstein on Disney*, p. 23.

48. Ibid., p. 36.

49. Ibid., p. 63.

50. Ibid., p. 43.

51. Ibid., p. 95.

52. Ibid., pp. 94–5.

53. Ibid., p. 46.

54. Ibid., pp. 50, 53.

55. Ibid., pp. 55–6.

56. Ibid., p. 57.

57. Ibid., p. 62.

58. Ibid., p. 89.

59. Sergei M. Eisenstein, *Non-Indifferent Nature: Film and the Structure of Things*, Cambridge University Press, Cambridge 1994, pp. 39–49.

60. Leon Trotsky, *Trotsky's Notebooks, 1933–1935*, edited by Philip Pomper, Columbia University Press, New York 1986, p. 44.

61. Max Eastman, *Marx, Lenin and the Science of Revolution*, George Allen & Unwin, London 1926, p. 32.

62. Ibid., p. 34.

63. Ibid., pp. 34–5.

64. Philip Pomper explores Trotsky's relation to animism in his introduction to Trotsky's notebooks. He notes that one of Trotsky's early articles, on a Russian 'Darwin', from 1901, criticised the scientist Solovev for his animism. See the introduction to Trotsky, *Trotsky's Notebooks, 1933–1935*, p. 46.

65. Leon Trotsky, *Trotsky's Diary in Exile 1935*, Faber & Faber, London 1958, p. 94.

66. Ibid., p. 95.

67. Trotsky, *Trotsky's Notebooks, 1933–1935*, p. 48.

68. Leon Trotsky, *The History of the Russian Revolution*, Pluto Press, London 1985, p. 1122.

69. Leon Trotsky, *Literature and Revolution*, Redwords, London 1991, pp. 282–4.

70. André Breton, *Manifestoes of Surrealism*, University of Michigan Press, Ann Arbor 1969, pp. 291–2. See also Maurice Nadeau, *The History of Surrealism*, Penguin, Harmondsworth 1978, pp. 236–7.

71. Written in 1977 for *New Society*, reprinted in John Berger, *About Looking*, Writers and Readers, London 1980, pp. 1–26.

72. Berger, *About Looking*, p. 12.

73. See Karl Marx, *Capital* Volume 1, Charles Kerr, New York 1904, p. 426.

74. See Benjamin, *GS*, vol. VII.1, pp. 243–9.

75. Breton, *Manifestoes of Surrealism*, p. 293.

76. Ibid.

77. Eisenstein, *Eisenstein on Disney*, p. 63.
78. Ibid., p. 66.
79. Reprinted in *The Eisenstein Reader*, pp. 80–81.
80. See Theodor W. Adorno and Hanns Eisler, *Composing for the Films*, Athlone Press, London 1994, pp. 40–43.
81. Eisenstein, 'The Dramaturgy of Film Form (The Dialectical Approach to Film Form)', in *The Eisenstein Reader*, p. 97.
82. Eisenstein, 'From Lectures on Music and Colour in *Ivan the Terrible*', in *The Eisenstein Reader*, p. 171.
83. Ibid.
84. Ibid.
85. Ibid., pp. 172–3.
86. Ibid., p. 184.
87. Eisenstein, *Non-Indifferent Nature*, p. 389.
88. Ibid.
89. Ibid., p. 390.
90. Ibid.
91. Ibid., p. 391.
92. Ibid.
93. Robin Allan indicates that it was indeed a Chinese-American artist, Tyrus Wong, who was largely responsible for the forest scenes that appeared in the film. He quotes Disney animator Jim Algar, who noted the 'moody oriental touch of never being tightly finished'. See Robin Allan, *Walt Disney and Europe*, Indiana University Press, Bloomington 1999, p. 183.
94. Eisenstein, *Eisenstein on Disney*, pp. 64–5.

techne-colour

1. William Wordsworth, *Poetical Works*, Oxford University Press, Oxford 1969, p. 62.
2. See Frederick Burwick, *The Damnation of Newton: Goethe's Colour Theory and Romantic Perception*, Walter de Gruyter, Berlin and New York 1986, pp. 198–9.
3. Wordsworth, *Poetical Works*, p. 383.
4. J.W. Goethe, *Theory of Colours*, MIT Press, Cambridge MA 1970, p. xxxviii. The *Farbenlehre* appeared in three parts between 1808 and 1810. The three parts were the didactic part, the polemical part and the historical part. It was originally titled *Zur Farbenlehre von Goethe: Nebst einem Hefte mit sechzehn Kupfertafeln*, J.G. Cotta'schen Buchhandlung, Tübingen 1810.
5. Newton, quoted in Milton Klonsky, 'Art and Life: A Mennipean Paean to the Flea; or, Did Dostoevsky Kill Trotsky?', in Klonsky, *A Discourse on Hip*, Wayne State University, Detroit 1991, p. 214.
6. Such an experiment had been carried out before by Descartes, who was also an observer and describer of rainbows. See René Descartes, *The Philosophical Writings of Descartes*, vol. 1, Cambridge University Press, Cambridge 1985, p. 166. See also Philip Fisher, *Wonder, the Rainbow and the Aesthetics of Rare Experiences*, Harvard University Press, Cambridge MA 1998.

For the benefit of Mickey Mouse continuity, it must be noted that one of Newton's first experiments as a boy was to build a little windmill whose sails were turned by a mouse placed inside. See Klonsky, 'Art and Life: A Mennipean Paean to the Flea', p. 215.

7. Dennis Sepper's account of Goethe's struggle against Newton defends Newton's experiments in a detailed examination of the arguments and the scientific understanding of the time. See Dennis L. Sepper, *Goethe contra Newton*, Cambridge University Press, Cambridge 1988.

8. Sepper maintains that Goethe had not read Newton when he performed this experiment, but knew his work only by hearsay. Ibid., pp. 16–17.

9. This is a term from Goethe's essay 'Der Versuch als Vermittler von Objekt und Subjekt' (1793), in *Goethes Werke*, edited by Erich Trunz, vol. XII, *Naturwissenschaftliche Schriften*, C.H. Beck, Munich 1981.

10. Goethe, *Theory of Colours*, pp. xxxvii–xxxviii.

11. Ibid., pp. xli–xliv.

12. J.W. Goethe, *Faust 1 and 2*, in *Goethe, The Collected Works*, Volume 2, edited and translated by Stuart Atkins, Princeton University Press, Princeton 1984, p. 154. (Subsequent citations refer to this edition.)

13. Sepper notes that Goethe was unable to explain the appearance of the rainbow. See *Goethe contra Newton*, p. 150.

14. Philip Fisher notes that Newton's summary of the characteristics of the rainbow in *Opticks* adopts the tone of God himself, echoing the instructions of an architect rather than the voice of a 'humble observer': '*Thus shall there be made* two Bows of Colours', Fisher, *Wonder, the Rainbow and the Aesthetics of Rare Experiences*, p. 104.

15. *The Aesthetic and Miscellaneous Works of Frederick von Schlegel*, Henry G. Bohn, London 1849, p. 419.

16. Novalis (Friedrich von Hardenberg), *Henry of Ofterdingen: A Romance*, John Owen, Cambridge 1842.

17. Goethe, *Theory of Colours*, p. 45.

18. Quoted in the 'Introduction' to J.W. Goethe, *Scientific Studies*, Suhrkamp, New York 1988, p. xix.

19. Burwick, *The Damnation of Newton*, p. 76.

20. See ibid., pp. 72–3. Later the abstract filmmaker Stan Brakhage developed a theory of hypnogogic closed-eye vision – physical, psychological, poetic – and he would imitate this with multiple layers of image, abstraction, surface scratching, bleaching and colouring.

21. Henri Bergson, *Matter and Memory* (1911), George Allen & Unwin, London 1919, p. 19.

22. Ibid., p. 31.

23. Walter Benjamin, *Gesammelte Schriften* (hereafter *GS*), 7 vols, edited by Rolf Tiedemann and Hermann Schweppenhäuser, Suhrkamp Verlag, Frankfurt am Main 1972–91, vol. IV.2, p. 1049.

24. See Benjamin, *GS*, vol. VI, p. 701.

25. See Benjamin, *GS*, vol. VII.1, p. 445.

26. Benjamin, *GS*, vol. VI, pp. 122–3.

27. Benjamin, *GS*, vol. VII.1, p. 23.

28. Benjamin, *GS*, vol. VI, p. 120.

29. Ibid., p. 110.

30. Ibid., p. 113.

31. Benjamin, *GS*, vol. III, pp. 10–11.

32. Ibid., p. 19.

33. Ibid.

34. Benjamin, *GS*, vol. IV.2, p. 609.

35. Goethe, *Theory of Colours*, p. 22.

36. For a list of devices, see Benjamin, *Passagen-Werk*, in *GS*, vol. V.2, p. 655; *The Arcades Project*, trans. Howard Eiland and Kevin McLaughlin, Belknap/Harvard University Press, Cambridge MA 1999, p. 527.

37. Benjamin, *Passagen-Werk* 2, p. 1031; *Arcades Project*, p. 861.

38. Benjamin, *Passagen-Werk* 1, p. 235 (my translation); *Arcades Project*, p. 173.

39. Benjamin, *GS*, vol. IV.2, p. 613; 'A Glimpse into the World of Children's Books', in *Selected Writings*, vol. 1, 1913–1926, Belknap/Harvard University Press, Cambridge MA 1996, pp. 442–3.

40. Benjamin, *GS*, vol. IV.2, p. 614.

41. Benjamin, *GS*, vol. IV.1, p. 263.

42. Benjamin, *GS*, vol. I.2, p. 630; *Charles Baudelaire: A Lyric Poet in the Era of High Capitalism*, New Left Books, London 1973, p. 132.

43. Benjamin, *GS*, vol. I.2, p. 628; *Charles Baudelaire*, p. 130.

44. Quoted from Adorno's study *Alban Berg*, Cambridge University Press, Cambridge 1994, p. 114. Benjamin quotes from the same passage of 'L'Art romantique' in his file on Baudelaire (file j, quotation 7), *Passagen-Werk* 1, p. 312; *Arcades Project*, p. 239.

45. Benjamin, 'Über das Programm der kommenden Philosophie' ('On the Programme of the Coming Philosophy'), *GS*, vol. II.1, pp. 161–2.

46. Benjamin, *GS*, vol. I.1, p. 60. In English in Benjamin, *Selected Writings*, vol. 1, 1997, p. 192 (translation altered). In *Pariser Passagen* 1 Benjamin notes that his formula for his arcades study is construction of facts with a total elimination of theory, as Goethe attempted in his morphological writings. Benjamin, *Passagen-Werk* 2, p. 1033; *Arcades Project*, p. 864.

47. Benjamin, *Selected Writings*, vol. 1, p. 279.

48. Ibid., p. 303. See Eisenstein's thoughts on these cave drawings as direct impressions and animistic attempts to bring to life an inanimate representation: Eisenstein, *Eisenstein on Disney*, Methuen, London 1988, p. 43.

49. Benjamin, *GS*, vol. VI, p. 67.

50. Sigmund Freud, 'A Note upon the "Mystic Writing-Pad"', *Pelican Freud Library*, vol. 11, Penguin, Harmondsworth 1984, p 430.

51. *Pelican Freud Library*, vol. 6, Penguin, Harmondsworth 1976, p. 252.

52. See Benjamin, *GS*, vol. VII.1, p. 368. See also notes for the second version of 'Das Kunstwerk im Zeitalter seiner technischen Reproduzierbarkeit', Benjamin, *GS*, vol. VII.2, p. 666.

53. Benjamin, *GS*, vol. VI, p. 127.

54. Miriam Hansen makes a point of the way that mimesis assumes a critical and corrective function vis-à-vis instrumental rationality in Adorno and Horkheimer's

work. It 'prefigures the possibility of a reconciliation with nature, which includes the inner nature of human beings, the body and the unconscious'. See 'Mass Culture as Hieroglyphic Writing: Adorno, Derrida, Kracauer', *New German Critique* 56, Spring–Summer 1992, pp. 52–3.

55. See Benjamin, *GS*, vol. VII.2, p. 792.

56. Ibid., pp. 792–794.

57. Walter Benjamin, 'Kleine Geschichte der Photographie', *GS*, vol. II.1, p. 385; 'A Small History of Photography', in *One-Way Street and Other Writings*, New Left Books, London 1979, p. 256.

58. Ibid.

59. Walter Benjamin, *GS*, vol. II.1, p. 380; *One-Way Street and Other Writings*, p. 252 (translation modified).

60. Benjamin, 'Der Sürrealismus', *GS*, vol. II.1, p. 297; 'Surrealism', in *One-Way Street and Other Writings*, p. 227.

61. Respect is due to Scott J. Thompson, director of research at the online Walter Benjamin Research Syndicate, for (amongst many other things) his extraordinary efforts in bringing to scholarly attention Benjamin's interest in intoxication.

62. Benjamin, *GS*, vol. VI, p. 609.

63. Benjamin, *GS*, vol. VI, pp. 562–3.

64. Benjamin, *GS*, vol. VI, p. 588.

65. Benjamin, *GS*, vol. VII.1, p. 445; *GS*, vol. VI, p. 704.

66. Benjamin, *GS*, vol. VI, pp. 126–7.

67. See Benjamin, *GS*, vol. VI, p. 561, and the repetition in *Passagen-Werk* 1, p. 286 (my translation); *Arcades Project*, p. 216.

68. For details about the three different versions of 'The Work of Art' and their place in Benjamin's thought, see 'The Work of Art in the Age of Unbearable Capitulation', chapter 6 of Esther Leslie, *Walter Benjamin: Overpowering Conformism*, Pluto Press, London 2000.

69. Benjamin, *GS*, vol. I.2, pp. 461–2; *GS*, vol. VII.1, pp. 376–7.

70. Benjamin, *GS*, vol. I.2, pp. 459, 496; *GS*, vol. VII.1, p. 374. 'The Work of Art in the Age of Mechanical Reproduction', in *Illuminations*, Fontana, London 1992, p. 227.

71. K.S. Malevich, *Essays on Art 1915–1933*, vol. 1, Rapp & Whiting, London 1971, pp. 233–8.

72. Ibid., p. 126.

73. Quoted in Giannalberto Bendazzi, *Cartoons: One Hundred Years of Cinema Animation*, John Libbey, London 1994, p. 13.

74. He was later the director of the only official futurist film – *Vita Futurista* (1916).

75. In 1925 Alexander Laszlo, who also had devised colour organs, wrote a book titled *Coloured Light Music*.

76. See *Film as Film: Formal Experiment in Film 1910–1975*, exhibition catalogue, Hayward Gallery, London 1979, p. 20.

77. Quoted in Cecile Starr and Robert Russet, *Experimental Animation*, Van Nostrand Reinhold, New York 1976, p. 36.

78. Ibid., p. 38.

79. Quoted in Jeanpaul Goergen, *Walter Ruttmann: Eine Dokumentation*, Freunde der

deutschen Kinemathek, Berlin 1989, p. 78.

80. It appeared in German and Italian. It is reprinted in Goergen, *Walter Ruttmann*, pp. 94–6.

81. See *Moholy-Nagy: An Anthology*, edited by Richard Kostelanetz, Da Capo, New York 1991, p. 155.

82. After the Second World War, when the Allies destroyed a number of German patents, Gasparcolor disappeared. The competition had been radically knocked out.

83. Quoted in Richard Neupert, 'Painting a Plausible World: Disney's Color Prototypes', in Eric Smoodin, ed., *Disney Discourse: Producing the Magic Kingdom*, American Film Institute/Routledge, New York and London 1994, p. 111.

84. Quoted in John Culhane, *Walt Disney's Fantasia*, Harry N. Abrams, New York 1987, p. 150.

85. See Neupert, 'Painting a Plausible World', p. 110.

86. Quoted in Culhane, *Walt Disney's Fantasia*, p. 159.

87. Martin Krause and Linda Witkowski, *Walt Disney's Snow White and the Seven Dwarfs: An Art in the Making*, Hyperion, New York 1994, p. 39.

88. Later on the palette changed – with the brighter, zanier colours of *Alice in Wonderland*, the nostalgic London postcard colours of *Lady and the Tramp*, the bold linear approach in *101 Dalmatians* with its flat patches of colour.

89. Quoted in Culhane, *Walt Disney's Fantasia*, p. 159.

90. See Neupert, 'Painting a Plausible World', pp. 107–8.

91. See Eisenstein, *The Eisenstein Reader*, p. 185.

winding up

1. See Michael Barrier, *Hollywood Cartoons: American Animation in its Golden Age*, Oxford University Press, Oxford 1999, p. 398.

2. See Steven Watts, *The Magic Kingdom: Walt Disney and the American Way of Life*, Houghton Mifflin, New York 1997, p. 330.

3. Cited in Alan Bryman, *Disney and His Worlds*, Routledge, London 1995, p. 25.

4. Frank Thomas, quoted in Barrier, *Hollywood Cartoons*, p. 398.

5. Richard Schickel, *The Disney Version*, Pavilion Books, London 1986, p. 178.

6. These are a critic's words, quoted in Watts, *The Magic Kingdom*, p. 285.

7. Barbara Deming, 'The Artlessness of Walt Disney', *Partisan Review*, vol. XII, no. 2, Spring 1945, pp. 226–31.

8. See Sergei M. Eisenstein, *Non-Indifferent Nature: Film and the Structure of Things*, Cambridge University Press, Cambridge 1994, p. 390.

9. J. Hoberman, in *Vulgar Modernism: Writing on Movies and Other Media* (Temple University Press, Philadelphia 1991), nominates Tex Avery's work as the quintessence of 'vulgar modernism' (p. 33).

10. Dudley Moore and other members of *Beyond the Fringe* narrated the completed version.

11. For one account, see Irving Sandler, *The Triumph of American Painting*, Icon Editions, Harper & Row, New York 1970.

12. See Jean Charlot, *Art from the Mayans to Disney*, Sheed & Ward, New York and London 1939, pp. 778–9.

13. Cited in Michael Denning, *The Cultural Front*, Verso, London, 1998, p. 419.

14. This somewhat obscured part of Reinhardt's career; its relationship to his later aesthetic stance has been uncovered by Michael Corris: 'The Difficult Freedom of Ad Reinhardt', in John Roberts, ed., *Art Has No History!*, Verso, London 1994.

15. See Robin Allan, *Walt Disney and Europe*, Indiana University Press, Bloomington 1999, p. 233.

16. Quoted in Leonard Maltin, *Of Mice and Magic: A History of American Animated Cartoons*, Plume, New York 1987, p. 74.

17. Milton Klonsky, 'Along the Midway of Mass Culture' (1949), in *A Discourse on Hip*, Wayne State University, Detroit 1991, p. 191. Dwight Macdonald, 'Masscult and Midcult' is reprinted in Dwight Macdonald, *Against the American Grain: Essays on the Effects of Mass Culture*, Vintage, New York 1962, p. 37.

18. Macdonald, 'Masscult and Midcult', p. 38.

19. See Klonsky, 'Along the Midway of Mass Culture', p. 192.

20. This reading of the Cézanne painting, the Philadelphia *Bathers*, is drawn from T.J. Clark's *Farewell to an Idea: Episodes from a History of Modernism*, Yale University Press, New Haven and London 1999, pp. 153–6.

21. See Clement Greenberg, 'The "Crisis" of Abstract Art' (1964), in *The Collected Essays and Criticism*, vol. 4, University of Chicago Press, Chicago 1993.

22. See *Potlatch* 29, 5 November 1957.

23. Quoted in Richard Taylor and Ian Christie, eds, *The Film Factory: Russian and Soviet Cinema in Documents 1896–1939*, Harvard University Press, Cambridge MA 1988, p. 59.

24. Clement Greenberg, 'Avant-Garde and Kitsch', in Charles Harrison and Paul Wood, eds, *Art in Theory*, Blackwell, Oxford 1992, p. 537. Greenberg's 1939 essay was published first in *Partisan Review*, a year later a second version appeared in *Horizon*. Since then versions have found inclusion in many influential collections: *A 'Partisan Review' Reader* (1944), *Mass Culture: The Popular Arts in America* (1957), Gilles Dorfles's *Kitsch: An Anthology of Bad Taste* (1969), *Pollock and After: The Critical Debate* (1985), and in various other anthologies of art criticism.

25. For a history of Coney Island amusement park, its push-me-pull-me relationship to gentility and Disney's dislike of this haunt of the lower classes, see John E. Kasson, *Amusing the Million: Coney Island at the Turn of the Century*, Hill & Wang, New York 1978.

26. Clement Greenberg, '"American-Type" Painting' (1955–58), in William Phillips and Philip Rahv, eds, *The Partisan Review Anthology*, Macmillan, London 1962, p. 165.

27. Ibid., p. 168.

28. Ibid., pp. 165–71.

29. Greenberg, 'Avant-Garde and Kitsch', p. 534.

30. Theodor W. Adorno, *Minima Moralia: Reflections from Damaged Life*, Verso, London 1978, p. 247.

31. This phrase echoes one in a letter from Walter Benjamin to Werner Kraft. See *Briefe*, vol. 2, edited by G. Scholem and T.W. Adorno, Suhrkamp Verlag, Frankfurt am Main 1978, pp. 698–9.

select bibliography

Abbott, E.A., *Flatland: A Romance of Many Dimensions*, Dover Publications, New York 1952.

Adorno, Theodor W., *Prisms*, trans. Samuel and Shierry Weber, Neville Spearman, London 1967.

————, *Ohne Leitbild*, Suhrkamp Verlag, Frankfurt am Main 1969.

————, *Philosophy of Modern Music*, trans. Anne G. Mitchell and Wesley W. Bloomsky, Sheed & Ward, London 1973.

————, *Negative Dialectics*, trans. E.B. Ashton, Routledge & Kegan Paul, London 1973.

————, *Minima Moralia: Reflections from Damaged Life*, trans. E.F.N. Jephcott, Verso, London 1978.

————, *Noten zur Literatur*, Suhrkamp Verlag, Frankfurt am Main 1981.

————, *In Search of Wagner*, trans. Rodney Livingstone, Verso, London 1981.

————, *Aesthetic Theory*, Routledge & Kegan Paul, London 1986.

————, *The Culture Industry*, trans. Juliane Brand and Christopher Hailey, Routledge, London 1992.

————, *Alban Berg*, trans. Juliane Brand and Christopher Hailey, Cambridge University Press, Cambridge 1994.

————, and Hanns Eisler, *Composing for the Films*, Athlone Press, London 1994.

————, and Max Horkheimer, *Dialectic of Enlightenment*, trans. John Cumming, Verso, London 1995.

Allan, Robin, *Walt Disney and Europe*, Indiana University Press, Bloomington 1999.

Aragon, Louis, *Paris Peasant*, trans. Simon Watson Taylor, Picador, London, 1987.

Arvatov, Boris, *Kunst und Produktion*, Carl Hanser Verlag, Munich 1972.

Baigent, Michael and Richard Leigh, *Secret Germany: Claus von Stauffenberg and the Mystical Crusade Against Hitler*, Jonathan Cape, London 1994.

Barna, Yon, *Eisenstein*, Secker & Warburg, London 1973.

Barrier, Michael, *Hollywood Cartoons: American Animation in its Golden Age*, Oxford University Press, Oxford 1999.

Bendazzi, Giannalberto, *Cartoons: One Hundred Years of Cinema Animation*, John Libbey, London 1994.

Benjamin, Walter, *Charles Baudelaire: A Lyric Poet in the Era of High Capitalism*, trans. Harry Zohn, New Left Books, London 1973.

————, *The Origin of German Tragic Drama*, trans. John Osborne, with an introduction by George Steiner, New Left Books, London 1977.

————, *Briefe*, 2 vols, eds G. Scholem and Theodor W. Adorno, Suhrkamp Verlag, Frankfurt am Main 1978.

————, *Illuminations*, trans. Harry Zohn, edited with an introduction by Hannah Arendt, Fontana, London 1973.

————, *One-Way Street and Other Writings*, trans. Edmund Jephcott and Kingsley Shorter, New Left Books, London 1979.

————, *Understanding Brecht*, trans. Anna Bostock, with an introduction by Stanley Mitchell, New Left Books, London 1973.

————, *Reflections*, trans. Edmund Jephcott, edited with an introduction by Peter Demetz, Schocken Books, New York 1986.

————, *Moscow Diary*, trans. Richard Sieburth, ed. with an afterword by Gary Smith, (originally an edition of the journal *October*), Harvard University Press, Cambridge MA and London 1986.

————, *Gesammelte Schriften*, 7 vols, edited by Rolf Tiedemann and Hermann Schweppenhäuser, Suhrkamp Verlag, Frankfurt am Main 1972–91.

————, *Das Passagen-Werk*, edited by Rolf Tiedemann, volume 5 of *Gesammelte Schriften*, 1982; *The Arcades Project*, trans. Howard Eiland and Kevin McLaughlin, Belknap/Harvard University Press, Cambridge MA 1999.

————, *Selected Writings*, 2 vols, edited by Marcus Bullock and Michael W. Jennings, Belknap/Harvard University Press, Cambridge MA 1996, 1999.

————, Collection of papers (newspaper cuttings, galley proofs, articles) on Disney, animation and fairy-tales, held at the Adorno archive, Frankfurt.

Berger, John, *About Looking*, Writers and Readers, London 1980.

Bergson, Henri, *Matter and Memory* (1911), trans. Nancy Margaret Paul and W. Scott Palmer, George Allen & Unwin, London 1919.

Bloch, Ernst et al., *Aesthetics and Politics*, Verso, London 1977.

Breton, André, *Manifestoes of Surrealism*, trans. Richard Searer and Helen R. Lane, University of Michigan Press, Ann Arbor 1969.

Bryman, Alan, *Disney and His Worlds*, Routledge, London 1995.

Burwick, Frederick, *The Damnation of Newton: Goethe's Colour Theory and Romantic Perception*, Walter de Gruyter, Berlin and New York 1986.

Canemaker, John, *Felix: The Twisted Tale of the World's Most Famous Cat*, Da Capo Press, New York 1996.

Carter, Huntly, *The New Spirit in the Cinema: An Analysis and Interpretation of the Parallel Paths of the Cinema, which have led to the great Revolutionary Crisis forming a Study of the Cinema as an Instrument of Sociological Humanism*, Harold Shaylor, London 1930.

Charlot, Jean, *Art from the Mayans to Disney*, Sheed & Ward, New York and London 1939.

Christie, Ian and David Elliott, *Eisenstein at Ninety*, Museum of Modern Art, Oxford 1988.

Clark, T.J., *Farewell to an Idea: Episodes from a History of Modernism*, Yale University Press, New Haven and London 1999.

Cohen, Karl F., *Forbidden Animation: Censored Cartoons and Blacklisted Animators in America*, McFarland, North Carolina 1997.

Comenius, Johann Amos, *Orbis Sensualium Pictus*, with an introduction by John E. Sadler, Oxford University Press, Oxford 1968.

Crafton, Donald, *Emile Cohl, Caricature and Film*, Princeton University Press, Princeton 1990.

Culhane, John, *Walt Disney's Fantasia*, Harry N. Abrams, New York 1987.

Culhane, Shamus, *Animation: From Script to Screen*, Columbus Books, London 1989.

Curtis, Barry, 'In-betweening: An Interview with Irene Kotlarz', *Art History*, vol. 18. no. 1, March 1995, pp. 24–36.

Debord, Guy, *Society of the Spectacle*, Black and Red, Detroit 1983.

Deming, Barbara, 'The Artlessness of Walt Disney', *Partisan Review*, vol. XII, no. 2, Spring 1945.

Denning, Michael, *The Cultural Front*, Verso, London 1998.

Descartes, René, *The Philosophical Writings of Descartes*, vol. 1, Cambridge University Press, Cambridge 1985.

Diem, Carl, *Olympische Reise*, Deutscher Schriftenverlag, Berlin 1937.

Downing, Taylor, *Olympia*, BFI Film Classics, BFI, London 1992.

Max Eastman, *Marx, Lenin and the Science of Revolution*, George Allen & Unwin, London 1926.

Eisenstein, Sergei M., *The Film Sense*, trans. and edited by Jay Leyda, Faber & Faber, London 1943.

———, *Yo – Ich Selbst*, trans. Regine Kühn and Rita Braun, Fischer Verlag, Frankfurt am Main 1988.

———, *Eisenstein on Disney*, trans. Alan Upchurch, Methuen, London 1988.

———, *Non-Indifferent Nature: Film and the Structure of Things*, trans. Herbert Marshall, Cambridge University Press, Cambridge 1994.

———, *The Eisenstein Reader*, trans. Richard Taylor and William Powell, edited by Richard Taylor, BFI, London 1998.

Eisler, Hanns, 'Film Music – Work in Progress', in Hanns Eisler, *Musik und Politik, Schriften, Addenda*, edited by Günter Mayer, Reklam, Leipzig 1983.

———, *A Rebel in Music: Selected Writings*, Kahn & Averill, London 1999.

Elderfield, John, *Kurt Schwitters*, Thames & Hudson, London 1987.

Eliot, Marc, *Walt Disney: Hollywood's Dark Prince*, André Deutsch, London 1994.

Engels, Frederick, *Dialectics of Nature*, Progress Publishers, Moscow 1976.

Feild, Robert, *The Art of Walt Disney*, Collins, London and Glasgow 1944.

Fisher, Philip, *Wonder, the Rainbow and the Aesthetics of Rare Experiences*, Harvard University Press, Cambridge MA 1998.

Forgacs, David, 'Disney Animation and the Business of Childhood', *Screen*, vol. 33, no. 4, Winter 1992, pp. 361–74.

Freud, Sigmund, *Pelican Freud Library*, 15 vols, Penguin, Harmondsworth 1973–86. 'A Note on the "Mystic Writing-Pad"' (1925), vol. 11, 1984; *Jokes and their Relation to the Unconscious* (1905), vol. 6, 1986.

Frisby, David, *Fragmente der Moderne*, Daedalus Verlag, Rheda-Wiedenbrück 1989.

Futurist Manifestos, edited with an introduction by Umbro Apollonio, Thames & Hudson, London 1973.

Gambino, Ferruccio, 'A Critique of the Regulation School', *Common Sense* 19, June 1996.

Goergen, Jeanpaul, *Walter Ruttmann: Eine Dokumentation*, Freunde der deutschen Kinemathek, Berlin 1989.

Goethe, J.W., *Theory of Colours*, trans. Charles Eastlake, MIT Press, Cambridge MA 1970.

———, *Faust 1 and 2*, in *Goethe, The Collected Works*, Volume 2, edited and trans. Stuart Atkins, Princeton University Press, Princeton 1984.

———, *Goethes Werke*, edited by Erich Trunz, vol. XII, *Naturwissenschaftliche Schriften*, C.H. Beck, Munich 1981.

————, *Scientific Studies*, Suhrkamp, New York 1988.

Gorky, Maxim et al., *Soviet Writers' Congress 1934: The Debate on Socialist Realism and Modernism in the Soviet Union*, Lawrence & Wishart, London 1977.

Graham, Cooper C., *Leni Riefenstahl and Olympia*, Scarecrow Press, Metuchen NJ 1986.

Grandville, *Bizarreries and Fantasies of Grandville: 266 Illustrations from 'Un autre monde' and 'Les Animaux'*, Dover Publications, New York 1974.

Greenberg, Clement, 'The "Crisis" of Abstract Art' (1964), in *The Collected Essays and Criticism*, vol. 4, University of Chicago Press, Chicago 1993.

Grimms' Fairy Tales, trans. L.L. Weedon, illustrated by Ada Dennis and E. Stuart Hardy and others, Ernest Nister, London 1898.

Hamon, Philippe, *Expositions: Literature and Architecture in Nineteenth Century France*, University of California Press, Berkeley 1992.

Hansen, Miriam, 'Mass Culture as Hieroglyphic Writing: Adorno, Derrida, Kracauer', *New German Critique* 56, Spring–Summer 1992.

Harrison, Charles et al., *Primitivism, Cubism, Abstraction: Modern Art Practices and Debates*, Yale University Press and Open University Press, New Haven and Milton Keynes 1993.

———— and Paul Wood, eds, *Art in Theory*, Blackwell, Oxford 1993.

Hartman, Geoffrey, *Wordsworth's Poetry, 1787–1814*, Yale University Press, New Haven 1964.

Hay, James, *Popular Film Culture in Fascist Italy: The Passing of the Rex*, Indiana University Press, Bloomington 1987.

Hayward Gallery, *Film as Film: Formal Experiment in Film 1910–1975*, exhibition catalogue, London 1979.

Hegel, G.W.F., *Logic*, trans. and edited by W. Wallace and J.N. Findlay, Oxford University Press, Oxford 1975.

Heide, Robert and John Gilman, *Disneyana: Classic Collectibles 1928–1958*, Hyperion, New York 1995.

Hoberman, J., *Vulgar Modernism: Writing on Movies and Other Media*, Temple University Press, Philadelphia 1991.

Horkheimer, Max, 'Art and Mass Culture', in *Zeitschrift für Sozialforschung*, Jahrgang 9 (reprint), Deutscher Taschenbuch Verlag, Munich 1980.

Huelsenbeck, Richard, *The Dada Almanac* (1920), English edn prepared by Malcolm Green, Atlas, London 1993.

Kasson, John E., *Amusing the Million: Coney Island at the Turn of the Century*, Hill & Wang, New York 1978.

Kater, Michael H., *Different Drummers: Jazz in the Culture of Nazi Germany*, Oxford University Press, Oxford 1992.

King, David, *The Commissar Vanishes: The Falsification of Photographs and Art in Stalin's Russia*, Canongate Books, Edinburgh 1997.

Klein, Norman M., *Seven Minutes: The Life and Death of the American Animated Cartoon*, Verso, London 1993.

Klonsky, Milton, *A Discourse on Hip*, Wayne State University, Detroit 1991.

Kolman, Vladimir, *Vom Millionär, der die Sonne Stahl: Geschichte des tschecoslowakischen Animationsfilms*, Deutsches Filmmuseum, Frankfurt 1981.

Kracauer, Siegfried, *Das Ornament der Masse; Essays*, Suhrkamp Verlag, Frankfurt am Main 1977.

————, *Kino*, Suhrkamp Verlag, Frankfurt am Main 1979.

————, *Straßen in Berlin und Anderswo*, Das Arsenal, Berlin 1987.

————, *Schriften*, vol. 5 part 3, *Aufsätze 1932–1965*, Suhrkamp Verlag, Frankfurt am Main 1990.

————, *The Mass Ornament: Weimar Essays*, Harvard University Press, Cambridge MA 1995.

Krause, Martin and Linda Witkowski, *Walt Disney's Snow White and the Seven Dwarfs: An Art in the Making*, Hyperion, New York 1994.

Krupskaya, Nadezhda, *Memories of Lenin*, Lawrence & Wishart, London 1942.

Kuenzli, Rudolf E., ed., *Dada and Surrealist Film*, Willis Locker & Owens, New York 1987.

Kurtz, R., *Expressionismus und Film*, Verlag der Lichtbildbühne, Berlin 1926.

Langer, Mark, 'The Disney–Fleischer Dilemma: Product Differentiation and Technological Innovation', *Screen*, vol. 33, no. 4, Winter 1992, pp. 343–60.

Laqua, Carsten, *Wie Micky unter die Nazis fiel: Walt Disney und Deutschland*, Rowohlt Verlag, Hamburg 1992.

Lenin, V.I., *Philosophical Notebooks*, in *Collected Works*, vol. 38, Lawrence & Wishart, London 1972.

Leslie, Esther, Introduction to a letter exchange between Adorno and Marcuse, *New Left Review* 233, January–February 1999.

————, 'Space and West End Girls: Walter Benjamin versus Cultural Studies', in 'Hating Tradition Properly', *New Formations* 38, 1999, pp. 110–24.

————, *Walter Benjamin: Overpowering Conformism*, Pluto Press, London 2000.

Lewis, Wyndham, *Time and Western Man* (1927), Black Sparrow Press, Santa Rosa 1993.

Macdonald, Dwight, *Against the American Grain: Essays on the Effects of Mass Culture*, Vintage, New York 1962.

Macpherson, Don, ed., *Traditions of Independence: British Cinema in the Thirties*, BFI, London 1980.

Malevich, K.S., *Essays on Art 1915–1933*, vol. 1, Rapp & Whiting, London 1971.

Maltin, Leonard, *Of Mice and Men: A History of American Animated Cartoons*, Plume, New York 1987.

Kazimir Malevich 1878–1935, catalogue published by the Armand Hammer Museum of Art and Cultural Center, Los Angeles 1990.

Marinetti, F.T., Bruno Corra, Emilio Settimelli, Arnaldo Ginna, Giacomo Balla and Remo Chiti, 'The Futurist Cinema 1916', in *Futurist Manifestos*, Thames & Hudson, London 1973.

Marx, Karl, *Capital* Volume I, Charles Kerr, New York 1904.

————, *The Revolutions of 1848*, trans. Rodney Livingstone, Penguin/New Left Review, London 1973.

————, *Early Writings*, trans. Rodney Livingstone, Penguin/New Left Review, London 1977.

————, *The Eighteenth Brumaire of Louis Bonaparte*, Lawrence & Wishart, London 1984.

———— (1885), *Capital* Volume II, Penguin Books, New York 1992.

———— (1894), *Capital* Volume III, Penguin Books, New York 1991.

————, and Friedrich Engels, *Marx and Engels Collected Works*, 50 vols, Lawrence & Wishart, London 1975–.

Merritt, Russell and J.B. Kaufman, *Walt in Wonderland: The Silent Films of Walt Disney*, Johns Hopkins University Press, Baltimore 1993.

Mespoulet, Marguerite, *Creators of Wonderland*, Arrow Editions, New York 1934.

Moholy-Nagy: An Anthology, edited by Richard Kostelanetz, Da Capo, New York 1991.

Montagu, Ivor, *With Eisenstein in Hollywood*, Seven Seas Books, Berlin 1968.

Moritz, William, 'Resistance and Subversion in Animated Films of the Nazi Era: The Case of Hans Fischerkoesen', *Animation Journal*, Fall 1992, pp. 4–33.

————, 'Oskar Fischinger', in *Optische Poesie: Oskar Fischinger, Leben und Werk, Kinematograph* 9, 1993, Deutsches Filmmuseum, Frankfurt am Main.

Nadeau, Maurice, *The History of Surrealism*, Penguin, Harmondsworth 1978.

Noake, Roger, *Animation: A Guide to Animated Film Techniques*, Macdonald Orbis, London 1988.

Noever, Peter, ed., *Aleksandr M. Rodchenko and Vavara F. Stepanova: The Future is Our Only Goal*, Prestel Verlag, Munich 1991.

Nordenfalk, C. and H. Richter, *Nationalmusei utställings-katalog no.178: Viking Eggeling 1880–1925*, Nationalmuseum Stockholm, October–November 1950.

O'Connor, Louise, *Viking Eggeling 1880–1925. Artist and Film-maker. Life and Work*, trans. Catherine G. Sundstrom and Anne Bibby, Acta Universitatis Stockholmiensis, Stockholm Studies in History of Art 23, Almquist & Wiksell, Stockholm 1971.

O'Pray, Michael, *Eisenstein and Stokes on Disney: Film Animation and Omnipotence*, University of East London, School of Architecture, Art and Design Working Papers, London 1995.

Optische Poesie: Oskar Fischinger, Leben und Werk, Kinematograph no. 9, 1993, Deutsches Filmmuseum, Frankfurt am Main.

Partisan Review Anthology, edited by William Phillips and Philip Rahv, Macmillan, London 1962.

Petric, Vlada, *Constructivism in Film: The Man with the Movie Camera; A Cinematic Analysis*, Cambridge University Press, Cambridge 1993.

Phillips, Christopher, ed., *Photography in the Modern Era*, Aperture, New York 1989.

Richards, Jeffrey and Dorothy Sheridan, eds, *Mass-Observation at the Movies*, Routledge & Kegan Paul 1987.

Richter, Hans, *Filmgegner von Heute – Filmfreunde von Morgen* (1929), Facsimile, Verlag Hans Rohr, Zurich 1968.

Hans Richter by Hans Richter, edited by Cleve Gray, Thames & Hudson, London 1971.

Richter, Hans, *Der Kampf um den Film*, Fischer, Frankfurt am Main; *The Struggle for the Film*, trans. Ben Brewster, Scolar Press, Aldershot 1986.

————, *Dada: Art and Anti-Art*, trans. David Britt, Thames & Hudson, London 1978.

————, Werner Haftmann and Werner Hoffmann, *Kurt Kranz: Early Form Sequences 1927–1932*, MIT, Cambridge MA 1975.

Riefenstahl, Leni, *Memoiren 1902–1945*, Verlag Ullstein, Frankfurt am Main 1987; *A Memoir*, St Martin's Press, New York 1993.

————, *Hinter den Kulissen des Reichsparteitagfilms*, Zentralverlag der NSDAP, Munich 1935.

Roberts, John, ed., *Art Has No History!*, Verso, London 1994.

Rose, Steven, *Lifelines: Biology, Freedom, Determinism*, Penguin, Harmondsworth 1998.

Royal Academy of Arts, *50 Years Bauhaus*, exhibition catalogue, London 1968.

Rubinstein, Joshua, *Tangled Loyalties: The Life and Times of Ilya Ehrenburg*, I.B. Tauris, London and New York 1996.

Sandler, Irving, *The Triumph of American Painting*, Icon Editions, Harper & Row, New York 1970.

Schickel, Richard, *The Disney Version*, Pavilion Books, London 1986.

Schlegel, Frederick von, *The Aesthetic and Miscellaneous Works of Frederick von Schlegel*, trans. E.J. Millington, Henry G. Bohn, London 1849.

Scholem, Gershom, *Walter Benjamin: The Story of a Friendship*, Jewish Publication Society of America, Philadelphia 1981.

Sepper, Dennis L., *Goethe contra Newton*, Cambridge University Press, Cambridge 1988.

Smoodin, Eric, ed., *Disney Discourse: Producing the Magic Kingdom*, American Film Institute/Routledge, London and New York 1994.

Stallabrass, Julian, *Gargantua*, Verso, London 1996.

Starr, Cecile and Robert Russet, *Experimental Animation*, Van Nostrand Reinhold, New York 1976.

Storm, J.P. and M. Dreßler, *Im Reiche der Micky-Maus: Walt Disney in Deustchland 1927–1945*, documentation of an exhibition in the Filmmuseum Potsdam, Henschel, Berlin 1991.

Stravinsky, Igor and Robert Craft, *Expositions and Developments*, Faber & Faber, London 1962.

Stravinsky, Igor and Robert Craft *Dialogues*, Faber & Faber, London 1982.

Talbot, Daniel, ed., *Film, An Anthology*, University of California Press, Berkeley and Los Angeles 1966.

Taylor, Richard and Ian Christie, eds, *The Film Factory: Russian and Soviet Cinema in Documents 1896–1939*, Harvard University Press, Cambridge MA 1988.

Taylor, Brandon and Wilfried van der Will, eds, *The Nazification of Art*, Winchester Press, Winchester 1990.

Thomas, Bob, *Walt Disney: A Biography*, W.H. Allen, London 1976.

Thomas, Frank and Ollie Johnston, *The Illusion of Life: Disney Animation*, Hyperion, New York 1981.

———, *Too Funny For Words*, Abbeville, New York 1997.

Trethewey, Richard L., ed., *Walt Disney: The FBI Files*, Rainbo Animation Art, Pacifica, CA 1994.

Trotsky, Lev, *Problems of Life*, Methuen, London 1924.

Trotsky, Leon, *Trotsky's Diary in Exile 1935*, Faber & Faber, London 1958.

———, *The History of the Russian Revolution*, Pluto Press, London 1985.

———, *Trotsky's Notebooks, 1933–1935*, edited by Philip Pomper, Columbia University Press, New York 1986.

———, *Literature and Revolution*, Redwords, London 1991.

Watson, Ben, *Art, Class and Cleavage: Quantulumcunque Concerning Materialist Esthetix*, Quartet, London 1998.

Watts, Steven, 'Walt Disney's Art and Politics in the American Century', *Journal of American History*, June 1993, pp. 84–110.

———, *The Magic Kingdom: Walt Disney and the American Way of Life*, Houghton Mifflin, New York 1997.

Wells, Paul, *Understanding Animation*, Routledge, London 1998.

White, Eric Walter, *Walking Shadows: An Essay on Lotte Reiniger's Silhouette Films*, Hogarth Press, London 1931.

Wilson, Catherine, *The Invisible World: Early Modern Philosophy and the Invention of the Microscope*, Princeton University Press, Princeton 1995.

Wordsworth, William, *Poetical Works*, Oxford University Press, Oxford 1969.

acknowledgements

Thanks: For access to the Benjamin papers, the T.W Adorno Archiv, Frankfurt am Main. For an excellent library, museum and film programme, the Deutsches Filmmuseum, Frankfurt am Main. For access to papers by Frankfurt Schüler, the Horkheimer–Pollock Archiv, Frankfurt am Main. For meticulous Goethe and picture research, Stiftung Weimarer Klassik/Goethe-Nationalmuseum. For generosity, the Fischinger Archive, Primrose Film Productions, Eva Riehl, Marion von Hofacker. For freely offered expertise, Philippa Dawson. For allowing the young me to be pump-primed with *Tom and Jerry*, *The Flintstones*, *Yogi Bear*, *Scooby Doo*, *Top Cat* and Disney Features at the Finchley Gaumont, my parents, Sheila and George. For everything, Ben Watson.

The author and publishers would like to thank the following for the use of illustrative material: pp. 13, 15, reprinted with special permission of King Feature Syndicate; pp. 27, 29, 173, 221, 249, C7, C8, © Disney Enterprises, Inc.; pp. 39, 43, 45, 220, by kind permission of Marion von Hofacker; pp. 48, 49, by kind permission of Primrose Film Productions; p. 93, by permission of the British Library (shelf number: 989/3785); pp. 125, 139, courtesy of Leni Riefenstahl; pp. 175, 176, C1, courtesy of King Features/Ronald Grant; p. 205, © Man Ray Trust/ADAGP, Paris and DACS, London 2001; pp. 259, 261, C6, courtesy of Stiftung Weimarer Klassik/Goethe-Nationalmuseum (photographer, Sigrid Geske); p. 294, © ARS, NY and DACS, London 2001; C2–3, © Fischinger Archive; C4–5, by kind permission of Eva Riehl/Image: Stiftung Deutsche Kinemathek.

index

With ruminations on drawing, colour and caricature, on the political meaning of fairy-tales, talking animals and human beings as machines, *Hollywood Flatlands* brings to light the links between animation, avant-garde art and modernist criticism.

Focusing on the work of a number of aesthetic and political revolutionaries of the inter-war period, Esther Leslie reveals how the 'animation' of commodities can be studied as a journey into modernity in cinema. She looks afresh at the links between the Soviet Constructivists and the Bauhaus, for instance, and at those between Walter Benjamin and cinematic abstraction. She also provides new interpretations of the writings of Siegfried Kracauer on animation, of how Theodor Adorno's and Max Horkheimer's film-viewing affected the development of their thinking, and of Sergei Eisenstein's famous handshake with Mickey Mouse at Disney's Hyperion Studios in 1930.

Hollywood Flatlands provides not only a complete history of animation but a reminder that convincing analysis requires both wide-angle and zoom shots, and a polemic against the limp sociological positivism that would like to erect impermeable bulkheads between mass culture and critique.

1916